BETWEEN PROHIBITION AND LEGALIZATION
THE DUTCH EXPERIMENT IN DRUG POLICY

STUDIES ON CRIME
AND JUSTICE
A SERIES FROM
THE RESEARCH
AND DOCUMENTATION
CENTRE

BETWEEN PROHIBITION AND LEGALIZATION

THE DUTCH EXPERIMENT IN DRUG POLICY

EDITED BY ED. LEUW AND I. HAEN MARSHALL

KUGLER PUBLICATIONS
AMSTERDAM / NEW YORK

Library of Congress Cataloging-in-Publication Data

Between prohibition and legalization : the Dutch experiment in drug
policy / edited by E. Leuw and I. Haen Marshall.
    p.   cm. -- (Studies on crime and justice)
  Includes bibliographical references.
  ISBN 90-6299-103-3
    1. Narcotics, Control of--Netherlands. 2. Drug abuse-
-Netherlands--Prevention. I. Leuw, Ed. II. Haen Marshall,
I. (Ineke) III. Series.
HV5840.N4B48 1994
363.4'5'09492--dc20

94-1664
CIP

ISBN 90-6299-103-3

Distributors:

For the U.S.A. and Canada:
Kugler Publications
P.O. Box 1498
New York, NY 10009-9998
Telefax (+212) 477-0181

For all other countries:
Kugler Publications
P.O. Box 11188
1001 GD Amsterdam, The Netherlands
Telefax (+31.20) 638-0524

CONTENTS

PREFACE TO THE SECOND PRINTING OF "BETWEEN PROHIBITION AND LEGALIZATION"

Ed Leuw and Ineke Haen-Marshall

Two years have passed since the first edition of this volume was published. During this relatively short period of time interesting developments have taken place, with regard to both the national and the international dimensions of the "Dutch Drug Policy". Discussions have focused just as much on the "pragmatic" drug policy approach as on the nature and extent of drug problems in The Netherlands. We will provide a brief update.

After a period in which a broad consensus on the issue seemed evident in Dutch society, drug problems and drug policy have again become more prominent on the political agenda and in the public consciousness. Debates and reports on the issue abound in the Dutch parliament, the mass media and in international exchanges within the European Community.

The current resurfacing of concern with drugs and drug policy should be viewed in the context of significant changes in the Dutch political landscape. Since the summer of 1994, the Dutch government has been comprised of a unique coalition of political parties. Christian Democrats who have "always" formed the core of Dutch governments are no longer represented in the government. The present Cabinet is made up of three "non-confessional" parties which tend to be more liberal on morally significant issues. The basic socio-philosophical notion that drug use is a liability for the individual rather than for the state is definitely more congenial to the present government of social democrats and assorted "liberals" than to the traditional Dutch government headed by a Christian Democrat. This is even more true in view of the fact that the two Ministries most involved in the regulation of morally significant issues, the Departments of Justice and of Public Health and Welfare, are headed by Ministers from the "left wing liberal" coalition party, that is traditionally most sceptical of state interference in issues involving private behavior.

With the new administration, expectations were raised that the most contradictory element of Dutch Drug Policy, the existence of semi-legal commercial outlets for the consumers" market of cannabis, would be more officially regulated. Most specifically, this concerned the disparity between the judicial policy of the "front door" and the "back door" of the "coffee shops". As is explained in this volume, coffee shops are more or less officially allowed to sell hashish and marihuana to customers at the front door. At the back door, however, the law "must be" violated in providing the coffee shop with their necessary stock. Back-door transactions may occur between the coffee shops and more or less organized "criminal" wholesalers. Along these lines, there is a risk that coffee shops will be appropriated and used as store fronts (possibly for other illegal activities) by such organisations.

The increasing awareness of the inconsistency of front-door and back-door policies coincided with signals from society that a number of coffee shops were generating problems. Complaints about coffee shops causing a nuisance in the neighborhood were more often being heard. Increasing suspicion arose that, in some coffee shops, "hard drugs" (particularly cocaine and XTC) might be available, and anxiety was expressed that those facilities could function as deviancy-producing sanctuaries for adolescents. Within the Dutch Drug Policy, coffee shops were intended to integrate and normalize a certain kind of drug consumption not considered to be very harmful. The degeneration of some of the coffee shops would obviously be contrary to this essential aim of Dutch Drug Policy.

There were, however, more areas of concern. Since the beginning of this decennium, the number of coffee shops has increased rather sharply to a total of about 2000 in 1996. A relatively large number of the new coffee shops was established in socially problematic neighborhoods. Many of them were owned or exploited by entrepreneurs from recently developed ethnic minority communities. Enterprises in the "gray" market between legality and illegality are, almost by definition, poorly regulated. Because, for their economic survival, marginal groups often (have to) rely on alternatives to the more exclusive conventional economy, this "gray" market offers easily accessible economic opportunities, especially for some ethnic minority groups. The ethnic minorities concerned (particularly the Turkish and North-African immigrants) come from traditional cannabis producing countries. This increases the probability that part of the coffee-shop branch will be supplied with cannabis by foreign-based (criminal) organizations. Because of their easy reliance on the facilities of their home countries, these organizations are fairly immune to the normal measures of social control. The normalization of the consumption market of cannabis is seriously complicated by such circumstances.

The recent concern that part of the coffee-shop branch might be degenerating, triggered strongly divergent ideas about possible solutions. An advisory committee from the Public Prosecutor's Office proposed that, in time, the coffee-shop practice should be completely abolished. The Christian Democratic party, considering drug policy as an important issue for expressing their (new) identity as an opposition party, also adopted this so-called "zero option". The majority of the coalition parties, however, favored the opposing solution of sanitizing the consumer market of cannabis, by allowing more legal opportunities for supplying coffee shops with cannabis. This possible solution was in line with the local coffee shop policy in several Dutch towns, where "gentlemen's agreements" are made between coffee shops and the local authorities. Coffee shops will be exempted from police interference in their "normal" business practice (among which is the presence of a realistic stock of cannabis) if they "guarantee" respectability in terms of public order, security and the absence of drugs other than cannabis on their premises. For instance, in the town of Tilburg, a limited number of coffee shops is allowed to exist on this basis. These establishments are actively supervised by the police to ensure a respectable mode of operation. At the same time they are protected by the local authorities from unfair allegations by the surrounding neighborhood, which are sometimes based on no more than clashes of lifestyle. Whether in favor of the gradual termination of the practice or further legalization and integration within the conventional economy, all parties in the current debate agreed that the Dutch consumption market for soft drugs should be more seriously monitored by the police and the civil authorities.

Interestingly, the Dutch explicit and unmitigated harm reduction approach to the use of hard drugs has not raised comparable controversy, either nationally or internationally. But here too, some shifting of priorities is noticeable. Complaints from citizens about the bothersome effects of more or less officially instituted free zones for hard drugs have, in some instances, resulted in a more repressive and less accommodating approach to hard-drug scenes. In such cases, a different balance has been struck between avoiding unnecessary marginalization of drug addicts and protecting the public from the adversities of a hard-drug consumption market. In Rotterdam and Maastricht, a "planned" (Platform 0 alongside the Central Railway Station) and an unplanned free zone (a "needle park" on the River Maas) were successfully removed by police action. It was felt that the major requisite for allowing a free zone - the ability to control the negative effects to security and public order - was no longer warranted. The almost inevitable relocation of the hard-drugs scene to a poor residential area of Rotterdam was met with an intensive police campaign to maintain security and public order. In effect, the Rotterdam situation represents a stalemate rather than a solution. Terminating the "official" free zone for hard drugs has resulted in the establishment of a subdued hard-drugs scene in a residential area. Many police are involved in containing this situation, and the public has certainly not stopped complaining about the nuisance the drugs scene creates.

In recent discussions about the priorities of the pragmatic Dutch drug policy, the international perspective has become more prominent. Here too, the picture is rather ambiguous. International opinion seems to have polarized. On the one hand, Dutch drug policy seems gradually to have earned more European understanding and approval, especially from those responsible for the "dirty" work of finding viable solutions to the urban, real-life problems of drug markets and drug addiction. However, on the other hand, some national governments, most notably those of France and Sweden, have fiercely criticized the Dutch practice of decriminalizing the use and the consumption market of illegal substances. During the past year, (drug) diplomatic relations between France and The Netherlands have become strained. The French government has maintained that its country is negatively affected by the relatively easy availability (close to its borders) of illegal substances. Within the European Community, France is exerting pressure to put an end to the Dutch coffee-shop practice. In response, the Dutch have asserted their right to autonomy in finding their own solution to an internal social and public health problem. Apart from this, the Dutch feel little responsibility for the bleak conditions in French suburbs, which make the use of and trade in drugs an attractive option for vast numbers of unemployed and disillusioned adolescents, often from ethnic minority communities.

But as has already been said, mounting European pressure on the pragmatic Dutch drug policy is only part of the story. In particular, many German states (in fact the majority) have adopted much of the Dutch harm-reduction and "normalizing" approach. Just as in The Netherlands, socio-medically supervised free zones for hard drugs are being tolerated, or have been instituted in a number of German states. In Frankfurt, public health officials from Amsterdam were invited to set up a large-scale methadone program. And, likewise, the use and retail trade of cannabis has been decriminalized in those German states. Germany's Constitutional Court in Karlsruhe has recently ruled that (just as in The Netherlands) possession of up to 30 grams of cannabis should not be punished. The rather favorable attitudes of many German states towards the Dutch drug policy is most clearly expressed in an "open letter" dated March 1996 from the governments of six (out of 15) German states, urging the Dutch government not to succumb to international pressure to redress decri-minalization and normalization of the use and retail trade of illegal sub-stances.

Both the national and international discussions on Dutch Drug Policy have culminated around the governmental Drug Policy Paper, "Continuity and Change", which was presented to parliament in September 1995. In an introduction to a recent issue of a journal published by the Ministry of

Justice, the Minister of Justice concluded that, according to the new drug policy plan, the Dutch practice of tolerance will be fully maintained. "Legal prohibitions on trade and production will be sustained, while some small-scale manifestations of this will be tolerated by law enforcement practice, in combination with civil administration measures" (Sorgdrager 1996). The drug policy paper, as well as the parliamentary debate on the drug policy plan, clarifies in some detail what this apparently delicate balancing of contradictions means in practice. On the hottest issue of the coffee shops, the new government has decided that this institution should be preserved, although it should be more intensively supervised to ensure respectable modes of business operations.

The government has acknowledged the desirability of counteracting the supply of foreign retail traders who purchase soft drugs from Dutch coffee shops. For this reason, the maximum amount for a single transaction has been reduced to 5 grams of cannabis. However, the limit of "non-interference" with the possession of cannabis still remains at 30 grams. Furthermore, local authorities have been given more power to resist the establishment or presence of a coffee shop within their jurisdiction. On the other hand, cautious hints have been given that arrangements at a local level might be contemplated when resolving the front door-back door discrepancy, by allowing coffee shops to obtain cannabis from non-criminal "home-growers". The Dutch parliament has supported this (perhaps mainly ritual) adaptation of the Dutch soft-drug policy by a large majority.

According to the Drug Policy Plan and the parliamentary debate, the policy concerning the demand side of hard drugs will remain largely unchanged. Again, a mixture of more repressive and decriminalizing measures has been proposed by the government and has been accepted in parliament. A new provision will be formulated to allow for the incarceration of highly criminal drug addicts in specialized therapy-oriented institutions. In practice, this provision will resemble penal law commitments to forensic psychiatric detention centers. The policy plan suggests one or two years as the maximum term for such commitment.

In itself, this intended penal law measure for "compulsory treatment" represents a new perspective in Dutch drug policy. It is in conflict with the more traditional rejection of any form of non-voluntary treatment for addicts. However, counterbalancing this more repressive innovation, the policy plan has also broken down another "taboo" in the Dutch harm-reduction approach to hard drug addiction: the start of some small-scale experiments with the medical prescription of heroin. The heroin maintenance programs will aim at older addicts in destitute psycho-social circumstances, those with a long history of addiction.

Small steps in different, sometimes opposite, directions may be typical of a drug policy which attempts to compromise between the apparent futility of drug prohibition and the unknown perils of legalization.

Reference

Sorgdrager, W.: Nederlands gedoogbeleid; pragmatisch en effectief. *Justitiële Verkenningen* 9:9-14, 1995

INTRODUCTION

In a period of two decades Dutch drug policy has evolved in partial opposition to the internationally dominant ideology of prohibitionism. The "normalizing" home policy, together with the compliance to law enforcement in the international arena, make up a rather complicated and ambivalent Dutch position in drug policy. The Dutch drug policy is fully in line with the international control practices against wholesale drug trafficking. As regards its social drug policy, however, it has become a rare dissenter within an increasingly unifying and compelling international drug policy context. This book gives an account of the national Dutch drug control strategy.

The course, the practice and the rhetorics of any drug policy are determined by its major theoretical premises. It is the final ideological position of the Dutch "pragmatic" or "non-moralistic" drug policy, that problems of deviant drug taking and drug selling are deeply and inescapably part of the society in which they occur. This stands in contrast to the more traditional prohibitionist notion which puts primary blame on users and sellers of illegal substances.

The assertion of "user accountability" has followed logically from the American prohibitionist "war on drugs". It assumes that drugs and addiction form an evil in itself, which can be purged from society by deterrence and by promoting total abstinence. The Dutch understanding of the social liability of illegal and addictive drugs is rather less straightforward. It painstakingly balances between the reciprocal notions of freedom and responsibility. This involves, on the one hand, the personal freedom of the individual (i.e., the right to self-determination) to use drugs and even to be addicted; on the other hand, it involves the personal responsibility of drug users for their own (mental) health and their own social behavior (criminality included).

In the Dutch view, then, accountability for the existence of drug and addiction problems is shared by drug users/dealers and society. This means that the responsibility of users of illegal drugs is mitigated by society's responsibility for criminalizing drugs and for the existence of social conditions that make using and selling illegal drugs a functional and rewarding practice for relatively large segments of the population. More specifically, within the framework of Dutch drug policy, drug users are not held accountable for the social marginality, deterioration and degradation that accompanies deviant addiction. These adversities are understood as consequences of society's choice to prohibit (the use of) certain psycho-active substances.

Criminalization of "drugs" is a public means by which society demarcates conventionality. "Drug accountability", for all but the most direct and primary psycho-pharmacological drug effects, should consequently be given to conventional society. More than anything else, this basic understanding may explain the course of Dutch drug policy towards harm reduction in the case of hard drugs and (*de facto*) "legalization" in the case of soft drugs (marihuana and hashish). This has been the consistent course since the adoption of the Revised Opium Act in 1976.

Perhaps more than with any other social problem, the extent and quality of drug problems are a reflection of a particular society's moral priorities and preoccupations, its political processes, the (in)equalities of its distribution of wealth and welfare among (ethnic) classes and the integrative (in)adequacies of its culture. Illegal drug taking, addiction and the viability of the illegal drugs trade are all symptoms and logical consequences of a national social-economic and cultural order. Granted, to a certain extent, the (illegal) drug problem may legitimately be perceived as a threat to a nation's health, its security or its young generation. But it would be a gross distortion of the nature of drug problems to conceive of them as alien and evil menaces forced upon an innocent society. Within Dutch social history it has become almost a truism that the "innate" alcoholism among Dutch working classes earlier this century could be attributed to their poverty and political powerlessness. Some decades later, in a more equitable society, alcoholism has become a normal and equally distributed (public) health liability (Gerritsen 1993). In similar vein, few people in our part of the world would doubt that the extent of problematic alcohol use in present Russia is a symptom rather than a cause of a stagnating society.

Consistent with this view, Dutch drug ideology has rejected the idea that present day drug addiction and drug trafficking, with its heavy concentration in socially deprived and culturally alienated population groups, could (or even should) be eradicated without reconsidering society's social-economic and cultural order. But obviously, staging a socio-cultural revolution in order to eliminate drug addiction is just as futile as staging a "war on drugs" in a society which gives abundant "good reasons" and opportunities for using drugs, abusing drugs and earning money with selling drugs.

Instead of staging a moral crusade for a "drug-free society", the Dutch drug policy model has favored more mundane objectives such as de-escalation and normalization of drug problems. During the last twenty years a rather coherent pattern of drug political instruments and practices has been developed to further this basic goal. They will be described and explained in the various chapters.

In line with the ideological presumptions sketched above, Dutch drug policy is firmly entrenched in social scientific knowledge. Drug control measures in the Netherlands are largely executed by the means of social work and welfare agencies. The doctrines of medical practice and legal deterrence are certainly not absent in the Dutch drug control system, but they are of less central importance than in more traditional modes of drug policy. Problematic drug use is accepted as an inevitable, but limited and manageable social and (public) health problem of modern society.

Law enforcement is viewed as an unsuitable means to regulate the demand side of drugs, as this instrument for control tends to aggravate rather than alleviate the public health and public order problems of illegal drug use. While using hard drugs and being in possession of these for one's own use are legally proscribed, in practice the Dutch criminal justice system does not intervene here. Employing law enforcement is restricted to the higher levels of the illegal drugs trade. The predominance of the social scientific view is also reflected in a relatively low level of medicalization of drug problems. Using drugs is primarily understood not as a disease, but as normally motivated (but often unwise) behavior, fitting in a certain lifestyle, personal development and social conditions. Accordingly "curing to abstinence" or primary prevention of drug use are not the central objectives of Dutch social drug policy. Instead of minimizing the number of users and the extent of illegal drug use, Dutch drug policy is first and foremost concerned with reducing the risks and hazards of drug taking.

Harm reduction is the core concept. It is implemented by extensive low level and non-conditional methadone prescription, social-medical assistance for drug users, large-scale free needle exchange programs, and the pragmatic acceptance of a number of "free zones" where the consumers drug market is left relatively undisturbed.

In a more general sense the principle of harm reduction is also implemented by abstaining from state interference with illegal but non-deviant drug use (i.e., kinds of illegal drug use which are not heavily frowned upon, or considered highly problematic by large parts of society). Although the recent increase of cultivation and commercialization of soft drugs has created (mainly drug diplomatic) policy concerns, Dutch society seems to have moved beyond the point that the repression and stigmatization of hashish and marihuana can be justified. Using soft drugs has in the course of two decades of "normalizing" drug policy evolved into a legitimate private choice. Use may be a possible concern for parents and educators, but no longer a credible case for state interference. To a lesser extent the same may apply to the fashionable recreational and largely non-problematic use of XTC or cocaine (Cohen 1990).

The ideological key concept of "normalization" deserves more clarification. Conceiving of the drug problem as a social problem in the true sense of the word implies that a "solution" can be achieved by gradually reversing the social construction of the drug problem, through a process of reduction of signficance and (moral) interest. "Normalizing" simply means a de-escalation of the social (drugs) conflict, in which both the socially added attractions and harmfulness of illegal substances are reduced. Drugs may inevitably produce a "funny" or even pleasurable feeling in the head. But, ideally, that should be their only inevitable consequence. Their economic attractions, the glorious defiance, the identity and (deviant) sense to life that illegal drugs confer are solely produced by repressive and stigmatizing social control. In this sense normalisation is synonymous to decriminalization.

Normalization not only requires the reduction of secondary harm and attractions of illegal substances, it also implies that the social and political rewards of the drug prohibition system itself are to be discarded. Under the conditions of normalization, no extrinsic moral or political interests should be served with the regulation of psycho-active substances. This is a far cry from reality under the present conditions of prohibition. In fact, the secondary moral and political rewards of drug prohibition probably offer the best explanation of the persistence of a social control system which so blatantly fails to achieve its professed aims. Prohibition is a success, not because it helps to limit the public health and security problems of society, but because it offers substantial and highly valued moral, political, economical and social rewards.

Political careers and professional careers are made through the drug control system, even those of the sociological detractors and castigators of the system. It helps to boost politicians' popularity by providing them with uncontroversial and gratuitous rallying themes and election platforms. It helps to simplify and neutralize the structural and cultural strains within society. Intractable adversities such as marginality, deprivation, alienation and ethnic tensions can conveniently be attributed to drugs as an alien evil. The drug problem even allows these adversities

to be attributed to a lack of willpower and morality within the most deprived population groups, where, invariably, drug addiction has settled
(Musto 1973; Scheerer 1993; Duster 1970; Lidz *et al.* 1980). Of course
the Dutch "pragmatic" drug policy has not completely exempted itself
from these self-deceiving lures. But, as will be explained in This Volume,
furthering moralistic and political aims by rallying on the drugs issue is
certainly less feasible within the framework of "pragmatic" drug policy.

The selection of the chapters in this book bear witness to the fact that
the Netherlands has a valuable and varied empirical research tradition
aimed at careful documentation of drug-related issues. Typically, the studies in this book combine careful empirical description with theoretical
analysis. Not only is most research described in this collection
theoretically grounded, it also represent a creative integration of different research methods (secondary analysis of available data, observations,
ethnographic accounts, repeated in-depth interviews). Another common
theme in the works presented here is that all the researchers, some more
explicitly than others, try to challenge common myths and mispercep-
tions about drugs and the effects of drug policy.

"All drugs are legal in Holland..." "In Amsterdam, drug-related crime
is rampant..." "The Dutch have lost all control over using and dealing
drugs..." — these are but a few examples of the incorrect or incomplete
beliefs about Dutch drug policy often expressed by foreigners. One of
the primary purposes of this book is to debunk some of these myths by
providing a complete and in-depth description of the facts about drug
policy in the Netherlands. To this end, the chapters in the Part I (Chapters
1 through 5) provide a detailed description of the legal, social, and philosophical foundations of the current pragmatic Dutch drug policy. A major
theme of the book is how and why Dutch drug policy is so different from
that of other European countries and the U.S. The first two chapters of
Part I address this question by providing the historical and socio-political
background of current Dutch drug legislation and policy. De Kort (Chapter 1) traces the development of Dutch drug policy back to the government's economic interests in the drug trade involving the Dutch colonies
in the 19th century and its resultant reluctant enforcement of the early
international drug treaties. He explains the Dutch emphasis on the medical-social care of users and prevention by referring to specific national
political, social and cultural circumstances (*i.e.*, drug use remained
limited to isolated groups, influential role of medical profession on
policy, lack of a moral entrepreneur, and integration of the youth culture

into the social and political mainstream). In Chapter 2, Leuw zeros in on the history of the political and cultural forces involved in the centerpiece of Dutch drug legislation, the 1976 Revised Opium Act and the crucial role of two expert committees in formulating policy. He emphasizes how in the Netherlands the drug problem has not been a confrontational issue between moral/political right and moral/political left, but rather has gone through a process of de-escalating significance, very different from countries like the U.S. and Germany. Modern Dutch drug policy is based on two principles: combatting large-scale drug trafficking (through law enforcement) and prevention and assistance to the drug user (through public health). Silvis (Chapter 3) gives an overview of the legal principles behind drug enforcement in the Netherlands; he highlights the role of the "principle of expediency" which provides the legal latitude to develop policy guidelines *not* to enforce particular drug law violations (*i.e.*, those involving users and small-scale dealing). Silvis also shows how the Netherlands has not remained immune to the erosion of due process protections often associated with drug enforcement. The Dutch view drugs primarily as a public health problem, and only secondarily as a criminal justice problem. Wever (Chapter 4) describes the public health approach to drugs, both in terms of its philosophy (with as key concepts normalization, risk reduction, and prevention) and its practical operationalization in treatment and services. Both Silvis and Wever speculate about the effects of international forces on drug policy. The discussion of the ideological foundations of Dutch pragmatism in Part I is completed by Erkelens and Van Alem (Chapter 5) in their analysis of the development and state-of-the-art of Dutch correctional policy. They show how this policy has developed within the changing perspectives of general criminal justice policy and the general drugs and crime problem in Dutch society. Of particular interest is their discussion of the so-called "drug-free units" (DFUs) in Dutch prisons, which in the view of many exemplify the Dutch pragmatic approach to drugs.

Different from the United States, where drugs are considered a problem of utmost urgency, the Dutch do not view drugs as a tremendously pressing problem. Consistent with this view, Dutch drug policy is best characterized as low key and minimalist. "Moderation" is the thread connecting the chapters in Part II of the book (Chapters 6 through 10). Swierstra (Chapter 6) chronicles the development of drug problems in the Netherlands over the last two decades. In addition to describing epidemiological developments in drug use, he asks whether Dutch drug use careers differ from those observed in other countries; and, if so, if these differences reflect the particular nature of Dutch drug policy. He bases his observations on the results of two empirical studies of the careers of hard drug users, and he concludes that the patterns and careers have changed over time, reflecting social, political *and* drug policy changes. He concedes that pragmatic Dutch drug policy has facilitated experimentation with drugs, and that methadone maintenance, although it may keep people addicted for longer periods of time, keeps people more socially integrated. Korf (Chapter 7) uses a field study of 382 drug tourists to study why foreign drug users come (and stay) in Amsterdam, how they generate their income, and what — if any — are the effects of the Dutch policy of "discouragement"? Van Gemert and Verbraeck's (Chapter 8) ethnographic account of two decades of drug dealing and use also is based on Amsterdam observations, with a particular focus on how the culture of the Amsterdam inner city provides a fertile and hospitable environment for drug users and drug dealers. Their account illustrates the important fact that one can only understand the nature of the local "drugs scene" against the backdrop of the cultural and economic context of the neighborhood. The chapter further shows that a sometimes tense, but generally peaceful cohabitation of the drug subculture with traditionally deviant and more conventional city life is feasible. Amsterdam is also the focus of Jansen's description (based largely on personal observations of transactions) of the "coffee shop" phenomenon (Chapter 9). Coffee shops are perhaps the most well-known examples of "liberal" drug policy known to foreigners; Jansen uses his description to show that Dutch society has successfully integrated soft drugs into mainstream society. Part II concludes the description of the restrained Dutch approach to drugs with Bieleman and Bosma's discussion (in Chapter 10) of the Rotterdam Drug-Related Crime Project, an experimental program emphasizing cooperation between local city government, the Prosecutor's Office, police, and drug assistance agencies, aiming to prevent drug-related criminality. Within a three-year time period (1988-1990), four (small-scale) DRC programs were implemented: a research study describing the extent and nature of the Rotterdam drug-using population, a work project aimed at the reintegration of addicts into society, a "target hardening" project to reduce drug-related property crime in parking garages; and a shelter for addicts near the Central Station aiming at the reduction of nuisance associated with the concentration of drug addicts in that area. Although not successful by all measures, Bieleman and Bosma document several accomplishments of this pilot project.

Most of the chapters of the book touch, in one way or another, on one of three key questions: (1) how is Dutch drug policy different from that of other countries; (2) how is the increasing internationalization of the world going to have an impact on Dutch drug policy, and (3) is there anything in Dutch drug policy that may be transferred to other nations. Part III makes these questions its central concern. First, in Chapter 11, Marshall and Marshall examine the philosophy of drug prevention as well as the major types of drug prevention programs in the Netherlands. Within the perspective of "normalization" drugs are a normal health education issue which, relative to for instance alcohol use or safe sexual practices, is of minor importance for general (young) population groups. Dutch drug prevention is contrasted with the U.S. as low-key and minimal and less likely to make use of fear arousal and/or moral appeals. Grapendaal, Leuw and Nelen (Chapter 12) present a field ethnographic study of Amsterdam to assess arguments pro and contra legalization and decriminalization. The drug legalization debate is one that crosses national boundaries and often manages to ignite international consternation among government officials and policy makers of the highest level. Grapendaal and co-workers' study is based on repeated interviews of a sample of Amsterdam opiate addicts about their drug taking and economic behavior over a period of 13 months; they examine the role of drugs in the initiation of the criminal career, the effect of methadone maintenance on property crime, and the (in)elasticity of demand. They interpret their data in a deviant career perspective: people who are attracted to drugs are looking not only for dope, but also for illegality. Blom and Van Mastrigt (Chapter 13) describe several international developments, more specifically those related to the ongoing process of European unification, which might affect the Dutch model of drug control. They discuss Dutch drug policy as it has developed since the mid-seventies in the context of the foundation of national and international developments in drug policy, the Single Convention. They do an admirable job in describing the rather chaotic world of international drug control bodies in Europe (including the United Nations). They speculate about the likelihood that the Dutch model will survive in the international War on Drugs, using relevant domestic developments in the Netherlands. Kraan (Chapter 14) analyzes Dutch drug policy from an economic perspective, employing a "public choice" approach to analyze the regulation of markets and the provision of services with regard to cannabis, cocaine, and heroin. His comparison of the relative importance of health care *versus* law enforcement costs between the U.S. and the Netherlands illustrates the utility of this model as a way to operationalize the philosophical principles underlying different social policies. This chapter suggests that the Dutch policy model allows better returns for substantially less public expenses. Consistent with the title of the book, Kaplan, Haanraadts, Van Vliet and Grund (Chapter 15) conceive of Dutch drugs policy as an "experiment" in the shift from a "more of the same" adaptation strategy to a "different goals" strategy. This concluding chapter represents an ambitious attempt to provide a pragmatic answer to the question of whether Dutch drug policy may be used as an example for other countries by identifying the "manageable bits" which are transferable to other countries. The authors argue that Dutch society presents a compact adaptation of broad socio-historical processes which all modern societies are now undergoing; Dutch society is an example of the new and innovative well-being state (De Swaan 1988). The emotional and cultural conditions for the technology transfer of Dutch drug policy are becoming more widespread. In view of the fact that Dutch drug policy is, by most measures, more humane and less costly than that of many other countries, it is appropriate to conclude this book with the optimistic note that Dutch drug policy, in the final analysis, although in many ways unique to the Netherlands, does have implications beyond Dutch national boundaries.

References

Cohen, P.: *Drugs as a Social Construct*. Utrecht: Elinkwijk, 1990
Duster, T.: *The Legalisation of Morality: Law, Drugs and Moral Judgement*. New York: Free Press, 1970
De Swaan, A.: *In Care of the State: Health Care, Education and Welfare in Europe and the USA in the Modern Era*. Cambridge: Polity Press, 1988
Gerritsen, J.: *De Politieke Economie van de Roes: de Ontwikkeling van Reguleringsregimes voor Alcohol en Opiaten*. Amsterdam: Amsterdam University Press, 1993
Lidz, C.M., Walker, A.L. and Gould, L.C.: *Drugs, Deviance and Morality*. Beverly Hills: Sage Publications, 1980
Musto, D.F.: *The American Disease: Origins of Narcotic Control*. New Haven: Yale University Press, 1973
Scheerer, S.: Political ideologies and drug policy. *European Journal on Criminal Policy and Research* Vol. 1, No. 1, 1993

PART I

IDEOLOGICAL FOUNDATIONS
OF "PRAGMATISM"

I. A SHORT HISTORY OF DRUGS IN THE NETHERLANDS

Marcel de Kort

1. Introduction

Dutch drug policy deviates substantially from drug policies in most other countries. It is not surprising, then, that Dutch drug policy has often met with severe criticism from abroad. Criticism from foreigners has become more pronounced during the last decade. For example, critics in the United States have objected to the low-threshold methadone programs and needle-exchange programs; Germany and Sweden have strongly criticized the decriminalization of the use of cannabis.[1] It is such controversial aspects – the attention to the medical and social care of drug users and the decriminalization of marihuana – which form the "deviant" core of Dutch drug policy.

If indeed Dutch drug policy deviates so much from drug policies in other countries, an interesting question presents itself: How can we explain the development of this unique Dutch way of dealing with drugs? How was the historical development of the Netherlands with regard to drug policy different from, say, the United States and Great Britain? This chapter attempts to answer this question as follows. In the first section, I provide a brief description of the highlights of the developments in Dutch drug policy: 19th century drug use, Dutch interests in the production and sale of drugs, the Dutch position in international opium conferences, the 1919 Opium Act and developments after the Second World War. In the second part of this chapter, I discuss the political and social conditions in the Netherlands which provided the foundation for the development of this much criticized policy. Illuminating in this respect is a comparison with the developments in the United States and England. The present chapter's emphasis is predominantly on the developments prior to the mid 1970s.

2. Self-medication and medicine in the nineteenth century

In the 19th century, quackery and popular healing had a dominant position in health care. Self-medication was so popular that around the end of the 19th century a large part of the population had never even visited a physician. The cause of this low level of consultation of physicians should not be located in a shortage of physicians or poor social-economic conditions of the Dutch population. Modern medical care was readily available through the system of poor relief or sick funds. In addition, there was an abundance of recognized medical doctors during the second half of the 19th century.

According to Verdoorn (1981), 19th century Dutch society knew two types of medicine: the "primitive-traditional" and the "rational-scientific". These two types were not integrated, but co-existed independently from one another. Based on popular healing practices, the believers in "primitive-traditional" healing rejected elements of modern medicine, such as physicians, hospitals and midwives. Those patients who did visit physicians accepted the modern "rational-scientific" way of thinking. These two separate groups, with their very own cultural pattern with regard to illness and health, existed side by side until around 1880 when the integration of these patterns begun. The gradual integration of "primitive-traditional" and "rational-scientific" approaches to healing continued well into the 20th century. Opiates played an important role in "primitive-traditional" medicine. Nineteenth-century books about popular healing contain many prescriptions with opiates. For example, one could fight toothache by placing a piece of opium in the hollow tooth or by rinsing one's mouth with opium solvent; hemorrhoids would disappear through the use of a poppy oil enema (Osiander 1854). Poppy oil or syrup could cure many ailments and was also used to keep children quiet and relaxed. The use of poppy syrup as a baby "pacifier" was the best-known and most infamous application of this drug until well into the 20th century. After a spoonful of poppy syrup, the baby would stop crying and quietly fall asleep. In 1854, giving poppy syrup to babies was still considered a "good habit". Half a century later, people began to reject it due to the risk of poisoning the children through an overdose. In the middle of the 19th century, however, the use of opiates was not yet taboo. The different remedies were readily available and cheap.

In the second half of the 19th century, a large variety of patent medicines (usually referred to as "specialités" or "specialties"), often containing opium, cocaine or marihuana, became part of "primitive-traditional" medicine. Numerous types with exotic names and helpful for virtually all ailments became available. From 1875 on, it was particularly the medicines containing cocaine which became popular, such as Vin de coca du Perou, Professor Dr. Sampson's coca preparations and the coca preparations of Doctor Jose Alvarez.

Opiates were also used frequently in the practice of "rational-scientific" medicine. Opium was virtually the only adequate remedy with a pain-killing effect. In the 19th century other pain killers such as aspirin were not yet available. Thus, physicians of that period did not have any alternative pain killers, had little understanding of the harmful effects associated with drugs, and freely prescribed drugs to their patients. In the middle of the 19th century, members of the medical profession were mostly positive about drugs: morphine was viewed as having no harmful side-effects and one was enthusiastic about Dover's powder, a "specialty" containing opium. Morphine, in particular, was used frequently. As early as the beginning of the 19th century, a German by the name of Sertuner managed to extract morphine from opium, but morphine did not become very popular until the invention of the hypodermic needle 50 years later. Injection of morphine by hypodermic needle was an application of "rational-scientific" medicine. Whenever they saw a need, physicians would inject large quantities of morphine in their patients for a variety of reasons, thereby creating a new group of addicts. In fact, physicians created a new disease, which may be characterized as iatrogenic dependency.

About ten years after the hypodermic needle was first used, physicians concluded that morphine was addictive. They called this addiction "hunger" or "desire" for morphine, "morphinomania" or "morphinism". Initially, French and German doctors spearheaded the study of the addictive effect of morphine; however, soon afterwards research on "morphinism" was done in large parts of Europe and the United States.[2]

In Dutch medical publications there were mostly references to foreign research, with the added note that "morphinism" was more of a problem in countries other than the Netherlands. It is possible that there were relatively fewer visible morphine addicts in the Netherlands than, for example, in Germany, France and the United States. Because of historical developments such as the French-German War (1870) and the American Civil War (1861-1865), the number of addicts in Germany, France and the US experienced an explosive growth. The rise of this "soldier's disease" stimulated the field of medicine in these countries to conduct research on the addictive qualities of morphine. The Netherlands, on the other hand, was not involved in a war during the second half of the 19th century, which made morphine addiction there a less noteworthy phenomenon than in other countries. Another possible explanation for these international differences in connection with morphine addiction may be found in the more prominent role of popular healing in the Netherlands as compared to other Western European countries and the US. Due to the importance of "primitive-traditional" medicine in the Netherlands, fewer people were at risk of developing an iatrogenic addiction through "rational-scientific" medicine (*i.e.*, hypodermic needle); rather, people could ingest liquid laudanum or a "specialty" containing opium.

In 1886, a dissertation entitled *Alcoholism, Morphinism and Chloralism* was published, the only extensive Dutch study of this topic in the 19th century. Broers, the author of this dissertation, concluded that this morphine "disease" was spreading in all countries, including the Netherlands, at a frightening speed. Broers based his conclusions primarily on information extracted from foreign publications. He managed to introduce only a few of his own patients as "Dutch morphinists". It is impossible to provide a reliable estimate of the total number of "morphinists" living in the Netherlands during that period. There simply are no statistics and extensive studies. However, we do know that around the turn of the century, articles on addiction to morphine and cocaine appeared regularly, primarily in the Dutch Journal of Medicine and the Pharmaceutical Weekly.

Around 1880, Dutch medical specialists began to examine cocaine more closely, as a result of the spread of "cocainism" in the Netherlands. Gradually, one started to distinguish between the use of drugs for medicinal or recreational purposes. If prescribed by the physician, opiates and cocaine were viewed as beneficial. On the other hand, the same drugs in the hands of the lay public were considered stimulants and thus harmful. In effect, physicians and pharmacists were simply attempting to obtain a monopoly on the prescription, administration and supply of drugs. This trend paralleled the professionalization of the medical and paramedical occupations taking place during that time.

The last decades of the 19th century thus witnessed a re-definition of drug use as problematic by the medical profession. After the medical profession had put a claim on opiates and cocaine, an "attack" on self-medication became inevitable. The "specialty industry", with its heavy reliance on drugs, was a thorn in the side of official medicine. Spearheaded by the Union against Quackery, physicians who were eager to professionalize their occupation initiated an offensive against the competition. Indeed, around 1900, the use of drugs had become a problem for the medical profession enviously eying the unrestrained sale of opiate-based or cocaine-based specialties.

The 19th century drug history of the Netherlands is not very different from what took place in other Western countries. In the United States, England, France and Germany, opiates and coca(ine) also played an important role, both in self-medication and in official medicine.[3] There was a considerable volume of concerned writing about addiction to morphine and cocaine in these countries. The Netherlands differed from the US and other Western European countries in that it did not have any addicted soldiers and there was hardly any scientific research on the nature and dimensions of the addiction. However, both medical and pharmaceutical sources strongly suggest that the Netherlands certainly was not a drug-free country at that time.

3. The Netherlands Indies, drug production and trade

It was not until the end of the 19th century that the Netherlands became concerned with the use of drugs as a stimulant. This concern must be understood in the historical context of the Dutch government's role in the production and trade of drugs, particularly in its colonies. In the former Dutch colony of the Netherlands Indies, recreative use of opium had been experienced for a much longer time. Indeed, the smoking of opium by the local population had resulted in huge profits for the Dutch for centuries. The Dutch used a system of "opium leasing" – that is, the government leased the right to sell opium to the highest bidder. Dutch ships transported the opium from Turkey and Bengal to the Malay Archipelago, where distribution was left primarily to Chinese opium lease-holders. According to Vanvugt (1985), the Dutch position regarding the trading and consumption of opium was determined by the financial interest of this trade for the national treasury. Colonial profits were, to a large degree, dependent upon opium profits. Between 1834 and 1875, the net opium profit was 3,369 million guilders (about 2,000 million dollars); between 1876 and 1915, the profits from opium were 7,033 million guilders (about 3,500 million dollars). Between 1816 and 1915 the total net profit from opium constituted approximately ten percent of the total income from the colonies for the Dutch treasury. By the end of the 19th century, when it became apparent that the profits from opium leasing were declining, the government decided to implement a state monopoly on the sale and distribution of opium in the Netherlands Indies. This state monopoly was referred to as the "regie-system".

The debate accompanying the transition from the leasing system to the state monopoly resulted in an enormous volume of books, flyers and pamphlets about opium. Typically, this literature was written in a polemic style and focused on three themes: (1) the problems of opium smuggling in the Dutch East Indies; (2) the possible harmful effects of opium use; and (3) the transition from the leasing system to the state monopoly. Financial considerations played an important role: for each proposed change in policy the financial consequences for the state's treasury were closely scrutinized. There was no question that measures should be taken against smuggling practices which would cut tax revenues. The advantages of a state monopoly were stressed heavily in this literature; a state monopoly would inhibit smuggling because the (legal) state opium with its own packaging would be clearly distinguishable from the (illegal) smuggler's opium. Second, a state monopoly would mean higher profits, in view of the fact that income from opium leasing had declined substantially by the end of the 19th century. Finally, it was argued that it would be easier to reduce the number of opium smokers by a state monopoly than by any other system. This last advantage was considered especially important by a group of authors who emphasized the harmful effects of the smoking of opium and who viewed it as the responsibility of the Dutch to decrease drug use.

In practice, however, the Dutch did not take any substantial measures against the consumption of opium in their colonies. Until well into the 20th century, the profits from opium were too substantial to permit any form of general prohibition. The Second World War and the subsequent independence of Indonesia marked the end of the Dutch opium trade in Asia.[4]

In addition to the financial interests of the opium trade, the production of coca leaves and cocaine also played a crucial role in contributing to the Dutch treasury. Around 1860, efforts to extract cocaine from coca leaves were successful, resulting in a fast rise in the popularity of this drug. Initially, the coca leaves came from Peru and Bolivia. The Dutch saw a new market, and in 1878 coca plants were transported from South America to the Dutch Indies, where beginning in 1886, important and continuously expanding plantations were established. In the beginning, coca from Java, the island with the largest number of plantations, could not compete with the leaves imported from other countries. However, the quality of the coca harvest improved steadily and considerable energy was devoted to the careful packaging and transportation.

The production of coca leaves increased sharply during the first decades of the 20th century. While in 1907 only 200 tons of leaves were produced in the Indies, in 1914 this had increased to almost 1,400 tons. During the First World War, the transportation to Europe became seriously impaired and export declined sharply (to less than one-and-a-half ton in 1916). After the war, however, the export of coca leaves quickly recovered and peaked in 1920 with more than 1,700 ton. At that time, the Netherlands had been the largest cocaine producer of the world for nearly ten years. By far the largest portion of the coca leaves was transported to the Netherlands. The largest customer was the Dutch Cocaine Factory in Amsterdam, established in 1900. The Amsterdam-based firm Cheiron as well as Brocades and Stheeman in the eastern part of the Netherlands also produced cocaine.

Although the Dutch maintained that its cocaine was produced exclusively for medical purposes, it is plausible to assume that an important portion was used purely for recreative purposes. In 1922, it was estimated that the world need for cocaine for medicinal purposes was some 12,000 kilos. The production of coca leaves in the Indies (1,283,503 kilos) alone would have been more than sufficient to satisfy this demand; similarly, the export of coca leaves from Peru and Bolivia together would also have satisfied the world demand (Gavit 1925). It should be noted, however, that the cocaine for recreational purposes, to a large extent, was brought into circulation through medical channels at that time, which made the medical need appear much more substantial than it really was.

The Netherlands was by no means the only country in the world which had important economic interests in the production and trade of drugs. Germany produced cocaine and codeine and England produced morphine. Persia (now Iran) had interests in the cultivation of the poppy and Portugal produced opium in Macao, while France made money on opium in Indochina. Yet, the Netherlands was viewed by the Americans as one of the worst "evil-doers", in particular because of its coca production. For example, Java and the Netherlands were mentioned in one breath with Peru and Bolivia (Musto 1987). As recently as 1931 and 1940, the League of Nations referred to the Netherlands as one of the most important producing and exporting countries (Chatterjee 1981). Yet, Dutch representatives attending international opium conferences at the beginning of the 20th century were not very cooperative. The reluctance of the Dutch to cooperate with international efforts to control drugs was not surprising in view of the potential loss of substantial profits for the Dutch treasury.

4. The International Opium Conferences and the Opium Act

In 1909, at the initiative of the United States, a commission convened in Shanghai to discuss the international opium trade and opium consumption in the colonies. With the exception of the United States, the participating countries were not at that time concerned with drug use in their own country. This lack of concern with domestic drug abuse was also true for the Netherlands. The chair of the commission, Bishop Brent from the United States, had hoped to assemble a conference (rather than a commission) – a diplomatic meeting which would result in official measures by the represented governments. At the request of Great Britain and the Netherlands, however, the Shanghai meeting remained limited to a commission: "a fact-finding body which could make only recommendations and not commitments" (Musto 1987:35). The opium commission formulated nine recommendations; the main impact of these recommendations was that they provided the foundation for further negotiations.

Again based on American initiative, an international opium conference met in The Hague in 1911 to translate the Shanghai recommendations into actual legislation. Organizing the first international opium conference was not a simple task. The United States felt that international regulations took much longer than anticipated. Under the leadership of Dr. Hamilton Wright, a physician with strong political interests, the United States began to express concern that a conspiracy existed against the American "crusade" against drug use. To add insult to injury, Germany, England and the Netherlands gave the impression not to have any real short-term need for such a conference. Wright decided to take the offensive against this apparent inertia: "(he) sought out the Dutch minister to the United States, then vacationing in Maine, and threatened that if the Netherlands continued to procrastinate, the United States might convene the conference in Washington" (Musto 1987:49). Ultimately, the Netherlands organized the first international opium conference, resulting in the Hague Opium Convention of 1912. The largest portion of this convention consisted of guidelines regarding the regulation of the production and trade of opiates and coca(ine). Article 9, which required participating countries to enact legislation to limit the production and sale of drugs to medicinal purposes only, is most crucial for the present discussion. This article provides the foundation for the 1919 Dutch Opium Act.[5]

It took several years, however, before ratification of the 1912 Opium Convention. Article 31 of the convention required the organization of another conference, if the agreement had not been ratified by all participating countries by December 31, 1912. It became apparent that individual governments, including the Netherlands, were not in any hurry to ratify the convention; consequently, a second and even a third conference, respectively in 1913 and 1914, were necessary to urge the participants to take appropriate action. At the 1913 and 1914 meetings, the Netherlands argued in favor of expedient ratification and swift adjustment of national legislation; yet, the Dutch government dragged its feet the longest. It was not until February 1915 that the agreement was finally ratified.

Vested economic interests in the production and trade of drugs may explain the Dutch reluctance to endorse strong international drug control. Clearly, the Netherlands attempted to protect these interests at the conferences (Wissler 1930) and did so successfully, at least temporarily. During the international meetings, the Dutch position was made very clear and explicit. At the first opium conference, the Netherlands argued in favor of a government monopoly on opium. The opium trade would need to be left solely to the governments; and smuggling needed to be combatted forcefully. The Dutch delegates characterized the smugglers as "our greatest enemies" (Chatterjee 1981). Indeed, the Netherlands maintained a government monopoly on opium in the Dutch Indies until the invasion of the Japanese army in 1942. In addition, the Netherlands also disagreed with attempts to regulate the cocaine trade. Ultimately, the international treaties did not harm the Dutch interests in this white powder for a long time. Incidentally, the Netherlands also objected to the inclusion of marihuana in the convention.

Chatterjee (1981) characterizes the Dutch position during this international discussion until the Second World War as "pseudo-obligation...neither self-induced nor genuine". The Netherlands, however, overestimated the possibility of guaranteeing its own interests. The Netherlands hoped to reserve the right to withdraw from the Opium Convention in case of conflicting interests, or not to ratify any international agreement which would threaten economic interests too much.

At the domestic front, the feasibility of employing legal measures and international cooperation to control illegal drug trade started to raise questions in the Netherlands as early as the 1920s. The majority opinion in the Netherlands was that the "war on drugs" (as we call it now) could not be won. Several Dutch sources from that period suggest that the illegal drug trade would be difficult to control due to the importance of the financial and economic interests involved in the highly priced, easily concealed drugs: "The simplicity of the restriction notion is, however, only superficial: one will encounter virtually unsurmountable difficulties in any attempt to implement this notion into practice" (Tan Tong Joe 1929:13-14; author's translation). The notion that it was possible to eliminate international illegal drug smuggling was referred to as the "American position" – a position which is "(virtually) unenforceable" (Tan Tong Joe 1929:13-14).

5. The reluctant and selective enforcement of the Opium Act

Other countries criticized the Netherlands for their lenient drug control measures. This may be illustrated in the following example, which caused an international stir. In 1928, when the Netherlands had not yet introduced a certification system to regulate international trade, the Chemical Plant Naarden was able to buy and sell about half of the world production of heroin. Meanwhile, other countries had already passed legislation to prohibit this, but in the Netherlands where this was still completely legal, the Chemische Fabriek Naarden obtained a government permit to produce and sell drugs. The Opium Commission of the League of Nations was very critical of this action.

After the enactment of the 1919 Opium Act, transportation of drugs and drug trading had become illegal. Although it was still possible for businesses to participate in drug trade through a system of permits, a substantial (extensive) smuggling trade could not be prevented.[6] Soon after the enactment of the Opium Act large quantities of illegal drugs were confiscated. For example, in the harbor city of Rotterdam in 1920, a shipment of morphine was found with an estimated value of 50,000 German Marks. Two years later, in a town near the German border, 700 flasks of morphine, which were intended to be distributed to different regions in the country, were confiscated. In 1925, there was an attempt to use safes to smuggle 50,000 Guilders worth of cocaine and morphine from the Belgian city of Antwerp to Rotterdam. In England, a 29-year-old Dutch citizen was convicted of the illegal possession of cocaine. According to the police, this Dutchman had been living in London for a few years, but he travelled repeatedly to the Netherlands and France to buy cocaine (Parssinen 1983). Interestingly, the Dutch were convinced that international organized crime was responsible for the large-scale smuggling. The introduction of the system of certification in 1928 was not able to suppress drug smuggling either. Ever more creative means were invented to transport drugs across national borders. It was close to the Belgian border that the first suitcases with false bottoms were discovered in 1930.

The fight against drugs became increasingly professionalized in the 1930s, at both national and international levels. During the 1930s, there were regular international meetings of police authorities to discuss how to combat drug smuggling more effectively. The Rotterdam police established a special Narcotics Division. At that time, the United States played an important role in the internationalization of the fight against drugs: "The Americans have built an organization in Europe to assist the European police in all possible manners and, of course, to also prevent the transportation of drugs from Europe to the United States" (*Nieuwe Rotterdamsche Courant* 1939; author's translation).

Not surprisingly, the Opium Act virtually did nothing to stop drug smuggling. The popular press repeatedly complained about the lack of effective measures. For example, in 1921, the *Pharmaceutical Weekly* predicted that "...the Netherlands will shortly become the center of a clandestine opium and cocaine trade".

The maximum sentence for violation of the Opium Act was increased from three months imprisonment and a 1,000 guilder fine in 1919 to one year imprisonment, with the same fine, in 1928. In practice, it was the smuggler who received the most severe sentence. For example, those involved in the smuggling of morphine and cocaine in safes received the maximum sentence. On the other hand, pharmacists who violated the law by selling opiates or cocaine without prescription received lighter sentences. To illustrate, the prosecutor asked for three months imprisonment of a pharmacist who had provided drugs to "morphinists" (*Pharmaceutisch Weekblad* 1938:1209). Addicts were typically not convicted under the Opium Act. There was one group of users, however, who was more likely to be prosecuted: the Chinese opium smokers. The first Chinese group of immigrants arrived in 1911 in Rotterdam to break the seamen's strike. After a few years, this group had developed its own "Chinatown" both in Rotterdam and Amsterdam. Opium smoking was very popular in the Chinese community; an estimated 75% of the Chinese smoked opium. The arrival of the Chinese introduced the use of opium in the Netherlands. After 1919 it was this particular group of users who was singled out for prosecution, because their method of consumption was foreign to European norms, not serving any medicinal purpose, and being used exclusively for recreational purposes. In addition, the Chinese were an easily distinguishable and isolated group for the police. The Chinese smoked their opium in opium dens, which were easy to locate by law enforcement officials. Generally speaking, rather mild sentences were given to Chinese who were prosecuted under the Opium Act. Possession of opium for personal use was permitted; however, if one was in possession of more than two grams, prosecution resulted. Fines varied from between 25 to 50 Guilders.

This does not mean that it was only the Chinese who used drugs. Police reports from the 1920s suggest a widespread use of cocaine by seamen congregating in certain neighborhoods attracted by prostitution and bars. Most of these users, however, obtained the drugs through a physician's prescription. A 1937 study indicates that physicians prescribed large quantities of cocaine, morphine, and the opiate Dilaudid for their patients. Very little heroin was used. The Opium Act could not be used to prosecute these users, because physicians were allowed to prescribe drugs.

6. Comparisons of drug policy in the Netherlands, Great Britain and the United States before the Second World War

I have already discussed the notion that vested economic interests were an important explanation for the apparent reluctance of the Dutch to fully endorse international agreements concerning drugs. It seems that the noted lack of a stringent enforcement at the domestic level, however, requires an explanation involving additional factors. In this context, it is useful to draw upon the work done by Parssinen (1983) who compares the American repressive approach of the 1920s with the more medically oriented approach of Great Britain. He explains the differences in approach by the presence of problematic recreational user groups in the United States while comparable problematic drug-using groups were virtually absent in England. In the United States, a large Chinese community existed from which recreational drug use gradually spread to other groups. Parssinen argues that the Chinese community in England was much smaller and more isolated than in the United States. When we include the Netherlands in this comparison, an interesting commonality with the English development may be noted. As in England, the Netherlands did not have a large group of recreational drug users who were viewed as causing social unrest. Although the Netherlands had the largest Chinese community in Europe, in comparison with the United States, this community was relatively small and isolated from other groups. It is noteworthy, however, that it was mainly Chinese users who were prosecuted in the Netherlands, in spite of a relatively permissive attitude. Yet, it may be argued that in the Netherlands, as in England, it was the absence of a large group of recreational drug users and the small size of the Chinese community which accounts for the absence of a repressive approach.

Another cause for the differences in policy between the United States, Great Britain and the Netherlands may be the differential impact of the medical profession on policy. According to Stein (1985), physicians in the United States had little influence at the federal level, where drug policy was formulated. In the United States, medical interest groups were active at state level, not at federal level. The medical profession in Great Britain was much more influential in setting public health policy than in the United States. This is reflected in the composition of the Roleston

Committee which was established in 1924 to answer the question of whether doctors should be allowed to prescribe opiates and cocaine to addicts. The Committee consisted mainly of physicians, who were able to implement a medical approach: "Above all, they were medical men who were defending the professional prerogative of the physician to exercise control over the drugs he administered" (Parssinen 1983:220).

In practice the Dutch policy on drugs was very similar to the British policy during the period of 1920 through 1955. However, there was no Roleston Report, so there has never been any mention of the "Dutch medical model". Enforcing the Opium Act was a task for the Justice and Health Departments. Police and the Justice Department focused on the prosecution of illicit trafficking and smuggling, while physicians were concerned with the addicts and were authorized to prescribe drugs to addicts. This separation of tasks and authorities between health and justice officials, due partly to regular interdepartmental exchanges of views, was well balanced. The moment the police and the Department of Justice concerned themselves with prescribing physicians and addicts, the Health Department would intervene. It did not allow the prerogatives of the medical profession to be violated. One such incident occurred for instance in 1937 when the police initiated an investigation of the use of drugs and the degree to which doctors prescribed drugs to patients. The police sent alarming reports to the Justice Department, allegedly indicating that doctors and pharmacists prescribed drugs on a large scale to supply addicts. The Health Department reacted furiously to the reports provided by police authorities. It charged the police with unauthorized interference in public health matters. Police officials were said to be unable to judge whether drugs were used for recreational purposes.

It was made abundantly clear that there were no violations of the Opium Act and the police were not authorized to investigate doctors. This was a task for the Health Department.

7. Developments after the Second World War

Shortly after the Second World War, Amsterdam established its own two-member Narcotics Division. The establishment of the Amsterdam Narcotics Division was triggered by increased smuggling by Germans from the supplies of drugs from the capitulated German Army. (As we already have seen, Rotterdam established its own Narcotics Division before the Second World War.) In the first few years after the war, drug use did not receive much attention. Drug enforcement officials apparently observed very little recreational drug use. There were few arrests and the amounts of confiscated cocaine and morphine were negligible. Opium smoking by local Chinese was generally tolerated. However, Chinese seamen who smuggled kilos of opium were prosecuted.

Before the war, there was virtually no use of marihuana in the Netherlands. Only artists and writers occasionally experimented with the smoking of hashish and marihuana. After the war, the use of these drugs was mostly associated with "...swing musicians, black and white musicians, who try to identify with this music. Trade is concentrated in the cosmopolitical downtown areas of Amsterdam and Rotterdam, the only places where the few black bands that exist in our country can find employment. This trade often involves swindling: all too frequently the so-called reefers are, for instance, opium cigarettes" (Van Wolferen 1949:323; author's translation).

After the Second World War, the trade in marihuana cigarettes increased. However, the police could not do anything about it, since the possession and sale of this drug was not yet illegal. In 1953, possession of marihuana became illegal under the Opium Act and in 1955 the first arrests took place among marihuana smugglers and marihuana users. Attention was focused primarily on American soldiers of the Allied Forces in West Germany, who would come to the Netherlands on "pay day". Marihuana was sold to the American soldiers by Dutch people, who obtained the drug from sailors. As far back as 1955 the Amsterdam Narcotics Division cooperated with the American Office of Special Investigation at Soesterberg Airbase. In that year, three American soldiers were arrested for possession of 60 marihuana cigarettes, a considerable amount for that time period. A painter was convicted to a three-month suspended prison sentence because of possession of two marihuana cigarettes. According to the annual reports of the Amsterdam Narcotics Division, the trade in "Indian hemp" was mostly in the hands of persons who came from the colony of Surinam.

The 1960s signaled a turn in drug use and drug policy in the Netherlands. Marihuana, and to a lesser degree, amphetamines were more visible and its use was no longer restricted to artists, students, and so on. During this time, the police would hunt intensively for a few grams of marihuana or hashish. The penalties were quite severe. Users with a minimum amount of marihuana in their possession were often sent to prison for a few months. However, this repressive approach could not prevent a fast increase in the use of marihuana, particularly with the rise of the 1960s' youth culture (*i.e.,* Provos or beatniks and hippies).

LSD was first imported from England in 1965 in relatively large quantities and its use spread quickly. As Cohen (1975) points out, this fast dissemination of LSD could only take place because of the presence of a large supply of the drug and the willingness of large groups of people to accept the drug. In 1966, there was a wave of sensational publicity in the newspapers which fueled the fear of LSD. The *Telegraaf*, a popular newspaper, argued: "A small lump of sugar quickly takes the user to a fantasy world but LSD causes insanity". Not even two weeks later the Opium Act was expanded to include LSD, together with another 18 psychedelic drugs.[7]

During the 1960s, use of opium in the youth culture was also expanding. Up to that time, the Chinese opium dens were more or less tolerated. However, as soon as Dutch youth began to buy their drugs at the opium dens, a more repressive policy was implemented against both the smoking and injection of opium. This situation continued until the arrival of larger amounts of heroin in 1972.

8. Decriminalization of marihuana

One of the most noteworthy aspects of Dutch drug policy in the 1970s was the *de facto* decriminalization of the use of marihuana and the small-scale dealing in youth centers and so-called coffee shops. This is a striking development in view of the fact that only ten years earlier the prosecution of users and dealers of this most frequently used drug was still a high priority for the criminal justice system. Furthermore, smoking of marihuana or hashish was by no means a socially accepted custom in the Netherlands of the 1960s. How, then, may we explain the development of the internationally "deviant" Dutch drug policy of the 1970s? A comparison with the United States may shed some light on this question.

A comparison between the United States and the Netherlands with regard to marihuana shows an important difference. Marihuana in the United States was associated with a "marihuana ideology"; first as a "killer weed", causing violence among its predominantly Mexican-American users, and later as a middle-class youth "drop-out drug" (see Himmelstein 1983). The Netherlands, on the other hand, lacked a specific ideology associated with marihuana. Before the Second World War, there was only a very sporadic use of marihuana. After the war, although there was some use in circles of jazz musicians and American soldiers, the use was so limited that an ideology never developed. The already noted repressive response to all drugs in the early 1960s reflected concern with law-breaking *per se*, rather than a strongly held belief system about the evils associated with marihuana use.

The Netherlands also lacked a moral entrepreneur, like the Federal

Bureau of Narcotics in the US, interested in criminalizing this drug. In the Netherlands marihuana use was not linked to a particular ethnic group, like the Mexican-Americans in the US. The "killer weed" ideology never existed in the Netherlands; the use by the youth culture in the 1960s was the first confrontation of society with marihuana. Marihuana did become a symbol of the counterculture and played, therefore, a role in this broader social and political movement. When confronted with the need to respond to increasing marihuana use, Dutch policy makers could thus develop new policy unencumbered by the weight of an already existing, emotionally charged ideology.

This does not address the question of why the Dutch "ideological answer" was not formulated in the obvious prohibitionist model, consistent with international norms. A possible speculative answer to this question may be found when we consider the political, cultural, and social changes which took place in the Netherlands in the 1960s. From about 1917 till the 1960s, pluralistic Holland may be characterized as a "pillarized" society. The pillarized society consisted of groups with their own ideology, philosophy of life, or religion. There was little contact between the firmly organized different pillars. Nonetheless, the Netherlands had a very stable democratic system. An important condition for this stability was that the elites of the different pillars made compromises at the political level. These compromises developed on the basis of the "consociational democracy" (Lijphart 1968). In this manner, conflicts within the pluriform and divided society were made manageable through the compromises reached by the elites, which resulted in political stability (cf. Van Schendelen 1984).

However, in the 1960s, this system more or less collapsed. Decreased religious involvement, expansion of the means of communication and increased prosperity all contributed to the process of de-pillarization. People no longer felt committed to their philosophical or ideological pillar and came into contact with other philosophies of life. This de-pillarization was also noticeable at the political level, which meant the demise of what may be called the "pacification democracy". These changes provided groups which did not belong to one of the pillars with a chance to play a role in the political and social world. At the political level, this was reflected in the emergence of new, relatively successful political parties, which broke through the relatively homogeneous political culture. Outside the realm of politics, new groups received the opportunity to influence social life. This was also true for the youth culture which, in this time of social change, was not relegated to a marginal social position. Unlike many other countries, in the Netherlands drugs and countercultures associated with drugs were thus not marginalized and combatted with criminal justice measures. These changes meant that the Netherlands could develop an alternative drug policy - within the parameters of international agreements. The Single Convention of 1961 did not permit legalizing cannabis. The only possibility within the margins set by the Convention was the *de facto* decriminalization of cannabis.

9. The Baan Commission

With the increasing recreational use of drugs in the 1960s, the need for alternative policies was recognized. In 1968 a committee (the Baan Commission) was appointed with the mandate to re-evaluate governmental drug policy. The composition and recommendations of the Baan Commission will be discussed in the next chapter; suffice it to say here that the report of this commission formalized the philosophical and legal foundation of current Dutch drug policy. The report made a distinction between soft drugs (*i.e.,* marihuana and hashish) and hard drugs. Generally speaking, soft drugs were considered relatively harmless; users and small dealers were essentially to be left alone. Addiction to hard drugs was viewed primarily as a medical problem; it was decided that hard drugs should remain illegal. The report supported a "two-track" policy: a medical approach to addicts and a criminal justice-oriented (repressive) approach to large-scale dealers of hard drugs.

One of the most important foundations of Dutch hard drug policy, as formulated by the Baan Commission, is that the emphasis be on the medical-social care of users and prevention. We may list three different reasons for this.

1. Dutch society has a well-established tradition of social legislation and good medical care. Building a system of social welfare legislation has been important since the early period of pillarization. It was believed that social legislation and good medical care for the lower classes would alleviate class conflict and promote unity within the pillar. The system of pacification democracy, in a sense, encouraged the implementation of government measures to promote social well being. It is not surprising that, in a country where the well being of the population in the form of social legislation and good medical care is an important government task, medical-social care plays an important role in drug policy. Increased prosperity after the Second World War brought in abundant tax income which enabled the Dutch government to implement an ever improving system of social legislation and medical care for its citizens.

2. The hard drug policy formulated by the Baan Commission did not represent a radical change, rather an adjustment and refinement of an already existing approach. Indeed, the emphasis on medical and social care was a continuation of the long established balance between a repressive and a medical approach. As the preceding brief overview has documented, the Netherlands has followed a two-pronged approach (repressive and medical) since the 1920s.

3. A possible third reason for the medical approach to hard drug use may be the absence of a heroin problem in the Netherlands at the time of publication of the Baan report. In the United States and Great Britain, the medical approach was abandoned during periods when recreational use of heroin became a main concern. Heroin was not found on a larger scale in the Netherlands until the summer of 1972, six months after the Baan report was published.

10. Conclusion

Dutch drug policies with respect to the supply side of the drug market reflect, to a certain extent, the international repressive norm. There are, however, important national differences with regard to policies related to the demand side. In this brief overview, I have attempted to demonstrate that the "alternative" Dutch drug policy with regard to the demand side is the product, to a significant degree, of national political, social and cultural circumstances. Our historical analysis clearly suggests that the formulation of drug policy is more than a rational weighing of different alternatives and developing political choices. Government policies are the product of national historical developments and circumstances. Caution must be used, therefore, in adopting the position that the Dutch policy should be used as an "example" for other countries. This will be discussed in more depth in the concluding chapter of this book.

References

Berridge, V. and Edwards, G.: *Opium and the People: Opiate Use in Nineteenth-Century England*. New Haven, London: Yale University Press, 1981

Broers, J.: *Alcoholisme, Morphinisme, Chloralisme*. Leiden: Uitgeverij Slotboom, 1886

Chatterjee, S.K.: *Legal Aspects of International Drug Control*. The Hague: Martinus Nijhoff, 1981

Cohen, H.: *Drugs, Druggebruikers en Drug-scene*. Alphen aan den Rijn: Samson, 1975

Courtwright, D.T.: *Dark Paradise: Opiate Addiction in America before 1940*. Cambridge MA / London: Harvard University Press, 1982

Diehl, F.W.: *The Opium Tax Farm on Java, 1813-1914*. Paper, 1993

Erlenmeyer, A.: *Die Morphiumsucht und ihre Behandlung*. Berlin, 1887

Gavit, J.P.: *Opium*. London: Routledge & Sons, 1925

Gunkelman, M.: *Vom Wunderheilmittel zum socialen Gift. Der Wandel des Kokaingebrauchs und seiner sozialen Bewertung in Deutschland bis 1930*. Diplomarbeit. Frankfurt/M, 1984

Himmelstein, J.L.: From killer weed to drop-out drug: the changing ideology of marihuana. *Contemporary Crises* 7:13-38, 1983

Kaplan, C.D.: The uneasy consensus: prohibitionist and experimentalist expectancies behind the international narcotic control system. *Tijdschrift voor Criminologie* 26:98-109, 1984

Kreutel, M.: *Die Opiumsucht*. Stuttgart: Deutsche Apotheker Verlag, 1988

Lijphart, A.: *The Politics of Accommodation: Pluralism and Democracy in the Netherlands.* Berkeley: University of California Press, 1968

Musto, D.F.: *The American Disease, Origins of Narcotic Control*. New York: Oxford University Press, 1987

Nieuwe Rotterdamsche Courant, 22 February 1939

Osiander, J.F.: *Volksgeneeskunde, of Eenvoudige Middelen en Raadgevingen tegen de Kwalen en Krankheden der Menschen*. Leeuwarden, 1854

Pharmaceutisch Weekblad, p 1209, 1938

Parssinen, T.M.: *Secret Passions, Secret Remedies: Narcotic Drugs in British Society 1820-1930*. Philadelphia: Manchester University Press, 1983

Rush, J.R.: *Opium Farms in Nineteenth Century Java: Institutional Continuity and Change in a Colonial Society, 1860-1910*. Dissertation. Yale University, 1977

Scheerer, S.: *Die Genese der Betäubungsmittelgesetze in der Bundesrepublik Deutschland und in den Niederlanden*. Göttingen: Verlag Otto Schwarz, 1981

Stein, S.D.: *International Diplomacy, State Administrators and Narcotics Control*. Hampshire, Brookfield: Gower Publishing Company, 1985

Tan Tong Joe: *Het Internationale Opiumprobleem*. Dissertation. The Hague, 1929

Van Schendelen, M.C.P.M. (Ed.): Consociationalism, pillarization and conflict-management in the low countries. *Acta Politica* xix, January 1984

Vanvugt, E.: *Wettig Opium*. Haarlem: In de Knipscheer, 1985

Van Wolferen, M.D.: Marihuana. *Tijdschrift voor Strafrecht* 308-323, 1949

Verdoorn, J.A.: *Het Gezondheidswezen te Amsterdam in de 19e Eeuw*. Nijmegen: Sun, 1981

Wissler, A.: *Zur Geschichte der Opiumfrage*. Dissertation. Jena, 1930

Endnotes

1. See, for example, Kaplan (1984).
2. A. Erlenmeyer (1887) counted between 1864 and 1886, 260 German, French or English language publications on this topic.
3. See, for example, for the United States: Musto (1987) and Courtwright (1982); for England: Berridge and Edwards (1981) and Parssinen (1983); for Germany: Scheerer (1981), Gunkelman (1984) and Kreutel (1988).
4. For more information on the use and trade of opium in the Dutch Indies see Vanvugt (1985), Diehl (1993) and Rush (1977).
5. The Dutch Opium Act was implemented in 1919. The Opium Act included opium and its derivates as well as cocaine. The Opium Act prohibited the preparation, sale, processing, delivery, import and export, and possession of drugs with intent to deliver. The Opium Act was revised in 1928, because of an international agreement signed in 1925, which in turn was a supplement to the 1912 agreement. The 1928 revision also included marihuana and cocaine derivates. In addition, the punishment was increased from a maximum of three months in 1919 to one year in 1928.

6. After the enactment of the Opium Act of 1919 several businesses obtained permits to produce and/or deal in drugs. The system of certification introduced in the Netherlands in 1928 was designed to regulate the importation and exportation of narcotics. For example, whenever a business wanted to export heroin, it had to produce a certificate from the receiving country to obtain a permit to export.
7. This publicity wave and the subsequent prohibition of LSD were probably related to the threat of the Provo's to interrupt the approaching wedding of the then Princess Beatrix and the German Prince Claus by poisoning the Amsterdam drinking water with LSD and by giving LSD-tainted lumps of sugar to the horses.

II. INITIAL CONSTRUCTION AND DEVELOPMENT OF THE OFFICIAL DUTCH DRUG POLICY

Ed. Leuw

1. Introduction

Modern drug use appeared in Dutch society at the end of the 1960s. During these early years, the recreational use of illegal substances by sometimes non-conformistic, but definitely non-marginal youth gained some prominence, although perhaps more in public awareness than in numbers. The nature of this drug use, a rather uninhibited and even somewhat ostentatious use of cannabis, implied that value conflicts rather than objective problems were at the core of the initial phenomenon. At the end of this period drug use had spread throughout the population to a certain extent. At the same time, as a consequence of the introduction of opiates and the emergence of some related social and public health problems, the drug issue now had become more than being just a "simple" value conflict.

During several years a drug policy debate took place among politicians, administrators and professionals on the principles of the social control of this problematic phenomenon. At the end of this initial phase of modern drug taking in the Netherlands the debate had come to a temporary conclusion regarding moral character and harmfulness. Ahead of popular opinion, professionals and political administrators increasingly adopted a morally dispassionate and, in terms of drug ideologies, more liberal and less prohibitionistic course.

The end of the process of establishing a "pragmatic and normalizing" drug policy was reached in 1976, when the Revised Opium Act was enacted in the Dutch parliament. This event marked the end of an era characterized by an ideology of prohibition and moral rejection of any kind of (illegal) psychotropic drug use. The social debate on the significance of drug use had evolved towards more pluralism and diversification.

The new drug legislation of 1976 laid the cornerstone of a comprehensive drug policy program. It involves education, prevention, general "youth policy" and measures specifically targeted at drug users, such as social assistance and psycho-medical therapy.

In a formal legal sense the Revised Opiate Act of 1976 may be understood as the penal law part of this more general drug policy program. The program as a whole reflects the central elements of Dutch drug policy: tolerance for non-conformistic lifestyles, risk reduction with regard to the harmful health and social consequences of dangerous ways of drug taking and, finally, penal law measures directed against the illegal economy of (hard) drugs. Reconciling these partly conflicting elements with one another has been (and still is) the really hard part of developing drug policy.

In retrospect, this multi-faceted framework of social control has firmly established the basic principles as well as the common practices of social and penal law drug policy in the Netherlands (Van de Wijngaart 1991). It has served this role until the present day, with surprisingly little emotions or public dissent in Dutch society. Since these early days, the national drug policy has become more a matter of technical and administrative concern than a matter of principles. In this Chapter, the social political process which has resulted in Dutch "pragmatic and non-moralistic" drug policy will be described and to some extent, explained.

2. Social and cultural backgrounds of the initial problem definition

Although opiates and cocaine have, to a limited extent, been present in Dutch society during the last 100 years, the issue of drug taking as a focal and public social concern hardly existed before approximately 1965 (De Kort 1989). The public and political awareness of addiction and substance use as a social problem was restricted to alcohol. Similar to the rest of the Western world, this traditional substance of pleasure and problems had a long history as a significant social problem. The social problem concept implies the presence of medical, mental health, moral, educational and criminal policy concerns. Alcohol used to be the one and only widely available substance for which possible misuse transcended purely individual problems, and as such alcohol qualified as a *bona fide* social problem. Drug taking and addiction only existed as rare phenomena of personal misfortune which could be dealt with by the medical profession and by an appeal to self-evident morality. For such problems, social control issues are either non-existent or they are taken for granted. In sum, there used to be no more need for social policy debate on drug taking than on suicide, heart diseases or insanity.

Starting from about 1965 things changed rapidly and radically. Drug taking as a social problem first came to the public consciousness in the much broader cultural context of the diversification of lifestyles and value systems. In this era, a broad variety of moral constraints and normative expectations was successfully challenged. This cultural process involved important issues of lifestyle, sexual behavior and the conventions of public appearance. It also involved a certain diminishing of traditional power differentials between groups in society, such as between generations, females and males, or the social-economic (and the political) status groups.

In this process of rapid re-orientation of social values the so-called counter-cultural "alternative" youth culture played a major role. Its growing social power manifested itself primarily in the traditionally liberal city of Amsterdam. During the last years of the 1960s the "Provo's", a loosely organized group of young cultural rebels, had gained some prominence in the city. They were highly visible and generally admired by otherwise more conformistic peers. The Provo-movement playfully provoked the Amsterdam city administration and police in various inventive ways. Stretching the borders of social and personal liberty was the movement's explicit aim. Challenging the public order regulations and some penal law prohibitions was its strategy. Weekly "happenings" downtown delighted the young, partying crowds, while making the authorities quite nervous. Publicly smoking pot was part of the provocation game. The movement's success in influencing the social and cultural order was reflected in the dismissal of both the mayor and the police commissioner of Amsterdam following the peaceful but effective turmoil the Provo movement created. Because of their overreactions to the provocations of the Provo's, the positions of both authorities were undermined.

It may be significant for further developments of drug policy (and other legislation in the sphere of "victimless crimes") that this movement was partly absorbed into the conventional political structure of the city of Amsterdam. Part of the Provo movement was transformed to a political "party" at the city level. It won some seats in the city council. Occasionally blowing pot during its meetings was one way to make it clear that simple prohibition would no longer do as the mainstay of drug policy. A few years later one of the leaders of the Provo movement was appointed as alderman in Amsterdam.

Perhaps because of this close identification with counter-cultural lifestyles and values, the initial concept of drug-taking as a social problem in the Netherlands has been fundamentally ambivalent. It incorporated appreciations of personal freedom and tolerance as well as depreciations of deviance, pathology and immorality. The original phenomenon of "drug-taking" (which in practice meant the use of cannabis) was one of the cases that passed the test of the often claimed relative permissiveness and tolerance of Dutch society, comparable to the normative acceptance of other moral value innovations in this same period: legalized abortion and pornography, and the more uninhibited manifestations of prostitution, homosexuality and hedonistic sexuality in general.

At the end of the decade of the 1960s the phenomenon of (illegal) drug use (LSD and amphetamines were not yet outlawed) had spread sufficiently to generate widespread confusion, anxiety and some moral outrage in general Dutch society. The public dispute mainly centered around the highly symbolically loaded use of psychedelics (cannabis and LSD) by a young non-conformistic, but non-marginal avant-garde. At the onset of this development the drug-takers could broadly be defined as young or even not-so-young bohemians (Cohen 1975). Later, with the flower-power revolution well on its way, those groups were referred to as hippies.

Social reactions to the drugs' symbolism intensified when it became inescapably clear to parents, educators and legislators alike, that the hippie lifestyle was appealing to broad segments of the "normal" young generation, perhaps even to their own children. This phenomenon was met with contradictory and ambivalent reactions. By some it was welcomed as a humanistic liberation from worn-out moral and social constraints. The hash-blowing "hippies" had many supporters among liberal new elite groups, such as the young university graduates who were taking positions in the rapidly expanding world of (mental) health, welfare and social policy institutions. To many of this (increasingly influential) group of policy makers the hippies appeared as the bearers of the key to a better world of love, understanding and carefree hedonism. In this context drug-taking (smoking pot) appeared as a sacred ritual which should be shielded from narrow-minded interference by conventional ("square") society.

On the other hand, several other groups in Dutch society of around 1970 were indignant about the hippie lifestyle and (psychedelic) drug--taking. Typically they were the older moral conservatives who were at a clear disadvantage as they had to ride against the high tide of fashionable tolerance and pluriformity. They appeared as rather unglamorous representatives of a silent moral majority, the so-called "concerned citizens" groups of medical doctors, parents and educators, and some law enforcement officials. The one and only cabinet minister (R.J.H. Kruisinga, a Christian Democratic state secretary for public health, a physician by profession) who actively sided with this moral opposition and rallied on the theme of radical prohibition, was cheerfully mocked by the flourishing underground press and by one of the major public radio networks.

Apart from the rapidly growing numbers of cannabis experimenters and users around 1970, serious drug problems were still quite rare. Social drop-outs, (mental) health troubles, and drug-related criminality were reported in the context of some LSD, opium and amphetamine use. But although they were seen as a disturbing prospect by many social policy officials, those cases were too small in numbers (no more than several hundreds) to be a genuine cause for concern.

As we will see, the first professional study and advisory groups, which were officially appointed around 1970, have been quite influential in the formulation and execution of what in recent years has come to be known as the "Dutch model" of drug policy. It is of utmost importance that these working groups were established in an era and in a society where drug use had come to the public consciousness against the backdrop of a relatively mild dispute of lifestyles and value systems, and not against a background of criminality, pathology and deeply rooted social conflict. The latter elements certainly did enter the Dutch drug problems field in later years; however, by then the tradition of non-moralistic accommodation and pragmatic risk management in drug policy was already firmly established.

3. The initial formulation of drug policies and the construction of the revised opium law of 1976

In the years 1969 and 1970 two expert committees, one private and one state committee were appointed, both charged with constructing a model for the social policy towards the use of illegal drugs. Essentially, their mission was to construct a definition and a normative orientation towards a hitherto non-existing social phenomenon. Culturally and historically many options were still available. Because this was a relatively new problem in Dutch society, the course of social policy had not yet been charted on the track of prohibition and moral rejection.

Both committees finished their task after about two years. The reports they produced were concise, each one of them can easily be read in less than two hours. They have, each in their own way, exerted much influence on the processes of formal law construction and the execution of social drug policy until the present day. The line of reasoning and the conclusions that were reached in those reports were not unlike the results of similar working groups in the US, Canada, and the UK (Advisory Committee on Drug Dependence 1968; National Commission on Marihuana and Drug Abuse 1973; Commission of Inquiry into the Non-Medical Use of Drugs 1972). The real difference is that the Dutch reports have been much more influential in shaping actual policy.

In 1969 the state-sponsored Institution for Mental Health appointed the working group that produced a report "Options in Drug Policy" ("Ruimte in het Drugsbeleid"). The committee was chaired by Loek Hulsman, a penal law professor reputed for his abolitionist's views. It consisted of 14 persons, who were representatives of scientific disciplines, high-ranking law enforcement officials, representatives of the ministries of justice and public health, and directors of mental health and welfare institutions. It is important that at least five members of this committee were social scientists. This committee had no officially recognized political status. Perhaps this is the reason that it reached more far-reaching liberal conclusions than the government-appointed committee known, after its chairman, as the "Baan Committee". The most striking fact of the second committee is, however, that its conclusions and recommendations were broadly accepted by the Dutch government as well as parliament, and that its recommendations to the present day have guided the practical implementation and execution of Dutch drug policies. In this respect Holland seems to be the exception to a general disregard that has typically been the fate of the advisory committees recommending decriminalization and relaxation of drug policies.

Because of its official status, the Baan Committee was, of course, the committee that really mattered. The more radical "Hulsman Committee" (named after its chair) was, however, influential because it was the first to finish its report, and because two of its members also participated in the official government-committee. This "Working Group on Narcotic Substances" (as the Baan Committee was officially named) had more high-ranking administrators of the ministries of public health and justice as well as penal law officials among its 15 members than the Hulsman Committee. Based on the differences in official status and composition of the two committees, one may speculate that the Hulsman Committee typically voiced the views of the traditional liberally minded social science and (mental) health professions, whereas the Baan Committee should in principle be considered to be more ideologically balanced. According to this logic a comparison between the recommendations of both reports may tell us how far a broad professional consensus about drug policies in Holland was removed from explicit permissiveness.

4. The Hulsman Report: Defining basic social attitudes

The Hulsman Committee based its risk analysis of illegal drugs (compared to legal recreational as well as medical drugs) mainly on the dependency-producing potential of the substances (Stichting Algemeen Centraal Bureau voor de Geestelijke Volksgezondheid 1971). While stressing the potential dangers of opiates, amphetamines (no one in the Netherlands even thought of the possibility of cocaine becoming a problem, since this drug was virtually absent) and barbiturates, it relativized the pharmacological risks of cannabis "...tobacco undoubtedly has stronger addictive properties than cannabis" (p 19-20). It disregarded the "stepping-stone" thesis of cannabis which around 1970 was still seriously considered by stating that "...one of the most important causes of escalation from cannabis to other, more dangerous drugs is the fact that cannabis is included in the Opium Act" (p 53).

Sociologically it interpreted drug (cannabis) use as a subcultural phenomenon, controlled by and fitting into a certain lifestyle, which in a modern pluriform society should not be judged by the norms of the subculture of "respectable citizens". It reasoned that moral rejection and repressive social control measures based on such a biased view would result in the marginalization of those non-conformistic subcultures. This line of reasoning was specifically applied to interference by the state: "The government should not take a censuring position based on the fact that a certain behavior does not fit into the life-concept of those who are holding state-power" (*Ibid.* p 40). The report especially warned against the harmful effects of law-enforcement practices in this respect.

Philosophically the report is based on the principle that the state should refrain as much as possible from interference with behaviors that have consequences for the individual person only. Indeed, John Stuart Mill's famous maxim from "On Liberty", used to be quoted a lot in those days. According to the report this maxim should certainly apply to repressive social control measures: "Although it is highly probable that the smoking of cigarettes will yearly make thousands of victims in this country, it can't well be imagined that the state would take forceful action against the tobacco-smoker" (*Ibid.* p 39). The Hulsman Committee warned strongly against putting more than very little reliance on the penal law in controlling drug problems. It predicted that the threat of law enforcement would not only fail to deter people from engaging in vice (victimless crime) in their private life, it would for various reasons also fail to control the supply side of the drug market. When penal law action is considered, so they reasoned, its possible or actual benefits should always be weighed against the costs, both in terms of money and law enforcement capacity, and in terms of the harmful social effects of law enforcement. Among the undesirable side-effects they mentioned the amplification of deviance and marginality of drug scenes; the symbiotic development of vigorous and violent specialized police forces and (organized) drug traffickers as opponents in an escalating war; and the gradual undermining of civil liberties and the legitimacy of penal law. In short, this early report on modern drug policy reasoned that law enforcement against the world of illegal drugs would be costly, would fail to really control the supply, would make the social and health problems of drug-taking worse than necessary, would reinforce the growth of powerful criminal organizations, and would undermine constitutionality.

One can hardly deny a certain amount of prophetic talent to the Hulsman Committee when the following citations from this almost 20-year-old report are compared to Wisotsky's more recent account of the results of the "war on drugs" in the US. (Wisotsky 1986) The commission contemplated on the risks of embarking on a predominantly repressive drugs-control policy: "The narcotic department of the police-force will develop into a big, well-trained and excellently 'armed' unit, which will have to be improved and increased permanently, to keep up with the never-ending escalation. The undoubtedly more vicious character of the drugs problem that will develop will deplete the administration of other options to react to the problem. The dealer of marihuana as we know him now will only survive as a memory of how it all started, in the romantic 1960s and 1970s" (p 49). The commission specified the social risks of primarily relying on law enforcement, which it qualified as an "inadequate and therefore extremely dangerous" choice for drugs control: "This instrument will fail again and again, which will induce its proponents to further increase the repressive measures ... law enforcement, will increasingly have to intrude into the spheres of private life ... (which) ... will further the polarization between several groups in society and may thus lead to increasing violence" (p 51).

The policy recommendations that concluded the report of the Hulsman Committee were more radical than those of the officially appointed Baan Committee, yet they were not as radical as the rhetorics of this report might have suggested. Even the relatively fervent liberals of this committee chose a more pragmatic course when relating to the practice of the developing Dutch drug policy. We will compare the policy recommendations of the two committees after a brief description of the report of the Baan Committee, which had a decisive influence on the formulation and further development of drug policies in the Netherlands.

5. The Baan Committee: Defining basic social reactions

The Hulsman Committee may very well have reflected the high tide of moral pluralism that dominated the Dutch social-cultural landscape around 1970, not only in the field of drug use but also in other areas of potential moral and social conflict. (Of course this was a much more general trend in the Western world.) Sexual morals and corresponding legal practices changed drastically. Homosexuality, abortion and pornography were more openly accepted. Traditional relations of authority (such as between the sexes and the generations) were seriously challenged. The same thing happened to religious and political power institutions. During that period one did not only see crowds of young American backpack tourists congregating on Dam Square or in the Vondelpark to openly share their joints, but also sex and abortion tourists from southern European countries, and on Friday-night crowded airplanes from London with gay people set out to partying in the gay bars of Amsterdam.

In this cultural climate the Hulsman Committee probably provided an ideological justification for the much more down-to-earth Baan Committee to break away from the single-minded prohibitionist regime that until that time had seemed to be the most natural Dutch (official) social policy approach to illegal drug use. The Baan Committee explicitly referred to the Hulsman report in its own policy paper, entitled "Background and Risks of Drug Use" (Werkgroep Verdovende Middelen 1972). Interestingly enough, the original assignment from the State Secretary of Social Affairs and Public Health to the "Working Group on Narcotic Drugs" was clearly phrased within this traditional prohibitionist's framework. It mentioned three main topics of concern. The first and the last were very briefly formulated as a study into the causes of the increasing use of illegal drugs, and the correct medical-social treatment of those addicted to such substances.

The second topic to be studied by the Baan Committee was more extensively qualified. It reads as follows:

"the counteracting of the irresponsible use of those substances by: (a) efficient criminal investigation of illegal trade channels; (b) efficient criminal investigation of and appropriate ways of dealing with users; (c) education on the dangers ... of use".

During the next two years the government, after discussion with parliament, broadened the working group's initial assignment, to give recommendations for social drug policy not necessarily within the prohibitionistic framework. The Baan Committee reached its final composition in 1970 and published its report in 1972. The conclusions of this report were almost completely adopted by the center/conservative government that was in office. A revised form of the strictly prohibitionist "Opium Act" (dating back originally to 1928) was ultimately developed by the center/left-wing government that took office in 1973. The revised Opium Act proposal was brought before parliament no earlier than 1976. The four-year time lapse between the development of the legal proposal and the ultimate passing of the legislation has probably been quite functional; the proposed decriminalization and relaxation of drug control were already introduced in social practice during this period. Consequently, the effects of the proposed law could first be tested in practice even before official new legislation was to be adopted. This was perfectly consistent with the committee's view that for the proper evolution of drug policy, frameworks for experimentation should be created. These experiments should be carefully evaluated: "...when sufficient faith in the safety of new positions exists, then the old ones can be left" (*Ibid.* p 74).

The Baan Committee did not indulge in philosophical or ideological digressions, but rather straightforwardly tackled two main issues. First, it debated whether or not a strictly prohibitionistic policy model should be retained for all drugs outlawed by the then existing national and international (Single Convention) legislation. Secondly, it tried to offer an outline for an integral social policy model in which diverse social (control) measures could be fitted. It specifically tried to link priorities of drug policy to available policy options such as repressive criminal justice measures, (psycho)-medical and welfare measures, education, and normalization.

The leading notion behind the recommended policy model of the Working Group was that the level of coerciveness and certainty of social reactions to using and trading drugs should be carefully linked to a risk-analysis of the kind of drugs and behaviors involved. According to this logic, the Working Group devoted special attention to cannabis and concluded that this substance should no longer be included in the category of drugs with "unacceptable risks". It argued that the social costs of criminal law repression of use and other-than-wholesale trade of cannabis would outweigh the possible benefits. In this concept of social costs, the committee included the dangers of unwarranted marginalization and fulfilling the conditions for the stepping-stone effect.

Before providing its final recommendations for the revision of the Opium Act, the report stated that "...penal law policy should take into account the more general aims of social drug policy" (p 67). General drug policy should, first and foremost, be aimed at primary and secondary risk prevention. In this context, the report stated that "...socially integrated use of drugs may be possible ... This does not mean that no risks are involved, but that those risks could be acceptable" (*Ibid.* p 66). Although phrased in different terms than the Hulsman Committee, the Baan Committee also rejected law enforcement as the main answer to the illegal drug problem. It put penal law policy in the context of general social drug policy, and it accepted the premise that particular forms of drug taking could be tolerated (and even integrated into society).

Both the Hulsman and the Baan committees stated their penal law reform recommendations in similar frameworks. They both distinguished between cannabis and the other illegal drugs, and they further distinguished between using and trading drugs. As mentioned before, the Hulsman Committee was most radical in its recommendations. It proposed that use of cannabis should be legalized and that trade of cannabis (on any level) should be made a misdemeanor which only would be punishable by a fine. This same legal status was proposed for possession and use of illegal drugs other than cannabis. However, dealing and trading in those drugs should remain a criminal offense. The Baan Committee recommended that use and "small-scale-trade" of cannabis should be made a misdemeanor. On the other hand, wholesale trafficking of cannabis (more than 250 gram) should remain a criminal offense, but there should not be a threat of imprisonment of more than one year. Using and trading other illegal drugs were proposed to remain criminal offenses. Although the Baan Committee stated that "...a penal law approach of drug users is inadequate" (*Ibid.* p 68), they also believed that in the foreseeable future this statute could not be missed as a possible means of exerting pressure on chronic users to seek treatment, and as a symbolic warning for prospective or experimental users.

In 1975 the new cabinet, in which the (more leftist) Social Democrats had replaced the Conservatives in a coalition with the Christian Democrats, introduced a revised form of the existing Opium Act to parliament. In this bill, the general recommendations of the Baan Committee had been translated into concrete provisions. The government provided three rationales for the proposed penal law reform: a more severe criminalization of the trade in amphetamines, a maximal separation between the trade in cannabis and the trade in drugs with "unacceptable risks" and, finally, the reduction from the status of criminal offense to the status of misdemeanor of the possession of cannabis for own use. After all was said and done, the revised Opium Act proposed by the government turned out somewhat less liberal than the Baan Committee had intended.

6. The parliamentary debate: Political acceptance of pragmatic policies

In 1976 the proposed revised Opium Act was discussed in parliament. Although formally this was a penal law bill, its primary endorser was the Minister of Public Health, social democrat Irene Vorrink, the first member of cabinet responsible for its defense in parliament. The Minister of Justice, the Christian Democrat Dries van Agt, was the secondary endorser. He played a less important role in the bill's defense. This order reflects the central notion in Dutch social drug policy that drugs are, first and foremost, a public health and welfare issue, where criminal law and law enforcement is of limited and secondary importance.

The bill was passed by parliament, not without some passionate discussions, but almost unscathed, with the addition of two minor criminalizing provisions. The right-wing opposition – mainly Christian fundamentalist parties plus some members of the Conservative Party (VVD) – ultimately voted against the bill. It was adopted by a large majority (approximately three to one), consisting of the left wing opposition, the majority of the Conservative Party plus the Social Democrats and the Christian Democrats. The latter two parties (the foundations of the coalition cabinet) unanimously supported the bill.

In spite of some individual disagreements, there was a remarkably broad acceptance of the central notion that the use of hard drugs is not a problem that should be controlled by criminal law. The members of parliament expressed an almost unanimous conviction that drug addicts should be helped or treated, and should not be targets for law enforcement. A spokeswoman for the Christian Democratic party went even further than the Social Democrats in asserting her preference for an eventual decriminalization of all drug use. The spokesman of a right-wing opposition party opposing the bill agreed with the government's view that the threat of criminal law against users of hard drugs should be moderate and only be used to put some pressure on them to seek treatment: "...there is a limit beyond which execution of punishment serves no reasonable end. This limit is reached when truly addicted people are concerned ... We favor medical treatment instead of criminal prosecution..." (Handelingen 1976:3021). He further seemed to imply (although he would not explicitly affirm) that addicts should be sent to mandatory treatment. The left-wing opposition also agreed with the depenalization of the use of hard drugs, but instead of forced treatment they advocated the possibility of medical prescription of heroin to addicts. There also was little disagreement about the proposed considerable increase of the maximum penalties for wholesale (international) illicit trafficking in drugs with "unacceptable" risks (*i.e.*, hard drugs), although the Social Democrats and the other left-wing parties warned against the social risks of escalating the war against the drugs trade. The Minister of Justice acknowledged that such undesirable effects (*e.g.*, more violence, more aggressive marketing tactics, higher prices and, consequently, more criminality) might occur. But that would be no reason not to fight more forcefully against the suppliers of illicit hard drugs, he stated. He added that a balanced two-track policy, aimed against the supply of and the demand for hard drugs would be necessary.

The opponents of the revised Opium Act mainly argued against it because of the proposed formal decriminalization of cannabis. This seems to indicate that this heavily symbolic issue was really the heart of the value dispute that the proposed new drug policy reflected. Generally, the opponents contested the government's conclusion that the individual and social risks of cannabis were "not unacceptable". A small and by now quite familiar battle of "scientific proofs" about the possible psychomedical and social harmfulness of cannabis raged in parliament. Only the two small religious fringe parties admitted their conviction that official "approval" of any kind of drug use was unacceptable for moral reasons. This argument was countered by Joop Voogd, the Social Democratic spokesman, who said he happened to possess in his house a 5-gram piece of cannabis "purely for curiosity's sake as I may reassure some of my colleagues" (Handelingen 1976:3067). He raised the question why young people with their recreational substance of preference should be vulnerable to the theoretical threat of four years of imprisonment, while alcohol, the functionally similar substance of "the silent majority", was not only accepted but even commercially exploited (Handelingen 1976:3067).

The Minister of Public Health asserted to the relatively small minority of principled opponents of the bill (*i.e.*, those against the decriminalization of cannabis) the government's intention to eventually arrive at the complete legalization of cannabis. She did recognize, however, that this could only be done if the regulations of the international Single Convention were changed to allow a complete absence of criminal law provisions against cannabis. The minister declared that the Dutch government would try to encourage such modifications in the international treaty: "...that countries will be free to draw up their own national regime" (Handelingen 1976:3098). With regard to the possible medical and social risks related to the decriminalization of cannabis, she argued, first, that the vast increase in cannabis use had occurred during a period of no distinction between cannabis and other drugs, and secondly, that in the absence of a clear indication of serious harmfulness of cannabis "...the final conclusion about the dangerousness of cannabis is not so much based on chemical or biological data, but more on our social evaluation of the substance" (Handelingen 1976:3096). Both ministers defending the proposed revised Opium Act asserted the important legislative principle that, in order to criminalize private behavior, the burden of proof of the unacceptability of such behavior should rest on the legislators. Apart from the main question of whether or not cannabis should be legalized there remained three controversial issues that were heavily contested: the 30-gram limit, the "house dealer" and the "Stock Exchange Reports". In only one of these issues (the Stock Exchange Reports), was the government eventually beaten.

6.1 The 30-gram limit

There was some opposition against the supposedly too liberal allowance of the quantity of cannabis (30 grams) that could be possessed before it would be considered a criminal offense. The 30-gram limit was based on the sympathetic calculation that this would allow a personal supply sufficient for two weeks that would also enable users to share some stuff with their friends. Some skeptical representatives rightly assumed that this would protect small-scale cannabis dealers from serious law enforcement. The government wisely did not try to refute this argument, but said that such a consequence should be accepted. In fact, the later development of the "coffee shop" phenomenon was based on this arrangement. The spokeswoman for the Conservative Party submitted an amendment directed against the 30-gram limit. It was rejected by a two-third majority.

6.2 The house dealer

Some animated discussions were devoted to the phenomenon of the so-called "house dealer". This is a person who is permitted by the staff and the board of a recreational or educational youth center to sell limited quantities of cannabis to the members and visitors of such a youth center. This practice had already been adopted by a small number of youth centers for some years, based on the recognition that their visitors were already in the habit of using cannabis as part of their recreational activities within the center. It had been noticed that some of them were attracted to other drugs and – consequently – that there was a substantial risk that dealers of hard drugs would try to develop a market in the youth center.

The designation of a house dealer served to prevent the diffusion of hard drug use into vulnerable groups of adolescents. The parliamentary opposition against it not only pertained to matters of criminal law (as the house dealer would probably violate the 30-grams limit), but also to the fact that those youth centers were fully funded by public means. Precisely at the time of the parliamentary discussions, criminal proceedings were taking place against a house dealer in the Hague. The Minister of Justice argued that the dilemmas involved in this case could not be solved by law or by a central policy. Decisions should be made by the law enforcement authorities who on the basis of the expediency principle could decide whether or not to act against a specific house dealer in specific circumstances. The minister acknowledged, however, that the house dealer could be very useful in realizing a central aim of Dutch drug policy, namely the separation of the markets and social contexts of hard and soft drugs. For this reason he said that "...law enforcement should take into account the interests of public health and welfare" when deciding about the legal position of the house dealer (Handelingen 1976:3116). In other words, law enforcement should refrain from interference with the institutionalized sale of cannabis (*i.e.,* through the house dealer) for the benefit of society.

Shortly after the adoption of the new Opium Act the issue of the house dealer became a subject of practical drug policy consultation at local levels between administrative and law enforcement authorities. Since then no more house dealers have been prosecuted. The issue would have been forgotten completely, were it not that an overzealous administration of a city near the German border decided to officially appoint and license a local cannabis house dealer, someone who had already operated in that capacity informally for some years in one of their youth centers. This was more than the German neighbors of the Netherlands were prepared to take and it resulted in some political confrontations between both countries (Kaplan 1984).

6.3 The stock exchange reports

The government lost its battle over the last of the three most controversial issues of the cannabis policy. The dispute around the Stock Exchange Reports was symbolically highly charged. It concerned a weekly feature in a very popular radio-program for young people, broadcasted by the Social-Democratic network, one of the major public networks in the Netherlands. This feature gave information on drug issues. It often contained non-moralistic warnings against the risks of hard drugs. But, most importantly, it was in outright defiance of prohibitionistic attitudes in its candid publication of the market prices of the different brands of hashish and marihuana. The presentator and author of this feature was the chief editor of a flourishing "underground" magazine. He was often alluded to as "the emperor of the alternative youth culture". He succeeded in maintaining his popularity in the hippie population by expressing imaginative ideas; for instance, the replacement of the hothouse agriculture of silly tomatoes by some good breeds of Indian hemp. Not surprisingly, his popularity was rather low among more conventional circles of society. It was widely known that this young man was the son of the Minister of Public Health.

This issue shows where the broad consensus on more tolerance for the social phenomenon of cannabis use ended. Many representatives in parliament, even many who were in favor of the new decriminalizing drug policies, disapproved of the Stock Exchange Reports. They were deemed to be a blatant propaganda for drug use. Some members of the right-wing parties fulminated strongly against the program and asked for law enforcement actions, or, at the very least, that this program should be banned from the air. They were most appalled by the fact that the program always ended by referring to the homegrown weed variety as "...'Lowlands Weed', our national pride", which, to my memory, was a very optimistic qualification for something that smelled like smoldering hay and which brought about sore throats more than kicks. None of the indignant representatives, however, even tried to imply that the family relationship had anything to do with the position of the minister primarily responsible for the defense of the new bill. The spokesman of the Social-Democrats tried to counter the accusations against "his own" Social-Democratic network by insisting that the program was actually intending to educate and warn against drugs. This however did not stop parliament from proposing and adopting an amendment. Against the intentions of government, provision 3b was added to the revised Opium Act, which made illegal "...any publication aimed at promoting the sale or delivery..." of all illegal substances. The Stock Exchange Reports however continued to be on the air some five more years. Then the feature died a natural death because of a lack of interest as the prices of soft drugs were beginning to be published on the "menus" of the coffee shops.

In June 1976, the new Opium Act was passed into law, with only minor alterations from the bill that was originally proposed to parliament.

7. Concluding remarks

This brief history shows that, apart from a short period at the very beginning of the 1970s, the drug problem has hardly been a confrontational issue between moral/political left and moral/political right in Holland. As a matter of fact, this relative "neutrality" of Dutch drug policy has been maintained until the present day. The drug issue has not served as a means of promoting political or moral power, nor has it served the specific institutional interests of law enforcement agencies. Political speeches elaborating on the abhorrence of illegal drugs have seldomly been staged. They would appear as quite misplaced in the Dutch political culture. Consequently, there are no votes to be won or positions to be conquered by rallying on the anti-drug theme.

In a comparative analysis of the development of drug policies in the Netherlands and Western Germany it was concluded that "...a low degree of politicalization of the issue was the most important prerequisite for successful decriminalization" (Scheerer 1978:603). In the decisive years for setting the tone of drug policies, around 1970, the general public in both countries was assumed to be quite similar in its (moral) rejection of drug (cannabis) use. Thereafter, according to Scheerer, social policy reactions departing from this public attitude strongly diverged. In Germany, the political parties, the police and the medical profession used the drug issue to further their own institutional objectives by a process of problem amplification. A contrary process of de-escalating the significance of the drug problem relativation occurred in the Netherlands. The Social Democrats were allowed to realize their "liberal" interests in moral issues because their Christian Democratic partners in the coalition cabinet did not choose to use the drugs issue "as a self-serving sociopolitical symbol" (Scheerer 1978:595).

The Dutch revised Opium Act of 1976 reflects the settling of a value dispute over personal preferences and collective prohibitions. This compromise over moral values has allowed a pragmatic and cost-benefit oriented drug policy to be developed and implemented in the 1980s and 1990s.

References

Advisory Committee on Drug Dependence: *Cannabis*. London: H.M. Stationary Office, 1968
Cohen, H.: *Drugs, Druggebruikers en Drug-scene*. Alphen aan de Rijn: Samson, 1975
Commission of Inquiry into the Non-Medical Use of Drugs: *A report of the Commission*. Ottawa: Information Canada, 1972

De Kort, M.: *De Problematisering van het Druggebruik in Nederland 1850-1940*. Rotterdam: Erasmus Universiteit, 1989

Handelingen Tweede Kamer 1976 (Proceedings of the House of Representatives). Den Haag: Staatsuitgeverij, 1976

Kaplan, C.D.: The uneasy consensus, prohibitionist and experimentalist expectancies behind the International Narcotics Control System. *Tijdschrift voor Criminologie* 98-109, 1984

National Commission on Marihuana and Drug Abuse: *Second Report of the National Commission on Marihuana and Drug Abuse*. Washington DC: US Government Printing Office, 1973

Scheerer, S.: The new Dutch and German drug laws: social and political conditions for criminalisation and decriminalisation. *Law & Society* 12:585-605, 1978

Stichting Algemeen Centraal Bureau voor de Geestelijke Volksgezondheid: *Ruimte in het Drugbeleid*. Meppel: Boom, 1971

Van de Wijngaart, G.F.: *Competing Perspectives on Drug Use: The Dutch Experience*. Amsterdam/Lisse: Swets & Zeitlinger, 1991

Werkgroep Verdovende Middelen: *Rapport van de Werkgroep Verdovende Middelen*. Den Haag: Staatsuitgeverij, 1972

Wisotsky, S.: *Breaking the Impasse in the War on Drugs*. New York: Greenwood Press, 1986

III. ENFORCING DRUG LAWS IN THE NETHERLANDS

Jos Silvis

1. The historical and international background

Occasionally, people seem to think drug policy has no history before the sixties. The actual shape and content of drug policy in most countries, however, has a direct link to the early days of this century. Moreover, the problematic relation of people with certain substances with psychotropic effects probably dates back a number of millennia.[1]

Drug policy in the Netherlands has some of its roots in its colonial past. The Dutch government used to have large monetary interests in the trading and consumption of opiate products in what is now the independent state of Indonesia. Though governmental intervention in that particular drug trade had a solid financial rationale, it was legitimated by the proclaimed goal of reducing drug consumption and production in order to protect the unfortunate addicted inhabitants of the colonies.[2]

This historical involvement in the struggle against drug misuse and the resulting knowledge about this problem is one explanation for the important role the Dutch played in the original international effort to universalize the repressive approach to (especially) narcotic drugs. Holland, together with China and the United States, entered into the agreement of Shanghai in 1909 acknowledging for the first time the need for an international approach to drug-related matters. Soon the earliest international drug treaty followed in the Dutch city of The Hague. The Treaty of The Hague (1912) established the foundation of the international legal approach to the so-called dangerous drugs.[3]

The historical background of the widespread participation of most countries in the drug treaties from 1919 on lies in a peculiar fact that has no direct connection with drug problems in the member countries, not even in their colonies. In fact, not many states signed the treaty of The Hague spontaneously. This changed quite dramatically when the First World War was ended by signing the Treaty of Peace 1919. Article 295 of the 1919 Treaty of Peace reads as follows:

"Those, of the High Contracting Parties who have not yet signed, or who have signed but not ratified, the Opium Convention (...) agree to bring the said Convention into force and for this purpose to enact the necessary legislation without delay (...). Furthermore, for those Powers which have not yet ratified the Opium Convention, ratification of the present Treaty should be deemed in all respects equivalent to the ratification of that Convention (...)".[4]

Ever since this creative legal move, drug treaties have had more participating countries than any other "non-political" treaty. After the Treaty of The Hague many other drug treaties were initiated. This resulted in an international institutional framework that is currently anchored in the organization of the United Nations.

In 1961, an effort to replace all existing treaties with a single one resulted in the Single Convention of New York, which is still the primary legal document in the international cooperative effort against the so-called dangerous drugs. The Dutch are a party in this Convention as well as in the Amendment that followed in 1972. The Dutch hesitated for a long time, however, before they signed the convention of Psychotropic Substances, which was drafted in 1971.[5] This hesitation was largely based on mere technical grounds. An interesting development occurred at a conference organized in preparation of the 1988 Vienna Convention on Illicit Trafficking where the Dutch Minister of Justice expressed full Dutch support for the international fight against drugs. Apparently, the initial objections against the treaty had withered away quite suddenly. By announcing that the Dutch had decided to adhere to the Convention of Psychotropic Substances, the Minister of Justice thus garnered the necessary credit to be considered a serious participant in the designing of the Vienna Convention. The focus of the Vienna Convention is on hurting drug traders and traffickers financially.[6]

Although the Netherlands was one of the early forerunners of the internationalization of drug policy, over the years it lost its leadership role in this regard. Gradually, the Netherlands became just one of the many countries that simply signed the treaties and acted loyally in the implementation of the agreements. International agreements form the (more or less freely accepted) external constraints within which a sovereign drug policy can be developed. The treaties (especially the Single Convention of 1961) may be quite strict in relation to the kind of legislation the member states should have, but in matters of daily criminal policy many options remain open. To a certain extent the international treaties have produced harmonious legislation all over the world; however, different types of *policy* are put into practice under similar criminal legislation.

Dutch drug policy has often been described as rather different from that of other Western countries. The following descriptive account of the role of the Dutch criminal justice system in Dutch drug policy will explain the Dutch approach to drug problems; focusing on the actual functioning of the criminal justice system will be more instructive than reading formal statements by diplomats or other representatives of the Dutch government on the background and rationale of the Dutch drug policy.

2. Law-on-the-books and law-in-action

In the Netherlands the distinction between "law-on-the-books" and "law-in-action" is remarkably clear with regard to drugs.[7] Possession of marihuana and hashish is forbidden,[8] but in virtually every town one can find coffee shops where consumers openly buy their illegal products without fearing interference from the police.[9] Also, in the big cities one can easily spot the places where heroin and cocaine are sold, although this takes place in a more tense atmosphere. Here the police may suddenly show up and make arrests.

However, it is too simplistic to conclude - as the skeptical observer of the highly visible drug trade and drug use will be tempted to do - that there is no law enforcement at all in the Netherlands. Countries where drug users are less visible do not necessarily have a lower level of consumption or a better system of handling problems surrounding consumption. Painting the cities blue with law enforcement officers will certainly take away the visibility of drug problems but definitely not the drug-related problems as such.

Important is what police officers actually do and how they carry out their function. Legal documents may be an important factor in guiding the police and the prosecution in their behavior, but other factors are also important.[10] This seems almost self-evident. Legal rules do not address the problem of limited resources such as personnel, cars, interrogation rooms, cells, and so on. When more cases are processed than the system can properly handle, mistakes occur and the criminal justice system derails. The criminal justice system must set priorities in order to prevent such a situation. This holds true for all countries, including those where the police and the prosecution are formally obliged to bring to court any crime that is detected (*i.e.*, countries based on the principle of legality).

Contrary to the principle of legality, which for example is incorporated in the German Code of Criminal Procedure, the Dutch have committed themselves to the principle of expediency (or opportunity) which formally allows discretionary powers to the police and the prosecution.[11] The use of this principle of expediency is not limited to the necessity of setting priorities in order to cope with scarcity of resources. In fact the main function of the principle of expediency is to prevent prosecutions that are not in the best public interest. Originally, this legal principle gave prosecutors an almost unlimited degree of personal discretion, but presently there are officially published guidelines on how to deal with certain cases under specified conditions. (See discussion in section 4 of this Chapter.) These guidelines bridge the gap between the law-on-the-books and the law-in-action, particularly with regard to illegal drugs.

3. The Opium Act: law-on-the-books

The current Dutch Opium Act dates back to 1928; however, many changes have taken place since. Only the name and some of the scheduled drugs remind us of the original document. The Opium Act of 1928 replaced the first Dutch legislation on illegal drugs that came about as a consequence of an international treaty in 1919. Prior to that there was only an 1885 statute, which curiously enough limited the sale of opiate products in amounts of less than 50 gram to medical practitioners and pharmacists, allowing everybody else to deal in larger portions.

Originally the Opium Act was a piece of health legislation. In some respects it still is, for instance by allowing the Minister of Health to license persons and institutes to prescribe particular drugs. A license to prescribe legally forbidden drugs is only provided if justified by scientific or medical goals. The Minister makes these licensing decisions, but the initiative to start such a program (*i.e.*, to prescribe legally forbidden drugs) is often taken at the local political or administrative level.[12]

Though originally the Opium Act may have been health legislation, today it is viewed primarily as criminal legislation. There is no question that this Act satisfies all demands of the international conventions, stating the punishability of possession, trade, cultivation, importation and exportation and a number of other acts and omissions in relation to narcotic drugs (including cannabis products).

Depending on whether the drugs are listed on schedule 1 or schedule 2 of the Opium Act, the law specifies different sanctions. The mildest approach is toward the drugs on schedule 2. This list only contains cannabis products. On schedule 1 one finds drugs such as heroin and cocaine. According to the explanatory report accompanying the Opium Act the government considered the drugs on schedule 1 to be an "unacceptable risk". Cannabis products on the other hand were not considered to involve unacceptable risk. The maximum punishments for acts and omissions in relation to the drugs on schedule 1 are much harsher than for the drugs on schedule 2. In fact the differentiation reflected in the schedules parallels the well-known distinction between soft and hard drugs. On schedule 1 you find "hard drugs" (heroin, cocaine, LSD, *etc.*) and on schedule 2 you find only hemp and derivatives of hemp like cannabis. A technically odd feature of the two schedules is that tetrahydrocannabinol (the working substance of hemp and cannabis) is listed on schedule 1. Tetrahydrocannabinol as well as cannabis resin are considered hard drugs (*i.e.*, drugs with unacceptable risk) when they are found in a form other than the "normal soft drugs" of schedule 2 (*i.e.*, marihuana, cannabis, hashish, esrar, chiras and djamba, all customary solid mixtures of cannabis resin to which no other substances have been added). These "sloppy" definitions of tetrahydrocannabinol and hemp products on the schedules of the Dutch Opium Act are theoretically quite unsatisfactory, but in practice this has never caused any problem.

Since the Dutch hemp production is of growing significance, we need to comment on the peculiar position of hemp growing in the Netherlands. The Opium Act forbids the growing of hemp unless it is to win seed, to shield gardens from the wind, or for industrial purposes like the production of rope. In practice it is hard to clearly establish the purpose of growing hemp. It is generally acknowledged that, under the umbrella of the above-named exceptions, the growing of hemp for drug recreational purposes has been flourishing for over ten years. The quality of Dutch hemp is the best in the world according to drug users: tetrahydrocannabinol levels of more than 30% are found (maximum measurement: 37%). In comparison: Moroccan hemp usually gives a tetrahydrocannabinol level in the range of 6% to 15%. The national production of hemp makes it possible for the Dutch to provide the coffee shops to a large degree with home-grown products. Though it is relatively easy to make hashish out of Dutch hemp, research shows that there is little Dutch hashish on the consumer market.

Another important distinction in the Opium Act is between suppliers and consumers of illegal drugs. Use of illegal drugs *per se* is not directly punishable under Dutch law, but possession for use is. The relatively low legal priority on cannabis enforcement is reflected in the maximum level of punishment for possession of small amounts of cannabis. Theoretically, a maximum of one month imprisonment is possible for possession of up to 30 grams. But in practice there usually is no punitive reaction at all. If there is any punishment, it is generally no more than a small fine or a simple discharge. The relatively privileged position of cannabis products in Dutch legislation is the result of the historical compromise between proponents of legalization and the government which feared international reaction to legalization. As mentioned earlier, punishments for crimes relating to the drugs on schedule 1 are much tougher. A trafficker of heroin or cocaine or any other drug on schedule 1 faces a maximum punishment of 12 years imprisonment with the possibility of accumulation of punishment to a maximum of 16 years.

The Dutch Opium Act with its distinctions between cannabis products and other illegal drugs has been in effect since 1976. The last significant change of the Opium Act took place in 1985 with the introduction of the criminalization of any preparatory act relating to serious drug offenses (such as importation). In Dutch criminal law, the preparation of crimes other than drug-related offenses is not criminal unless there is a beginning of execution of the intended crime. The criminalization of preparatory acts in relation to drug crimes makes it easier for the police to use their powers in a pro-active manner. On the other hand, this possibility of early intervention makes it more likely that police activities intrude into everyday life. Also, the risk of legal errors is greater when the law covers preparatory acts that also might serve quite legitimate undertakings. Though the criminalization of preparatory acts is limited to operations related to the drugs on schedule 2 ("hard drugs"), the prosecution has developed techniques by which mere preparation of drug offenses involving cannabis (schedule 1 drug) may also be dealt with under legislation related to participation in forbidden organizations (paragraph 140, Dutch Penal Code).

4. Guidelines for law in action

The Opium Act may give some idea of the priorities in Dutch drug legislation, but it does not reflect, of course, the actual practice of drug law enforcement. In the Dutch legal system prosecutors are hierarchically placed above the police, they can give orders to implement a certain enforcement policy. In order to harmonize drug law enforcement in the different regions, the prosecutors of the High Courts produced guidelines for law enforcement and prosecution of drug crimes.[13] Although more accurate than the Opium Act, these guidelines also do not describe actual practices. The guidelines are a kind of pseudo-legislation, intended to guide officials, rather than clearly defined legal rules for citizens.

According to the guidelines, controlling the hard drug trade should have a high priority among police and prosecutors. This should be implemented by specialized law enforcement agencies, consistent prosecution policies, pretrial detention, and clearly specified sentences (minimal three years for dealers; two years for traffickers). In judicial practice, several criteria - such as the magistrates' "kilo policy" for importation traffickers in which prosecution demands one year per kilo hard drugs, up to the maximum of 12 years - have gradually developed. Personal circumstances ("how much did they know about their role in the illegal transport?") of individual traffickers are not very relevant in such a policy. This particular practice was never written down as an official guideline and ultimately did not survive criticism: it disappeared as quietly as it had appeared.

With regard to cannabis, the guidelines create a certain form of *de facto* decriminalization consisting of an officially agreed upon non-intervention in the retail market of cannabis under certain circumstances. This includes the practice of the so-called house dealer in the controlled setting of youth centers. Such agreement not to intervene may be made by the police, the prosecutor and the mayor in their regular discussion of what kind of criminal justice policies to pursue in a town or region. This system of triangular consultation allows the flexibility necessary to integrate the policies that flow from different responsibilities of the three parties involved (*e.g.* the partly conflicting interests of law enforcement, public order and public health). Though the guidelines only recognize the legitimacy of the house dealer phenomenon in youth centers, most deliberations have resulted in accepting cannabis dealing in coffee shops. In some cases the courts have acknowledged that prosecution of cannabis dealers in coffee shops should not be encouraged as long as they act according to a number of negative criteria, like[14]:
- not selling to youngsters who are under 18 (in some towns: 16) years of age; not promoting the business by advertisements;
- not selling in other than small amounts; not selling other illegal drugs;
- not selling to foreigners;
- not causing other public disturbances.

Whenever disturbances take place on a regular basis in a coffee shop, typically the local government takes administrative action in order to close the coffee shop.[15] The fact that soft drugs are involved has appeared to be irrelevant to Dutch administrative courts.[16] Local government is not allowed to close a shop or pub merely because of the retail trade in soft drugs. This socio-legal practice which has developed over the last 15 years shows that use and selling of cannabis products has gained a pseudo-legal status in the Netherlands, in spite of the Opium Act, which defines cannabis possession as a minor misdemeanor and drug dealing as a felony. At this point a closer look at the legal construction of allowing dealing in coffee shops may help explaining the somewhat confusing concept of a pseudo-legal status.

There are about 1500 coffee shops in the Netherlands where soft drugs may be bought.[17] How is that practice reconcilable with international obligations? The Single Convention and the obligations of the Illicit Trafficking Convention of 1988 do demand criminalization of possession, trafficking, dealing, cultivating and producing of soft drugs as well as of hard drugs. This obligation is met in Dutch legislation in the Opium Act. But there are no clauses in the relevant UN drug conventions that concern the actual *enforcement* of the legislation. The Single Convention acknowledges explicitly that enforcement of statutes may be limited on the basis of principles that are a fundamental part of a nation's sovereignty. This clause provides the latitude the Dutch have been using in their drug policy: by interpreting the legal principle of expediency as a fundamental sovereign principle, the Dutch have been able to develop a policy of (partial) non-enforcement of violations of the Opium Act. The expediency principle includes the discretionary powers of the prosecution (paragraphs 167 and 242 of the Criminal Procedure). The Dutch Supreme Court demands a degree of consistency in the use of discretionary powers. Earlier we referred to the guidelines for law enforcement and prosecution of drug crime produced by the prosecutors of the Courts of Appeal. These guidelines are intended to structure the use of discretionary powers of the prosecution in a consistent manner. According to the Dutch Supreme Court, a practice that follows these prosecutorial guidelines in a consistent manner has the status of "law". The guidelines explicitly allow the presence of a soft drugs dealer in youth centers. The guidelines imply that decisions concerning enforcement of drug laws are to be made at the local level through regular deliberations between the mayor, the prosecutor, and the police. Although the coffee shops are not dealt with in the guidelines, case-law based on Dutch Supreme Court decisions states that a consistent practice, even if not formally included in prosecutorial guidelines, also obtains the status of "law". Thus, "practice" creates new laws.

Because coffee shops have been consistently tolerated since the late seventies in most parts of the Netherlands, now a specific motivation is required to successfully prosecute dealing in soft drugs in a coffee shop.[18] This specific motivation could be that certain conditions which guide the acceptance of coffee shops in most parts of the Netherlands are not met in the coffee shop under scrutiny. As a consequence of the way in which coffee shops have become accepted, it is likely that other forms of dealing in soft drugs eventually may gain a similar pseudo-legal status. An example may already be found in the case of a "blow-home-courier-service" where a person had organized a local delivery service for cannabis users. He distributed small amounts of cannabis in the region of 's Hertogenbosch.[19] According to the court the prosecution had no adequate justification for prosecuting this particular person in view of its overall lenient policy in soft drug matters. The prosecution lost this case.[20]

In spite of these developments, it must be noted here that legal evolution towards tolerance is by no means inevitable. Legally it is very well possible that a gradual retreat from the earlier policy of tolerance may take place. Mounting external pressure on the Dutch government may be an important factor. Partners in the Schengen Agreement have legitimate grounds to challenge Dutch drug policy, because the Schengen Agreement not only demands repressive legislation but also repressive *practice* in relation to soft drugs (Article 71). On the other hand, the Schengen Agreement also acknowledges respect for national sovereignty (Article 72).

Let us return to the guidelines. Though a low priority is given to the prosecution of possession of cannabis products, it may happen that a person gets caught with it. What will happen? The guidelines state that when an individual is caught with cannabis products for private use, it is possible to prevent prosecution through a transaction of 50 guilders (approximately US $25). The guidelines set 30 grams as the maximum amount one can possess for private purposes, but in practice prosecution virtually never takes place for possession of less than 50 grams; even at this level 90% is not prosecuted.[21] The police are not asked to take any pro-active initiatives to detect possession of small amounts of cannabis for private use. When larger amounts are involved, imprisonment becomes more likely, in particular for possession of one kilo (or more) of cannabis. According to Rook and Esser's study of the prosecution of drug-related offenses, seventy-seven percent of people convicted of possession of less than one kilo of cannabis only received a fine.

The tolerance shown for use of and trading in soft drugs is partly extended to hard drugs (*e.g.*, heroin or cocaine). Users of these drugs do not have to fear direct intervention by the police in search of drugs. This is also a consequence of the guidelines, which give low priority to investigating possession of small amounts of hard drugs for private use. As a matter of fact, actual sentences for possession of up to 10 grams of heroin (or other "hard" drugs) are considerably below the guideline term of one year. However, importation or exportation of illegal drugs is met with a more strict enforcement of the law.

In spite of the restrained approach of law enforcement toward illegal drug use, many drug users are prosecuted because they come in contact with the police for ancillary crimes (shoplifting and other thefts, robberies, burglaries and so on). According to the prevailing law enforcement philosophy, drug addiction is not to be considered an excuse or a mitigating circumstance for cases of secondary criminal involvement.

Differently, the guidelines of the prosecutors explicitly recognize that a medical or socio-medical approach is preferred for people who violate the rules with regard to possession for private use. The guidelines are more than empty words; they are supported by a strong network of drug-related social services. Be that as it may, still a large percentage of the prison population is addicted to drugs, which shows that the Dutch intention to deal with drug dependents primarily outside the criminal justice system is not altogether successful.

5. Consequences of a criminal justice approach

Clearly, the Dutch criminal justice system shows considerable flexibility in dealing with the drug issue. However, the picture would not be complete without an examination of the consequences of current law enforcement policy on (1) the drug market and drug use, and (2) on the criminal justice system itself.

The impact of the Dutch emphasis on attacking the supply side of the drug trade on the drug market is quite similar to the effect of such approach in other countries.[22] The drug prices for consumers are, without a doubt, considerably higher than would be the case in a non-intervention market. The exact nature of the impact of criminalization of drug trafficking on the price of drugs is unknown; the proposition that drug prices follow a log function (*i.e.,* 10 times as much in the town as on the field in the country of cultivation, ten times as much on the boat as in the town, and 10 times as much for the users in the place of destiny) at least has the credit of elegance and some self-fulfilling truth (even dealers read books). It is a well-documented fact that drug use in the illegal market brings about ancillary crimes of a secondary nature (*i.e.,* a variety of criminal acts to raise money to buy drugs). Furthermore, the circumstances of drug use in an illegal context – despite the many assistance services available in the Netherlands – are still more risky than they would be in a legal context where there is no need to conceal use. In fact, to a large extent Dutch drug-related social services do no more than try to remedy the negative effects of the illegal context in which use takes place, rather than the negative effects of use itself.

The criminal justice approach definitely has an impact on the illegal drug trade. The high-risk/high-profit characteristics of a black market enterprise are, of course, an outgrowth of a repressive law enforcement approach to drug trade. This brings along a system of money laundering, firms that function merely as a front to cover up illegal activities, corruption in banking, bribery of police and customs and so on.[23] In similar fashion, the illegal nature of drug dealing encourages the use of violence by operators in the drug market. These effects are of a general nature and by no means specific for the Dutch situation. Although the intensity of these effects may differ from one country to the other, they exist worldwide.

A repressive (*i.e.*, criminal justice approach) to illegal drugs has also consequences for the functioning of the criminal justice system. The peculiarities of enforcing drug laws cause concrete problems in police investigations. Drug crimes are essentially victimless crimes; under normal conditions nobody is interested in informing the police of knowledge concerning drug transactions. This necessitates some forms of infiltration, or the buying of information; the police must rely on deception, and deal with informants with questionable credentials. Another problem is that drugs are relatively easy to get rid of when things get hot. Consequently, the police needs to move fast to "freeze" situations. Hazardous events, like crossing borders, are foreseeable and dealers have many means of shifting risks to naive or innocent traffickers. Even in the relatively low-key drug policy approach of the Netherlands, the fight against drugs has, occasionally, had a destructive effect on constitutional safeguards. This erosion of due process is based on the misleading but persistent notion that procedural safeguards frustrate the fight against drugs. It is misleading because a criminal justice system that shrinks away from due process is threatened in its very existence. In the next section, I will elaborate on this point by discussing a few Dutch Supreme Court cases related to police powers and drug users.

6. Police powers and drug users

As stated before, the Dutch fight against illegal drugs is primarily directed at the dealers. That has been the official policy from 1976 onwards. Nonetheless, many cases in Dutch courts are about possession of relatively small amounts of drugs. In order to search a person, Dutch law demands objective individualized grounds for suspicion; however, in the case of drugs, the mere presence in a place generally known for drug use and dealing provides sufficient grounds to allow the police to search anyone at that particular location (Ruimte, HR 14-1-1975, NJ 1975, 207). This may bring about searches at public places like railway stations, where drug users regularly hang out. This move from individualized to generalized suspicion is a major breakthrough in norms of criminal procedure. The search and arrest of drug users is not an aim in itself, but allows the police to gather information about dealers. Many drug users are under some sort of permanent suspicion and can be taken from the street any moment the police has time and energy to do so. When several statements from drug users implicate a certain person as a dealer, according to the Supreme Court it is no longer necessary to find drugs in the possession of this suspected dealer to obtain a conviction. In this way, again, the normally required objective grounds for suspicion and prosecution are reduced to a minimum, which opens the risk for manipulation of the criminal justice system. Though some drug users are under permanent suspicion when search and arrest are involved, in other situations it suddenly appears expedient *not* to view them as under suspicion (*e.g.* when the police questions them in the street without first cautioning about the right to remain silent (HR 29-9-1981, NJ 1982, 258)).

At the same time that the police appears to get more power with regard to drug-related activities, officers show a growing reluctance to arrest drug users, either for public order reasons or for trying to use their information to arrest dealers. Given the spread of the HIV virus among drug users, physically searching these people is considered to be hazardous. Moreover, it brings little job satisfaction to push the same unfortunate young people through the revolving door of the criminal justice system time and again. Therefore, many police officers favor some form of medically controlled prescription of drugs.

7. Police powers and dealers

Specific characteristics of the fight against illegal drugs make it necessary to employ "creative" investigative means, because of a lack of spontaneously reported information on drug-dealing to the police.[24] In 1979, the Dutch Supreme Court established a number of conditions for the operation of undercover agents. An undercover officer may not incite anyone to commit drug crimes unless the person involved was already predisposed to do so. The presumed predisposition of a person is based on his criminal record and on facts drawn from the operational reports of the undercover agent (HR 4-12-1979, NJ 1980, 356).

An undercover agent need not be a Dutch policeman. As a matter of fact, in the Supreme Court case just mentioned the undercover was a US DEA agent, with official diplomatic protection. Undercover agents normally work in a special task force for short-term infiltration. They seek to buy drugs, preferably in large amounts, and to arrest on the spot. Normally the Public Prosecutor agrees in advance on the type of procedure the task force follows; however, retroactive acceptance may also be sanctioned by the court. In a number of cases the undercover agent operates in connection with anonymous sources; the reliability of these sources is underscored by the sustained reputation that such a source has as a police informant. This is rather paradoxical, as it is hard to grasp how such a source can function for a prolonged time period without some foul play, which in turn would undermine the presumed reliability.

The position of anonymous informers and witnesses in Dutch law has come under attack as a consequence of rulings of the European Court of Justice. Accepting statements of anonymous witnesses as evidence of legal guilt may run contrary to the provisions of fair trial (Article 6 (1) and (3)(d)) of the European Convention for Human Rights): Unterpertinger, Kostovski.[25] But as long as the anonymous informers can be used by the police without formally using their statements as legal evidence, then there is no restriction to do so. In the Brandstetter case,[26] the European court suggested that the identity of the witness could remain a secret as long as the defense did not seek to question him or ask for his presence in court, and his testimony was of only minor evidential value. In the Lüdi case,[27] the European Court of Justice was more open to the possibility of allowing anonymous statements of undercover-agents in drug cases as evidence, but only if the defense maintains the right to cross-examine the witness (provided this can be done in a way that protects the identity of the undercover agent).

Because of the specific difficulties in gathering information about drug dealing, tapping telephones has a growing popularity. More than 50% of the telephone taps in the Netherlands are related to drug investigations. Very often these taps are used in a prospective manner and not as a means to solve cases that have already occurred. This makes sense, since dealers are not likely to evaluate past transactions by phone; however, constitutionally the Dutch police should only use phone taps as a tool for solving (not preventing) crimes.

There are times when ordinary citizens have the duty to inform the police of suspected drug dealing activities; if they fail to do so they run the risk of being considered a participant in a drug crime. The Supreme Court made this ruling in a case against a taxi-driver who went 60 miles from Rotterdam (the Netherlands) to Antwerp (Belgium) at night in order to pick up a person from a boat. The person who had asked for the taxi from Rotterdam had some boxes and sacks with him. The taxi-driver did not inquire about the content of the luggage. When customs and police caught them on the way back to Rotterdam, the taxi-driver stated he did not know that his passenger was transporting illegal drugs. In spite of this defense, the taxi-driver was convicted for "culpable trafficking". The court ruled that the defendant should have considered the fact that his passenger was a foreigner with unconventional luggage in the context of the general knowledge that foreigners use taxi-drivers for illegal transports. Based on this general knowledge, he should have inquired about the content of the luggage.[28]

This case not only reflects an expansionist dynamic in criminal justice when drugs are involved, but also a discriminatory bias toward ethnic groups. That last aspect is shown in other cases as well. The Dutch Supreme Court has decided that contact between a "German white and a Dutch black person in the Warmoesstraat Amsterdam" may serve as a ground for police action on the suspicion of drug dealing (HR 6-12-1983). This case illustrates the discriminatory character of police actions against the drugs trade.

As the above examples illustrate, the Netherlands has not been exempted from the gradual retreat from the norms of due process resulting from the criminal justice fight against illegal drugs.[29] And yet there is no indication that this has contributed to solving drug problems.

The willingness of the Dutch courts to expand police powers in fighting drug crimes has met with very limited success. Illegal drugs keep coming in, just as drug dealing keeps going on. Therefore, the police continue to ask for more powers, more financial means and a wider definition of what is a (drug) crime. This has already brought about legislation on the punishability of preparatory acts related to drugs. This 1985 legislation makes it possible to prosecute those who organize drug deals from a distance (with money and contacts) but who manage never to actually get caught with any drugs in their possession. The most recent proposal involves laws to punish dealers financially; legislation on money laundering and confiscation of illegally obtained proceeds (especially from drug dealing) is in preparation.

Our discussion of the impact of drug enforcement on the functioning of the Dutch criminal justice system suggests an analogy with its effects on drug-related social services. The relevant Dutch service agencies mainly work to redress the negative consequences of the illegality of drug taking; similarly, the criminal justice system mainly focuses on the

confiscation of the profits that came about as a consequence of the illegality of drugs. It appears that some form of legal availability of currently prohibited substances would solve many problems, just as it inevitably would also bring about new problems.

In this context it is interesting to note that a remarkable number of
people in strategic positions in Dutch criminal justice drug policy have
spoken out for radical decriminalization of currently illegal substances.[30]
For instance, the Chief of Police of Utrecht, one of the largest cities in
Holland, is a strong supporter of complete legalization of all drugs. His
view is that the supra-national war on drugs has generated a multiplier
effect in crime rates.[31] Some members of the judiciary have also been
outspoken about the destructive effects of the law enforcement approach
to drugs. The vice-president of one of the District Courts has repeatedly
and publicly stated that the current criminal justice approach is a disaster.
"We are trying to win the fight against drugs the wrong way", he said
addressing a conference on drugs. He did not come to this conclusion by
reading scientific material on the drug war, but by observing the daily
practice of criminal justice.[32] During this same conference, a high-ranking official in the Ministry of Justice proposed to deal with drug offenses
through administrative (instead of criminal) law.[33] Finally, the solicitor-
general of the Dutch Supreme Court has argued that the criminal justice
approach to drugs has no serious future and may very well dissipate quite
suddenly, just like the Berlin Wall.[34]

8. The effects of European harmonization

The effects of international developments on Dutch drug policy are
discussed in Chapter 13 (Blom and Van Mastrigt). Therefore, we will
only very briefly touch on some issues related to the current trend in the
direction of European unification. The European economic and political
integration has undoubtedly already had consequences for drug policy in
Holland, though there is a debate on its actual significance. Some argue
that European integration leaves enough discretion for the Dutch to go
their own way. Others think this optimism is unjustified, and I do agree
with them. Germany and France are hard liners on the drug issue, even
where cannabis is concerned. Whenever Dutch drug policy could have
any potential effect in Germany or on German citizens, German officials
will remind the Dutch government of its obligation under the Schengen
Treaty. In anticipation of such pressure Holland is already preparing for
a harmonization of drug policy. Recently, the Dutch government endorsed a study which suggested giving priority again to the arrest and

prosecution of persons in possession of small amount of soft drugs, especially when involving so-called drug tourists. But drug tourists do not only come to Holland for its permissiveness. They are sometimes motivated to come to the Netherlands because of lack of primary care facilities in their home country. The types of easy available services for drug dependents in the Netherlands (methadone programs, needle exchange) as well as the relatively mild punishments for drug crimes have been criticized by some of the other European countries. It seems unlikely that other European countries will open their borders without demanding adjustments in Dutch drug policy to make it more consistent with the European context. On the other hand, there are also indications of a contrary development, a shift from debating drug policy in an ideological manner to debating it in pragmatic terms. There are some indications that European drug policy harmonization will increasingly focus on the limitation of risks, as regards the health situation of users, the level of use, and the spread of AIDS in relation to drug use and prostitution. An international shift from ideology to pragmatism may save the peculiarly effective permissiveness that characterizes the Dutch criminal justice system, at least in some respects.

No one can claim to have the final solution to problems surrounding illegal drugs, but there is a growing understanding in the Netherlands that repression (even when it is focused on hard drugs) is not the most pragmatic option for drug policy. Unless, of course, one simply wants to stick to an internationally well-established habit.

Endnotes

1. Social and cultural aspects of drug use and historical origins of the use of opium. In: Chatterjee, S.K. (Ed.), *Legal Aspects of International Drug Control*, p 3. The Hague/Boston/London: Martinus Nijhoff, 1981.
2. Meijring, J.H.: *Recht en Verdovende Middelen*. The Hague: VUGA, 1974.
3. Stein, S.D.: *International Diplomacy, State Administrators and Narcotics Control: the Origins of a Social Problem*. Hampshire, UK: Gower Publ, 1985.
4. Similar provision may also be found in: Article 230 of the Treaty of Peace with Hungary, dated 4 June 1920; Article 174 of the Treaty of Peace with Bulgaria dated 27 November 1919; and Article 280 of the Treaty of Peace with Turkey dated 10 August 1920. See Chatterjee, S.K.: *Legal Aspects of International Drug Control*, p 67; Endnote 1.
5. Convention on Psychotropic Substances of 21 February 1971 (Geneva).

6. United Nations Convention Against Illicit Traffic in Narcotic Drugs and Psychotropic Substances, 19 Dec. 1988, UN Doc E/CONF 82/15. See: Chief Bassiouni, M.: Critical reflections on international and national control of drugs. In: Den *Int'L & Pol'Y* Vol. 18:3, pp 311-337, 1990; Stewart, David P.: Internationalizing the war on drugs: the UN convention against illicit traffic in narcotic drugs and psychotropic substances. In: Den *Int'L & Pol'Y* Vol. 18:3, pp 387-404, 1990; DeFeo, Michael A.: Depriving international narcotics traffickers and other organized criminals of illegal proceeds and combatting money laundering. In: Den *Int'L & Pol'Y* Vol. 18:3, pp 405-415, 1990.

7. See for this distinction: Van Dijk, J., Haffmans, C., Rüter, F., Schutte, J., Stolwijk, S. (Eds.), *Criminal Law in Action. An Overview of Current Issues in Western Societies.* Arnhem: Gouda Quint, 1986. In relation to drugs in that collection: Rüter, F.: *Drugs and the Criminal Law in the Netherlands*, pp 147-166. See also: Downes, D.: *Contrasts in Tolerance. Post-War Penal Policy in the Netherlands and England and Wales.* Oxford: Oxford University Press, 1988.

8. Opium Act Section 3.

9. See about the coffee shops in Amsterdam: Jansen, A.C.M.: *Cannabis in Amsterdam. A Geography of Hashish and Marihuana.* Muiderberg: Coutinho, 1991.

10. Not a recent phenomenon, see Emsley, C.: *Policing and Its Context, 1750-1870.* London: MacMillan, 1983. See also Davis, K.C.: *Police Discretion.* St. Paul, MN: West Publ Co, 1975; Stead, P.J.: *Pioneers in Policing.* Montclair, NJ: Patterson and Smith, 1977; Reuss-Ianni, E.: *Two Cultures of Policing: Street Cops and Management Cops.* New Brunswick, NJ: Transaction, 1983; Toch, H. and Douglas Grant, J.: *Police as Problem Solvers.* New York: Plenum Press, 1991, especially Ch. 12: A Problem-Oriented War on Drugs.

11. A recently proposed change in the German Narcotic legislation (paragraph 31) introduces the expediency principle for the prosecution in a range of drug crimes. The German parliament has accepted the proposal.

12. A recent example: In September 1992 the Rotterdam police and the City administration announced that a heroin prescription program was being considered for a small group of "addicts". The execution of such a program is nonetheless the full responsibility of the medical doctor who ought to decide on medical criteria.

13. The official document is called: Richtlijnen voor her opsporings- en strafvorderings-beleid inzake strafbare feiten van de Opiumwet (Strct. 1980, 137).

14. Arr. Rbank Groningen 11 December 1986, see: Silvis, J.: Kroniek rechten en criminologie. In: *Tijdschrift Alcohol en Drugs* 13(2):59-60, 1987. Arr. Rbank Zutphen 2 mei 1986, NJ 1986, 667.

15. An example of such action is a decision by the Dutch Supreme Court (November 25 1985 ARB 1986, no. 248). The court stated that direct intervention by the local authorities in order to close the coffee shop is allowed in cases where there is a direct threat to the quality of life in the neighborhood of a coffee shop where soft drug dealing takes place. In this case soft drugs were being sold to very young children.

16. The Court has decided that dealing soft drugs in a coffee shop is not necessarily detrimental to the living conditions in that neighborhood (Afdeling Rechtspraak van de Raad van State 8 May 1984 (Arb. 1984, 442).

17. Cannabisverkooppunten in Nederland, NIAD, Utrecht 1991.

18. HR 12 Juni 1990, NJ 1991, 44; HR 5 maart 1991, NJ 1991, 694.

19. Rechtbank 's-Hertogenbosch (Politierechter) 16 april 1992, Parketnummer 01/023997/91: distributing soft drugs by car is not substantially different from selling soft drugs in a coffee shop.

20. The prosecutor has recently re-opened the case against the same person on similar grounds. Either the prosecutor has reason to believe that the court has changed its opinion, or the prosecutor has decided to fight the case through to the Appeal Court and perhaps to the Supreme Court.

21. These statistics are drawn from a study of A. Rook and J.J.A. Essers about the period 1977-1982, published in 1988 (*Vervolging en Strafvordering bij Opiumwetdelicten*, Staatsuitgeverij, 1988).

22. Körner, H.H.: *Betäubungsmittelgesetz*, München: Verlag C.H. Beck, 1990; Caballero, F.: *Droit de la Drogue*, Paris: Dalloz, 1989; De Choiseul Praslin, C.-H.: *La Drogue: Une Économie dynamisée par la Répression*, Paris: CNRS, 1991; Albrecht, H.J. and Van Kalmthout, A.M.: *Drug Policies in Western Europe*, Freiburg: Eigenverlag Max-Planck-Institut, 1989.

23. De Choiseul Praslin, C.-H.: *La Drogue: Une Économie dynamisée par la Répression*, Paris: CNRS, 1991.

24. See for the US situation on this issue, Marx, G.T.: *Undercover. Police Surveillance in America*. Berkeley/Los Angeles/London: California Press, 1990.

25. Unterpertinger *vs* Australia, European Court of Human Rights, Series A, Vol. 110. Judgement of 24 November 1986, Application no. 9120/86; Kostovski *vs* Netherlands, European Court of Human Rights, Series A, Vol. 166. Judgement of 20 November 1989, Application no. 11454/85. 12 EHRR 434.

26. Brandstetter *vs* Austria 1991, European Court of Human Rights, Series A, Vol. 211. Judgement of 28 August 1991, Application nos. 11170/84, 12876/87 and 13468/87.

27. Lüdi *vs* Switzerland, European Court of Human Rights, Series A, No. 238, 1992. In this case the infringements of privacy (Art 8(1)) by undercover agents were justified as being necessary in a free society (Art 8(2)).

28. HR 16-2-1982, NJ 1982,425. The Dutch Opium Act differentiates between intentional and non-intentional but culpable trafficking. The taxi-driver was sentenced for culpable trafficking. Most Western European countries have no punishment for culpable trafficking, except the Netherlands, Germany and Greece.

29. See Rüter, F.: *Drugs and the Criminal Law in the Netherlands*, o.c.; Trebach, Arnold S.: The loyal opposition to the societies. In: Van Dijk (Ed.), *Criminal Law in Action*. Arnhem: Gouda Quint, 1986.

30. Baanders, A.P.: *De Hollandse Aanpak. Opvoedingscultuur, Druggebruik en het Nederlandse Overheidsbeleid*. Assen: Van Gorcum, 1989.

31. Wiarda, J.: Mogelijkheden en beperkingen van de repressie-strategie. In: Groenhuijsen, M.S., Van Kalmthout, A.M. (Eds.), *Nederlands Drugsbeleid in Westeuropees Perspectief*, pp 49-59. Arnhem: Gouda Quint, 1989.

32. Böcker, B.F.N.: Rechter en rechtspraak in de drugsproblematiek. In: Groenhuijsen, M.S., Van Kalmthout, A.M. (Eds.), *Nederlands Drugsbeleid in Westeuropees Perspectief*, pp 89-96. Arnhem: Gouda Quint, 1989.

33. De Beaufort, L.A.E.J.: Strafrechtelijke marktbeheersing. In: Groenhuijsen, M.S., Van Kalmthout, A.M. (Eds.), *Nederlands Drugsbeleid in Westeuropees Perspectief*, pp 69-87. Arnhem: Gouda Quint, 1989.

34. Leijten, J.: *NRC*, December 1991.

IV. DRUGS AS A PUBLIC HEALTH PROBLEM: ASSISTANCE AND TREATMENT

Leon Wever

In the Netherlands, present government policy on drug abuse is based on the view that drugs are primarily a problem of public health and welfare. In this Chapter, a short description is given of the policy developments with regard to assistance and treatment of drug users in the last decade. Particular attention is given to the results of two policy evaluations, followed by a discussion of recent trends in drug policy. The final section speculates on the future direction of Dutch drug policy.

1. Background of a social drug policy, the 1970s

When heroin entered the Netherlands in the early 1970s, most policy makers felt very uncomfortable with the idea that they had to rely on law enforcement in order to reduce drug supply and demand. These uneasy feelings may be explained by several distinct features of Dutch society in the 1970s. First of all, the early seventies were characterized by movements to decriminalize a variety of behaviors, which were considered private and expressive of a personal lifestyle. In particular, many legal provisions regulating sexual behavior were abolished. This resulted in a search for alternative ways of controlling social problems. At the same time, the proliferation of heroin use became especially noticeable among groups of immigrants from former Dutch overseas colonies - immigrants who were experiencing all kinds of social problems in a period of fast growing unemployment. Both developments prevented the drugs issue from being conceived as a single, isolated phenomenon; rather, drugs were viewed against the backdrop of adjustment problems of new immigrants and the general decriminalization movement.

Starting in the mid-seventies, the larger cities were very much involved in the process of urban renewal of deteriorated areas, where the problems of drug use and drug dealing were concentrated. Despite diverse attempts to solve the problems of the modern big cities by means of urban renewal and welfare programs, the drug trade soon became an inevitable element of urban problem areas. In addition to the socio-medical realities of addiction to illegal drugs, many people became economically dependent on the drugs trade in Dutch cities.

During the seventies, one conclusion became crystal clear to academics, law enforcement personnel and social service professionals: the criminal justice system was definitely not the appropriate institution for solving drug addiction problems, particularly in view of the fact that drug problems appeared to be closely intertwined with other social developments. This awareness resulted in a call for a welfare-oriented approach: preventive measures on the one hand, and providing assistance and treatment to drug users on the other.

An institutional framework for drug treatment was already in place: throughout the country, there were a variety of both inpatient and outpatient alcohol dependency clinics. Initially, these alcohol dependency clinics were seen as the most adequate facilities for the treatment of drug users as well. However, it soon became apparent that the nature of drug addiction – with all its social complications – made the traditional treatment approach – directed at total abstinence – unworkable for most drug users. This was the major reason for the development of so-called "client-centered" facilities. In the bigger cities in particular, grassroots organizations and "alternative" youth assistance institutions (such as "Release" and the "SDI", the "Amsterdam Foundation for Drug Information") provided assistance directed at the immediate needs of people in trouble, such as providing shelter, daycare services, and basic medical care. These organizations proved to be better able to reach drug addicts and to take care of them. Providing "care" for a large number of drug users was found to work better than trying to "cure" a small group into abstinence. Fierce debates on the philosophy underlying the assistance and treatment of hard drug users accompanied these social policy developments. The more informal, low threshold, peer-oriented care and assistance approach competed with the more traditional, medico-therapeutic approach. The latter soon lost ground to the former. Within a relatively short period of time the new, "alternative" approach of providing care and assistance to drug users was officially accepted and incorporated into the national and municipal funding structures.

Dutch social drug policy has developed as part of a more general social and health policy – a policy which represents an important dimension of a much-encompassing social security system. Put simply, the Dutch state legally guarantees a reasonable income to anybody not capable of earning a living (due to unemployment or illness). Furthermore, virtually all income groups participate in a comprehensive and publicly controlled system of health care insurance. This means that, for the large majority, all medical needs are covered. In addition to the social security and health insurance system, the Netherlands has developed a tradition of fully subsidized social and welfare services, ranging from social work agencies, youth support services to community centers. The development of Dutch drug policy has to be understood against the tradition of large-scale government involvement with social and health services. In addition, it should be noted that Dutch criminal justice policy has created the necessary "legal room" for the development of non-abstinence oriented drug treatment services.

2. The development of drug treatment policies in the 1980s

Present drug policy was fully developed and implemented in the 1980s. Three periods can be distinguished: 1. a radical policy shift in the early 1980s; 2. a time of policy evaluation in the mid-eighties; and finally, 3. the period dominated by AIDS and crime.

2.1 A radical shift

In the early eighties, downtown areas of the larger Dutch cities (*i.e.*, Amsterdam, Rotterdam) became increasingly dominated by a highly visible drug population, creating feelings of uneasiness and annoyance among the public. It became apparent that many addicts were not reached by any public service. Furthermore, drug addiction had become increasingly a problem of the lower social-economic groups – groups that already were confronted with other social problems, such as unemployment, bad housing and crime. Ethnic minority groups, in particular, appeared to be hit hard by both drug addiction problems and unemployment, crime, and poor housing. Many drug treatment services were still only focusing on abstinence, without much regard for the social needs and manifest demands of the addicts.

It was during this time period that the urge for more direct and immediate ameliorative measures to deal with drug problems caused a major shift in national and local drug policies. The target of drug treatment was broadened. Increasingly, services were funded which focused on improvement of the physical and social situation of addicts, even when they maintained their drug use. These new services or new approaches within the existing facilities were mainly of an ambulatory, outpatient, or "low threshold" nature, for example, street corner work, open door centers or methadone maintenance facilities. Furthermore, they now explicitly attempted to address the problems as perceived by the clients: acute health problems, including withdrawal effects, money, housing, education and work. To phrase it in more general terms: this new approach focused on the reduction of social and medical risks related to the use of hard drugs, rather than on the termination of drug use. "Harm reduction" as the principal aim of drug policy was being practiced in the Netherlands before the concept was officially defined in the international drug policy context.

In addition, policies changed within the more traditionally oriented residential facilities. Cooperation with the outpatient services improved. Crisis- and detoxification centers were created, which also functioned as a connection between ambulatory and residential treatment. Treatment modalities – which typically had been of a long-term nature – became diversified; a variety of conceptual frameworks was introduced. Short-term treatment and part-time treatment were established.

During the first half of the 1980s, this complex network of drug treatment and assistance facilities was established throughout most regions of the country. Any city with drug problems developed drug policies in which social assistance and diversified treatment played a dominant role.

2.2 Two evaluation reports

In the mid 1980s, two large-scale evaluations of drug policy were conducted. The reports were written by groups of government officials with an administrative responsibility for drug policy. The first report, entitled the "1986 Review of Alcohol and Drug Policy" (Ministry of Finance 1986) attempts to evaluate drug treatment and assistance policies after the period of development and re orientation discussed above. The second report is entitled "Drug policy in motion, towards a normalisation of drug problems" (Interministerial Steering Group on Alcohol and Drug Policy 1985). In this document, the more fundamental problems and contradictions of drug policy are discussed and an effort is made to provide a rational theoretical foundation theory for future drug policy.

The 1986 Review was designed to provide cost-cutting arguments. Because of the lack of hard data and the political popularity of the drug demand-reduction approach, the government decided not to reduce funding. Instead, a program of evaluation research was started in order to draw conclusions about the effectiveness and efficiency of drug treatment and governmental treatment policy.

Of much more importance for the development of drug policy in the Netherlands was "Drug policy in motion". This report was written by a coordinating and advisory body consisting of top government officials (Interministerial Steering Group on Alcohol and Drug Policy). To a large extent, the report was based on a sociological study of life histories of heroin addicts (Janssen and Swierstra 1982). The analysis of the heroin problem and the policy recommendations resulting from this research greatly influenced the ideas on social policy within the Interministerial Steering Group on Alcohol and Drug Policy. Its report contained a number of critical remarks about the effectiveness of drug policy in general. Furthermore, alternative policy options were discussed, ranging from legalization of drugs to compulsory treatment of drug addicts.

The report concluded that a coherent set of policy objectives and the required means for an overall drug policy were lacking. It was noted that policy objectives were often conflicting. It made a distinction between the primary problems which are caused by the use of drugs, and the secondary problems which are caused by the social context in which the substances are used. For instance, the primary problem of opiate use may be the mental and physical dependence it produces. In addition, this substance suppresses physical pain and emotions. These primary drug effects make users vulnerable for all sorts of physical and mental problems. However, there are additional (secondary) drug problems related to opiate use – a wide variety of undesirable phenomena, which do not exclusively bear upon users themselves. These secondary drug effects include a set of health problems caused by malnutrition and contaminated drugs and needles. There are also drug problems which are essentially unrelated to any property of the substance itself. These secondary effects include crime and prostitution, public expense for treatment and law enforcement and, not least, the infringement of civil liberties. All these additional, secondary individual and societal problems are inexorably linked to the world-wide prohibition of certain substances. The report argues that this has resulted in an international out-of-control black market, with high profits for the traffickers, and many risks to society.

The report concludes that most Dutch aid and treatment facilities deal with these secondary drug problems. This may be true even to the extent that one part of the drug policy is occupied with solving the problems caused by another part of the drug policy.

The report "Drug policy in motion" acknowledged the drug phenomenon as an inevitable, always present, aspect of modern society, with an established infrastructure of illegal and legal interest groups. It concluded that the existing traditional policy measures for reducing supply and demand were rather unsuccessful. Consequently, it considered the potential of two radical alternatives to existing practices: (1) legalization of illicit drugs, and (2) compulsory treatment.

The report argues that legalization of drugs would probably solve most of the secondary problems associated with drug use. Many drug problems directly related to the black market economy would disappear if the availability of drugs were less restricted. For obvious reasons, however, most notably the international conventions on drugs and the uncertain effects of legalization, the report deemed legalization out of the question.

Compulsory treatment was rejected for reasons of human rights and effectiveness. Because there is no guarantee that a particular treatment is successful, compulsory treatment would be reduced to a disguised form of mere detention. It is a fundamental Dutch legal principle that no-one can be forced into accepting treatment.

The report proposed a compromise between a policy leading to a war on drugs, and the other extreme of drug legalization. On the one hand, the war on drugs unwarrantedly denies the societal reality that drugs have become a normal, although undesirable, part of our culture. Legalization, on the other hand, tries to avoid the secondary problems as much as possible, yet fails to take into account political realities. The pragmatic policy proposed by the report is not aimed at total elimination of all drug problems, but rather at initiating a gradual process of controlled integration of the drug phenomenon in modern society.

Pragmatic drug policy calls for a process of "normalization" which involves managing the risks of psychotropic substance use in society, rather than getting involved in futile attempts at its complete elimination. This is not to deny that severe individual and family problems frequently result from hard drug use. Normalization requires, however, that "supposedly collective problems are demystified and socially redefined as primarily individual problems" (Engelsman 1989). At the end of such a process, the drug problem should be viewed as a "normal" problem, one of the several health and social problems a society faces and tries to control. Moreover and importantly, criminalization of the consumer is considered a harmful way of discouraging the use of hard drugs. Consequently, the normalization process requires de-stigmatization of drug users. "This does not mean that this phenomenon has been spirited away. But it has been put in another perspective in order to enable society to face the problems from a realistic point of view, unobscured by moralistic coloring" (Engelsman 1989).

The fact that pragmatic drug policy relies on factual and realistic means and steers away from a dramatized and over-emotional approach is clearly reflected in the Dutch prevention policy. The drugs issue is not addressed as an isolated issue by fright-invoking means. Instead, this subject is mainly discussed in school programs, where it is part of an integrated approach aimed at the promotion of healthy lifestyles. The main issue is not the radical abstention of illegal substances, but learning to cope with risk-involving behavior (including alcohol and tobacco use), and learning how to be responsible for one's behavior and choices.

This "normalization approach" regarding drug problems as proposed in the report "Drug policy in motion" was adopted as the formal foundation of drug policy by the Government in 1985.

2.3 Crime and AIDS

In the mid-1980s, two new themes began to emerge in drug policy: crime and AIDS. Crime was on the increase. Drug-related crime, such as shoplifting and burglary by addicts who needed money to support their habit, appeared to continue, despite the readily available treatment and assistance facilities in the cities. Consequently, although, in theory at least, drug policy was to minimize the role of law enforcement in the lives of drug users, in practice many addicts still were confronted with the criminal justice system. It should be noted that Dutch drug users did not enter the criminal justice system because of illegal drug use or possession, but because of (drug-related) property offenses.

The crime problems in the cities and the drug problems in the prisons led to the adoption of a policy by which drug treatment and assistance became more oriented towards the needs of law enforcement. New policy measures inside and outside the prison were implemented, such as treatment as part of a conditional sentence, or a pre-treatment phase in detention in order to be released earlier.

The different policy adjustments had – again – one thing in common: the diversion from punishment to treatment, the voluntary character of treatment (it is the addict's decision to turn to treatment or not; the alternative is imprisonment just as for anybody else who has committed a serious crime), the use of existing legal instruments (e.g., conditional sentencing), and the use of all available treatment and assistance modalities, outpatient and inpatient.

The easy accessibility of the (voluntary) treatment and assistance system – more than 70% of addicts are estimated to be in contact with this system – proved to be of vital importance when AIDS began to emerge as a problem among drug users. It is a well-known fact that the lifestyle of many drug users, where needle sharing and unprotected sex with different partners are common phenomena, puts this group at a high risk for the spread of the HIV virus. When confronted with this new crisis in public health, existing drug policy was adjusted with "risk reduction" as its primary aim; an AIDS policy with realistic and feasible preventive targets was deemed essential for any pragmatic social policy.

The main target of the drug-related AIDS policy is to limit the spread of the HIV virus by attempted modification of risky behavior. This mainly implies safe sex and safe drug use, both of which may be achieved by reasonable changes of lifestyle. It is unlikely that reduction (let alone termination) of unwanted behavior can easily be achieved; therefore, a reasonable alternative is to teach safer techniques of involvement in the (still risky) behavior (drug use, sex). Thus, if drug use cannot be stopped – and we all know the limitations of intervention in this regard – using drugs in safer (non-intravenous) ways should be encouraged. And when this is not feasible – as practice sometimes shows – encouraging safe injection may be the most effective method. Health education for drug users is therefore being accompanied by the availability of sterile needles and syringes, as well as condoms.

Due to the fact that drug users form a well-defined high-risk group, efforts can be directly aimed at reaching these groups. This necessitates a large variety of drug treatment and assistance services which are easily accessible, an out-reaching approach of these services (street work, fieldwork in hospitals and jails, low-threshold "open-door-centers") and realistic, pragmatic intervention goals (i.e., not primarily directed at kicking the habit but at risk reduction). In the Netherlands, ambulatory drug treatment and assistance services, such as the Consultation Bureaus for Alcohol and Drugs and the Municipal Health Services (see section 3) fulfill a central role in AIDS prevention. It is not difficult to see why. They form a dense network throughout the country (in 60 cities, more than 100 outpatient services); they have already established contact with most of the drug-addicted population, and they are experts in influencing the behavior of drug addicts.

Although the majority of drug addicts were (and are) in more or less regular contact with drug treatment institutions, there remained a sizeable, more elusive group of intravenous drug users. Therefore, a need was felt to explore other ways of getting the health message across. Initial attempts were made to delegate the promotion of risk-preventive measures to the organized consumer groups of drug users, the so-called "junkie-unions". In 1987 junkie-unions existed in 31 cities. Unfortunately, it soon became apparent that most of these groups were too weakly organized, and too institutionally isolated to be able effectively to tackle the job of AIDS prevention among the drug addicts. Subsequently, innovative health education and behavior modification measures were integrated within the traditional treatment and assistance facilities. A quick start of AIDS prevention among drug users was facilitated by the prompt and ready cooperation of the treatment and assistance services involved. Moreover, these agencies were willing to take unorthodox measures, such as the distribution of clean needles, or providing injectable methadone. They also accepted the idea of adapting their drug treatment efforts towards the aim of AIDS prevention.

The cities of Amsterdam and Rotterdam had already had some experience with the dispensing of sterile needles because of earlier efforts to prevent the spread of hepatitis among drug users. The needles were sold to drug users by the junkie-unions. In many cities, needles can easily be obtained from pharmacists, but in other places pharmacists are reluctant to accept drug users as clients. That is why, in Amsterdam, the first needle exchange program was set up by the junkie-union. A few years later, the project was adopted and extended by the Drug Abuse Treatment Department of the Municipal Health Service. Several other treatment and assistance services also started to include free needle exchange programs, sometimes within the context of methadone maintenance programs. At the present time, some police departments even provide needle exchange facilities for arrested addicts.

The national federation of drug treatment services (followed by the Netherlands Institute on Alcohol and Drugs) started an AIDS prevention program for all Dutch treatment services, financially supported by the Ministry of Health. This program has established a national network of AIDS prevention officers within the drug treatment facilities, in order to communicate new developments and to coordinate preventive actions.

In retrospect, three conditions – a network, consensus on preventive measures, and cooperation – have been essential in the successful implementation of an extensive and far-reaching national AIDS prevention program for drug users. Needle-exchange programs appear to lead to safer injection practices. Feared negative side-effects, such as increased use of needles because of increased availability, have not occurred (Hartgers et al. 1989). On the contrary, only 25-30% of Dutch heroin addicts use drugs intravenously. The percentage of intravenous drug using AIDS patients among the total group of AIDS patients is relatively low (Netherlands: 9%; all European countries: 36%; USA: 28%; WHO 1992).

3. Drug treatment services

Because of the emphasis on the reduction of risks of drug use in Dutch drug policy, most policy efforts have been directed towards the development of assistance and treatment services for addicted drug users. Treatment for alcohol or drug problems by these agencies is free. Four types of services can be distinguished: 1. out-patient Consultation Bureaus for Alcohol and Drugs (CADs); 2. municipal methadone programs; 3. social welfare services for drug users; and 4. residential treatment facilities. This section includes a brief description of the major organizational and operational characteristics of these institutions.

3.1 The Consultation Bureaus for Alcohol and Drugs

The Medical Consultation Bureaus for Alcohol and Drug Problems (CADs) are autonomous, non-governmental, but publicly funded institutions, the entire costs of which are borne directly by 23 municipalities and 19 probation boards. Seventy-five percent of these funds are provided by the Ministry of Welfare, Health and Cultural Affairs through these municipalities. The remainder is financed by the Ministry of Justice through the probation boards. The nationwide network of CADs comprises 16 main branches, 44 subsidiary branches and 45 consulting rooms. The total budget amounts to Dfl. 80 million* per year.

The CADs are (mental) health institutions specifically oriented towards addiction problems. The institutions operate on the principle that the care, treatment and assistance they provide should ignore the legal (or moral) status of the object of addiction. Although the CADs primarily provide non-residential mental health care, their services are strongly oriented towards social welfare, as the majority of their staff (1000 in all) are social workers. The objectives of individual CADs may vary somewhat from overcoming addiction through treatment to stabilizing the condition of addicts by supplying methadone on a "maintenance basis". A variety of methods is used, including psychotherapy, group therapy, material assistance, family therapy, counselling, and advising groups of parents.

An increasingly important area of the CADs' work consists of advising and training teachers and members of more general health and welfare services, such as general practitioners and youth workers. This part of the work aims at enhancing the competence of the more general agents in the field of public health and welfare as far as (drug)addiction problems are concerned. Most recently, the CADs also fulfill major preventive tasks in the field of AIDS control (needle exchange, information and education).

Operationally as well as organizationally, the CADs are linked, in part, to the judicial system. This is of special importance in the field of drug

* One US Dollar is Dfl. 1.80

addiction. The CADs cooperate with the general probation services in a program of early assistance to arrestees. Drug-using arrestees are visited in the police cell within the first 48 hours of their arrest. Arrested heroin addicts are offered methadone and efforts are made to establish contacts which will lead to the acceptance of assistance and counselling during and after detention in penal institutions.

3.2 Municipal methadone programs

In several of the larger cities, municipal authorities have set up their own methadone programs, administered by the municipal health services. The Ministry of Health provides the municipal methadone programs with a budget of about seven million Dutch guilders annually.

Methadone may be supplied on a reduction basis (the dose is gradually reduced) or on a maintenance basis (a constant dose). Methadone is now supplied either by a CAD or the municipal health service in virtually all population centers with a drug problem. As with the CADs, the municipal health programs have a central role in the field of AIDS prevention. At the present time, methadone is being provided to 7000 addicts daily in approximately 60 municipalities. Roughly three quarters of the clients receive methadone in a maintenance scheme. This means that, on average, about 40% of the drug-addict population in the Netherlands is in daily contact with methadone treatment. It is further estimated that, on an annual basis, about 75% of the addict population has been in contact with treatment or assistance facilities for drug users.

3.3 Social welfare services for drug users

The social welfare projects for drug users are part of a wide range of social welfare services aiming especially at young people. Traditionally, these institutions target multiple-risk groups where addiction problems may occur together with unemployment, ethnic minority status and other indicators of marginality. These welfare projects are typically subsidized on a local level, where facilities may be optimally suited to meet the most urgent needs. Some 550 people are employed in these services. The services are intended to be easily accessible and to have the widest possible outreach. They concentrate on different types of aid, often for young problematic drug users. Typical social welfare drug-oriented programs are: open door centers for specific groups (such as street prostitutes or homeless people), street-corner work, ethnic or religious therapeutic communities, night centers for homeless addicts, and social rehabilitation projects for (former) addicts, including supervised housing, vocational and social aptitude training, assistance in adjusting to a life-style that includes regular work, and possibly aftercare following some form of treatment.

A number of services is targeted to specific groups on the basis of their religious affiliation or ethnic and cultural identity. Some of these work nation-wide. The Ministry of Welfare, Health and Cultural Affairs has a budget of approximately 55 million Dutch guilders for almost 90 projects in 45 municipalities. Roughly one half of the total sum spent on these kinds of assistance to addicts is allocated to the four major cities: Amsterdam, Rotterdam, The Hague and Utrecht. Approximately one third of the total budget is earmarked for projects for ethnic minorities from former Dutch overseas colonies (living both within and outside the four main cities). The focus on different minority groups more or less mirrors demographic and drug-epidemiologic developments within the Dutch society. Consequently, assistance to addicts of Surinamese origin (Latin America) has increased considerably, while it has decreased sharply where Moluccans are involved. Most recently, more social welfare programs for young drug users are being directed at (children of) migrants from Mediterranean countries, who are turning to drugs in increasing numbers.

3.4 Residential facilities

Residential facilities for the treatment of drug addicts and alcoholics are located throughout the Netherlands, providing a total of 1000 beds. These facilities exist either as independent clinics or therapeutic communities, or as special units in general (psychiatric) hospitals.

Two major types of treatment are available: (1) crisis intervention and detoxification (which may last between two days and three weeks); and (2) clinical treatment (lasting from three months to a year, aimed at overcoming addiction). These facilities cost about 100 million Dutch guilders per year and are funded from contributions made under the Exceptional Medical Expenses (Compensation) Act, which is part of the Dutch public health insurance system.

4. Trends and perspectives

During the last two decades, Dutch drug policy has more or less continuously adapted to the changing drug problem and to changing policy assessments. This process will undoubtedly continue.

Developments in recent Dutch drug policy may be characterized by several trends. The first trend is the acceptance as a matter of fact that drug use and drug trafficking will be an ever-present and inevitable aspect of modern society and, consequently, the understanding that large-scale attempts at the "war on drugs" will be futile. A policy of zero tolerance may be seen by some people as morally just; however, for social policy purposes, it is deemed neither realistic nor effective. Therefore, a pragmatic policy has been developed aimed at reducing the personal and social risks of drug use, without necessarily expecting to terminate drug use at the individual or social level.

The second trend may be called a built-in flexible response of Dutch social drug policy which allows for adaptations to the changing needs of society. The specific problems of ethnic minorities, the growth of crime and the threat of AIDS are examples of these changes, requiring a re-evaluation of aims and instruments in social drug policy.

Expansion is the third trend. The budget for drug abuse treatment and prevention, contrary to that for many other welfare and health services, has increased constantly.

The fourth trend is integration and rationalization. At the present time, a rather strong consensus has emerged on the objectives and means of drug treatment and assistance. Normalization, resocialization, risk reduction and prevention are the key concepts within this broad consensus of social drug policy.

The fifth trend is a re-appraisal of the role of the criminal justice system. If drug users are approached as normal citizens with rights and duties, they should be held accountable for their behavior just as anyone else. Addiction is no excuse for undesirable social behavior. At the same time, re-appraising the role of the criminal justice system implies acknowledging its usefulness in facilitating the achievement of treatment goals, for example, by conditional sentencing or in-detention preparation of treatment.

Finally, the sixth trend is decentralization. Since 1990, municipal authorities have had the primary responsibility for the development of ambulatory (outpatient) treatment policy. These authorities are most directly confronted with the practical social consequences of drug use. Consequently, they are considered to be the most suitable for making the practical policy choices.

Have these policy trends had an effect in terms of reducing the drug problem? There is some evidence available on the effects of drug policy.

As will be shown in Chapter 6, the use of illicit drugs (cannabis, heroin) has stabilized since the early 1980s, as has the number of drug-related deaths. The average age of drug addicts is rising, as is the age of first use of heroin. The number of young drug addicts is decreasing. There is no indication whatsoever that the use of cocaine has increased rapidly or that non-deviant cocaine use presents severe addiction problems for a substantial number of people (Cohen 1989).

A growing number of drug addicts is in contact with drug treatment facilities. Both methadone maintenance and withdrawal treatment have become more popular. Currently, 75% of all heroin addicts are involved in some way with methadone programs. Ten years ago this percentage was closer to forty. The demand for residential withdrawal therapy has also doubled in the last ten years (Driessen 1990; Buning 1990). The needle-exchange programs appear to lead to safer injection practices.

These trends indicate that it is possible to manage and contain drug problems with an extensive policy aimed at drug demand and harm reduction, and a reduced enforcement of the law against consumers of drugs. However, there are also some trends which give a more negative picture. For instance, there is a small but growing group of "revolving-door" patients with a long addiction career and often psychiatric problems. Poly-drug use has become more prevalent, which makes drug abuse treatment more difficult (*e.g.*, there is no substitution therapy available for cocaine addiction or heavy use of tranquilizers). Drug use among groups in a relatively disadvantaged social and economic position, particularly ethnic minorities, remains the most resilient problem. Despite the relatively favorable figures on the relation between intravenous drug use and HIV infection in the Netherlands, the spread of HIV among and from the drug-using population is still a threatening prospect.

What has the present decade in store? Undoubtedly AIDS will remain the most important social and health concern in connection with drug use.

AIDS undoubtedly constitutes a major social risk. AIDS and addiction give a double stigma, decrease the opportunities for resocialization and for leading a normalized life, and increase marginalization. Preventing this from happening will be an increasingly important challenge for drug treatment and assisting facilities. There is no use trying to treat a group for drug abuse only, while ignoring the fact that this group (and others) are taking deadly risks, are going to die or be expelled by society.

As far as the other trends described above are concerned, they will most probably persist in the foreseeable future, except perhaps for the expansion of services. The growing group of hard-core, psychiatric addicts will have to lead to an adjustment of treatment policy in terms of cooperation with psychiatric facilities.

The socio-economic position of several marginal groups in larger Dutch cities calls for increasing efforts to improve the level of education and employment. This is as important for social policy in general, as it is for social drug policy. Without improving these social conditions, attempts to make people stop using illicit drugs will be doomed to failure.

Current political forces within Dutch society strongly favor the present social drug policy of "normalization". In fact, the need to focus drug policies on harm reduction is no longer a topic of political debate. This large-scale political support of present drug policy may be threatened, however, by the increasing internationalization of drug policy.

The official United Nations drug policy strategy is based on both supply and demand reduction. In international political conferences and within international organizations, a growing number of resolutions are calling on national governments to develop demand reduction programs (Wever 1992). Since drug problems and the possibility to decrease demand for drugs are heavily influenced by local or national social and cultural factors, it is very important that the responsibility for this part of the drug policy lies primarily with the national states and local communities.

The international level is traditionally ill suited for developing demand reduction programs. The international drug policy strategy, as formalized in international conventions, almost completely focuses on the control of international trafficking of illicit drugs. The international institutional framework has the same built-in limitations. The few international organizations interested in demand reduction, such as the World Health Organization or the Council of Europe (Pompidou Group), have neither the political power nor the funds to compete with supply reduction as the most obvious and dominant part of international drug policy.

This situation may present two problems for national drug policy: one of a legal, the other of a financial nature. The legal problem might be that increasing efforts to reduce the supply of drugs by means of law enforcement and international cooperation reduce the freedom of individual states (*i.e.*, the Netherlands) to continue their own pragmatic and non-moralistic drug policy. An example of this trend may be seen within the European Community, where the development of a common drug policy currently is a focal issue, with clear implications for the freedom of involved individual countries.

The financial problem may be a result of the attention that international drug policy is presently receiving from government leaders. The implementation of internationally agreed policy costs money. It is very well possible that public money will be allocated to those items of government policy that gain most political weight. In the case of drug policy, this may very well be the international cooperation in matters of law enforcement. This could mean that funds for law enforcement will be allocated at the expense of funds for social drug policy.

In the Netherlands, drug abuse is still seen mainly as a public health and welfare problem. But we have to accept the fact that this perspective is vulnerable in an international political debate where the drug phenomenon is seen as an object of warfare. History has shown that welfare and warfare do not get along very well. The Dutch experience also shows that a social drug policy, directed at demand and risk reduction, is capable of containing and even diminishing the problems connected with drug use.

Acknowledgment

The author wishes to acknowledge the help of Ton Cramer (Ministry of Welfare, Health and Cultural Affairs) in checking some of the figures in this Chapter.

References

Buning, E.C.: *De GG&GD en het Drugprobleem in Cijfers, Deel IV*. Amsterdam: GG&GD, 1990

Cohen, P.D.A.: *Cocaine Use in Amsterdam in Non-Deviant Subcultures. Amsterdam: University of Amsterdam, Institute of Social Geography, 1989*

Driessen, F.M.H.M.: *Methadonverstrekking in Nederland*. Rijswijk: Ministerie van Welzijn, Volksgezondheid en Cultuur, 1991

Engelsman, E.L.: Dutch policy on the management of drug related problems. *Br. J. Addiction* 84:211-218, 1989

Hartgers, C., Buning, E.C., Van Santen, G.W., Verster, A., Coutinho, R.A.: The impact of the needle and syringe-exchange programme in Amsterdam on injecting risk behavior. *AIDS* 3:571-576, 1989

Interministerial Steering Group on Alcohol and Drug Policy: *Drug Policy in Motion, towards a Normalisation of Drug Problems*. Rijswijk: Ministry of Welfare, Health and Cultural Affairs, 1985

Janssen, O.J.A., Swierstra, K.: *Heroïnegebruikers in Nederland, een Typologie van Levensstijlen*. Groningen: Criminologisch Instituut Rijksuniversiteit, 1992

Ministry of Finance: *1986 Review of Alcohol and Drug Policy*. The Hague, 1986

Wever, L.J.S.: Drug policy changes in Europe and the USA; alternatives to international warfare. *Int. J. Drug Policy* 3/4: 1992

V. DUTCH PRISON DRUG POLICY: TOWARDS AN INTERMEDIATE CONNECTION

L.H. Erkelens and V.C.M. van Alem

1. Introduction

It is a well-known fact that Dutch drug policy has several unique features, setting it apart internationally. Although the Netherlands has a different way of handling drug problems, there are some problems Holland shares with other countries. One major problem common to virtually all Western countries is the pervasive influence of drugs in the sphere of criminal justice, especially in prison.

It was only recently that an explicit "penitentiary drug policy" developed (Van Alem et al. 1989). For a number of years the focus of drug policy excluded prisons. The issue of drugs and the correctional system scarcely got the attention of policy makers, neither from the field of public health nor from the penal law field.

However, by the end of the seventies a critical stage was reached; drug problems in prison were perceived as increasingly detrimental to both the addicted offenders, the prison climate as a whole, and to the goals of imprisonment. Currently (1991), about 50% of the population is classified as addicted to hard drugs (mainly heroine, but also cocaine and amphetamines).

This chapter is concerned with the development and state-of-the-art of Dutch correctional drug policy. This policy has developed within the changing perspectives of general criminal justice policy and the general drugs (and crime) problem in Dutch society. Consequently, we will first take up the issue of recent developments in criminal justice policy and look at the corresponding changes within the Dutch penitentiary system. Next, we will elaborate on penitentiary drug policy and its implementation.

2. Developments in Dutch criminal justice policy

During the late 1960s and 1970s, the socializing and integrative elements (the so-called "denominational allegiances") in Dutch society progressively weakened (Van Dijk 1985; Downes 1988). These factors, in conjunction with demographic factors (*i.e.*, mainly the post war "baby boom") and the emergence of long-term unemployment among segments of the younger generation, contributed to a change in criminality and criminal justice in Holland. There was a gradual, but consistent increase in the crime rate: the number of offenses reported to the police rose from 1,100 per 100,000 in 1950 to 7,100 per 100,000 in 1985. (By the end of the 1980s, crime rates started to level off.) Between 1950 and 1980, the crime rate increased by more than 700%; the number of crimes solved by arrest declined from 50% in the 1950s to below 20% in the 1980s (Buikhuisen 1989).

These factors contributed to a gradual change in opinions about crime, criminals, and criminal justice policy. Until well into the 1970s, criminality was primarily viewed as a problem of social deprivation; or alternatively, inspired by the "labeling theory", offenders were seen as the products of repressive means of social control (Buikhuisen 1989; Van Dijk 1985). Not only were these views shared by most criminologists, they were also quite strongly represented in the discussion of politicians and administrators dealing with criminal justice policy. The dramatic rise in criminality and criminal victimization transformed political (and public) opinion: there was a marked decrease in the general level of tolerance for crime in Dutch society.

Thus, the early 1980s saw the dawn of a new era in Dutch criminal justice policy. Part of the "toughening" of attitudes should be understood as a recognition of the (negative) side effects of earlier, more lenient policies. This resulted in a different official (*i.e.*, governmental) perspective on crime, sentencing policy and judicial organization.

With regard to sentencing policy, for example, the number of prisoners with a sentence of more than one year increased markedly; in the period 1986 till 1992 by 44% (Vegter 1993). On the other hand, so-called back and front door options for diversion out of the prison system were offered to relieve some of the pressure. Moreover, a more prevention-oriented approach was implemented in criminal justice policy. An example are the measures directed at decreasing the rate of vandalism, for instance by means of techno-prevention or increasing the level of social control in some vulnerable areas. The "tougher" attitudes soon had consequences for the Dutch penal system. A government report "Society and Crime" (1985) was presented as a comprehensive policy plan to improve the maintenance and enforcement of law and order. The report suggested that drug-related crime was one of the main contributing factors to the sharp increase of petty criminality. In this context, more or less coercive (ranging from compulsive treatment to exerting some pressure) forms of treatment of drug addicts within the criminal justice system were mentioned as a policy option.

3. Dutch prison policy

The main foundations of the current Dutch prison system were laid after World War II. New legislation, embodied in the Prison Act of 1951 and the Prison Statute of 1953, gave rise to a differentiated prison system. Different kinds of prisons (from open to closed) were established, where offenders could be placed according to length of sentence, personality, type of offense and potential for rehabilitation.

The principle of rehabilitation is incorporated in Article 26 of the Prison Act. This Article states as the system's primary goal the orderly and safe execution of punishment, and preparing the inmate's return to society as its secondary goal. The concept of rehabilitation as such has changed over time. Until the end of the 1950s, rehabilitation was viewed mainly as a personal affair. In those days, the concept of rehabilitation had a strong moral dimension, dating back to notions derived from 19th century prison ideology. This ideology stated that incarceration was meant to bring on new moral insights among inmates. Inmates were expected to reflect upon their crimes and wrongdoings. To that end every prisoner was locked up alone, in one cell. There was virtually no contact possible between inmates in this so-called cellular system (Auburn system).

With some slight adjustments, this cellular system persisted until the early 1950s. However, with the Prison Act of 1951 a new principle was introduced. The new approach recognized that prisoners were social beings. (This recognition had a lot to do with prison experiences of many Dutch people who had been incarcerated as members of the resistance movement during World War II.) Rehabilitation was no longer considered a purely personal affair of moral redemption, but instead was primarily understood as a social process: prisoners had to be resocialized. They should learn proper social norms and values by staying together in more or less homogeneous groups. Prison work was seen as an important tool for resocialization. Prior to the prison Act of 1951 prisoners worked alone, each in his own cell. With the new Act they started to work together in workshops, approximating normal work processes.

The resocialization mission of the prison system was believed to be equally valid for all prisoners, but its implementation was thought to require differentiated means. All prisoners were placed in more or less homogeneous group regimes where they could start learning the social norms they were thought to be missing. For reasons of security and safety, prison institutions were differentiated according to criteria like age, gender, length of sentence, and legal status of the detainee. Youthful offenders were separated from adults and men from women. The prison system was differentiated into two levels of freedom of movement. Within the highest security level, prisoners were only permitted to operate as groups in the course of structured activities such as prison work. Otherwise prisoners had to stay in their own cell. Within the second level of security conditions, inmates only had to stay in their cell during the night. Any other time they were free to socialize and move about the ward.

At the end of the 1970s, one had become more sceptical about the potentially resocializing effects of group regimes within a differentiated penal system. The growing scepticism echoed the often cited conclusion that in the field of correctional rehabilitation "nothing works" (Lipton *et al.* 1975). This changing attitude was also influenced by the disappointing results of Dutch evaluation studies of different prison regimes (Van der Linden 1978).

Starting in the early 1980s, the conventional prison ideology of resocialization for all inmates began to lose its importance. Replacing the lofty aim of rehabilitation, more elementary goals for the treatment of offenders were formulated: namely, the principle of a humane confinement, and the principle of minimizing possible negative side effects of imprisonment. Both principles were to apply to all inmates. They may be considered as the Dutch minimum standards for dealing with offenders. A third and more ambitious principle was added to the two previous ones: to offer inmates opportunities to work on their personal development and psychosocial problems. This third principle may be understood as an updated operationalization of the resocialization ethic included in Article 26 of the Prison Act. This desirable end result of incarceration is no longer expected to be produced under all circumstances, but is viewed more as the outcome of a detention process shaped, to a large degree, by the inmates' own choices and motivation. Resocialization is now viewed primarily as a matter of providing options and chances within the prison environment, where it is up to the inmates to chose whether they want to take advantage of these chances.

Related to the introduction of these principles, new modalities of imprisonment have emerged. For several categories of problematic inmates, such as drug addicts, drunken drivers, mentally ill inmates, and inmates representing high security risks, special wings have been established. These developments are consistent with the framework provided by the 1951 Prison Act. Over the years, the principle of one inmate per cell has been maintained. The function of the single prison cell was transformed, however, from an instrument for moral redemption into a requisite for warranting minimal privacy of inmates within the prison walls.

4. Some quantitative features of the Dutch penal system

The increase of the crime rate in conjunction with the call for stricter law enforcement and longer sentences resulted in a shortage of prison cells in the 1980s. A long-term plan to expand penal capacity was developed and prison space has been significantly expanded during the last decade (Ministerie van Justitie 1989).

Table 1 gives an overview of the current capacity of the different prisons.

Table 1. Number of cells of the Dutch prison systems on 1-7-1991

	N	%
Detention centers (jails)	4973	65.1
Closed prisons	1223	16.0
(Half-) open prisons	1099	14.4
Prisons for females	345	4.5
Total	7640	100.0
Total number of institutions	58	

The detention centers (jails) are intended primarily for persons facing criminal charges, but they also house sentenced offenders serving short sentences or awaiting transfer to a prison. Prisons are reserved for convicted offenders. There is a wide differentiation in prisons and in strictness of regime. There are a number of maximum security prisons for long-term offenders and a number of half-open and open prisons. The latter two types help ease the transition from the prison community to free society. Only a small proportion (less than 100 cells) within this minimum security category is of the "open" kind, in which prisoners are permitted to find work in the outside world and live with their families during the weekends. There is also a special group of offenders who are not placed in remand centers after their trial and sentencing; instead they are sent home to wait for a directive to report to a particular institution at a certain day. Indeed, it is quite common that, due to lack of capacity in the remand centers, defendants who should be incarcerated are actually sent home (Brand-Koolen 1987).

Prison capacity on January 1, 1981 was 3,798 cells; in ten years' time the overall capacity more than doubled to 7,640 cells. Proportionally, the closed prisons show the largest increase in capacity. The main cause of this development has been the increase in the average sentence length, which almost doubled from 3.2 months in 1982 to 5.7 months in 1989. In 1990, the incarceration rate (*i.e.*, the number of people incarcerated per 100,000 inhabitants), was 48 – still one of the lowest in Europe. The mean incarceration rate in 1988 for 23 European countries was 62 per 100,000 (Van der Goorbergh 1990). During the past few years this number has gradually risen; at this moment the Dutch rate is about 50 per 100,000.

In 1991, about 40% of the detained population was in the pre-trial phase, 3.6% of the population was female and about 15% of the prison population was younger than 23 years of age; foreign prisoners made up about one-fifth of the total prison population.

The nature of the detained population has changed quite dramatically over the last decade or so. Perhaps one of the most prominent qualitative changes in the correctional institution in Holland has been the introduction of the drug-addicted offender. The drug-using inmate population has shown a steady growth since the mid-1970s; this has had an enormous influence on penal treatment policy. The remainder of this chapter describes the unique features of Dutch correctional drug policy, formulated in 1983.

5. The rise of penal drug problems

"...one of the main unintentional effects of the use of criminal law to combat drugs has been the considerable growth of drug-abusers and drug-related problems (smuggling, dealing, use) within .... the Dutch penitentiary system" (Rüter 1986).

We wholeheartedly agree with this conclusion. In 1980, 23% of the prison population was estimated to be drug users; in 1982 this estimate had increased to 25%-30%; the most recent figure for 1991 is approximately 50% (Jaarverslag 1992). This 50% figure has to be used with caution: remand centers, half-open prisons and closed prisons show markedly different rates (sometimes as high as 60% or 75%). Because of the fact that registration is based on self-reports or/and needle mark inspection by correctional medical personnel, these figures probably underestimate the extent of drug use.

The increase in drug problems in penal institutions also results from the rising numbers of detained narcotic drug traffickers, who contribute heavily to the lengthening of the average time of imprisonment. About 25% of all inmates in Dutch prisons are sentenced for offenses against the Opium Act. The average length of prison sentences of drug traffickers rose steadily from almost seven months in 1982 to over 11 months in 1989.

The categories of addicted inmates and incarcerated Opium Act offenders (drug traffickers and dealers) are, of course, not mutually exclusive. Research has shown considerable overlap of more than 35% between the two categories (Rook 1982).

Furthermore, there is empirical evidence that not all drug addicts in prison are equally inclined to smuggle drugs into the prison. Perhaps it is not surprising that prisoners who are addicted to drugs *and* sentenced for both an offense against the Opium Act *and* for another crime (*e.g.*, some property crime), are most inclined to continue drug dealing within the prison walls. It are these petty, opportunistic traffickers who have become addicted to their own stuff and who have subsequently committed property crimes who are most likely to smuggle drugs into prison.

The large influx of addicted inmates confronted the prison system with a range of new problems for which it was quite unprepared. These problems had to do with drug use, as well as drug smuggling and dealing, and the social tensions among inmates and between inmates and correctional personnel created by these illicit practices. In addition to these internal order and control problems, many new problems of a medical and psycho-social nature emerged for which prison personnel felt totally unprepared. The next section describes the way these problems have been dealt with by the Dutch correctional system.

6. Main tenets of Dutch penitentiary drug policy

Penitentiary drug policy may be viewed as a continuous learning process, partly the result of deliberate planning, partly shaped by trial and error. Since the early 1970s, Dutch policy makers have taken advantage of a variety of tools to obtain knowledge and insight into the problems of drugs in prison. The main elements in this process have been: practical experience of people working in the penal institutions; performing and evaluating experiments; specific training programs for prison personnel; and organizing seminars and task forces on specific aspects of correctional drug problems.

The direction of this developmental process may be described in terms of distinct policy stages. The first phase started about twenty years ago when, in 1972, the first hard drug addicts appeared in the prison system. During the first seven years (1972-1979), the whole process was strongly treatment-oriented. Drug problems in prison were first and foremost approached from the addictive-disease perspective (Van Alem *et al.* 1989). Because addicted inmates were a new phenomenon, nobody knew how to deal with withdrawal problems, nor how to react to drug-seeking and drug-taking behavior. Prison doctors were bombarded with questions, from addicts as well as from prison staff. During that period the predominant view of addicts in prison was that of sick people whose crimes were the result of their illness. They were primarily viewed as patients, sick people who were actually out of place in prison.

This first socio-medically oriented stage of penal drug policy eventually led to two experiments in 1979, in remand centers in Amsterdam and Rotterdam. The goals of both experiments were: adequate detoxification, providing medical and psycho-social assistance for solving short-term problems and, finally, transferring addicted inmates as quickly as possible to outside treatment programs. The crucial role of two teams of drug consultants of the Consultation Bureaus for Alcohol and Drugs (so-called CADs) was significant in both experiments. For the first time, personnel of a private and professional drug treatment organization was accepted and integrated into the prison system. One of the main outcomes of these first experiments was the institutionalization and further expansion of the role of external drug assistance professionals within the prison system.

Almost simultaneously with the start of the Rotterdam and Amsterdam experiments a fundamental change in penitentiary drug policy perspectives occurred. Establishing and maintaining control over drug trafficking and drug subcultures in penal institutions became a focal point of concern. A second phase of penitentiary drug policy started, during which the drug problem was primarily defined as a liability for order and security within the prison, specifically threatening relations among inmates and between personnel and inmates. Thus, in this phase (which also lasted some seven years, from 1980 to 1986), a control model prevailed. Typically, during this period a special prison was designated for prisoners who had been caught dealing drugs in prison.

Further, a special procedure was established to inform the Ministry of Justice as well as the public prosecutor about drugs confiscated in prison (including, if possible, the owners of the contraband). In this manner, criminal procedures against suspected inmates could be initiated. Finally, measures such as bodily searches and closer control of incoming mail and packages were either established or used more frequently. In theory at least, even defense attorneys, social workers and prison staff were no longer immune from scrutiny to prevent the importation of drugs into prison.

Over time, the two dominant views - the socio-medical and the security control perspective - slowly merged into the third (and still prevailing) stage of penitentiary drug policy. The primarily control-oriented era came to an end in 1987, with the publication of a new policy plan called "Drug-Free Detention"*. The new plan was built on the idea that managing the drug problem and caring for the detained addicts should be compatible and mutually reinforcing.

7. Drug-free detention

The policy of drug-free detention is based on three goals:
1. To prevent as much as possible *but not at any cost* drug use and drug dealing within the prison walls.
2. To offer medical and psychological aid to inmates to overcome the direct effects of drug withdrawal.
3. To promote further assistance and treatment for those addicts who have shown to be genuinely motivated to do something about their addiction. Diversion to outside socio/medical institutions is a preferred means to reach this goal.

In other words, both drug control *and* providing primary care for addiction-related problems of prisoners are major tasks for the prison system. The policy assumes that more fundamental therapy, aiming at a "drug-free" life should be provided by the mental health system, but only when requested by the detainee.

These goals were formulated during the control-oriented period (in a policy document from the State Secretary of Justice to the Dutch Parliament in 1983**), but it took some years before conditions were in place to implement the last two of these goals. Personnel had to get practical experience with working with addicted inmates and detained drug traffickers. Specific training and education programs had to be instituted as part of the general training of the prison staff. Finally, drug workers of the Consultation Bureaus for Alcohol and Drugs (CADs) had to be integrated into the prison system. In 1986, these CAD professionals obtained a structural position within the Dutch prison system. As part of a general

---

* Brief van de staatssecretaris van Justitie (Letter of the State Secretary of Justice), 7 april 1987. Over verslavingsproblematiek in de inrichtingen van het gevangeniswezen, TK 1986-1987, 18 174, nr. 9.
** Brief van de staatssecretaris van Justitie (Letter of the State Secretary of Justice), 29 november 1983. Over verslavingspolitiek in de inrichtingen van het gevangeniswezen, TK 1983-1984, 18 174, nr. 1.

reorganization of the probation organizations in the Netherlands, it was decided that now 25% of the probation staff in the prisons had to be employed by the CADs.

The CAD organization has some characteristics which make it especially suitable for its role within prisons. Formally as well as professionally it combines the functions of a probation and a mental health organization. It is subsidized jointly by the Ministry of Health and by the Ministry of Justice. The "double" orientation of the CADs results, inevitably, in some tension but also has several distinct advantages. The organization is in a good position to mediate between the demands and needs of the criminal justice system and the mental health system. CAD workers are expected to provide new incentives to the further professionalization of drug care in prison.

The integration of the control and the care model was promoted by the 1987 introduction of two new mechanisms: the Drug-Free Unit (DFU), and urinalysis. Both measures were meant to support the goals of control and care in an integrated and mutually reinforcing way. The next sections will clarify this in some more detail.

8. Urine testing

A system of urine testing of incarcerated addicts was established in 1987 as part of the newly established Drug-Free Units (DFUs); participation in urinalysis within the DFU is contingent on a voluntary choice of the inmate to be detained in a DFU. One year later (in 1988), urine testing was introduced as a general investigative device for the presence of drugs anywhere in prison. One reason for the introduction of mandatory tests among the general prison population was simply to counteract the impression created by the designation of a DFU that drugs would be tolerated in other parts of prison. In addition, it was believed that levels of control inside and outside DFUs should not be too divergent, otherwise addicts would be less likely to opt for involvement in a DFU. Finally, it was feared that working conditions of prison personnel and probation workers might deteriorate in the absence of this form of control.

Mandatory urine tests outside the DFUs are not to be applied at random, but only in purposeful, functional and specified ways. As a general investigative device to detect drugs in prison, urinalysis may be imposed upon the inmate for several reasons. In the first place, urinalysis can be used as a method of gaining information on the prevalence of illegal drug use within prison. Secondly, urinalysis serves as an evaluation instrument for (violation of) furlough regulations. And, thirdly, these tests can produce the objective evidence in case somebody (for reasons of order and climate within the institution) is seriously suspected of drug use. In the first case, no disciplinary measures are attached to positive outcomes of urine tests; however, in the other two cases confirmation of drug use by urinalysis does call for sanctions.

No scientific evaluation of the effects of these mandatory urine tests has been done yet. Figures from the medical prison services in the first quarters of the years 1988 and 1989 indicate a sharp increase of urine testing, while the proportion of positive outcomes remains at a relatively low level. The data on urinalysis in Dutch jails and prisons are summarized in Table 2.

Table 2. Number of tests and percentage of positive outcomes of urinalyses for non-medical drug use in the first quarters of 1988 and 1989

Substance	1988		1989	
	N	%	N	%
Opiates	1812	2.1	2996	5.5
Amphetamines	341	0.0	947	0.3
Cocaine	1895	2.5	3574	3.3
Barbiturates	273	3.1	860	0.9
Tranquilizers	248	7.7	1230	3.7
Methadone	351	0.0	622	7.1
THC (cannabis)	626	11.6	1555	11.5

The table shows that marihuana/hashish (THC) is the most frequently detected substance, and tranquilizers (benzodiazepines) to a lesser degree. The data further suggest that the numbers of positive outcomes have increased in this period.

9. Drug-free units

In 1985 the policy report "Drug-Free Detention" was published (Drugvrije Detentie 1985). One of its main proposals was the creation of "Drug-Free Units" within the prison system; the implementation of this policy was initiated by the secretary of Justice, in a letter to parliament in 1987 (TK, 1986-1987, 18 174, nr. 9). These DFUs were intended to provide protection and care to imprisoned drug addicts. DFUs were to protect addicts against drug dealers, provide assistance to help addicts overcome withdrawal problems and help them start preparations for a drug-free life. Institutions with high proportions of addicts among their inmate population were asked to design proposals for DFUs. Extra staff and extra resources for conducting urine tests were made available. A procedure for urinalysis was developed by the Ministry of Justice. Addicted inmates who apply to be placed in the DFU are required to submit to urinalysis before being accepted. There are no set standards with regard to the frequency of these tests and the possible consequences of a positive urine test. Additional probation officers of the CADs have been made available to DFUs to provide professional advice and support. Prison administrators were asked to develop specific treatment regimes aimed at the goals of protection and care. A system of urine tests, in addition to the provision of aid, assistance, and education on a daily basis were considered necessary elements of these regimes.

The decentralized approach (*i.e.,* the request that prison administrators develop their own plans) proved to be rather successful. In a relatively short time the old "experiments" in the remand centers of Amsterdam and Rotterdam were reorganized and other DFUs were established. By the end of 1990 a total of thirteen DFUs were in operation: in jails (6), in half-open prisons (2), and in closed prisons (5). They offer a total of 333 places; their average capacity is about 25 places (minimum of 11, maximum of 40). Assuming that there are about 2,400 addicts in the penitentiary population, we may conclude that this amounts to one drug-free cell for every seven addicts. Up till now, there are no DFUs for female addicts. The average stay in a unit differs and depends on the length of the sentence. In jails and in half-open prisons the stay generally does not exceed six months. In prisons the average is between 6 and 12 months (Boekhoudt en Verhagen 1990).

One of the new DFUs, with a capacity of 30 places, is located in a half-open prison. It serves as a follow-up for addicted prisoners who come from other prisons, to serve the last half year of their term. This unit forms part of a so-called "drug-free detention route". Its program is strongly oriented toward the post-detention phase. To that end, contacts have been developed with outside residential and ambulatory drug programs. A week-end leave policy provides the opportunity not only to go home but also to stay, for example, in an outside clinic to get an idea about what it means to enter a therapeutic community.

After five years of experience with the DFUs, what conclusions regarding effectiveness and feasibility may be drawn? From a correctional point of view, the question is important whether these units contribute to a reduction of drug use and drug trafficking in prison. The short- and long-term effects of a stay in a DFU on the drug addiction career are also of utmost importance. Other questions relate to the characteristics of participating inmates, the effect on prison personnel, and so on.

Although there is no conclusive scientific evidence as of yet, anecdotal information and qualitative interpretations of experiences with the DFUs indicate that the new facilities do offer new opportunities for addicted inmates; furthermore, the DFUs do appear to decrease the pressure of drug problems on the prison system in general. In these drug-free settings, correctional personnel have been trained to work together with the drug care professionals of the CADs. Opportunities are being created for several kinds of counseling, and for initiating contact with external drug clinics. There is more and more emphasis on the importance of follow-up treatment within the prison system (the so-called "drug-free detention route" we referred to earlier).

10. Methadone treatment in prison

A number of general practitioners (GPs) working in Dutch prisons prescribe methadone to addicted prisoners. This generally concerns only reduction programs, in which prescription of methadone is reduced to zero in the course of a few weeks. There are virtually no methadone maintenance programs inside prisons. Prison physicians operate as independent experts within the prison; they have the authority to decide whether or not methadone is supplied. No methadone is provided to prisoners in DFUs. A small recent survey gives some data on the number and kind of methadone programs in jails. Of the 30 remand centers, 24 provided methadone and six did not. All of the programs were short-term reduction programs with a maximum dose range between 30 and 50 mg. Most of the remand centers (20) had a 1- to 4-day reduction program with a 5-mg reduction per day (Kools 1992).

Many addicts are clients of community-based methadone programs when they begin their incarceration. This explains the tendency of the Dutch prison system to use detoxification by means of methadone reduction, instead of a "cold turkey" approach. Dutch medical jurisprudence has established that prison doctors are obliged to verify a prisoner's claim that he or she has been a client of an outside methadone program. After confirmation of prior enrollment in a methadone maintenance program, it is then up to the prison physician to decide whether or not to prescribe methadone.

A 1986 conference for Dutch prison physicians on the topic of methadone suggested consensus on several points. A system of effective supervision and management is considered essential to prevent abuse (*i.e.,* to prevent the dealing of methadone in prison). Urine testing was proposed as an indispensable tool for monitoring illegal drug abuse. Conference participants unanimously rejected methadone maintenance for prisoners with sentences over six months. All agreed that no particular medical arguments (*i.e.* harmful detrimental effects of methadone) were available against overcoming physical dependence by means of a methadone reduction program; however, the attitudes on prescribing methadone varied markedly. Some prison doctors reasoned that the prescription of methadone is only necessary in some extreme cases to alleviate withdrawal symptoms. Others were convinced that it should be the addicts' own responsibility to take methadone or not. In this view, detoxification makes only sense if an addict is really motivated to become drug free. This implies that the addicts determine the moment they want to stop using methadone. However, all agreed that continuing illegal drug use would be sufficient reason to stop the prescription of methadone.

One leading Dutch (former) prison physician experimented with the "methadone on demand" approach. According to his experience, the large majority of addicted inmates stopped using methadone after approximately two months. This may be interpreted as positive support for the "own responsibility approach", at least within the coercive context of the prison. According to this prison physician (Roorda 1990a), two types of drug addicts tended to choose for methadone maintenance. One category may be described as the "extremely problematic" drug addicts, often characterized by co-morbid psychiatric disorders. The other category consists of young addicts who are still in their "honeymoon" phase. For the first category detoxification is (medically) not advisable. For the "honeymoon" type of addict a reduction program is seen as most appropriate. Both categories, however, only constitute a small segment of the detained addict population. The largest, most challenging group, according to Roorda (1990a), consists of addicts who, once in prison, are willing to detoxify but are afraid to make this decision because of anticipated withdrawal problems. They tend to prefer to start the detoxification process on a methadone maintenance basis. Roorda argues that it would be unwise to try to persuade these addicts to "go cold turkey", to move directly into abstinence. An "open" attitude of the prison doctor, which includes acceptance of the addict's possible relapse, is considered necessary for succeeding in the long run.

At this point, there exists no registration of the prescription of methadone in Dutch prisons and detention centers.

From the 1991 statistics provided by the chief medical officer of the correctional system it can be concluded that about one third (3,131) of the drug users entering the prison system (total in 1991: 10,745) get some form of methadone treatment (Jaarverslag 1992). Clearly, lower doses of methadone are prescribed to detained drug addicts as compared to non-detained drug addicts, averaging respectively 20.1 and 41.3 mg (GG & GD 1990).

Up to now there has been no thorough discussion about methadone as an instrument for prison health policy among professionals and administrators in the correctional field. For some subgroups of the prison population - *e.g.*, older addicts who have been using prescription methadone for a long time - methadone could be a viable option to keep them from "drug-seeking" behavior in prisons, to alleviate their symptoms, to stabilize their "pharmaceutical pattern" and thus to meet the objective of continuity of care. Obviously methadone could also prove to be an important health safeguard for IV users "at risk" of HIV infection because of their needle-sharing and/or risky sexual behavior.

11. Recent developments

Drug policy in Dutch prisons has gradually evolved towards an (attempted) balance between control and care measures. The gradual, incremental development of prison policy is, partly at least, a result of the decentralized nature of prison administration; prison staff has a fair amount of freedom to develop their own initiatives.

The care of addicts in prison (which expressly deliberately stops short of treatment to abstinence) is of limited use, however, when adequate connection with drug treatment outside prison is lacking; there must be some continuity between the prison experience and the outside world. One of the options to improve the connection between the prison and the community-based drug assistance system is the "article 47" clause; this provision allows addicted prisoners to be diverted to a treatment clinic outside prison after half of the sentence has been served. They can opt for completing the other half in a residential setting with an upper limit of half a year. If, after admission to the treatment center, they fail to comply with the conditions, they will have to return to prison. In 1989, 116 applications to "article 47" were made; 95 were granted. At present, this arrangement is considered the main tool for implementing the (third) goal of Dutch prison policy: providing real therapy for motivated addicts outside the prison system.

Analysis of article 47 transfers (Roorda 1990b) during the period 1982-1989 has shown that both the applications and the actual number enrolled in treatment have increased: in 1982, there were 38 transfers to outside treatment agencies, in 1989, there were 95 transfers. The mean number of days in treatment has remained fairly constant over the years, between 70 and 80 days. However, the percentage that drops out of treatment within two days after enrollment has gradually declined from 24% in 1982 to 16% in 1989.

Another method to enhance the continuity between the prison and drug-related community services is the further implementation of "drug-free detention routes". The communication and relationships between the different DFUs have to be improved. For example, in the selection process where detainees from remand centers are sent to closed prisons and – if possible – from a closed prison to a half-open or open prison, an important (early) criterion is the addict's motivation to "kick the habit". It makes sense that the initial steps made in a DFU in the first phase of detention (*i.e.*, in the remand center) should be followed by other ones, building on earlier decisions and experiences. In the final phase of the period of incarceration, prison programs must be available which offer opportunities for the social re-integration of the (former) addict. (In this context, we want to mention again the special half-open prison for drug addicts.)

In a recent government document, some guidelines for DFUs were proposed (Contourennota 1990). The following conclusions reflect the state-of-the-art philosophy of Dutch prison policy with regard to drug addicts:

1. DFUs in jails and half-open prisons serve a different function than DFUs in prisons. DFUs in prisons function as follow-up facilities for offenders transferred from jails. DFUs in jails are more general because of the heterogeneity of the population and the broad spectrum of (often acute) mental health problems.
2. The objectives of DFUs must be more clearly stated; the units should be open only for addicts who actively choose for participation in the program. This requires clear and unambiguous criteria for the required motivation.
3. Urine testing should remain as a protective tool, both for the addicts and the staff. However, the frequency of the urine tests should increase.
4. An additional forensic addiction clinic may be needed to complement the range of other available addiction treatment facilities.

These conclusions are still open to debate; however, the main message is clear. The Dutch want to give DFUs a fixed place within their prison system, define a clear target group, and place these DFUs in a broader spectrum of treatment alternatives both within and outside the prison system. Meanwhile, the focus on drug addiction problems within the prison population should not blind us to the fact that these problems are often part of a complex syndrome of socio-psychiatric disorders. A survey in one specific facility for juvenile offenders showed that about 80% of the inmates could be qualified as addicted to substances, while about 50% of those addicted to drugs had recent psychiatric problems (Bulten *et al.* 1992) This means that DFUs should not only be linked to the drug care and treatment systems, but also to general mental health institutions in the outside society. Up till now there is no such linkage.

12. Back-door and front-door options

In this chapter, we focus on the treatment of drug-addicted detainees and the measures directed at preparing them for the post-detention period. This policy is referred to as the "back-door option" for criminal drug addicts. By implication there must also be a "front-door option" offering an alternative way out of drug addiction. This alternative can be realized in the framework of community-based sanctions.

Within the Dutch criminal justice system, custodial sentences are officially considered as sanctions of last resort. If the social order has been severely disturbed or if victims of a crime need to be protected, incarceration is often viewed as unavoidable. Nevertheless, the harmful side effects of imprisonment, such as loss of occupation or the deterioration of social relationships – placing marginal people in even worse circumstances – should be minimized. The judge and the public prosecutor have different legal instruments at their disposal to apply sanctions other than imprisonment. In the pre-trial phase the public prosecutor may waive prosecution or put an end to remanded custody under certain specific conditions, depending on personal characteristics of the suspect. The prosecutor, for example, may require an offender who is a drug addict to have himself committed to a drug assistance or treatment program, either inpatient or outpatient.

Especially for juvenile delinquents there are various community-based sanctions available, but community service orders (CSOs) for adult offenders are also frequently applied. For example, in 1990 about 7,000 CSOs were issued against adults. Furthermore, for short custodial sentences, there is the option of so-called weekend enforcement. It should be emphasized that in the Netherlands community service orders are applied only as an alternative to imprisonment, that is, only when otherwise unconditional prison sentences (max. 6 months) would have been imposed. They constitute no sanctioning alternative in their own right.

Therefore, a failure to comply with the terms of a CSO will almost inevitably result in the enforcement of the prison sentence the order was meant to replace.

Experience has shown that without special support drug addicts almost invariably fail to comply with the conditions of a CSO For that reason some special projects have been implemented to make diversion to treatment and assistance programs a more viable option for criminal drug addicts. Examples of such projects are the Drug-Related Crime Project in Rotterdam (see Chapter 10 in this book) and the Street Junk Project in Amsterdam. Both are fairly small projects, using a mix of work, training, and medical assistance, and they are developed in close cooperation between probation agencies and the office of the public prosecutor.

Front-door options certainly have distinct advantages, compared to back-door options; however, front-door options for criminal drug addicts in the Netherlands are only just beginning to develop.

13. Conclusion

The drug problem has had a pervasive influence on the Dutch correctional system in a quantitative as well as qualitative sense. There has been a tremendous increase in the available prison capacity the last ten years, mainly because of the increase in the average sentence length. The qualitative changes relate to the change in the composition of the incarcerated population and the increase of drug-related problems, such as smuggling, dealing, drug use and (mental) health problems. Especially because of these qualitative changes it has taken considerable time to find a right mix between drug treatment and assistance and custodially oriented measures.

It is only recently that a more balanced penal drug policy has been developed. This policy tries to merge care and control goals. It aims at creating a detention climate which makes it easier for the addict to get help; the policy intends to create a linkage with civil treatment and assistance modalities. At the same time a number of control measures have been implemented to ensure a safe execution of the sentence. One of the most important remaining tasks is to improve the organizational framework for special drug-free facilities. Importantly, the different DFUs in different penal institutions need to be transformed into a better integrated (sub-)system.

Current prison drug policy is consistent with the pragmatism typical for Dutch drug policy in general: one learns by doing, from experience, fully aware of the fact that striving for a drug-free environment at all costs is an unrealistic goal. An additional reflection of the pragmatic attitude is that DFUs are viewed as having an educational and motivating function, rather than a treatment function. A main concern remains the question if prisons are suitable places for treating drug-addicted offenders in the first place. That is why many strongly believe that the search for other, less restricting sentencing options and non-institutional options (*e.g.*, CSOs) has to continue.

Prison drug policy is faced with a number of constraints. First, it develops as a by-product of drug policy in general. This implies that prison drug policy can never develop as an independent entity, detached from drug (treatment) policy in general. That is why so much emphasis is given to the development of the linkage function of prison drug care, both with community drug treatment and with community mental health treatment programs. Secondly, the goal of the orderly and safe execution of the sentence puts serious boundaries and restrictions on the treatment and care objective. Thirdly, the need for treatment is not limited only to drug addicted offenders; many other offenders have (mental) health or social problems in need of assistance.

Although important initiatives have been taken, Dutch prison drug policy is maturing only slowly. In a general sense, the drugs problem has forced the correctional system to re-think and to re-operationalize the ambiguously defined goals of incapacitation and rehabilitation. It is evident that penitentiary drug policy can only develop in a desirable and fruitful direction if penitentiary drug problems are seen as part of the total drug problem of society, not as a separate entity.

References

Boekhoudt, A. and Verhagen, J.J.L.M.: *Drugsvrije afdelingen in penitentiaire inrichtingen.* The Hague: Ministerie van Justitie, 1990

Buikhuisen, W.: Imprisonment in Holland: Some comments. *International Journal of Offender Therapy and Comparative Criminology* 33:154-158, 1989

Bulten, E., Van Limbeek, J., Wouters, L., Geerlings, P. and Van Tilburg, W.: *Psychische Stoornissen in Detentie; een Onderzoek naar de Prevalentie van Psychische Stoornissen bij Gedetineerden van de Jeugdgevangenis Nieuw Vosseveld.* The Hague: Ministerie van Justitie, 1992

Brand-Koolen, M.J.M.: The Dutch Penal System and its prisons: an introductory note. In: Brand-Koolen, M.J.M. (Ed.), *Studies on the Dutch Prison System.* Amsterdam: Kugler Publ, 1987

Contourennota: *Drugsvrije Afdelingen in Penitentiaire Inrichtingen.* Coördinatiegroep Drugsbeleid; Directie Delinquentenzorg en Jeugdinrichtingen. The Hague: Ministerie van Justitie, 1990

Downes, D.: *Contrasts in Tolerance; Post-War Penal Policy in The Netherlands and England and Wales.* Oxford: Oxford University Press, 1988

Drugvrije Detentie. Rapport van de werkgroep Drugvrije Afdelingen. The Hague: Ministerie van Justitie, november 1985

Dwang en drang in de hulpverlening aan verslaafden. Tweede Kamer, 1987-1988, 20 415, nrs. 1-2, 1988

GG & GD: *Methadonverstrekking in Amsterdam in 1989*. Jaaroverzicht van de Centrale Methadon Registratie. Amsterdam: Gemeentelijke Geneeskundige en Gezondheidsdienst Amsterdam, Stafbureau Epidemiologie en Documentatie, 1990

Jaarverslag 1991 van de Geneeskundig Inspecteur bij het Ministerie van Justitie. The Hague, 1992

Kools, J.P.: Methadonbeleid HvB's in schema ("Cold turkey in de bajes"). *Mainline* 2(4):14-17, 1992

LADIS (Landelijk Alcohol Drugs Informatie Systeem). Jaarverslag (1986). Utrecht: Nederlandse Vereniging voor CADs (NVC), 1987

Lipton, D., Martinson, R., Wilks J.: *The effectiveness of correctional treatment, a survey of treatment evaluation studies*. New York: Prager Publ, 1975

Ministerie van Justitie: *Rapport Voorzieningenbeleid 1990-1994. Delinquentenzorg en Jeugdinrichtingen*. The Hague, 1989

Rook, A.: *Probleemgroepen in Inrichtingen voor Langgestraften; een Inventarisatie*. The Hague: Ministerie van Justitie, Wetenschappelijk Onderzoeks- en Documentatie Centrum, 1982

Roorda, P.: Methadon in penitentiaire inrichtingen. In: Van de Wijngaart, G., Verbraeck, H. (Eds.), *Methadon in de Jaren Negentig (WGU-cahier 12)*. Utrecht: Rijksuniversiteit Utrecht, 1990a

Roorda, P.: *Artikel 47 van de Gevangenismaatregel bij de Behandeling van Verslaafden; Verslag over 1988-1989*. The Hague: Ministerie van Justitie, Directoraat Generaal Jeugdbescherming en Delinquentenzorg, 1990b

Rüter, F.: Drugs and the Criminal Law in the Netherlands. In: Van Dijk, J., Haffmans, C., Rüter, F., Schutte, J., Stolwijk, S. (Eds.), *Criminal Law in Action; An Overview of Current Issues in Western Societies*, pp 147-166. Arnhem: Gouda Quint, 1986

Van Alem, V.C.M., Erkelens, L.H., Schippers, G.M., Breteler, M.H.M. and Becking, J.M.: Verslavingsproblematiek in penitentiaire inrichtingen. *Justitiële Verkenningen* 15(2):39-61, 1989

Van Dijk, J.M.M.: Beleidsimplicaties van criminologische theorieën en implicaties van het beleid voor de theoretische criminologie. *Tijdschrift voor Criminologie* 27:320-345, 1985

Van der Goorbergh, J.: Persconferentie opening Huis van Bewaring Sittard, 16-02-1990, 1990

Van der Linden, B.: *Regiem en Recidive*. The Hague: Wetenschappelijk Onderzoeks- en Documentatie Centrum, Ministerie van Justitie, 1978

Vegter, P.C.: De toename van lange gevangenisstraffen: malaise voor het gevangeniswezen. *Nederlands Juristen Blad* 29 (26 augustus) 1993

Verhagen, J.J.L.M.: Veranderingen in de gedetineerdenpopulatie in de afgelopen tien jaar. *Justitiële Verkenningen* 15:7-16, 1989

PART II

LIMITED PROBLEMS AND
MODERATE MEASURES

VI. THE DEVELOPMENT OF CONTEMPORARY DRUG PROBLEMS

Koert Swierstra

1. Dutch drug problems 1970-1990

1.1 Introduction

Prior to the 1960s, drug use in Holland was limited to opium smoking by the Chinese community - a habit well known from the former Dutch colonial age in Indonesia and tolerated by the authorities provided the practice remained confined to the Chinese community - and the smoking of marihuana and hash within small subcultural circles in Amsterdam. During the 1960s, however, things were to change. First, the use of marihuana and hash became more common among young people in the whole country. And second, around 1965, the first young Dutch opium users presented themselves in the cities of Amsterdam and Rotterdam. In addition, Dutch youth discovered that amphetamines could be used for other than strictly medical applications. Although LSD played a modest part as well, the prelude of hard drug problems in the Netherlands was characterized by opium and amphetamines.

These early developments notwithstanding, it is fair to say that until the end of the 1960s, there were no genuine drug epidemics in Holland. This is reflected in the fact that the Dutch professional literature of that time only mentioned heroin as simply an opium derivate (methadone was still unknown at that time); American writings, on the other hand, already discussed these substances.

The use of hard drugs in Holland as a fairly significant social problem dates back to the beginning of the 1970s. It was the introduction of heroin in 1971/1972 which produced an explosive growth in the use of hard drugs in Holland. The Dutch development paralleled earlier experiences in the United States and later Britain, and occurred simultaneously with the introduction of heroin in (former) Western Germany. There is no question that the contemporary hard drug problems must be traced back to the introduction of heroin in Holland. During the 1970s, then, hard drug use spread fast, making it a structural social problem. The 1980s, however, were characterized by new trends and developments in the patterns and extent of drug use in Holland. Can we speak of specific Dutch drug use careers? Is there a uniquely Dutch history of drug problems? What is the role, if any, of drug policy in this? Is it possible to identify uniquely Dutch factors involved in recent developments? This Chapter attempts to address these questions by tracing the history of hard drug use and problems in the Netherlands over the last two decades.

1.2 Epidemiology

According to our best estimate, the number of opiate addicts in Holland had grown to approximately 25,000 by 1980. Between 8,000 and 10,000 of these addicts were thought to live in Amsterdam, the capital of the Netherlands. (These figures are accepted by most drug researchers and policy makers as correct, although some have arrived at higher estimates.) However, estimates of developments during the last decade have systematically been lowered. Current national estimates range between a minimum of 15,000 and a maximum of 20,000 opiate addicts. Moreover, several sources indicate that the mean age of addicts – another measure of the seriousness of drug use – has been consistently rising. Recent studies in Amsterdam and Rotterdam arrived at an average age of 30 years. (This finding is consistent with observations in the much smaller city of Heerlen.) Amsterdam Municipal Health authorities reported that the mean age of their drug clients increased from 27 to 30, between 1981 and 1987. In the same period, the proportion of addicted clients under the age of 22 decreased from 14% to less than 5%.

These figures strongly and consistently suggest that the number of opiate addicts in Holland indeed is declining. Although drug use in general appears to be decreasing, it is likely that drug use figures for specific (ethnic) subgroups such as Moroccan youth from North Africa will continue to rise. It is also important to realize that lower estimates of drug addiction have to be handled with caution. For instance, in the United States, lower estimates of opiate users (Des Jarlais and Uppal 1980:336; Inciardi 1986:71) fail to reflect a real diminishing of hard drug addiction in general. Among other things, the picture may be distorted by a temporary shift to other hard drugs.

1.3 Drug use patterns: from heroin to methadone, pills, cocaine

Opiate addiction (including prescription methadone) has formed the core of drug problems in the Netherlands since the introduction of heroin in the early 1970s. Currently, however, the dominant pattern for the opiate addict is to use various drugs, alcohol, and/or prescription drugs in addition to heroin and methadone. Similar to the situation in other countries, this poly-drug use is occasionally supplemented with new trendy substances such as XTC. Interestingly, popular American drugs such as crack and PCP have not taken firm root in the Netherlands.

Two important aspects of the current multiple drug use pattern are: the decreased significance of heroin and the increased significance of co-caine. The first development has already been illustrated for the situation in New York in the 1970s by Preble and Miller (1977). They showed how the predominant use of heroin was replaced by a pattern of multiple drug use of methadone, cheap wine, and pills. These substances are not only cheaper, but also easier to get; for the addict it takes less (income-gener-ating) crime. This consumptive pattern better matches the way of life of the older addict, who gets more or less burnt out after years of a rough drug life. It is reasonable to argue that this is especially important for the Dutch situation, with its aging addict population. Indeed, studies among hard drug users over the last years consistently find multiple drug use the predominant pattern. Drug addicts now use less heroin and more pills and alcohol; for approximately two out of three, prescription metha-done is the primary opiate drug. Heroin, the good old original, may be used more during the one weekend in the month when social security payments are paid.

The second process complements the first: cocaine has replaced heroin, at least to a certain degree. The popularity and myths of cocaine are well known, not the least in the United States. Cocaine makes you bigger, more self-assured, it keeps you sharp and part of the world; heroin, on the other hand, makes you lethargic and spaced-out. With coke, one can achieve, be a winner in social competition. As cultural symbols, the myths of opiates belonged to the 1970s, those of cocaine to the 1980s. Today, if drug addicts have enough money, they use both sub-stances together; if they lack the money, they prefer cocaine. Recent stu-dies conducted in Rotterdam and Amsterdam mention cocaine use in nine out of every ten opiate addicts. Moreover, preference for cocaine is typi-cal for recent hard drug incidence patterns (Intraval 1989:98; Korf 1987:71). Research among Rotterdam addicts indicates that most of the relative novices (who had used hard drugs for no more than two years), started with cocaine before getting involved with heroin use. Several stu-dies suggest that drug addicts who use a lot of cocaine are more crimi-nally active than addicts who use a lot of heroin. With the exception of Cohen (1989), the question of cocaine use outside the deviant world of multiple drug addicts has not been studied in the Netherlands. (A few studies are currently in progress.)

Before evaluating the developments of Dutch drug problems over the last 20 years, we will take a brief detour to look into the social make-up of the phenomenon of hard drug use.

1.4 Hard drug careers: addicts and the drug world

It is only normal that most (if not all) people occasionally seek distraction or pleasure in order to escape the daily routine, to solve conflicting demands, or whatever. For adults with close bonds to society, the institutional order and dominant culture provide various non-deviant ways of doing this: for example, through alcohol, use of medicine, gambling, and so on. For young people, on the other hand, who typically have fewer social bonds and less vested interests than their adult counterparts, it is more likely that their options will become deviant. Their environment often responds to this youthful deviance, thereby further reducing their options. One way of coping with the resulting problems is to get involved with drug-using peer groups. Hard drug use reinforces deviance.

In addition to a negative social response from the environment, the phenomenon of hard drug use is shaped by the criminal economy of the drug world, the relationship with deviant behavior among youth, and the addictive qualities of the substances. Habitual use of hard drugs is related to a specific way of life, a way of life which may become even more addictive than simple drug use. The notion of a social "addiction" to the drug way of life was introduced a long time ago by a number of American authors in the field. The tradition goes back at least to Becker (1963:53) and includes among others Lindesmith (1968:49), and Preble and Casey (1969:21). A related notion is the concept of the deviant career. This concept includes a socialization process into the drug world, different phases of drug use, a series of institutionalized contacts with mainstream society (e.g., police, courts, drug treatment and care programs), and an eventual termination of the career because of burn-out. For drug addicts with a long history of addiction, the police record begins to take on the same social function as a curriculum vitae in conventional society: as some type of calling card (Abrams 1982:296). (See also Waldorf 1973; Maddux and Desmond 1981; Biernacki 1986.)

The commitment to the drug way of life should be viewed in relationship to the degree of integration in conventional society. The addict to illegal drugs lives in both worlds, taking reference points from both the deviant world of drugs and regular society. The stronger the bonds to conventional society, the greater the sociological distance towards an integrated position within the drug world. And, as we will see later, the balance between the two worlds is not the same in the different stages of the drug career.

2. Incidence in the 1970s

2.1 The impact of subcultural backgrounds

The first large-scale generation of heroin addicts in the Netherlands was described, among others, by Janssen and Swierstra (1982). We analyzed how some specific youth subcultures contributed to the spread of heroin use in Holland, and how individual careers progressed from the subcultural phase of initiation into hard drug use into a fully fledged junkie way of life. In this respect, a new opportunity structure of heroin addiction took the place of the former deviant youth subcultures from the 1960s and 1970s. In retrospect, these youth subcultures may be seen as a pre-eminent expression of that particular period of time. Like anywhere else in the Western world, young people became economically more independent, resulting in greater freedom from the dominant culture. Different modalities of youth subcultures emerged, but it was specifically some of these which were to encourage, among other things, hard drug use. These subcultures functioned as necessary conditions for the beginner to progress toward a hard drug career.

2.1.1 Autochthonous white youth

We distinguished three distinct types of addicts among the white male Dutch drug users: the cultural rebels, the weekend adventurers, and the social marginals (Janssen and Swierstra 1982).

The cultural rebels, probably because of their middle class background and some education, were subculturally orientated toward self-development and individualism. Like the old hippies, they emphasized subjectivism and a spiritual escape from the status quo. For them the drug lifestyle was a full-time job. After years of addiction, experimental rule-breaking turned into criminal behavior.

The second category, the weekend adventurers, came from the working class with its material limitations and with a culture of the desirability of a respectable workers' life. For these people, regular work and family represented the core values. This particular subculture embraced values like masculinity, solidarity among men, vandalism for kicks, and the use of alcohol and amphetamines. Deviance, for them, was a form of social escape. Their addict life was dominated by feelings of ambivalence. While living a heavy and criminal junkie life, they retained parents, a stable job, and the clean society as their positive frame of reference.

The social marginals were characterized by a structurally marginal background (*i.e.*, parents with little education, often unemployed), often dating back generations. For them, their primary contacts with conventional society were with police and the courts, rather than with the institutions of education and the labor market. From an early age, these were street-wise youngsters, involved with non-drug-related criminality. Subcultural values of "old hands in the business" of criminality were accompanied by a sharply demarcated us/them perspective toward conventional society. As an addict, one was fully integrated into the hard drug subculture, culturally as well as economically.

The white Dutch females in our study came into contact with hard drugs through the predominantly masculine subcultures. We distinguished two types: the home-leavers and the social marginals. First, the home-leavers had either a middle class or working class background, with traditional gender expectations. Within their female role, social independence through formal education and/or a job would be only temporary; getting married and raising children was their long-term conventional option. Getting involved with "alternative" boyfriends was a way of escaping from these narrow role expectations. Paradoxically, it turned out that there was not much room for independent female behavior for them as addicts in the masculine drug world. One could survive as an addict through relationships with dealers and competent junkies, or through prostitution; often that meant being dependent on the male friend's position in the drug world.

The social background of the female social marginals was comparable to that of their male counterparts, but their position was inferior. They were supposed to stay at home, and their parents were not interested in motivating them to do well at school or to get a decent job. A street-life among peers provided more esteem and a chance to act independently. Contacts with members of so-called ethnic minorities marked their deviance. The street-wise subculture entailed delinquent or semi-illegal skills such as prostitution. As addicts, their position in the drug world remained marginal. Conventional society existed mainly through social control institutions.

2.1.2 Black and brown youth

Surinam is a former Dutch colony in South America. During the years preceding its independence in 1975, many young Surinamese people in their teenage years came to Holland. As in many other Western countries, problems resulting from their immigration primarily consisted of inadequate socio-economic opportunities (education, work), and the weakening or even disappearance of the extended family and related forms of informal social control. Instead, the street-corner culture of Surinam revived as a deviant phenomenon in the streets of the big cities of Holland. The street-corner culture offered them protection against their alienated existence as an immigrant. In addition to this cultural function, the subculture also offered economic opportunities such as drug-dealing, mostly at street level. This development was facilitated by the fact that in the 1970s the Dutch retail market for heroin was still expanding. Consequently, the tradition of "hustling", known from Surinam, was continued.

Surinamese drug careers can be differentiated into three groups; the hangers-on, the quarter-ounce dealers, and the home returners (Janssen and Swierstra 1982).

The hangers-on already belonged to the lower socio-economic class in Surinam. Their education and labor skills were very low, and after arrival in Holland, marginalization set in quickly. Hustling and smoking and dealing marihuana were regular activities. Hard drugs were viewed as an – albeit strong – kind of marihuana. Throughout years of heroin addiction, the original street-corner subculture remained the only social system in which they actively participated. For this group, conventional society remained at a great distance.

Among the quarter-ounce dealers the socio-economic position of the family and the level of their formal qualifications were somewhat higher. They were partly successful immigrants, and they saw opportunities to further improve their material wealth through illegal activities. Regular work was supplemented by joining their "own culture", the Surinamese street-corner subculture. These people were well suited to being middlemen in drug dealing: they had some knowledge of Dutch society; they had a place of their own, or at least were free of too much parental control; and they had earned enough capital to start a business. As addicts, they were also rather successful immigrants.

The home returners became well integrated into Dutch society, both economically and culturally – until the street-corner culture emerged. Because of their education and/or employment, this group lived within the mainstream Dutch society for years. However, the development of new problems in life, such as the pressures of living up to the image of being a successful immigrant, led to a turn to the Surinamese street subculture. For this group, cultural identity became a major preoccupation. After years of addiction, the position of these people was still marked by ambiguity. Although they had reclaimed their Surinamese roots, the conventional ties to institutional Western society had not been totally severed.

Research has also been done on drug use among another ethnic minority group in the Netherlands: people from the South Moluccas, an Indonesian island (Blom and Janssen 1987). Indonesia was a Dutch colony until the end of the Second World War; the Moluccans represent a special case for historical reasons. Many Moluccans served as soldiers in the Dutch colonial army, fighting against the Indonesians. After Indonesia became an independent nation, many South Moluccans were more or less exiled to Holland. Starting around 1950, the notion of establishing their own state, independent from Indonesia, became their focal concern. Over a period of time, however, political reality changed. The children of these Moluccans, born in Holland in the 1950s, encountered problems typical to second-generation immigrants. Frustrated in their original national aspirations, some of them turned to radical political action during the 1970s. The Dutch authorities responded rather severely to their political terrorism; and the original ideal lost much of its exciting appeal for new recruits into the political movement. Consequently, the political involvement of the South Moluccans diminished rapidly; one of the expressions of an "inner emigration" has been hard drug use.

This research on drug use among South Moluccans reveals certain similarities with the Surinamese hard drug addicts as discussed earlier. Here again, economic marginality and cultural problems were at the core of the addiction process. A significant difference between the two groups is, however, that the South Moluccans represented a historical specific generation of youth; a generation torn between Moluccan culture and Dutch culture. It is possible to distinguish two types of Moluccan drug addicts in the drug world of the 1970s: the Moluccan-oriented and the Dutch-oriented. For the Moluccan-oriented youth, deviance in relation to their parents still implied a social-cultural affiliation with Mollucan peers. Pre-drug delinquency was common. Typically, females came in contact with drug use through a Moluccan boyfriend. This group lived in ethnic Moluccan neighborhoods. To a certain degree, their involvement in drugs did cause a split, but even after years of addiction, they stuck to Moluccan relatives and culture as much as possible. Dutch dominant culture and conventional society were the real "them".

The Dutch-oriented youth rejected Moluccan culture. This group tended to have a somewhat more formal schooling than the Moluccan-oriented addicts; their primary affiliation was with white subcultures where they encountered hard drugs. The females were involved with white boyfriends - in clear conflict with the expectations of the Mollucan extended family. As addicts, the men functioned side by side with both white and Surinamese addicts, often dealing in drugs for the closed Mollucan circles. Importantly, these addicts did not live in Moluccan neighborhoods; rather, they lived among autochthonous (white) Dutch people.

2.1.3 Subcultural deviance of the 1970s and drug careers

We have shown how specific youth cultures in the 1970s encouraged the development of hard drug careers. In all cases, some form of deviance was already present prior to initiation into hard drug use. Initial hard drug use was consistent with an already established lifestyle of rules developed to respond to the problems of fighting an uphill battle with conventional society. Deviant drug careers were the result of this process. How the phenomenon of drug addiction developed after these first ten years is discussed in the next section.

3. Incidence in the 1980s: Diffusion of social settings

In a study of a more recent generation of youth who began to use heroin around 1980 (Swierstra *et al.* 1986), some interesting differences with earlier patterns were found. Generally, we observed a diffusion of the hard drug opportunity structure. It was no longer necessary to participate in any subcultural setting in order to become familiar with hard drugs. Of special importance was an increase in recreational hard drug use among various groups of youth. This trend was separate from the noted hardening of the marginal and criminal drug world.

The diffusion of the opportunity structure of hard drugs meant that the deviant career preceding the initiation into heroin use was generally shortened; young people arrived at hard drug use more quickly than before. Furthermore, the rationale for a life on hard drugs had become blurred and had lost its ideological focus. During the 1980s, a life on drugs became more of simply one of those lifestyles - one of several possible alternatives to choose from: heroin, why not (for a while)? In addition, this diffusion also manifested itself in a wider range of ages among users just starting; initiation into hard drugs occurred both at a younger and at an older age than previously.

Paralleling these developments on the consumer side, the supply structure also grew significantly. For instance, hard drugs began to appear in social clubs, community centers and discotheques catering to mainstream youth. This resulted in a diversification of patterns of drug use. In addition to the stereotypical social outcasts with a completely deviant pattern of behavior, socially respectable youth experimenting with illegal substances appeared on the scene. For them, initial drug use had nothing to do with choosing any particular lifestyle. In this respect, the subcultural phase of the social history of the phenomenon of drug use has apparently become a relic of the past.

It is interesting to note that the process of de-ideologicalization of hard drugs resembles what happened to soft drugs some fifteen years earlier. For students and teenagers in the first half of the 1960s, hash and marihuana were a symbol of cultural rebellion within an esoteric subculture; in the 1970s, an expansion of the soft drug use took place among lower-class youth, marginal youth, and ethnic minorities. At the same time, people in their 30s and 40s, economically and socially integrated, continued their use outside any specific social-cultural users' setting. They smoked at home, after work, and with their neighbors when having a drink. It should be noted that this process of normalization or de-symbolization of soft drug use was one of the intended effects of the Dutch Opium Act of 1976.

The diffusion of hard drug use in the 1980s was characterized by the following: (1) reproduction of subcultures; (2) diversification of deviance; and, (3) individualization of drug use.

3.1 Reproduction of subcultures

The first trend was a replica of the subcultures of the 1970s among a new generation of 1980s youth. For instance, our study again identified the category of "weekend adventurer" for a number of male drug users, and that of the "home-leaver" for a number of the females. There was one exception to this trend, however: the hippie subculture was gone. We found no instances where the cultural rebel has become involved in hard drug addiction.

3.2 Diversification of deviance

In the 1980s, a new category of marginal youth emerged. They came from a great diversity of socio-economic and cultural backgrounds; before their initiation into drug use, they were already regularly involved in delinquency. They were marginal with regard to the family, educational system, labor market, and institutionalized forms of leisure activities. Their deviance was not directed against any specific sector of society (*e.g.,* education or work), but rather evolved into a form of existence in its own right. Subcultures lost their power to recruit: a subcultural ideology was superfluous. For this category of youth, a life on hard drugs could fulfill several basic functions. First, it allowed them to acquire a social identity – something they lacked because of their marginal position in society. Second, hard drugs opened opportunities for an alternative, mostly criminal, career. And third, a life on drugs provided a rationalization for an already deviant lifestyle.

Our study showed a shift in pattern of use for the Surinamese young people between the 1970s and the 1980s. Most of the newly initiated Surinamese hard drug users had come to Holland at an earlier age than their predecessors in the 1970s, often within a few years after birth. Consequently, these second-generation immigrants had become so westernized that they shared the same social settings as many of their white contemporaries. Their doorway to hard drug careers was through predominantly white youth settings, and followed the same path as the marginal white Dutch youth. Marginalization preceded first drug use. These young Surinamese people were found, together with their white peers, in diverse social groups with a deviant lifestyle.

Another ethnic minority appeared in the drug world of the 1980s: young people from Morocco. They came from North Africa mostly to join their fathers who had been working in Holland for several years; some of them came on their own, to find a materially better existence, or for reasons of more personal freedom. The social situation of the Moroccan youth closely resembled the Surinamese youth situation from a decade before: most of them came to Holland during their teenage years; they were in a marginal position because of their inferior educational and employment opportunities; their families had lost most of their integrity and control functions. The resulting vacuum was often filled by a street subculture characterized by "hustling" activities such as small-scale drug dealing, other forms of delinquency, and hard drug use. A life on drugs provided an alternative "career", preferred over an alienated existence in Western society. Family reunions in the Western country caused additional problems, especially between son and father; some youth left home at an early age. Studies in the cities of Amsterdam (Van Gelder and Sijtsma 1988), Rotterdam (Intraval 1989) and Utrecht (Kaufman and Verbraeck 1986) showed that a strikingly large number of young Moroccans were living a more or less nomadic urban life, forming relatively tight-knit groups sticking together, quickly integrating newcomers.

3.3 Individualization of drug use

The other new variant of drug use was based on the role that the use of various drugs had taken in the recreational activities of otherwise "respectable" youth. In the 1980s, heroin had became part of the social setting of young people who had strong ties with conventional society. These young people had not developed a deviant way of life prior to their involvement in drug use. Their deviance was pretty much limited to the use of drugs, and was combined with family obligations, school and/or work. Their social background was mostly middle-class. There was no social-cultural involvement in the deviant drug world; they tried to abstain, as long as possible, from criminal income-generating activities. After years of addiction, the critical moment occurred when they had to make a decision in that regard; hard drugs now began to threaten their normality. For this group, addiction problems represented an isolated phenomenon within their predominantly conventional lifestyle (Swierstra et al. 1986).

We were not able to document this process of individualization of drug use in the life histories of the Surinamese youth. Indeed, for the Surinamese young people, problems of acculturation and cultural identity continued to play an important role in their life histories. Drug use still functioned to represent symbolically their deviance within conventional Western society.

Our observations regarding the white Dutch "respectable" user raise serious questions. For instance, was (is) this "socially respectable" category of hard drug users only a temporary phenomenon? Was the emergence of this type of hard drug user the result of Dutch drug policy (see below, paragraph 6). Or did this diffusion simply reflect the growing to maturity of the hard drug problem in Holland? The following takes a closer look at these (and other) questions.

4. Deviant drug careers and conventional social bonds

It is only to be expected that studies of the drug world will find drug addicts who have a deviant lifestyle, no matter what method of data collection is used. It is the addicts with a deviant lifestyle, after all, who are most easily identified. This was again the case in the recent study of Rotterdam (see Chapter 10). This study focused on persons who had been using opiates for less than two years at the time of the interview. Strikingly, these addicts either came from Moroccan backgrounds, or they went through a decidedly marginal, delinquent experience prior to their hard drug career. Delinquency was already a fixed pattern prior to their initiation into hard drug use. Of the 90 opiate addicts in this study, only eight (9%) could be classified as non-criminal users: addicts who were not involved in crime at any time prior or during their hard drug career. For this small group, conventional bonds with society remained mostly intact. However, consistent with other studies, it was found that addicts with criminal involvement had not completely severed conventional ties with society either.

For addicts with relatively strong bonds with conventional society, the social distance toward a full-blown junkie life is greater than for those who do not (any longer) have these bonds. Addicts with ties to conventional society apply a double standard with respect to their way of life: the standards of both mainstream society and the drug world. In a sense, they lead a double life. They find justifications for their addictive behavior; for example, they view drug addiction as an illness, or as an unfortunate consequence of a wrong choice which blocks the way back to "normal" society. On the other hand, those who do not have strong bonds with conventional society have a much less ambiguous attitude toward being addicted.

Examination of the already discussed addict types in the 1970s and 1980s shows that commitment to conventional society may be weak or absent for several different reasons – with different implications for drug careers. It is possible to identify groups whose bonds with regular society are strong enough to keep them from persevering with a very long-lasting deviant drug career. Examples from the 1970s are: the "weekend adventurers" among the white Dutch males, the "home-leavers" among the white Dutch females, and the "home returners" among the Surinamese men (see above, paragraph 2). Youngsters involved in predominantly recreational hard drug use in the 1980s form an additional category whose ties to conventional society remain fairly strong. However, we have also identified categories without such bonds with conventional society, where seriously deviant drug careers are a more plausible alternative: in the 1970s, the "social marginals" among Dutch males and females, and the Surinamese "hangers-on" (paragraph 2); and in the 1980s, the new marginal youth (paragraph 3.2). In these categories, to a high degree, their social position and their position in the drug world coincide. Regular society plays a subordinate role in their lives.

5. Drug careers in the long term

The original dissimilarities between the different types of users do not necessarily produce totally different drug careers. Indeed, examination of the successive generations of addicts shows that, after the initial phase of the hard drug careers, there is a strong tendency to uniformity in career development. This may be called the "standard junkie phase". Based on the Rotterdam study, we distinguish several structural elements of drug addiction typical for the "standard junkie phase" (Intraval 1989). Nearly all addicts were not working at the time of the interview and they lived of welfare. Either they had never had any regular work or else they had lost their, usually temporary and unskilled, job. More than three-quarters of the addicts had not finished their education. About nine out of 10 addicts was involved in some way with illegal forms of income generation. Virtually all addicts had been in contact with a methadone program some time during their addiction career. Their housing situation tended to be very unstable. Only very few had a partner who did not use drugs. Although one-third of the users had one or more children, only those with a non-using partner raised their child(ren) themselves. And finally, many of the addicts had had one or more clean periods in the course of their drug career, and relapsed. These structural similarities in addiction patterns were found in spite of the fact that there were very varying backgrounds prior to the onset of hard drug use. Thus, the determinants of the onset of drug addiction surely do not have to be the same as the determinants of drug careers in the highly active phase.

In order to understand the dynamics of drug careers in the long term, we conducted a follow-up study into the respondents of the 1982 study (Janssen and Swierstra) seven years later. The onset of hard drug use had been some 13 years before, in the 1970s. Through this research, we discerned three features of hard drug careers: mortality, abstinence and criminal activity. These features have also been described in studies in other countries, particularly the United States.

5.1 Mortality

Not every addict survives his risky habit. Specific immediate causes of death include a decrease in physical resistance, overdoses of the drug itself or of adulterated substances, suicide, violence, and AIDS. By inferring mortality rates from some 20 longitudinal studies from different countries, it was found that the mortality risk compared to non-drug-taking contemporaries is substantial: at least 10 times higher (Swierstra

1990:78). In our sample of 90 addicts from several cities in the Netherlands, six deaths (6.6%) have occurred since the first interview, seven
years before. This is a rather small proportion compared to other countries, where about 12% mortality after seven years is common. A possible
explanation for this relatively low mortality rate may be the relatively
tolerant and pragmatic attitude towards drug use in Holland. As has been
explained in other Chapters, Dutch drug policy places emphasis on health
care, rather than on repression and criminalization. For instance, many
addicts are involved in outpatient methadone maintenance programs including basic medical care. Furthermore, there is also a large safety net
of welfare facilities in Holland. This enables addicts to stay visible for
drug care and other welfare programs, without being forced to kick their
habit or else go to prison. These factors may promote the continuation
of moderate drug lifestyles over an extended period of time – more so
than in other countries.

Provisional figures for HIV among Dutch drug addicts indicate that
they are rather low, compared to other European countries and the United
States. We speculate that the higher visibility of the Dutch addict is of
great importance here: education and prevention programs as well as
needle exchange projects seem to contribute significantly to the containment of the HIV virus. Finally, the number of violent deaths in the Dutch
drug world appears modest, especially when compared to the United
States (Swierstra 1990:126).

5.2 Abstinence: quitting drug life

A classic thesis in the field is Winick's "maturing out" (1962 1964):
most drug addicts naturally stop before reaching their mid-30s. Winick's
figures seem to be too optimistic, however. Our review of some dozens
of hard drug studies, primarily from the United States and England, indicates a much lower rate of abstinence: less than 40% will have terminated use 15 years after first use. Around the mid-30s, only approximately one-third of drug addicts will have stopped altogether. In our
study we defined as genuine abstinents those who had not been using
drugs for at least one year while "on the streets", (i.e., outside prison or
clinic). By this standard, after seven years, about 25% could be defined
as having terminated their drug careers (Swierstra 1990:135).

Our findings are consistent with the results of our review of other studies, conducted in other countries. We speculate that this points to an
empirical regularity: in Western countries, the proportion of addicts who
terminate their career after several years is fairly constant (around 25%).

Contrary to the noted differences in mortality rates, termination rates may point to a more general pattern. This general pattern suggests that national or historical differences may not be very significant in determining termination rates; more importantly, perhaps, this empirical regularity may transcend the effects of various drug policies as well. This pattern cautiously suggests that the traditional medical notion of a natural history of drug addiction should not be neglected (see also Stall and Biernacki 1986:18).

Not unlike other studies, our study revealed varying pathways away from drug addiction among the sample: the temporary substitute addiction to alcohol, the abstinence-oriented therapeutic drug treatment, and accidental situational changes. In all cases, a gradual process of transition seems to occur into a more conventional way of life. The respondents in our study who had persisted in hard drug use often lived in Amsterdam and Rotterdam, two big cities with an extensive hard drug structure which is likely to make it more difficult to terminate drug use.

5.3 Decreasing criminality, increasing conventionality

The criminal behavior of the hard drug addicts in our studies has shown a clear pattern over the years. About only half of the sample had committed a serious criminal act prior to addiction; however, during drug addiction, most addicts were criminally very active. The high-activity criminal phase of the drug career typically lasted about 10 years. The last few years of the follow-up study, however, unmistakingly showed decreasing criminal activity, not only among the former addicts who had terminated their drug use, but also among a large number of those still addicted. The ex-addicts had stopped using drugs after eight years, around the age of 27. For this group, termination of drug use implied immediate cessation of criminal behavior. Those who were still addicted at the time of the follow-up study (average age was slightly over 32) had a drug career of over 13 years behind them. Their ongoing addiction notwithstanding, their involvement in criminality generally ceased between the ages of 30 and 35. Also among this group of addicts, a certain stabilization in their lifestyle took place, in anticipation of the termination of their criminal career. In this respect, their involvement in criminal behavior appeared to be independent of their drug career (Swierstra 1990:178).

Those still addicted may not end their drug career before their 40s, if ever. The older drug addicts stay in outpatient methadone maintenance programs. In addition to the daily dose of methadone, they are more likely to use alcohol and pills, rather than the more difficult to obtain substances of heroin and cocaine. Heroin and cocaine are expensive and demand a high level of income-generating crime. After years of police and prison experiences, the older addict now increasingly becomes concerned with trying to avoid further contact with the legal system. They have the option of using sedatives and barbiturates prescribed by the general practitioner; there is no longer the need for crime to support one's habit. Consequently, apart from their ongoing addiction, their way of life begins to differ less and less from that of people who have never used drugs. They are unemployed and have remained relatively uneducated for all these years; the lifestyle of the drug world provided an enticing alternative. However, once the bonds to the deviant drug world begin to weaken, what remains is simply unemployment and little schooling. They are now members of the lower-class, but they have lost the solace, comfort, and illusions hard drugs used to provide. Only when welfare payments are received (once a month), do they have the fleeting joy of a dose of heroin and/or cocaine (*cf.* Preble and Miller 1977). As part of the adjustment process, the conventional bonds with significant others outside the drug world begin to intensify: they renew contacts with relatives, start their own family life with partner and children, and establish social contacts within their neighborhoods. Gradually, these ties with the conventional world are substituted for the old bonds to the drug world.

In conclusion, in the sample under study (both ex-addicts and current addicts), there is an ongoing process of steady decrease in criminality and a steady increase in abstinence rate. Intensification of conventional bonds keeps these people from relapsing into their previous, criminally addictive, behavior. The ex-addicts do not only strengthen their ties with significant others in conventional society, but to the education and job market as well. Accompanying this is a conventional turn in moral beliefs: the rules of the existing social order are increasingly accepted. We may then conclude that, in the end, the vast majority of drug addicts appears to dissolve into conventional Dutch society.

6. Developments in the light of Dutch drug policy

6.1 Drugs and the spirit of the times

In the 1980s, public opinion on hard drugs in Holland shifted to the problem-causing behavior of the addict. In the 1970s, a hard drug user was viewed primarily as somebody experimenting with a cultural alternative way of life; during the decade of the 1980s, they were viewed as criminals and/or psychopaths. Scientific research put more emphasis on the criminality and public order aspects of drug problems. The policy counterpart was a more criminal justice oriented approach to drug problems, where the individual addict is held more personally responsible for drug-related problems. Methadone maintenance programs (the traditional public health response) are now complemented by a well-coordinated criminal justice response to their income-generating criminality and other public order problems. For instance, Amsterdam and Rotterdam developed projects designed to remove the annoying drug addicts from the streets; more so than before, the public prosecutor played an important role in these efforts.

The shifts in scholarly and policy focus are consistent with the current mood, both nationally and internationally. The American "War on Drugs" exemplifies the more repressive, less tolerant approach to the drug problem. In addition, as a product of European unification, more uniform (and quite probably, more repressive) international rules are forthcoming for the Netherlands. Yet, the Dutch approach to drugs remains characterized by several unique features.

6.2 Extent and nature of recent Dutch drug problems

Looking back over the past few decades, we may conclude that Dutch drug policy has possibly had a distinct effect on the character of drug problems in Holland. In terms of available figures, it seems that the pragmatic national policy did not produce the results that some of its hardline opponents predicted: *i.e.,* higher numbers of addicts. Neither international comparisons, nor developments within the Netherlands over the last two decades, could reasonably justify such an inference. Qualitatively, the effect of the Dutch drug policy may be assessed as follows. First, the use of heroin was tolerated in Holland, particularly in the larger cities. This policy was consistent with the intent of the 1976 Opium Act which was designed to avoid the marginalization of the user by concentrating on drug dealing and drug-related crime. Complementary to this approach is a policy emphasis on the health care of the addict. It seems reasonable to conclude that these conditions may have facilitated experimenting with hard drugs, particularly for those young people who otherwise would not have become involved in a deviant way of life. (In paragraph 3.3 we described this process as a component of the individualization of drug use.)

A second and related hypothesis is that the easy availability and the nature of the methadone maintenance programs in Holland have contributed to the Dutch drug problem. The highly visible Dutch addict, who is able to avoid withdrawal symptoms from heroin through easy access to low-threshold methadone programs, may have weakened the deterrent effect which normally radiates from a "dope fiend". Perhaps the image of a marginal and tough criminal drug life has been softened. Following this line of reasoning, for some of the experimenting drug users (particularly those from middle-class social backgrounds and/or with a lack of criminal experience – those who actually might have been deterred by the prospect of legal sanctions and/or a miserable life), the Dutch policy may have made it easier to become more involved than it would have been under a tough, repressive, drug policy.

Of course, in the final analysis it is simply impossible to determine exactly the effects, if any, of the specific Dutch approach to drugs on the nature and extent of the drug problems in Holland. What can be established, however, is that a higher degree of acceptance of the drug addict by society implies a higher visibility of the addict for conventional society, and *vice versa*. We expect that this will affect drug careers, especially in the long term. It is not the highly deviant and criminally highly active phase of the drug career which makes for important international differences; of more interest is what happens after this phase, when the curve of deviant vitality in human lives takes a downward turn. Our findings on long-term opiate addicts in the Netherlands illustrate this point.

6.3 A Dutch variant of drug careers?

Methadone maintenance programs may be an important condition for addicts in order to retain their bonds with institutional society over the years, or in order to repair them, after many years. Methadone maintenance programs reach the majority of the addict population in the Netherlands. Recent Amsterdam and Rotterdam studies indicate that every year about 70% of opiate addicts are involved in one of these programs (Intraval 1989:12). In addition, there is the safety-net of general welfare facilities in Holland. We may speculate that in countries with a more repressive drug policy it would have been very hard to find a substantial number of addicts in their 30s who are no longer criminally active, as we did in our study. In countries other than Holland, we would expect them to be either a criminally active drug addict, to have terminated their drug habit altogether, or, of course, to be dead. Moreover, prison sentences in countries like the United States are significantly longer than in the Netherlands. Dutch policy keeps addicts out of prison for most of the time during their active drug-using career.

As we already noted, the termination rates in Holland do not seem to differ from the international picture; however, mortality rates are lower in Holland. Addicts are "on the streets", *i.e.,* out of prison most of the time; yet, the criminally active phase of their drug-using careers appears to be more limited than elsewhere. In short, Dutch drug policy may, possibly, keep people addicted for a longer period of time, but in a more socially integrated way. This variant of the hard drug career might then be termed a product of the Dutch welfare society and its pragmatic drug policy.

7. Conclusion

The Dutch drug phenomenon has past its infancy; the subcultural phase in the social history of the phenomenon belongs to the past. The world of hard drugs has become tougher, more criminal, and is fought by law enforcement agencies more severely than ever before. However, compared to other Western countries (particularly the United States), Dutch drug policy is still pragmatic. The Dutch addict is kept socially visible by treatment and care programs. The shift in the direction of a more unambiguous approach over the last few years has resulted in a further articulation of the pragmatic, "normalizing" aspects of Dutch drug policy. Two important components of this policy are: the prevention of marginalization and of further criminalization; and the maintenance of a livable situation for all parties, including the addicts.

Dutch drug policy is gaining in popularity in other Western countries and the United States. To a large extent, the AIDS epidemic (especially among non-deviant groups) and the relative success of the Netherlands in containing the spread of the HIV virus is responsible for the growing appreciation of the Dutch approach to drug control. Indeed, some skeptical voices have expressed the fear that the international appreciation of Dutch drug policy may not survive the invention of the first effective medicine against AIDS. In our view, however, apart from its apparent success in the fight against AIDS, the unique Dutch approach to drugs deserves an open-minded, non-biased, and fair evaluation. In comparison to recent developments in other industrialized countries, Dutch drug problems have remained relatively minor, both quantitatively and qualitatively. At the very least, Dutch drug policy has not resulted in a fast escalation of the drug problem.

References

Abrams, Ph.: *Historical Sociology*. West Compton House: Open Books, 1982

Becker, H.S.: *Outsiders; Studies in the Sociology of Deviance*. New York: Free Press, 1963

Biernacki, P.: *Pathways from Heroin Addiction; Recovery without Treatment*. Philadelphia: Temple University Press, 1986

Blom, M. and Janssen, O.J.A.: *Molukse Heroïnegebruikers in Nederland; een Typologie van Levensstijlen van Molukse Heroïnegebruikers*. Rijks Universiteit Groningen, 1987

Cohen, P.: *Cocaine Use in Amsterdam in Non-Deviant Subcultures*. Institute for Social Geography, University of Amsterdam, 1989

Des Jarlais, D.C. and Uppal, G.S.: Heroin activity in New York City, 1970-1978. *American Journal of Drug Alcohol Abuse* 1, 3, 4, 335-346, 1980

Inciardi, J.A.: *The war on Drugs; Heroin, Cocaine, Crime, and Public Policy*. Palo Alto: Mayfield Publishing Company, 1986

Intraval (Bieleman, B., Bruggink, G. and Swierstra, K.): *Hard Drugs en Criminaliteit in Rotterdam*. Groningen: Intraval, 1987 (Separate extended summary in English: *Hard Drugs and Crime in Rotterdam*. Groningen: Intraval)

Janssen, O.J.A. and Swierstra, K.: *Heroïnegebruikers in Nederland; een Typologie van Levensstijlen*. Rijks Universiteit Groningen, 1982

Janssen, O.J.A. and Swierstra, K.: *Heroïnegebruikers in Nederland; een Typologie van Levensstijlen*. Rijks Universiteit Groningen, 1987

Kaufman, P. and Verbraeck, H.: *Marokkaan en Verslaafd; een Studie naar Randgroepvorming, Heroïnegebruik en Criminalisering*. Gemeente Utrecht, 1986

Korf, D.J.: *Heroïnetoerisme. II: Resultaten van een Veldonderzoek onder 382 Buitenlandse Dagelijkse Opiaatgebruikers in Amsterdam*. Universiteit van Amsterdam, 1987

Lindesmith, A.R.: *Addiction and Opiates*. Chicago: Aldine, 1968

Maddux, J.F. and Desmond, D.P.: *Careers of Opioid Users*. New York: Praeger, 1981

Preble, E. and Casey, J.J.: Taking care of business – the heroin user's life on the street. *International Journal of Addiction* 4(1):1-24, 1969

Preble, E. and Miller, T.: Methadone, wine and welfare. In: Weppner, R.S. (Ed.), *Street Ethnography; Selected Studies of Crime and Drug Use in Natural Settings*. Beverly Hills, CA: Sage Publications, 1977

Stall, R. and Biernacki, P.: Spontaneous remission from the problematic use of substances: an inductive model derived from a comparative analysis of the alcohol, opiate, tobacco, and food/obesity literature. *International Journal of Addiction* 21(1):1-23, 1986

Swierstra, K., Janssen, O.J.A. and Jansen, J.H.: *De Reproductie van het Heroïnegebruik onder Nieuwe Lichtingen; Heroïnegebruikers in Nederland, Deel II*. Rijks Universiteit Groningen, 1986

Swierstra, K.: *Drugscarrières; van Crimineel tot Conventioneel*. Rijks Universiteit Groningen, 1990

Van Gelder, P.J. and Sijtsma, J.H.: *Horse, Coke en Kansen; Sociale Risico's en Kansen onder Surinaamse en Marokkaanse Harddruggebruikers in Amsterdam. I: Surinaamse Harddruggebruikers. II: Marokkaanse Harddruggebruikers*. Universiteit van Amsterdam, 1988

Waldorf, D: *Careers in Dope*. Englewood Cliffs, NJ: Prentice Hall, 1973

Winick, C.: Maturing out of narcotic addiction. *United Nations Bulletin of Narcotics* 14:1-7, 1962

Winick, C.: The life cycle of the narcotic addict and of addiction. *United Nations Bulletin of Narcotics* 16:1-11, 1964

VII. DRUG TOURISTS AND DRUG REFUGEES

Dirk J. Korf

1. Introduction

"Even the streets are of two kinds: the touristy shopping street cluttered with neon signs, and the long and narrow sidewalk alongside the canals, marked by a street light, docked houseboat, parked car, locked bike, and falling leaves. Often they are only a block apart; the two styles of Amsterdam side by side" (Holleran 1990:11).

The introduction of illicit drug use in the Netherlands after World War II is frequently associated with foreigners and migrants: older people from Chinese descent who continued opium smoking as they had done in earlier decades, American sailors, black jazz musicians from (former) Dutch colonies in the Caribbean smoking marihuana, American soldiers stationed in West Germany who came to Amsterdam to buy marihuana. These groups, however, did not significantly increase illicit drug use among the local population. Rather, the spread of illicit drug use in the Netherlands is primarily associated with youth tourism, which strongly influenced the atmosphere in the capital city of Amsterdam in particular.

Tourism is a primary and continuously increasing source of income in Amsterdam.[1] In the 1960s, a new kind of tourism emerged. Young people met at the National Monument in front of the Royal Palace and in the Vondelpark. They slept in the open air. Within a short period Amsterdam became the European capital for the hippie generation. Sleeping in the open air was not particularly appreciated by the local authorities, and soon cheap alternative sleeping accommodation became available in houseboats, youth hostels and a municipal sleep-in. Youth tourism strongly contributed to Amsterdam's new reputation of being the largest drug metropolis on the continent.

This Chapter addresses a particular type of marginal youth tourism: frequent heroin users. After a short historical overview, findings from a field study among foreign daily opiate users are presented. Travelling behavior will be explained by a push-pull model. Special attention will be paid to political complications and the effects of a specific policy directed towards heroin tourists. Recent developments are summarized and explained by the local drug policy and shifting perceptions abroad of what has been called "the Dutch experiment" (Baanders 1989; Kaplan 1984).

2. From drug mecca to last stop

Until the mid-1960s illicit drug use was not perceived as an important social problem in the Netherlands (De Kort and Korf 1992). However, significant changes took place at the end of that decade. Arrests by the Amsterdam Narcotic Squad for possession or dealing rose steeply: 15 in 1961, 34 in 1965, 451 in 1969. This increase of arrests continued up to the mid-1980s (more than 5,000 in 1985) and then decreased again to approximately 3,000 per year. Originally, it was mostly cannabis, but soon heroin, perceived as a much stronger threat to Dutch society, became a primary target for the police.

Although in recent years more than two-thirds of the arrests by the Amsterdam Narcotic Squad concern Dutch citizens (including a substantial number of Surinamese), until the mid-1970s, the majority of arrests involved foreigners (Korf and De Kort 1990). It is not only police data which indicates the importance of foreigners in contributing to the spread of illicit drug use in the Netherlands. In a study on American drug refugees in Amsterdam and London, the Dutch capital city was characterized as the "mecca for the turned-on" (Cuskey et al. 1972). Although the authors had discovered that the Dutch people did not especially want the drug tourists, they did note that "Amsterdam does not hate the turned-on crowd. It may wish that they would go somewhere else, but offers them more friendly tolerance and acceptance than perhaps any other city" (Cuskey et al. 1972:3). Next to American drug tourists, Italians, French, Swiss, Germans "...and long-haired representatives from many other countries" were observed (Cuskey et al. 1972:22).

In the beginning drug tourists were mainly hippies, restricting their illicit drug use to cannabis, LSD and other psychedelics. Social workers, doctors, nurses and, more typically, lay people were involved in crisis intervention. New and non-traditional institutions evolved, partly influenced by American experiments (e.g., the Free Clinic in San Francisco). They claimed more solidarity with youth than traditional institutions, were able to gain respect from policy makers and were increasingly subsidized by the local and national authorities (e.g., Leuw 1984). A common intervention was to "talk down" a tourist on a "bad trip" after taking LSD. Soon the helping professions were confronted with foreign opium and somewhat later, heroin users (Werkgroep 1972; Ten Have 1973; Koda 1975; Leuw 1973).

Americans (hippies, soldiers deserted from Vietnam and bases in West Germany) and Germans belonged to the clientele of the first small-scale methadone program, initiated by the Jellinek Center. At that time, detoxification in West Germany was mainly restricted to inpatient treatment in old-fashioned psychiatric hospitals. The untraditional therapeutic communities and the Municipal Free Medical Care Program in Amsterdam had more German clients than Dutch (Hesser 1979; Koda 1975).

The "Deutscher Hilfsverein," a special center for social assistance to Germans in Amsterdam underwent drastic changes. For many years it had primarily helped tourists who had run out of money, elderly who wanted to return to their native country, and so on (Hesser 1983). Now they were confronted with a totally different group: youth tourists. In 1973 the center registered about 40 German heroin addicts among its clientele. In following years the number increased each year, reaching its peak at almost 800 in 1984.

Since the Netherlands went its own way in following a policy of decriminalization of cannabis use, it has been internationally criticized. Neighboring countries, West-Germany in particular, complained about the "lenient" Dutch drug policy, which was said to lead to an increase of drug abuse in surrounding countries. For example in January 1975 the state government of Northrhine-Westfalia requested that the Netherlands follow a more repressive policy towards cannabis, "...since it had been proven that these drugs meant the gateway to hard drugs".[2] The substantial number of German heroin users in particular gave Amsterdam its reputation of being the "Drug Mecca".

For more than a decade, news about the Dutch drug policy in the German media concentrated on German addicts in Amsterdam, mostly to illustrate the failure of a so-called tolerant policy. This media-hype reached its peak in 1984, when the city council decided to start an experimental heroin-on-prescription program for extremely problematic users. Along with the news about "Free Heroin" and the increasing number of German drug deaths in Amsterdam, the city's reputation changed into "Endstation für Fixer" (last stop for drug users). "Behind the border they hope to find paradise. What a terrible misunderstanding. They drive to Amsterdam to die!" (Bach 1984). Often the situation of German heroin users in Amsterdam was presented as an illustration of inhumane liberalism and capitulation of Dutch drug policy (Goos 1979). However, young Germans seldom started their heroin career in Amsterdam. According to Hesser (1979), they "... not only carried their drug problem from Germany, but also problems with the Germans legal authorities".

On the other side of the border, in the Netherlands, irritation about

German drug policy reached its peak in the mid-1980s. In 1975, a 26-year-old Dutch man, who supposedly sold hashish to Germans in the Netherlands, was lured over the border by a German undercover agent. He was arrested and sent to prison. Prior to that incident Dutch citizens had been arrested in Germany for selling illicit drugs to Germans in the Netherlands, but now the first case was documented, where German police had been active in the Netherlands without the permission of the Dutch authorities (Volkskrant July 30, 1976). In the following years, several cases led to furor in the Dutch parliament and to diplomatic friction (Eikenaar 1986; Kaplan 1984; Rüter 1988). In addition, Dutch officials perceived the growing presence of the many German heroin users in Amsterdam as a direct result of the repressive drug policy in Germany, where methadone programs were completely taboo and treatment was almost exclusively restricted to inpatient therapeutic communities. German officials attributed this heroin tourism to the "lenient" and "liberal" Dutch drug policy. Within this context, German heroin users became the target of comprehensive political activism (Wimmer 1990).

3. Towards a new policy

During the 1970s, among professionals from service agencies there was a growing consensus about the necessity of minimizing access of foreign drug users to treatment facilities in the Netherlands. Foreign heroin users, as a general rule, were not allowed to participate in methadone programs and inpatient treatment programs, partly because of the fear that such services would encourage additional heroin tourists to come to Amsterdam, but also for financial reasons (who would pay the treatment in a drug free therapeutic community?). When in treatment, foreigners primarily participated in methadone programs run by a general practitioner, or they lived in one of the religious drug free communities (*e.g.,* Jesus People).

During the following years, the local drug policy became more structured and coordinated (Leuw 1984). This had an effect on the treatment facilities for foreign heroin users. Because some of the Christian communities had closed, it became even more difficult for them to find treatment in Dutch drug free therapeutic communities. However, a number of general practitioners continued to prescribe methadone to a substantial number of foreigners. In fact, the means available to obtain methadone increased.

The Drug Department introduced its methadone-by-bus program at the end of the 1970s, mainly for Surinamese users and prostitutes (Vasseur

1990). Methadone-by-bus was not intended as the first step towards a drug free life, but rather its primary objective was to reduce the risks associated with illicit drug use. Since heroin-using street prostitutes ran many health risks, foreign female users constituted a significant portion of the first generation of bus clients.

Although the City Council was aware of the phenomenon of heroin tourism, it did not implement a specific policy with regard to this particular segment of the heroin-using population in Amsterdam. This changed in 1984. The City Council decided that the public health orientation (*e.g.*, low threshold methadone programs) and the repressive approach (tackling nuisance from street dealing and other drug-related crimes) should be integrated into a two-track policy. With regard to foreign heroin users, two specific goals were defined as part of a "policy of discouragement": to reduce their number and to decrease drug-related crimes. In order to realize these goals, methadone programs were supposed to "sharpen" their intake criteria for foreign users and the police should intensify their activities targeting foreign criminal users. In addition, officials visited a number of neighboring countries in order to explain the new policy to their counterparts and the media, thus hoping that foreign users would refrain from coming to Amsterdam.

The policy of discouragement was not a new invention. To some extent it had already been implemented by treatment facilities, but not as a consequence of official policy. Treatment staff had expressed some concern about the increasing numbers of foreign addicts. City officials had participated in a conference "Drugs over the Border", where German and Dutch experts extensively discussed the problems of German heroin tourists in Amsterdam (Goos 1979). After several years of discussion, in 1978 the City Council decided to financially support the "Deutscher Hilfsverein" - which had now changed its name to the Amsterdam Ecumenical Center (AMOC). Because the organization did extensive outreach work, it had a good reputation among German heroin users in Amsterdam. Also, it had built up a wide network of contacts with the legal authorities and treatment facilities in their native country. Many German heroin users in Amsterdam had a hard time surviving in the city and wanted to return to Germany. Because AMOC assisted German addicts in their attempts to return to their native country, the Amsterdam City Council decided to subsidize this agency.

The initiation of a new official policy with regard to foreign drug users in 1984 was based on a number of assumptions. First, Amsterdam was supposed to work as a magnet for foreign heroin users: they would come to the city because of its liberal climate, low drug prices and easily accessible methadone programs. Second, it was assumed that foreign heroin users were responsible for a large part of the most inconvenient and annoying petty crime (*e.g.*, shoplifting, theft of car-radios and bikes). Third, it was expected that a "tougher" legal approach would decrease the number of heroin tourists (Drugsbeleid 1985).

4. An epidemiological field study

Along with the introduction of the two-track policy, the City Council decided to implement a three-year drug research program. A field study among the so-called heroin tourists was a first priority, which clearly illustrates that the local authorities perceived the presence of foreign heroin users in Amsterdam as a serious problem. During April and July of 1985 and 1986 we interviewed four samples of approximately 100 foreign daily opiate users.[3] Our study was guided by four main questions: (1) What is the size of the drug-using population and which are its main sub-categories? (2) Which factors explain why foreign users come to and possibly remain in Amsterdam? (3) How do they generate their income? (4) What are the effects of the policy of discouragement?

Very often studies among frequent heroin users relate to captive samples (*e.g.*, inpatient treatment, prisoners, probation clientele, methadone patients). Consequently, the degree to which these samples are representative is often questionable. Apart from this general problem, in our case we had to assume that the target population was predominantly hidden and that heroin tourists were strongly under-represented in most of the captive samples.[4] Heroin tourists belong to a specific kind of hidden population; we introduced the concept of "floating population" to describe this particular group of people (Kaplan *et al.* 1990). Floating populations are characterized by their socio-geographic mobility.[5] Most often, hidden populations are studied with a qualitative research orientation, *e.g.*, ethnographic methods. In the drug field, ethnographers tend to concentrate on the most visible segments of the drug market.[6] Therefore, from an epidemiological point of view the representativeness of findings is frequently questionable.[7] Snowball sampling is a common method in qualitative studies, but methodological problems are often ignored and remain unsolved (Morrison 1988). In many studies, snowball sampling means not much more than recruiting new interviewees by referrals; *i.e.*, with the assistance of those who have been interviewed already. A first methodological problem is: Where to start with the process of sampling? It has been suggested that chains of referral be initiated within as many different subgroups of the target population as possible (Biernacki 1986;

Biernacki and Waldorf 1981).

The major methodological problems and possible solutions at this "zero stage" in snowball sampling have been extensively discussed by Watters and Biernacki (1989). First the districts in which to conduct the research must be defined (initial mapping). Second, extensive ethnographic mapping is necessary to uncover and analyze the social organization of target groups within the selected district. Third, an initial target plan for each district must be developed. Fourth, it is usually necessary to revise the target plans once in the field in order to meet social conditions and participation rates. During the last step, the preliminary findings shape research questions and instruments. This particular strategy was also applied in our study on heroin tourism.[8] We decided not to initiate snowballs in methadone programs and the like. Instead first contacts were initiated at private addresses, in public buildings, cafes, in the streets, and so on.[9] This could only be done by experienced field workers, who were not only familiar with specific districts, but who were also well-known to specific subcultures.

The next problem is: How to build up chains of referral systematically? In her study "Life in the Working-Class Family", Rubin (1976) applied the snowball technique. In order to limit the bias inherent to referrals, she asked the female interviewees to refer her to "the most distant connection" in the network instead of her closest friend. The Rubin method motivated us to look for a strategy that would help us to systematically avoid selection bias after the "zero stage".

In our study we introduced the concept of "randomized chain referrals".[10] Respondents were asked to nominate the other heroin tourists known to them, with a minimum of five and a maximum of 25 names or nicknames. This was strictly confidential and respondents were not supposed to let us keep their list of nominees at the end of the interview.[11] From this list we randomly selected the next respondent and asked the interviewee to assist us in finding that person. Although respondents were usually very cooperative in finding the selected nominee, it sometimes took us several days and nights of "hanging around" before this next respondent in the snowball chain was found.

This selection procedure resulted in rather heterogenous samples. The snowball sampling with randomized chain referral brought us in contact with types of users who had remained unknown to methadone programs and field workers (e.g., Italian housewives) and most would probably never have been reached with traditional snowball sampling procedures. Although this appears to be one of the great advantages of our method and suggests a substantial improvement in representativeness, we cannot claim that our respondents represent a fully random selection of the target population.

We used a multilingual structured questionnaire. Interviews lasted approximately one hour. Respondents were paid 25 Dutch guilders.[12] With regard to reliability of the self-report data we found significant consistencies between scores on different variables (*e.g.*, criminal career, illicit drug use).[13]

5. Findings

Among the 382 respondents we found 34 nationalities; 88% came from West-European countries. West-Germany, Italy, the United Kingdom and Spain were represented most frequently. One-third of the respondents were female. The largest nationality group, the Germans, consisted of 40% females. Ages ranged from 16 through 46 years, with an average of 27.4 years. Despite the dominant depiction of adolescents in the media (*e.g.*, young heroin prostitutes), daily opiate use was found not to be a juvenile problem; minors actually were a rarity with the age cohort late 20s/early 30s most strongly represented.

Most respondents were (primarily) raised by their natural parents and only 4% grew up with their grandparents, in foster families or in institutions. All socio-economic classes were represented. About 40% reported lower class, one-quarter lower/middle class, and one-third upper/middle or upper class as their background. These percentages did not vary significantly between the four samples.

Although the respondents in the field study lived or stayed throughout the city, the highest concentration was found in downtown Amsterdam. Other concentrations were found in neighborhoods with lower quality housing and in renovation areas.[14] Only one-quarter of the respondents said they were legally registered in Amsterdam. As far as respondents who had a place to stay were concerned, there was a wide variety in the quality of their housing. Some lived in clean and "bourgeois" apartments, while others stayed in dirty places without electricity, gas or water. Less than one-third had their own permanent address in Amsterdam; one out of ten was homeless.

In general, surveys do not allow us to reliably estimate the prevalence of frequent heroin use.[15] Several other methods can be applied to estimate opiate use in a city.[16] In our study, the number of heroin tourists per month was estimated with a capture-recapture technique and through extrapolation from the percentage of respondents participating in the Municipal Methadone Program.[17] The best approximate estimate of the size of the population was 1,500 heroin tourists per month during the summer of 1985 and slightly higher in 1986. Although Germans made up the largest category (one-third), their number was much lower than assumed by policy makers.[18] Italians constituted the second largest category; users from the United Kingdom were the third largest category. A secondary analysis of treatment and police data, together with mobility indicators from our field study, indicated that the number of heroin tourists decreased to approximately 800 per month during winter.

Respondents appeared to live rather isolated from the local population. Westermeyer (1982) came to the same conclusion with regard to western opiate users in Asia. For the majority of our respondents, other heroin users (mainly other foreigners) were the primary group of reference. Only a small category primarily lived in a world of non-users.[19]

Analysis of the snowball chains showed that nationality was an important variable in structuring the population of foreign users. Most respondents primarily lived within rather closed "scenes", basically limited to users from the same country and/or sharing their language. German users referred to other Germans; Austrians and Swiss – sharing German as their native tongue – were part of these snowballs. Italians also built a relatively separate group, although we found some overlap with users from other Latino countries (Spain, Portugal, Latin America). The Anglo population (UK, USA, Australia, New Zealand, South Africa) showed the strongest overlap with smaller "scenes" (*i.e.*, Ireland, Scandinavia), although some others seem to be more restricted to one nationality (*i.e.*, Yugoslavia, Greece). German female prostitutes appeared to be one of the most isolated groups within the population.[20]

Many respondents had a long history of illicit drug use; only 3% had a heroin career shorter than one year and one-third used heroin for the first time ten or more years ago. Apart from opiates, almost all respondents had been using cannabis and cocaine. Many also used LSD, amphetamines and pills (barbiturates, tranquilizers, and so on). The majority referred to themselves as heroin addicts, but only seldom had they been using heroin continuously. About one-third had had inpatient treatment. Half of the respondents had, at least once, kicked their habit voluntarily and did not do hard drugs, methadone or pills for a shorter or longer period; about one-quarter stayed "clean" for six months or more.

Approximately three out of four respondents were intravenous users. Application techniques correlated with nationality. Intravenous use was most dominant among Italians (94%) and Germans (90%). However, most respondents who used their first heroin in Amsterdam were non-intravenous users and preferred to chase the dragon ("to chinese").

The way respondents administer heroin correlated with the place where they used the drug for the first time. Experimenting in Italy and West Germany predominantly took place within a needle-oriented environment, whereas during initiation in Amsterdam other techniques (nasal, oral) were primarily learned. Only a minority of the respondents did not use drugs other than opiates. About half of the respondents reported cocaine use within the last 24 hours. The same was true for cannabis and more than one-quarter drank alcohol. Within the last seven days three-quarters of the respondents had used cocaine.

The data on recent drug use were analyzed for the combination: opiates (including methadone), cocaine, alcohol and pills: 20% had used three or four different drug types within the last 24 hours; 55% of the respondents used at least three of the four different drugs within the last seven days.[21] These findings indicate that among daily opiate users in Western Europe, poly-drug use is highly prevalent and that "pure heroin addiction" is very rare.

6. A push-pull model

Heroin users in Amsterdam show a high level of mobility. Many spend more time in neighborhoods other than where they reside. They also frequently change apartments, and move to other parts of the country. A small segment is homeless for a longer period (Korf and Hoogenhout 1990). A considerable proportion of the interviewed heroin tourists had been living in Amsterdam for quite a while. Among the interviewed heroin tourists one-third were "short-term visitors" (maximum of 90 days), almost two-thirds were "settlers" (three months or longer for a minimum of four days per week) and a small percentage were "swingers" (they visited Amsterdam more than six times per year).

The presence of foreign users in Amsterdam has been explained by the relatively low drug prices and the availability of methadone programs. Our data do not support such theories. It is indeed true that there were no methadone programs in Germany at the time of our study, and that heroin and cocaine were usually more expensive in Germany than in Amsterdam (although prices in Frankfurt and Amsterdam were not significantly different). However, users from Italy made up the second largest group, in spite of the fact that heroin and cocaine were cheaper in Italy than in Amsterdam and methadone programs were available in most parts of Italy. Another reason to question the importance of low drug prices is that a significant price decrease for heroin and cocaine in most European countries between 1985 and 1986 did not reduce the influx of new drug tourists into Amsterdam.

In order to come to terms with the motivations of heroin tourists for coming to Amsterdam, a push-pull model has been constructed. Push factors relate to the reasons why they leave their own country, such as unemployment; unavailability of methadone; poor-quality heroin; and legal problems. The pull factors that theoretically could attract heroin tourists to Amsterdam include: job market, availability of methadone; high-quality heroin which is cheap and easy to find; relaxed atmosphere; and friends. Three categories of answers were given to the question "Why did you come to Amsterdam the last time?": (1) Liberal climate for drugs users; (2) Work and living; and (3) Legal and political problems.

With regard to the more liberal climate for drugs users, respondents mentioned the (supposedly) less severe harassment in Amsterdam as the main reason. In the words of a local police officer: "The whole lifestyle is different here, easier. They feel better here, life is more bearable. In Germany you are far more isolated as a user. It's the German mentality: if you don't behave as you should, you will be expelled."

Respondents who gave work and living as the main reason for their coming to Amsterdam were unemployed in their own country and came to find work in Amsterdam; others came to visit relatives or to join their partner. A female Italian user explained: "I came here about three years ago with my boyfriend. We wanted to earn a lot of money by working hard. I have always worked abroad. I wanted to work the whole year, also in wintertime, but this is not possible at home. There are no tourists in Sardinia. In Amsterdam we found work in a pizzeria."

The majority of the respondents who mentioned legal or political problems ran away from their country because they either, had to go to court, were on probation, had to go to prison or mandatory treatment; others were political refugees (i.e., from Iran, Chile). Legal problems were most frequently mentioned by the German users and least frequently by the Italians. A German user (30 years old) told the following story: "Since I was 15 law enforcement has been after me. They started "caring" for me before I even used heroin. Got caught with some hash. Every time they had their reasons: the probation officer who wanted to talk to me once a week, the therapeutic communities, prison, psychiatric hospital. They were always after me. They arrested me to force me to provide information about my dealer. He is an asshole and can be put in prison for a decade. But he could kill me, so I keep my mouth. Why don't they leave me alone, all I do is use drugs. I work for my money, do some drugbizz, was a prostitute. Why do they treat me as a criminal when I never steal or something. I did not come to Amsterdam to use drugs, definitely not, but I had no choice. I just want to live my own life."

Table 1 shows the results of our study. We classified the responses by whether the (push or pull) factor was drug-specific (*e.g.*, price and purity of drugs) or non-drug-specific (*e.g.*, employment). The push and pull factors have also been compared over time. That is, the responses regarding the reasons for the first visit to Amsterdam are compared with those of the last visit.

Table 1. Push and pull factors by first and last time in Amsterdam

	First Time (285)*	Last Time (240)**
Pull Factors	74%	44%
* Drug-Specific	22%	32%
* Non-Specific	52%	12%
Push Factors	10%	24%
* Drug-Specific	8%	21%
* Non-Specific	2%	3%
Non-Specific Push and/or Pull	17%	32%
Total	100%	100%

*: These questions were only asked of the last three samples.
**: Forty-five respondents were interviewed after their first visit to Amsterdam.

Most of the reasons for visiting Amsterdam appeared to be not drug-specific: examples given were student visits and holidays with parents. Often the reported reasons could not be clearly categorized as either pull or push factors: examples include unemployment in their own country and hoping to find a job in Amsterdam. Whereas tourism and the general atmosphere in Amsterdam were important non drug-specific factors at the first visit, they played an insignificant role at the last visit. Work and housing gradually became more important. Among the reasons for the first visit, one-third could be categorized as drug-specific factors; among the reasons provided for the last visit, the importance of drug-specific factors increased to approximately 50% (*i.e.*, 32% designated as pull factors; 21% designated as push factors). Drug-specific pull factors increased slightly (from 22% to 32%); however, drug-specific push factors increased more strongly (from 8% to 21%). A general conclusion is that the importance of non-drug-related factors decreases during the drug career, but they still remain important reasons for drug users to come to Amsterdam.

In summary, in our field study among heroin tourists, data concerning several drug-specific variables were collected and analyzed. The magnet effect (lower drug prices, methadone programs) often pointed out by politicians and the media could not explain trends in heroin tourism. Moreover, trends in heroin tourism often correlated positively with trends in general youth tourism: for example, the increase in Italian heroin tourists parallelled the substantial increase of Italian youth tourism in general.[22] The respondents apparently were rather fond of travelling. They had often visited not only Amsterdam, but also other European metropoles (Paris, Barcelona, Berlin, Frankfurt, Rome). Almost one-quarter, for example, had lived in London for at least one period of more than three months. While Italian users seem to reflect a general trend and to be part of the growing number of "youth tourists" from this country (non-drug-specific pull factor), German users left their country mainly because of legal problems (drug-specific push factor). A closer look at legal problems indicates that this pull factor might be even more important than Table 1 suggests. Before they came to Amsterdam the last time, 51% of the Germans had legal problems in their own country (problems with the police; were on probation; had to go to court, had to go to prison and/or into mandatory treatment), significantly more than the other respondents (38%).

7. Drug use and economic behavior

The money spent on living (rent, food, clothes, *etc.*) during the last seven days preceding the interview varied strongly. While some users had a high standard of living, spending up to several thousands of guilders per week, others had hardly anything to eat. More than one-third of the respondents did not spend more than 100 guilders in the last seven days, while some could afford a luxurious lifestyle (expensive apartment, trendy clothes, Mercedes); the median was almost 200 Dutch guilders. The average amount of money spent on drugs (including alcohol, pills, methadone) in the last seven days far exceeded the amount of money spent on other living expenses. About one-quarter of the respondents did not spend more than 250 guilders on drugs during the last week; the median was slightly over 500 Dutch guilders.

Respondents were also asked how they had generated their income during the last seven days. We presented them with nine categories: work; sex business; welfare/unemployment; parents and relatives; drug business; pills and methadone; other illegal activities; and other legal activities. The source of income which generated the most money is defined as the primary source, others as secondary sources.

The drug business was the most important source of income. Four out of ten generated their primary income from steering, touting, copping and selling drugs and pills. Two-thirds earned at least some money this way. About half of the respondents received money from their parents, relatives or partner. Ten percent lived primarily off their partner and five percent off their parents or relatives. More than a quarter survived primarily (or secondarily) through work-generated income, other legal activities (street music, street theater, selling handmade jewellery, and so on) or welfare/unemployment. One-quarter of the respondents was supported by the sex business. For 18% of the respondents, prostitution or work in topless bars, floor and peep shows meant the main source of income. For 11% of the respondents, property crime was the main source of income and for another 15% these "other illegal activities" were a secondary source.

These findings do confirm that daily opiate use is strongly related to criminal behavior. The majority of the criminal activities, however, are to be categorized as "victimless crimes" (drug business and sex business). We found only one-quarter of the interviewees had committed crimes with victims (mainly property crimes) within the last week. As far as female users were concerned, they almost exclusively committed crimes without victims, in the sex business in particular (primary source for 40% of the females versus 9% of the males). Male users were mainly involved in earning money through drugs, but they also committed far more crimes with victims than females.

The economic behavior of daily opiate users is thus strongly dependent on gender. In addition, we found that users who were arrested some time before and/or after the beginning of the heroin career, and who also used alcohol frequently, were more likely to be involved in property crime. Respondents who (also) had been arrested for crimes other than violations of drug laws before they started using heroin reported property crimes as a source of income during the past seven days almost three times more than those who had not been arrested at all before their first heroin use. Users who had been in methadone treatment showed the opposite pattern. Respondents who did not participate in a methadone program were twice as likely to report property crimes than methadone clients.

During the field study, the official drug policy in Amsterdam with regard to heroin tourists was primarily directed towards reducing drug-related property crimes. A growing number of police officers were on the streets, where they kept the "scene" moving (Verbraeck 1988). The proportion of heroin tourists in the methadone program decreased. Our findings do not only suggest that a lower level drug dealing became more

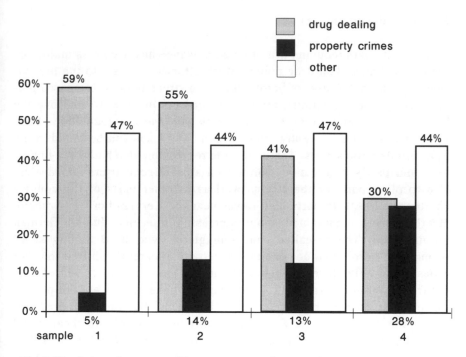

Fig. 1. Trends in main sources of income among male respondents.

dispersed throughout the city, but also that a decreasing proportion of the foreign users earned money in this branch. We did not find any significant change in economic behavior among females.[23] However, as a result of increased police activity, several of the users who were formerly involved in drug dealing now shifted to property crimes. As a matter of fact, the percentage of male respondents generating income from the drug business decreased by half from the first to the fourth sample. The figures for property crime showed the opposite trend: the proportion of male respondents who primarily lived from "other illegal activities" was far higher at the peak of the tourist season (July) than at the beginning (April), but in the long run an increase could be clearly observed (Fig. 1). Although we have only collected data from two successive years, the findings are not consistent with the popular assumption that an intensified law enforcement policy leads to a decrease of drug-related property crimes.[24] These findings were supported by later field studies in Amsterdam (Van Gemert 1988; Verbraeck 1988), showing that more police on the streets changes the structures of the drug market, but not necessarily reduces the number of dealers and users.

8. Recent developments

In recent years reducing drug-related nuisance has become a major target of the Amsterdam drug policy. Much attention is paid to the prevention of social gatherings of heroin users and street dealers. Increased police patrol is one technique, renovation projects in order to improve the quality of housing in problem areas is yet another technique. Consequently, a lower concentration of dealers and users can be found in the most problematic streets. The increasing repression also had some important, and partly predictable, unintended side effects: users and dealers fled to other parts of the city as well as to other parts of the country (Verbraeck 1990). In particular, towns near the German border (Arnhem, Heerlen) have complained about increasing nuisance due to German heroin users. The so-called "ant smugglers" who used to buy small amounts of heroin and cocaine in Amsterdam apparently shifted to other cities, preferably closer to their home town. These users are very different from their counterparts in Amsterdam. In general they are not pushed out of their country because of legal problems, but they are predominantly small-scale dealers who come to buy drugs which are cheaper and of better quality than in their home town (Grapendaal and Aidala 1991).[25] There are still German heroin users who come to the capital, stay for a short time, buy drugs and go back home, but the majority stays longer. Some have been living in Amsterdam for many years and often feel more Dutch than German.

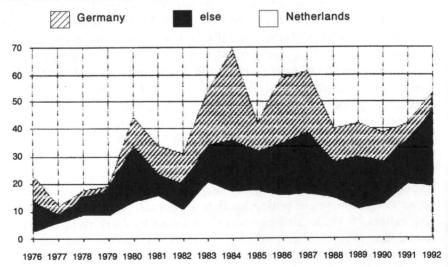

Fig. 2. Heroindeaths in Amsterdam by country of birth (1976-1992).

Local authorities in Amsterdam claim that the number of German heroin users has decreased (Buning 1990). A significant decrease of German drug deaths seems to support this conclusion (Fig. 2). Some years ago more German than Dutch heroin users died in Amsterdam. In recent years, the number of German drug deaths has decreased. This trend could be an indication of a general decrease in the number of German heroin tourists in Amsterdam. However, there are several intervening variables.[26] Firstly, most of the Germans who died did so within the first two weeks after their arrival (Cobelens et al. 1990). This means that "overdose" figures primarily relate to particular segments of heroin tourists, more so than to the population as a whole. Secondly, in recent years, more attention has been paid to the prevention of "overdose". Since the mid-1980s leaflets with instructions for foreign users of how to avoid a lethal overdose and how to help those who are in trouble ("keep them awake", "call an ambulance", "don't be afraid of the police") are distributed in youth hostels and other relevant locations. Also, ambulance personnel started using Narcan, an opiate antagonist; most probably this has saved lives. Thirdly, assuming that media news about suicides stimulates others to commit suicide, the local authorities stopped informing the media about every individual drug death. Instead of reporting every individual case, the number of drug deaths was reported only once a year.[27] Fourthly, the purity of heroin in Germany has improved in recent years; differences in purity between Germany and the Netherlands have been presented as a major reason for the high number of German drug deaths in Amsterdam (Cobelens et al. 1990). Whereas the number of German drug deaths in the Netherlands has decreased, there has been a tremendous increase in drug fatalities in Germany (up to 1,463 in 1990).[28]

At the same time, the number of foreign arrestees and methadone clients has declined. But again, we are confronted with some complications when trying to interpret this. As mentioned before, the policy of discouragement was directed towards limiting the possibilities of foreigners to enter methadone treatment. Furthermore, the number of arrests is also consistent with the increased intensity of police activities. (Special police projects were carried out in downtown Amsterdam during the summer of 1986 and 1987 (Verbraeck 1990) and later implemented in a decentralized way in other neighborhoods.)

An additional factor confounds our attempts to make sense out of these different indicators: While the number of foreign drug deaths, methadone clients and arrestees has decreased, the number of German heroin addicts among the AMOC clientele has remained rather stable (approximately

700 per year). Although drug policy is changing in Germany (methadone is no longer completely taboo; needle exchange programs were started in several cities), the push factors mentioned earlier still continue to exist. The AMOC annual reports indicate that German heroin users continue to run away from their country, mostly because of legal problems.

It seems that heroin tourists from Germany can roughly be divided into two categories: "swingers" who come to buy drugs in the Netherlands and others who run away from a problematic situation. For the first category, Dutch cities just across the border (Arnhem and Heerlen) are closer than German cities (Frankfurt am Main; Hamburg) where they can also buy heroin and cocaine relatively cheaply and of good quality.

Amsterdam is further away and it has become more difficult to buy drugs in the streets.[29] Consequently, this kind of "ant smuggling" has shifted from Amsterdam to cities closer to the Dutch-German border. The second category does not come for quick transactions, but with the intention of staying in the Netherlands. These people apparently still prefer Amsterdam. Only a few German heroin users live in Arnhem and Heerlen; the same is true for Rotterdam and the other large cities.

Thus, German drug refugees still come to Amsterdam. According to the Municipal Health Organization, their physical condition keeps deteriorating: they often need inpatient treatment in a general hospital, many are seropositive and a growing number has AIDS (PPP 1989). It is probable that German heroin users in Amsterdam are a strongly selective subsample of the total population of heroin users in Germany. Many have legal problems in their own country, but only a few hundred of an estimated total of 100,000 German users come to stay in Amsterdam. Life in Amsterdam has become increasingly problematic, e.g., it is more difficult to participate in methadone programs (in particular those administered by general practitioners), their physical condition has become worse and the number of AIDS patients among them has grown (AMOC 1990). In a sense, their unfavorable situation in Amsterdam has evolved into a push factor itself: they seem more motivated to return to their home country.

Since December 1987 a special Repatriation Project has been funded by the German government. This project, in close cooperation with AMOC, has returned a few hundred German heroin users to their home country, e.g., to general hospitals, for inpatient drug-free treatment, or to their parents. This project symbolizes a shift in the political arena. Instead of blaming each other for their "wrong" drug policy, cooperation and mutual respect is growing. On World Drug Day, in June 1988, Professor Süssmuth (1989), then German Minister of Youth, Family, Women and Health, stated: "With its policy of discouragement towards foreign drug users Amsterdam lost its reputation of being the "Drug Mecca" some time ago."

Another explanation applies to the Italian heroin tourists in Amsterdam. According to the Municipal Health Organization their physical condition is significantly better and repatriation is much easier to realize (PPP 1989). They have fewer legal problems and methadone programs are not unusual in Italy. Moreover, most of the Italian heroin tourists in Amsterdam are "short stayers". Data from methadone programs, needle exchange programs and police arrests indicate a continuing growth of Italian heroin tourists (Buning 1990; Reijneveld 1991). This finding is consistent with the conclusions from our field study in 1986. Due to the higher level of inflation in Italy it has become more attractive to them to spend a holiday in the Netherlands. This tourism was strongly stimulated by Dutch tourist campaigns and travel agencies in Italy. In the last decade the number of Italian tourists in the Netherlands has increased from 105,000 in 1980 to 230,000 in 1989 (Heering 1990). Apparently, drug tourism can be a side effect of general tourism; this is particularly the case when the younger generations are involved.

9. General outlook

Heroin tourists were defined as foreigners who used opiates for at least six days per week. The users in our study had many things in common, but also showed significant differences. In fact, the term "heroin tourist" can be quite misleading. First of all, it was not always appropriate to define our respondents as "tourists". Some had been living in Amsterdam for a decade or more. Second and more importantly, many interviewees did not come to Amsterdam only because of heroin. If we defined everybody who takes drugs and travels as a drug tourist, then not many people would be excluded from our definition. We would have to define a large proportion of the Swedes taking the ferry to Denmark or Germany as alcohol tourists, many young people visiting Amsterdam as hash tourists, simply because they drink alcohol on the Swedish ferry or smoke hash in an Amsterdam coffee shop. If we restrict ourselves to heroin users, many travel rather frequently, not only to other countries, but also within their own country. A heroin user who lives in a town near Rotterdam will sometimes go to that city and buy heroin. However, he or she could also go to Rotterdam to do shopping or go to a concert. Consequently, most heroin users should be defined heroin tourists. Clearly, such a definition does not make much sense. I will not propose any alternative here; I just want to point out that labeling a person as an heroin tourist implicitly carries the risk of forgetting that his or her heroin use not always dominates daily life, but may be but one of many other characteristics.

In his novel "In the Dutch Mountains" Nooteboom (1984) pointed to something that strikes the eye of many visitors. "Dutch people do not merely meet; they confront each other. They bore their luminous eyes into another person's and weigh his soul. There are no hiding places. Not even their homes can be described as such. They leave their curtains open and regard this as a virtue." Illicit drug use is rather visible in Amsterdam. The same is true for prostitution and other social phenomena. This visibility easily leads to the conclusion that things are worse in the Netherlands. However, simply because in other countries the problems may not be as visible, it does not mean they do not exist.[30]

In general the reputation of Amsterdam's drug policy abroad has changed. It has gained respect for its public health approach: low-threshold methadone programs, syringe exchange, and so on. While the city of Amsterdam expands such harm reduction facilities, it does not like foreign users in its programs. There are some indications that the policy of discouragement has resulted in a smaller number of German heroin users in the city. On the other hand, they still come and stay in Amsterdam. This will most likely continue as long as the German drug policy is dominated by the paradigm of drug-free inpatient treatment and continues to be rather reluctant to implement methadone programs (Gerlach and Schneider 1991; Schneider 1989). This creates a major conflict in Dutch drug policy: harm reduction implies methadone for foreigners, whereas methadone programs are perceived as a stimulus for foreign users to come and stay in the Netherlands. It is undoubtedly far easier to decide that heroin tourists should be kept out of the domain of drug programs at the political (abstract) level than "down in the trenches". For doctors, nurses and social workers confronted with unsafe sex and unsafe use practices and other health problems it is not always possible to refrain from doing what they consider to be in the best interest of prevention and treatment.

Even when push factors in other countries would decrease significantly, it does not seem plausible that heroin tourism would completely disappear. As shown for the Italian subgroup, to some extent heroin users are not very different from "normal tourists". They like to travel and visit cities which are beloved by young people, e.g., London, Paris, Berlin, Barcelona and Rome. Consequently, heroin tourism is unavoidably part of general youth tourism and exists in all larger cities in Western Europe.

References

Adler, P.A.: *Wheeling and Dealing. An Ethnography of an Upper-Level Drug Dealing and Smuggling Community.* New York: Columbia University Press, 1985

AMOC: *Jahresbericht/Jaarverslag 1989.* Amsterdam: AMOC, 1990

Avico, U. and Mariani, F.: *Diffusione di Oppiacei e altre Psicodroghe e Profili degli Assuntori tra i Giovanni della Leva Militare 1982.* Rome: Istituto Superiore di Sanità, 1983

Baanders, A.: *De Hollandse Aanpak.* Assen, the Netherlands: Van Gorcum, 1989

Bach, K.: Sie fahren nach Amsterdam um zu sterben. *Das Neue* 45, November 5, 1984

Biernacki, P.: *Pathways from Heroin Addiction; Recovery without Treatment.* Philadelphia: Temple University Press, 1986

Biernacki, P. and Waldorf, D.: Snowball sampling: problems and techniques of chain referral sampling. *Sociological Methods and Research* 10:141-163, 1981

Brinkman, N.: *Over Dood en Dosis. Een Literatuuronderzoek naar Sterfte onder Heroinegebruikers.* Utrecht: NcGv-reeks 80, 1985

Buning, E.C.: *Het Drugprobleem in Cijfers. Deel IV.* Amsterdam: Municipal Health Service, 1990

Clayton, R.R. and Voss, H.L.: *Young Men and Drugs in Manhattan: A Causal Analysis.* Rockville, MD: NIDA (Research Monograph 39), 1981

Cobelens, F.G.J., Schrader, P.C. and Sluijs, Th.A.: *Acute Dood na Druggebruik in Amsterdam.* Amsterdam: Municipal Health Service, 1990

Cohen, P.D.A.: *Cocaine Use in Non-Deviant Subcultures.* Amsterdam: University of Amsterdam, Institute of Social Geography, 1990

Cuskey, W., Klein, A.W. and Krasner, W.: *Drug-Trip Abroad: American Drug Refugees in Amsterdam and London.* Philadelphia: University of Pennsylvania Press, 1972

De Kort, M. and Korf, D.J.: The development of drug trade and drug control in the Netherlands; a historical perspective. *Crime, Law and Social Change* 17:123-144, 1992

Drugsbeleid: Problemen, Taken en Doelstellingen. Amsterdam: Bureau Voorlichting van de Gemeente Amsterdam, 1985

Eikenaar, A.: Hoe Nederlandse drugshandelaars in de val worden gelokt. *De Tijd*, November 8, pp 8-11, 1986

Gerlach, R. and Schneider, W.: Abstinence and acceptance? A commentary on the problematic relationship between the German abstinence paradigm, low threshold oriented drug work, and methadone. *Australian Drug and Alcohol Review* 3, 1991

Glaser, B. and Strauss, A.: *The Discovery of Grounded Theory: Strategies for Qualitative Research.* Chicago: Aldline, 1967

Goos, C.: *Drogen über die Grenze. Zur Drogensituation in den Niederlanden und der Bundesrepublik Deutschland. Probleme deutscher und niederländischer Drogenabhangiger im Nachbarland*, pp 3-5. Arbeitsgemeinschaft für Jugendhilfe, 1979

Grapendaal, M. and Aidala, R.: *Duits Drugtoerisme in Arnhem.* The Hague: Ministery of Justice (WOCD), 1991

Hartnoll, R., Lewis, R., Mitcheson, M. and Bryer, S.: Estimating the prevalence of opioid dependence. *The Lancet*, January 26, 1985

Heering, A.: De Italianen komen! *Intermediair* 26(15):21-29, 1990

Hesser, K.-E.H.: Deutsche Jugendliche mit Drogenproblemen in Amsterdam. In: *Drogen über die Grenze. Zur Drogensituation in den Niederlanden und der Bundesrepublik Deutschland. Probleme deutscher und niederländischer Drogenabhängiger im Nachbarland*, pp 103-107. Arbeitsgemeinschaft für Jugendhilfe, 1979

Hesser, K.-E.H.: 100 Jahre Deutscher Hilfsverein in Amsterdam. In: *Hundert Jahre Deutscher Hilfsverein.* Amsterdam: AMOC/DHV, 1983

Holleran, A.: Gluurders in Amsterdam. *Clique* 1:11-15, 1990

Johnson, B.D. *et al.*: *Taking Care of Business. The Economics of Crime by Heroin Abusers.* Lexington, MA: Lexington Books, 1985

Kaplan, C.D.: The uneasy consensus: Prohibition and experimentalist expectancies behind the International Narcotics Control System. *Tijdschrift voor Criminologie* 26(2):89-109, 1984

Kaplan, C.D., Korf, D.J., Van Gelder, P. and Sijtsma, J.H.: *Floating Drug-Using Populations in Europe: Comparative Reflections with the Americas.* Proceedings of the Community Epidemiology Work Group. Rockville, MD: NIDA, 1990

Koda: *Inventarisatie Rapport van de Projectgroep Buitenlanders.* Amsterdam: Kontinu Overleg Drugs Amsterdam, 1975

Korf, D.J.: *Heroïne Toerisme II.* Amsterdam: University of Amsterdam, Institute of Social Geography, 1987

Korf, D.J. and De Kort, M.: *Drugshandel en Drugsbestrijding.* Amsterdam: Bonger Institute of Criminology, 1990

Korf, D.J. and Hoogenhout, H.P.H.: *Thuis op Straat.* Amsterdam: GGZ-reeks, 1989

Korf, D.J. and Hoogenhout, H.P.H.: *Zoden aan de Dijk.* Amsterdam: University of Amsterdam, Institute of Social Geography, 1990

Korf, D.J., Mann, R. and Van Aalderen H.: *Drugs op het Platteland.* Assen, the Netherlands: Van Gorcum, 1989

Korf, D.J., Van Aalderen, H., Hoogenhout, H.P.H. and Sandwijk, J.P.: *Gooise Geneugten.* Amsterdam: SPCP, 1990

Leuw, E.: Drugsgebruik in het Vondelpark 1972. *Tijdschrift voor Criminologie* 15:202-218, 1973

Leuw, E.: Door schade en schande. De geschiedenis van drugshulpverlening als sociaal beleid. *Tijdschrift voor Criminologie* 28(2):128-136, 1984

Morrison, V.L.: Observation and snowballing: Useful tools for research into illicit drug use?. *Social Pharmacology* 2(3):247-271, 1988

Musterd, S. and Kersloot, J.M.: *Environmental Quality and the Perception of Drugs in Neighbourhoods in Amsterdam.* Paper presented at the 16th ICAA Conference, May 30-June 5, Lausanne, 1987

Nooteboom, C.: *In the Dutch Mountains.* Baton Rouge, LA: Louisiana State University Press, 1984

PPP: *Passanten en Prostituées.* Jaarverslag over 1988, evaluatie en onderzoek. Amsterdam: Municipal Health Service, 1989

Plomp, H.N. and Van Oers, M.L.: *Roken, Alcohol- en Drugsgebruik onder Jongeren in het Nederlandse Euregiogebied.* Amsterdam: Free Reformed University, Institute of Social Medicine, 1989

Preble, E. and Miller, T.: Methadone, wine and welfare. In: Weppner, R.S. (Ed.) *Street Ethnography*, pp 229-248. Beverley Hills: Sage Publications, 1977

Reijneveld, S.A.: *Methadonverstrekking in Amsterdam in 1990.* Amsterdam: Municipal Health Service, Epidoc, 1991

Rubin, L.: *Worlds of Pain. Life in the Working-Class Family.* New York: Basis Books, 1976

Rüter, C.F.: Die strafrechtliche Drogenbekämpfung in den Niederlanden. Ein Königreich für Aussteiger? *Zeitschrift für die gesamte Strafrechtswissenschaft* 100(2):385-404, 1988

Schneider, W.: Das deutsche Abstinenzparadigma am Scheideweg. *Drogalkohol* 13:104-116, 1989

Skarabis, H. and Patzak, M.: *Die Berliner Heroinscene. Eine epidemiologische Untersuchung.* Weinheim: Beltz Verlag, 1981

Sterk, C.E.: *Living the Life. Prostitutes and their Health.* Rotterdam: Erasmus University, 1990 (Dissertation).

141

Süssmuth, R.: *Amsterdam längst kein "Drogen-Mekka" mehr.* Bonn: Pressedienst des Bundesministers für Jugend, Familie, Frauen und Gesundheit, 1989

Ten Have, P.: Jeugdtoerisme als Amsterdams probleem. *Maandblad voor Geestelijke Volksgezondheid* 28(9):375-386, 1973

Van Gemert, F.: *Mazen en netwerken.* Amsterdam: University of Amsterdam, Institute of Social Geography, 1988

Vasseur, P.: *The Amsterdam Approach of the Drug problem.* Paper presented at the European Conference on Drug Addictions, Barcelona, January 24-26, 1990

Verbraeck, H.T.: *De Staart van de Zeedijk.* Amsterdam: University of Amsterdam, Institute of Social Geography, 1988

Verbraeck, H.T.: The German bridge: A street hookers' strip in the Amsterdam Red Light District. In: Lambert, E.Y. (Ed.) *The Collection and Interpretation of Data from Hidden Populations,* pp 146-155. Rockville, MD: NIDA (Research Monograph 98), 1990

Watters, J.K. and Biernacki, P.: Targeted sampling: Options for the study of hidden populations. *Social Problems* 36(4):416-430, 1989

Werkgroep Verdovende Middelen: *Achtergronden en Risico's van Druggebruik.* Rapport van de Werkgroep Verdovende Middelen. The Hague: Staatsuitgeverij, 1972

Westermeyer, J.: *Poppies, Pipes and People. Opium and its Use in Laos.* Berkeley: University of California Press, 1982

Wiebel, W.W.: Identifying and Gaining Access to Hidden Populations. In: Lambert, E.Y. (Ed.) *The Collection and Interpretation of Data from Hidden Populations,* pp 4-11. Rockville, MD: NIDA (Research Monograph 98), 1990

Wimmer, F.: *Tätigkeitsbericht 1989 Bundesprojekt Rückkehrhilfe.* Münster, Germany: Landschaftsverband Westfalen-Lippe, 1990

Endnotes

1. The city has approximately 700,000 inhabitants. In 1989 almost eight million tourists were registered.
2. Northrhine-Westfalia is the German state (Bundesland) with the highest density of population. It is situated east of the Netherlands (*Parool,* January 22, 1975).
3. The target population was defined as non-Dutch persons who use opiates at least six days a week. Users from the Dutch Antilles, Surinam and Indonesia were excluded (since they are considered Dutch citizens).
4. According to Wiebel (1990:4) this term refers to "a subset of the general population whose membership is not readily distinguished or enumerated based on existing knowledge and/or sampling capabilities".
5. The mobility may be vertical (*e.g.* upward and downward social mobility in the drug trade) or horizontal (*e.g.* homeless).
6. For example, street prostitutes (Sterk 1990) or street dealers (Van Gemert 1988). Such studies can contribute to a better understanding of illicit drug use, lifestyles, networks, and so on, and may be applied to test hypotheses or to generate theories. Adler's exemplary study on upper level drug dealing clearly illustrates that ethnographic studies do not have to be limited to the visible segments of the drug market (Adler 1985).
7. This problem can be illustrated by two American examples. Is it legitimate to generate a developmental model from comparing a street sample of mainly black and Puerto Rican heroin users with a white sample ten years later, as was done in the famous study "Methadone, wine and welfare" (Preble and Miller 1977)? Can the contribution of heroin addicts to property crime in a city or country reliably be estimated from a sample interviewed in a store front in one of the most problematic neighborhoods in New York City (Johnson *et al.* 1985)?

8. Dr. Patrick Biernacki, a medical sociologist from San Francisco, was very helpful in finding solutions for the zero stage problem in our study.

9. Next to ethnographic knowledge, the concept of theroretical sampling (Glaser and Strauss 1967) was very helpful to complete the process of mapping. For a more detailed description, see Korf and Van Poppel (1986) and Korf (1987).

10. At a later date, the same procedure was used in a study among frequent hard drug users in an urbanized region (Korf *et al.* 1990), and homeless youth in the inner city of Amsterdam (Korf and Hoogenhout 1989). In doing the field work for a study among non-deviant cocaine users (Cohen 1990), we applied a slightly different procedure.

11. In practice almost all respondents did give their list to us.

12. This is a virtual necessity if one wants to obtain cooperation and meaningful data from community-based research samples (Wiebel 1990).

13. A panel of 38 heroin tourists was followed for more than a year and interviewed every three months. Test-retest analysis indicated that they do not remember their exact age of initiation (first use of various drugs) but the mean scores for the whole panel were rather stable. Income and expenditures for drugs and living during the past seven days were measured by two different questionnaires; self-report data appeared to be quite consistent.

14. In a household survey on the perception of the spread of drug use over the city, Musterd and Kersloot (1987) presented some interesting socio-geographical theories to explain why drug use is more prevalent in such parts of a city than in others.

15. There are some exceptions. Avico and Mariani (1983) analyzed urine from a large sample of male Italian recruits; 1.7% of the urine samples were positive for opiates. Clayton and Voss (1981) conducted an extensive prevalence study in a High Drug Use Area in Harlem (New York City).

16. Skarabis and Patzak (1981) described a number of techniques based on the assumption that most users know each other. Estimates can be generated from statistical computations based on spacial distribution, *e.g.* the distance between the place users live (density estimates). This kind of method seems more useful for rural than urban areas. Another technique to estimate the prevalence of frequent opiate use is to extrapolate the size of the populations from indirect parameters, *e.g.* hepatitis and overdoses.

17. This technique stems from ethology and is known as the capture-recapture technique. In order to estimate the number of fishes in a lake, a first sample is caught. The fishes are tagged and put into the lake again. A second sample is caught, including tagged fishes from the first sample. Assuming that both samples are independent, the population size can be estimated ($N = ni * jn/nij$. N = population size; ni = size of sample i; nj = size of sample j; nij = size of both samples i and j). The capture-recapture technique was applied to the drug field by Skarabis and Patzak (1981) in Berlin and by Hartnoll *et al.* (1985) in London. In our case, the samples were foreign methadone clients in the Municipal Methadone Program and foreigners receiving methadone after arrest at police stations.

18. Their number was thought to be higher because they were greatly over-represented among clients in the methadone programs as well as among arrestees and drug deaths. Apparently, German opiate users have a higher risk of lethal overdose than other subgroups (Cobelens *et al.* 1990).

19. This finding results from the answers to the question: "Who are the five persons in Amsterdam you know best?"

20. In later field studies we discovered comparable patterns. Surinamese users were mainly found in snowballs together with other Surinamese. The same was true for white Dutch users in Amsterdam. Although there was somewhat more overlap between the different ethnic groups in the local population of daily opiate users, we found that female prostitutes were rather isolated and seldom found in snowballs with non-prostitutes. Male prostitutes appeared to be more integrated in other segments of the heroin using population (Korf and Hoogenhout 1990).

21. The most prevalent combinations were: opiates and cocaine, but no alcohol or pills; opiates, but no cocaine, alcohol or pills; opiates and alcohol, but no cocaine or pills; opiates and cocaine and alcohol, but no pills.

22. Every year about 350,000 to 400,000 of those tourists (15-34 years old) visit the Dutch capital. Between 1980 and 1986 the number of Italian tourists in youth hotels and youth hostels in Amsterdam doubled.

23. Prostitution remained the most important source of income. Police activities apparently did not substantially affect the number of female street prostitutes. Where did they have an affect? Women had to leave their working area in the Red Light District and move to a more dangerous public location (Verbraeck 1990).

24. In a later field study among local daily opiate users we found that those living from drug business, blacks in particular, were more frequently arrested than those living from property crimes (Korf and Hoogenhout 1990).

25. A similar phenomenon was found among Dutch users in rural areas (Korf *et al.* 1989; Korf *et al.* 1990)

26. Estimates on such a parameter are not very reliable (Brinkman 1985). Changes in purity, police arrests and (lack of) methadone treatment appear to correlate with mortality (Korf 1990).

27. This seems a trivial change in policy. Although it is not possible to estimate the proportion of suicides among drug deaths, suicide certainly plays a role (Cobelens, Schrader and Sluijs 1990).

28. (*Badische Zeitung*, January 4, 1991). This number does not include statistics from the former German Democratic Republic. Consequently, the number is related to a population which is approximately five times larger than in the Netherlands. As a comparative indication: in cities with 2-3 times more citizens than Amsterdam much more heroin deaths were registered (135 in Berlin and 128 in Hamburg, mainly Germans; versus 13 Dutch heroin deaths in Amsterdam).

29. A comparable trend was found in other field studies. Heroin users in rural areas often bought small dosages of heroin in their home town, and slightly larger dosages in larger towns in the neighborhood. For some grams they would travel 50 miles or more. However, they would seldom go to Amsterdam (Korf *et al.* 1990). In a region closer to the Dutch capital, we found a larger proportion of users who also bought smaller dosages of heroin in Amsterdam. Public transport facilities appeared to be important: users from towns with good public transportation connections with Amsterdam would buy heroin there more often than those from towns with better connections to the largest town in the region (Korf *et al.* 1990)

30. For example, in a school survey conducted in a Dutch-German region, it was found that a small group of German students had been offered illicit drugs while in the Netherlands; however, the same survey also showed that several Dutch students had the same experience in Germany (Plomp and Van Oers 1989).

VIII. SNACKS, SEX AND SMACK
THE ECOLOGY OF THE DRUG TRADE IN THE INNER CITY OF AMSTERDAM

Frank van Gemert and Hans Verbraeck

1. Introduction

Law enforcement officials, custom agents, academic researchers or people who like to use drugs – in short, people with a more than average interest in illegal drugs – tend to strain their ears when hearing the magic word "Amsterdam". Amsterdam, and in particular the old center of the town, is viewed by many as a "dope fiend's paradise". In spite of fierce efforts by the City Council to change the city image, the center of Amsterdam is still known as an area where it is easy to buy illegal drugs. This image is only partially correct; many Amsterdam drug users now simply buy their drugs at their dealer around the corner and no longer go downtown for drugs. Besides, for the somewhat adept drug user it is equally easy to obtain illegal drugs in other Dutch, European and American cities. Yet, for a considerable length of time now, drug dealing has been closely intertwined with the daily reality of the old town center of Amsterdam.

In this Chapter we provide an ethnographic account of drug dealing in downtown Amsterdam from 1970, zeroing in on two streets: the Zeedijk and the Damstraat. It is our purpose to disentangle the *modus vivendi* in this complex habitat. From our chronological description it will become evident how drug dealing has left a mark on this section of town. We provide the context for understanding the nuisance resulting from the drug trade. In addition to discussing the national and international drug conjuncture, we focus attention on local factors; specifically, we argue that the same informal codes which have characterized the tolerant nature of the neighborhood have also provided the seeds for drug-related nuisance and problems in this area.

In addition to published scholarly and journalistic sources, we rely primarily upon our own data: fieldwork experiences and many conversations with drug users, drug dealers and local residents. The bulk of our fieldwork was done in the second half of the 1980s (Van Gemert 1985, 1987, 1988; Verbraeck 1988). A map of the central Amsterdam area is provided to complement our ethnographic account (Fig. 1).

Central Station

↑

Dam Square

←

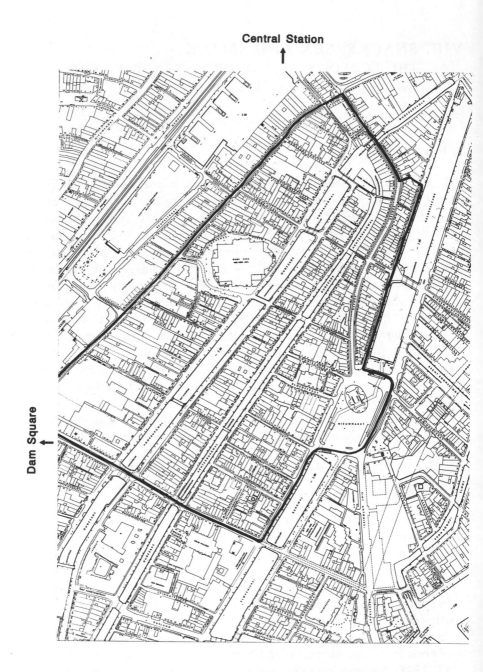

Fig. 1. Map of the central area of Amsterdam ("drugs and prostitution area" within the solid line, scale 1:5000). Reproduced by courtesy of the "Dienst Openbare Werken Amsterdam".

2. The history of the old city

The history of the Amsterdam city center dates back into the Middle Ages. Amsterdam became wealthy through overseas trade. All activities in earlier centuries were closely linked to shipping and trade. The Zeedijk, at present still the most infamous copping street of Europe, was then directly connected to the Amsterdam IJ harbor where the entire sailing world appeared to set foot ashore. A network of narrow streets and alleys, intersected by canals, emerged. Because of its busy harbor, the old town center soon became populated with bars and prostitutes. Still, throughout the centuries this old town center remained a residential area with many small shops and businesses. These small neighborhood stores continue to exist. Residents came from all possible directions. Many population groups exiled from other areas settled there and foreign merchants and sailors also permanently established themselves in Amsterdam. Part of this last category was made up of Chinese who successfully introduced the Chinese food culture to the city during the Depression. The Chinese established their own permanent community in several blocks within the center of town. Not only did they bring a new culinary experience, they simultaneously introduced the smoking of opium to Dutch society. In the Binnenbantammerstraat, between the restaurants and shops, a few opium dens emerged. Unlike the United States, after the introduction of opium legislation (Musto 1973), such opium dens were initially tolerated and were not harassed or abolished.

What exactly triggered the demise of the neighborhood is not clear. In any case, in the course of the 20th century, the Amsterdam harbor continuously became less important and the Second World War gave a serious blow to the neighborhood. Before the war, the Nieuwmarkt neighborhood was 40% Jewish. In 1942, a section of this neighborhood was made into a "Judenviertel" by the occupying forces and afterwards many Jews were deported. Following the Second World War, the city developed a plan to demolish the deserted and dilapidated streets and to establish a commercial center. However, local residents had different plans; they wanted to keep the neighborhood essentially residential. For about 30 years, city and residents were pre-occupied with the issue of the destination of the neighborhood. Ultimately, the wishes of the residents were realized (Van Breenen *et al.* 1987; Koster 1987).

The heart of a western city tends to consist of modern business buildings or, conversely, is characterized by large older buildings, reflecting a rich history. Unlike New York or Paris, Amsterdam does not have millions of residents and, thus, the old center of the city resembles in no way a major world capital. No enormous buildings, old or new, but a few canals and a maze of streets and alleys packed with houses, seldom counting more than three floors. In the old town center, one finds the grocer and the used book store next to the cafe and the snackbar. Around the corner, there may be a gambling hall and, within a stone's throw, sparsely clad women seated behind the windows, "Hi honey, how about it?" It is in this area, an area which more closely resembles a village rather than a metropolis, where the drug trade, eventually known far across national borders, began to develop.

Initially it was primarily sailors who sought their entertainment in this neighborhood; however, students, intellectuals, artists, jazz musicians and homosexuals gradually began to frequent the area. Consequently, the customers of the opium dens began to change. In addition to the customers who had been coming there for decades (in the Chinese community opium is a common old-age provision), members of the above-mentioned groups also began to experiment with opium. This development, beginning in the 1950s, continued into the next decade. Of course, youths all over the world began to use a variety of drugs during the 1960s (Cohen 1975; Perry 1985). Speed, cannabis, hallucinogens and cocaine now became part of the scene. In the Binnenbantammerstraat, a growing number of users waited daily until a Chinese resident would emerge willing to sell opium for ten guilders per gram.

"I remember the sound of the dice from the gambling house, tens of Chinese standing in the door opening. And myself waiting for the opium den at number 16. Or in front of the den across the street...... The grandfathers were addicted themselves. Very striking types.

It was quite an art to get the drugs, badgering, asking, it did not just happen..... We called him Pepper and Salt because of his hair. From a worn billfold he would get the packet. Was wearing a silk, quilted robe (Verhey 1985:27)."

In the winter of 1971-1972 it became increasingly difficult to obtain opium (Stoute 1985). The production of opium was halted in Turkey, and more and more opium from the Golden Triangle was transformed into heroin (Fromberg *et al.* 1976).

In the summer of 1972, there was suddenly an increase in the supply of heroin for sale in Amsterdam, which had been very seldom the case in the late sixties. Young tourists, among them a remarkable number of Americans, easily spent their money on the dirt cheap horse ($10-$20 per gram). At that time, drug enforcement agents had other priorities, among other things cannabis and opium. Heroin was thus sold very publicly and without any interference in the city, among other places in a few cafes at the Nieuwmarkt. Financial interests appeared non-existent; in the summer of 1972 horse was freely shared and distributed.

The honeymoon, during which the Amsterdam scene became acquainted with the ridiculously cheap heroin, lasted only one year. The police became interested in this particular drug (in 1971 only 50 grams of horse was confiscated; in 1973 this was 23 kilos) and the bars at the Nieuwmarkt where heroin was sold were closed, one by one. The price of heroin increased, the purity decreased, and more and more organized Chinese criminal groups got involved in the trade and imported ever-increasing amounts.

An illustration of the typical criminal group member is provided by Verhey (1985:27). "Hard flashy fellows from Singapore, guys who don't use themselves, golden toothpick in the mouth, pushy."

In the downtown area, the manner of doing drug business changed in order to spread the risks. The Chinese bosses were looking for intermediaries and they found what they were looking for in the young Surinamese immigrants, who came to the Netherlands in large numbers in the second half of the 1970s. They provided an important retail market and belonged to a category who smoked heroin and cocaine by heating a dose on aluminum foil and sucking up the smoke through a straw. From this point in time, the Zeedijk plays a crucial role in the drug trade; in a later stage, the Damstraat also began to emerge as an important area for the drug business.

3. Drug dealing in the inner city

Gradually, then, illegal drug dealing became more common in the inner city. Although the illegal drug business maintained an uneasy and tense relationship with the respectable order, it managed to become firmly entrenched in two streets: the Zeedijk and the Damstraat. On the Zeedijk, drug dealing began to overshadow everything else; on the Damstraat, drug dealing took place in the middle of other functions.

3.1 The Zeedijk

3.1.1 Heroin cafes

Young Surinamese visited the inner city and the South American street corner culture was centered around the bars and nightlife in the Nieuwmarkt area. They frequented the cafes on the Zeedijk where heroin was sold from behind the counter. These cafes were soon referred to as "heroin cafes". Using and dealing became a daily routine for the immigrants. The sale from the bars at the head of the Zeedijk was left undisturbed in the mid 1970s. By 1978, there were seven heroin cafes in the Zeedijk area, when the police initiated the first actions against these cafes. For a brief period, the Surinamese dealers and their customers were chased away from the Zeedijk. They came adrift, taking over a Surinamese social service agency which was consequently closed, forcing them to move through the city from one cafe to the next. At the local level, the Zeedijk lost its prominent drug trade position. During the time that the Surinamese dealers and their customers moved through the city, drugs were sold more and more from private homes. Only a small group of users, consisting primarily of Surinamese users, was not able to find a steady address for buying drugs. After a while, this group returned to the Zeedijk. The number of cafes where dealing took place rapidly increased to about 30 establishments in the entire street by 1981. Now Chinese intermediaries and Surinamese were fighting for dominance on the Zeedijk. Before the Chinese intermediaries completely disappeared from the retail trade, the street was split up: the Surinamese dealt in one section of the Zeedijk (from the head to the Stormsteeg) and the Chinese in another (from the Stormsteeg to the Nieuwmarkt).

The heroin cafes were usually Surinamese family businesses. One person, the head of the enterprise, was in charge of buying the drugs, while about every six months new sales people were hired to replace the old ones. Dealing from such establishments was conducted with a maximum concern for safety. Outside, people on the lookout warned those inside by pounding on the rain pipes whenever they saw potential trouble. Because only a little dope was kept in the house and because often there were hidden food elevators and secret exits, it was virtually impossible for the police to find contraband. This allowed such establishments to remain virtually impregnable vestiges.

Ordinary citizens began to avoid this street because of its sinister atmosphere. Those passers-by who were lost, were invariably "vacuum-cleaned" on the Zeedijk: robbed of money, cameras, and jewelry. Meanwhile, the police obtained authority to close those cafes where dealing took place; however, this measure had a limited effect since an evicted dealer was easily able to find another location to continue his business. Property owners realized that there was only one type of renter left on the Zeedijk – the drug dealer with a large amount of money. A rent of 1,200 guilders (some $600; half of that amount would be considered high under normal circumstances) was paid without any problem for a simple apartment; if it were not for the drug money, such a high rent would not have been affordable. It was not until the city gained control over the distribution of housing and began to systematically purchase the properties that such retail locations disappeared. Drug dealing increasingly began to take place in the streets; and the system of Surinamese family-run heroin cafes collapsed.

In that period, the bulk of the heroin in Amsterdam came from the Golden Triangle, but by the end of the 1970s another type of heroin was introduced into the local market place. At a high level in the heroin trade a war was fought between Chinese dealers from Singapore and Chinese dealers from Hong Kong. Afterwards, a second connection increased in importance; Turkish organized crime started to import increasing amounts of very potent horse from Pakistan. In contrast to earlier years, heroin was transported primarily over land with cities in Middle Europe gaining increased importance as distribution centers. Amsterdam retreated somewhat to the background of the drug distribution scene. At the same time, low-threshold methadone maintenance programs were implemented in Amsterdam and several other Dutch cities. Users applied for these programs in large numbers. Although many had already experimented with other drugs, the introduction of methadone programs resulted in the increased importance of cocaine and other psychopharmaceutical drugs in the inner city. In addition, alcohol received a more dominant position on the menu of the user.

3.1.2 Street trade

The strategy of street dealing was quite different from the strategy used in the heroin cafes. Some street dealers operated individually and protected their safety merely through a few places on the street where they hid their goods. They approached potential customers themselves. Other dealers worked on a larger scale; they decided to spread the risk and hired assistants – several people who sold drugs, one person who kept his drug supplies and another who safeguarded his money. They also hired "messenger boys" who were continuously on the lookout for potential customers, whom they sent to a dealer or his agent in exchange for drugs or money. Occasionally a person was hired as a lookout. As compensation he would receive drugs, provided he did his job well. The dealer himself simply observed the trading without any visible involvement.

Although the Zeedijk was seriously decaying, Amsterdam residents continued to reside there and a part of the neighborhood infrastructure remained intact. The butcher, the fishmonger, the grocer, the "normal" cafes remained, as did the Chinese restaurants and shops. In the early 1980s, the city in conjunction with the business community developed a plan to restore the century-old buildings for use by new shops, businesses and residents. As a result, in the second half of the 1980s, there were several buildings in scaffolds and the area was buzzing with construction and renovation activity.

Along with the economic restoration projects the police were also given more legal power to intervene in drug-related activities. The city took several administrative emergency measures primarily geared towards dealing with the problems on the Zeedijk. A "no knives" ordinance was implemented in 1981. Other local ordinances authorized the police to prohibit individuals or groups from assembling (1984) or from entering the area for a certain time period (1983). Furthermore, the police expanded its surveillance significantly. A special police team was established, the "local unit", which focused exclusively on street dealing; additional police officers and undercover agents began to patrol the Zeedijk area. Mounted police and police officers with dogs appeared. In 1985 a special Zeedijk team was established and in 1987 (the year of our most intensive fieldwork in the area) no fewer than six police officers were on patrol 24 hours a day on the Zeedijk - a street no more than 500 feet long! The battle between the scene and the police was grim and sometimes resulted in chaotic scenes:

"The corner of the Zeedijk and the Molensteeg is crowded, here are at least 50 users and dealers. A police van drives by. The first time it passes by, a part of the group simply stays. When they do not obey the request to move, one of the officers gets out with a German shepherd dog. A peculiar parade then develops: a big wave of users and dealers who quickly make a few more deals, behind them the police officer with the dog and finally the van with the barred windows. When the van passes by for the second time, the corner area begins to fill up again. This cat-and-mouse game is repeated three more times before the users and dealers finally retreat to the Nieuwmarkt."

Although the reader would perhaps expect differently after reading the foregoing account, the battle on the Zeedijk is not over yet. Even as this is written, a lively drug trade continues; one can hear people advertising their merchandise while scanning things like "big and small brown" (referring to consumer doses of heroin of $20 and $10) and "big and small white" (doses of cocaine at the same prices). The dealers who stay around in the neighborhood continuously adjust their strategies. Presently, anybody passing through the Zeedijk area will see a very conspicuous, public and drab tip of the iceberg of heroin dealing and heroin using Amsterdam: a continuously shrinking, yet unceasingly problematic remaining group of street junkies and dealers continue their daily presence in the inner city.

3.2 The Damstraat

3.2.1 Street dealers, house dealers and messenger boys

In contrast to the Zeedijk which has always been a noisy "party" street, the Damstraat is characterized more as a shopping street. Beginning at Dam square, the street provides an important pedestrian connection to the Stopera (city hall and opera under one roof). Many pedestrians, in particular tourists, are "sucked into" this street, either by design or by coincidence.

Even in the 1970s visitors bought their hash from street dealers in the Damstraat. These dealers earned gold during the vacation periods. They approached every potential buyer muttering the words "hash, hash". Several restaurant and bar managers realized that they could attract more customers by allowing people to "smoke" in their establishment. Not surprisingly, drug dealers also started to hang out in these places. Trying to prevent all drug dealing required enormous effort by the management of these establishments. After a while it became clear that some businesses had made a virtue of necessity. No longer did they resist cannabis dealing; instead, they began to actively participate in it.

This introduced a novel phenomenon: coffee shops where one could buy hash. Around 1980 there were only about four such coffee shops, however this number has expanded explosively since then. The growth has been so tremendous that presently, for many Amsterdam locals, the first thing that comes to mind with the word "coffee shop" is marihuana, not coffee.

The users preferred to buy in a quiet coffee shop, where one did not need to be on the constant look out for the police. Furthermore, they soon realized that the chance of buying furniture polish or other fake hash was considerably smaller in a coffee shop than on the streets.

In these establishments, the management usually appointed one person who was the only person authorized to sell hash and weed. As a rule, the management took care of the drug supply. Particularly in the early days of the coffee shop, this "house dealer" was presumed to conduct business with the utmost caution. However, once it was realized that dealing in these places was left virtually undisturbed, more publicity became the rule. One advertised in the local paper and the coffee shops were easily recognizable by the large marihuana leaves on the windows. Selling no longer occurred in secret. It used to be typical that a customer would discretely ask for the house dealer and then proceed to buy inconspicuously a small packet from this house dealer, who "just happened to be there". At present, customers simply walk up to the counter and ask what is for sale. Either they are shown the different types or they are referred to the "menu" which is clearly visible hanging on the wall.

In November 1987, when a few of the coffee shops experienced tax-related trouble and it was announced that strict measures would be taken against public advertising of the hash business, a shock reverberated throughout the world of the coffee shops. The marihuana leaves were removed from the windows or hidden behind stickers, but soon it was business as usual when there was absolutely no evidence of a mass persecution.

By the mid 1980s, hash was only seldom sold on the streets. The street dealers lost the competition with the house dealers in the coffee shops. Thus, those people who used to deal in hash on the streets were forced to start selling other drugs or to stop street dealing completely. This resulted in a separation of the drugs market.

"Two dealers who for years on end had only sold hash, disappeared from the streets and started to concentrate on growing "Netherweed". Both of these men presently supply several Amsterdam coffee shops with this drug. Thus, although they turned their backs on street dealing, they have remained faithful to their line of business."

While the hash trade continued from the coffee shops, the dealing in hard drugs flourished on the streets. It remained primarily the tourists who provided the market for these drugs. Due to the changed nature of their merchandise, the dealers were now guilty of more serious offenses than before. Moreover, one was no longer limited to selling one type of drug. The successful dealer had to be able to supply several drugs at short notice. As a result, the street dealers began to work with messenger boys, who operated basically in the same fashion as their counterparts on the Zeedijk.

Only the more reckless street dealers remained active. The newcomers were also willing to take greater risks, resulting in a changed composition of this group. Initially it was mostly Dutch hash smokers who tried to sell their beloved "Libanon, Afghan or Marok", but later there was a growing number of addicts who also attempted to get rid of horse and coke. Most of them, however, had empty pockets and hoped to find customers as messenger boys. This group included an increasing number of foreign people. "Ripping off" increased and street dealing developed a bad reputation. The street was no longer "respectable" for dealing in hard drugs. Although Dutch users still buy their horse and coke mainly on the Zeedijk or from private addresses, buyers in the Damstraat are usually, at most, only two handshakes away from a person who can supply a considerable dose of any desired drug.

3.2.2 Pill trade

During the summer of 1985 as the newly established Zeedijk police team began to enforce the law in a more stringent fashion, several Dutch users moved to the Damstraat. Near the bridge at the Oudezijds Achterburgwal, a meeting place was established for predominantly older heroin users. Typically, passers-by felt pity for them and there was virtually no initial objection to their increasingly conspicuous presence. Gradually, more "sick" users came to this meeting point. There was always somebody among those present who was willing to sell a few methadon pills. Starting in the summer of 1986, this bridge was commonly referred to as the "Pill Bridge". More and more people were attracted by the pill dealing. Not only "sick" addicts came here, but also a growing number of dealers took advantage of this readily available market. Dependent upon the presence of the law, they praised their merchandise in loud or subdued voices: "Metha", or "Rooie Knol" – a Dutch version of the sleeping pill called Rohypnol. Such transactions took place on the streets with little effort to conceal business. The pills were counted out in the hand of the buyer who paid in cash. In this manner, every addict who received methadone in pill form could thus sell his own dose. As soon as they were rid of their pills, the addicts would no longer hang around at the bridge, rather they would disappear in the direction of a horse dealer at the Zeedijk. Often the person who had sold methadone earlier would get in trouble himself a few days later and rush to the bridge to take his turn buying methadone pills. This short-term planning and the small profit margins resulted in a relatively low status of those involved in selling pills. Among those involved in the drug scene were the pill sellers; one does not speak of "pill dealers" – a term which provides a certain amount of status – but rather of "pill sellers". Pill sellers were not afraid to be picked up by the police; it involved only minor violations and they would be released very quickly again. Consequently, for a number of years, this trade was very visible in the Damstraat. More recently, however, it seems that the selling of pills has moved somewhat underground as a result of renewed intensive police intervention.

3.3 The Zeedijk and the Damstraat: Drug monoculture vs transitional zone

The shopkeepers who refused to leave the Zeedijk were forced to accept the conspicuous presence of the illegal drug business. The visitors of the street were nearly always involved with drugs. If one were to refuse them as customers, many of the shops would no longer have been profitable. Many shopkeepers compensated for their loss in revenue by fencing stolen goods or by subletting their building. Slowly but surely the respectable order on the Zeedijk disappeared in the monoculture of drug dealing.

On the other hand, the Damstraat continues to serve functions other than illegal drug dealing; it provides a transitional zone between the dominant culture and the culture of drug dealing. In this street, young tourists are customers of both shops, restaurants, bars and drug dealers. Snackbars, headshops, t-shirt shops, cafes and coffee shops are legitimate enterprises, however, they do profit from the appeal of the drug culture. This transitional zone has the advantage that the drug user is able to obtain illegal drugs without being stigmatized. After all, both (legitimate) shopping and buying (illegal) drugs are plausible activities in this area. This explains why novice users or users from out of town are mainly found in this street.

3.3.1 Neighborhood nuisance

By the early 1970s, Amsterdam had become a mecca for students, tourists and dropouts; the National Monument at the Dam square became a popular gathering place for hash-smoking "hippies". In 1971, members of the Royal Dutch Navy, upon their own initiative, and with a great show of force, attempted to remove these hippies from the square. Without a doubt, this action was an unambiguous expression of disapproval of the non-conformism of these so-called "dam sleepers". Although this action took place in the inner city, it was neither initiated nor supported by the local residents. At that time, there were virtually no feelings of nuisance caused by drug using or drug dealing in the neighborhood. A great deal of time passed before the tolerant attitude of the neighborhood was transformed into protest.

"A restaurant manager in the Zeedijk area scrubbed his sidewalk every day during the 1970s. A few times a day he stood in front of his door with a baseball bat and on a regular basis he used this weapon to refuse admittance to members of the scene. It was the consensus of the other people in the neighborhood that this was going too far and he encountered a wall of misunderstanding."

3.4 The Zeedijk

Initially, the nuisance associated with the heroin cafes remained limited. Throughout the 1970s, occasional police actions against such establishments were not the results of local complaints, but were mainly inspired by the fact that the Dutch Opium Act contained severe penalties for heroin, the main drug on the Zeedijk at that time.

Local complaints and protests gained momentum, however, when the scene – after making many detours through the city – returned to the Zeedijk and drug dealing on the street increased substantially. In earlier days, local business made money from the rough sailors (sex and booze), but now it was mostly the dealers who profited from the daily visitors to the Zeedijk. The revival of the heroin trade mainly harmed the residents of the northern section of the Zeedijk. They felt that the boundaries of tolerance had been crossed and they organized themselves in the Crisis Committee Zeedijk. However, the Zeedijk residents who lived closer to the Nieuwmarkt were not yet ready for mobilization into action (see next paragraph). In the Fall of 1981, the Crisis Committee Zeedijk distributed posters with a cynical text. Some time later, these angry locals occupied the council chamber in City Hall during a city council meeting; in protest, they threw fake heroin (detergent) and needles all over the place.

The number of businesses selling drugs grew and now virtually all residents had some unpleasant experience with the drug scene. A drug monoculture developed. The shopkeepers lost most of their income and street robbery occurred frequently. The problem at the head of the Zeedijk now became a problem for a large part of the neighborhood, thus causing solidarity to grow. A neighborhood committee, called "The Old Town", was organized. This committee included several leftist academicians and functioned as a tolerant mouth-piece for the neighborhood; for example, the distribution of heroin was proposed as a possible solution. Taking up the national discussion concerning this, they explicitly asked for government distribution of heroin. In the view of the neighborhood, the users were sick. Voices also argued in favor of creating "sanctuaries" for users: carefully selected places where people could use hard drugs without interference by the police.

Distribution of heroin never became a reality. Yet, an important point is that local policy was not aimed only at maintaining public order; there was also much concern with the well-being of addicts. With explicit approval of the neighborhood, treatment and assistance played an important role in the approach to the drug problem.

When the economic restoration plan Zeedijk began to take shape and most of the drug distribution locations were closed, numerous buildings were targeted for extensive restoration work. The street acquired a desolate character, which not in the least affected the drug street trade.

In 1984, the "junkboat" (a sanctuary for addicts) was closed, resulting in a growing presence of addicts on the Zeedijk. It was at this moment that the neighborhood, for the very first time, initiated plans to use force against the scene. City Hall responded by instructing the newly established police team to rid the Zeedijk area of addicts. The addicts dispersed throughout the inner city, but when it became obvious that the police action was only a temporary effort, the scene returned to the Zeedijk. Meanwhile, the viewpoints hardened and the addicts became criminals in the eyes of many local residents.

3.5 The Damstraat

During the same period, the shopkeepers in the Damstraat complained bitterly about the decay of their street. During the many meetings of the association of shopkeepers and at neighborhood meetings (where often the police were also represented) it became obvious that public confidence in official measures had been reduced to nil. Trying to get rid of shabbily dressed junkies in front of one's windows had become a daily routine.

"On May 21 1985, angry neighborhood residents hung posters with pictures of needles all over City Hall. The text, "Amsterdam's got 'it'" used by the city to emphasize the appeal of the city, changed to "Amsterdam has had it".

"In September 1985, the residents of the Damstraat protest, somewhat playfully, against the presence of a group of junkies. They retrieve old bicycle wrecks from the canals and use these to barricade the bench on the Pill Bridge. However, by the next day, the now quite popular cry of "Metha, methadon" can be heard all over again."

It was not only the junkies who gave the inner city a bad name. The "ball ball" game (a variant of the three card game), duping hundreds of ignorant passers-by, was also a thorn in the side of the neighborhood. Characters involved in this game were considerably more capable in defending themselves than the junkies. Some shopkeepers were prepared to chase addicts away; however, upsetting the gambling criminals was an entirely different story. Before any steps against the "ball ball" game were taken, cries of distress were heard repeatedly in the national newspapers.

"The "ball ball" game is very often played in front of a particular cafe in the Damstraat. The gamblers do not honor the barkeeper's request to move to another spot. In early June 1986, two large flower boxes appear in front of the business. The game is now played somewhere else. Very soon it becomes apparent that wire-netting has to be installed over the boxes, as passers-by express their appreciation by taking the plants."

In November 1986, city government provided a permit to place a fritter stand on the Pill Bridge, precisely on the spot where the junkies tended to sit. Mysteriously, at the same time, a person appeared whose job consisted of trying to get rid of the addicts. This person was also of questionable reputation; and initially it was not clear who paid his salary. Very soon, however, it became apparent that a number of neighborhood shopkeepers had been reaching into their wallets to pay this person. Although the "bouncer" had no legal authority, he threatened with violence and, occasionally, he suited his action to his word. The simple result was that the pill family moved less than one hundred meters to the next bridge.

When it became clear that other shopkeepers now ended up with junkies in front of their door, it was decided to hire a few more "dumb muscle men". In February 1987, following the example of the fritter stand, a candy stand was set up on the bridge over the Oudezijds Voorburgwal - the bridge that functioned as a meeting place for addicts. In March 1987, a few muscle men appeared; thus, the junkies moved to the bridge over the Kloveniersburgwal - their last station for now. Meanwhile, one thing was becoming very clear: the addicts would not disappear, but only move to another spot. Although in November 1987, a hamburger stand was placed here, this third bridge has remained the place where pills are sold.

These developments received extra attention in the summer of 1987 due to citizen disapproval of a wave of publications concerning Rohypnol, a sleeping pill sold daily on the Pill Bridge. It was claimed that the most horrible crimes had been committed under the influence of this drug; soccer vandals, allegedly, had also discovered it. Temporarily it seemed as if a new criminal drug problem presented itself in the Netherlands which resulted in deliberations in parliament to take this product out of circulation. However, because this pill is not essentially different from other benzodiazepines, one soon realized that this would only be a spurious solution to the problem.

"For several days in the Spring of 1987, a few neighborhood residents collected the wrappings of the pills sold on the bridge.

Because the names of the users were printed on the boxes, it could be determined, without question, that the pills came from the drug-assistance programs."

Paralleling developments on the Zeedijk, all residents and shopkeepers of the Damstraat were now convinced of the gravity of the situation. At this moment, for the first time, actions were not only possible; they were also supported by the entire inner city. At different meetings the neighborhood vocalized its demands, and the city agreed to implement the "Summer Plan". The Summer Plan (implemented between April and September of 1987 in downtown Amsterdam) involved an increased police presence on the streets and more enforcement against illegal drug trade. The priority of police drug policy was to maintain public order. The cat-and-mouse game became more grim and thus the "dealers guild" more alert.

"Details of the appearance of the undercover police officers made it possible to determine their identity irrefutably. Because undercover officers never patrolled on a bike, it appeared a smart move to start using bicycles. However, service bicycles in perfect condition are very conspicuous in the city center, even with an undercover police officer instead of an officer in uniform. That is why the dealers easily recognized these officers. After a while, they started to use older bikes."

After the 1987 summer period, the police force was reduced to its former size and according to many, the situation remained essentially the same, except, perhaps, that the junkies had become more mobile. They now covered a larger territory; those who were formerly only active on the Zeedijk were now also found in the Damstraat.

In October 1988, the neighborhood once again expressed its displeasure with the city. It was said that, although police were willing to act, their hands were tied. Consequently, an administrative solution to the problem was demanded. The tolerant position had now definitely disappeared; the neighborhood committee, "The Old Town", rejected its former position and turned forcefully against drug use and trade in the area. A large number of area residents and shopkeepers assembled and a long parade, armed with banners, went directly to City Hall. *En route,* the group was joined by several classes of school children, a group from a nursing home and a delegation from the Chinese business community.

"Between familiar faces of shopkeepers, bar managers and women from the neighborhood, I also saw one which amazed me tremendously, "German Hans", a hash and coke dealer and a more-than-average user, walked with a sign saying "We don't take it anymore". Later I heard that he had opened a coffee shop close to the Nieuwmarkt."

On foot, the parade progressed to City Hall to a city council meeting which had the drug problem on its agenda. Once in the council chamber, the parties involved expressed their discontent until everything became so disorderly that the meeting was adjourned.

Two weeks later, the neighborhood once again felt the need to emphasize its demands. During rush hour one evening, a blockade of burning car tires was set up at the Prins Hendrikkade. There were no further incidents, but traffic was completely stalled for two hours.

Thus, public feelings of nuisance increased and the government apparently was not able to respond efficiently and effectively to this problem. It is commonly assumed that public annoyance is a direct result of drug use and drug dealing. To a degree this is true; however, one cannot help wondering how it was possible for the drug trade to become so firmly entrenched in the city center in the first place. It is our hypothesis that local behavior codes provided an important and fertile ground for the drug trade, which is why the neighborhood needs to take some responsibility for its own problems.

4. Codes, crime and crisis

It may be argued that the proverbial Amsterdam tolerance originated in its central downtown area. A number of free spirits played a vital part in this process.

"In the middle of this century, Bet van Beeren was the queen of the Zeedijk. In cafe "Het Mandje" which she managed, everybody was welcome, not in the least homosexuals of both sexes. If intimate scenes threatened to be witnessed by the wrong eyes, Bet gave a warning. Even before the spoilsport entered, everybody was informed."

"Zwarte Joop" was born in the neighborhood and his career started with the illegal showing of pornographic movies in a small theater. In the 1970s and 1980s, this self-made man owned a sex and gambling empire at the Walls. He himself established a security service to ensure a smooth visit for those who entered his business. Virtually everybody, including the police, overlooked the occasional use of violence.

"About eight men were stationed at each bridge and everybody who dealt (drugs) was beaten up. Everybody who was black and out on the street after two o'clock was thrown into the canal. Once this group pursued a Surinamese who had knifed a Swede, all the way to the Oudekerksplein, like a kind of posse, and then proceeded to break his nose with a baseball bat. The next day, police chief Nicaise paid a visit to Joop to ask if he could lay off a little" (Middelburg 1988:162).

"Joop died on July 13, 1986. His empire was about to collapse due to large tax debts and in December 1983, a large part of his nightclub was reduced to ashes because of a revenge-motivated arson."

Although both their activities went against respectable order, both Zwarte Joop and Bet van Beeren were celebrated people in the neighborhood. Both were bending the rules, but not only to their own benefit. Many bars attracted extra customers since the city center allowed homosexuals the opportunity to move around freely, and safety in the neighborhood was more important for local residents than the fact that the police did not have the monopoly on the use of force.

People who elsewhere would have been damned, taunted, or barred, thus found a supportive environment for their practices in the inner city of Amsterdam. That is why this area, for a long time, housed a colorful collection of non-conformists who, attracted by the tolerant climate, live in a symbiotic relationship with the other locals residents. How may we explain this? Are the rules different in this area? We have already shown that it is possible to break the law without violating the codes of the neighborhood. The opposite, however, is also possible.

"In early September 1986, a souvenir shop on the Zeedijk and a barbershop a few streets away were vandalized and occupied by neighborhood residents. This was a protest against the sale of drug paraphernalia from these premises (needles for $1.25; a quarter of a lemon, indispensable to dissolve Pakistan heroin, and pieces of tin-foil, both for $0.50)...... The barber relented and gave up the sale of drug paraphernalia; however, the legal sale of needles from the souvenir shop was only briefly interrupted by the neighborhood action and continues until this day. In this manner, the manager of this shop has isolated himself permanently from the rest of the neighborhood."

What is considered right or wrong by the neighborhood and what has been described by law as such are not necessarily one and the same. In addition to this substantive difference, legal codes tend to have unambiguous boundaries, while neighborhood codes know more gradual distinctions. The already-mentioned "ball ball" game is a case in point.

"As early as 1980 a few Yugoslavs played the "ball ball" game at the Walls and near the Oudemanhuispoort. The gambling game drew attention, but was only occasionally played in the summer. In 1985, a few Moroccan boys show up in the Damstraat who introduced the game again. They made good money, but they were not able to deal with unhappy losers."

"Therefore they came to an agreement with several Dutch criminals who participated in the game and who, if necessary, used force to protect the profits. Because of the profits and the limited resistance encountered, the players became reckless and more and more unsavory situations developed: traffic jams, fights and arrogant behavior with the large amounts of money."

In 1988, the police received permission to deal more harshly with the participants. The game is no longer played in Amsterdam. In principle, there was little resistance to this illegal gambling game; however, as it began to occur on a large scale and began to dominate the street, considerable opposition developed. As opposed to those who had introduced it, the newcomers used the game in an excessive fashion, thus offending residents of the neighborhood.

What do the codes of the inner city entail? What is allowed and what is not? We may distinguish three criteria. First, it is important that there is not an unacceptable amount of neighborhood nuisance and disturbance associated with the activity. Second, the situation is affected by whether there are recognizable victims. It is no coincidence that "permissible" deviant behavior primarily centers around "crimes without victims": gambling, drugs, sex, fencing. A third criterion is that it has to involve activities that can also be carried out by non-offenders. Thus, the nature of the violations does not result in the stigmatization of the offender and the social removal of the offender from the non-offenders. Fencing, in particular, is closely intertwined with the everyday realities of the inner city, and many cannot stop themselves from taking advantage of stolen goods.

"In a downtown cafe, virtually every day drug addicts come by to offer stolen goods for sale. To prevent confusion, the names of the two "salesmen", both named Peter, received an addition referring to their specialty: Peter "Bike" and Peter "Book"."

That dealing in soft drugs also takes place within the reach of the ordinary citizen becomes apparent from the following reflections by a bar manager:

"All day I tried to keep the street dealers out. I had become a thief from my own wallet. On the street everything was sold, the police did nothing. And I kept on trying to keep my business clean. Frequently, Germans came in and asked for 20 grams or an ounce, but also a pound or a kilo! Then I decided to get a house dealer..."

"Snitches" are very unpopular here. Most people are reluctant to report violations, particularly if they themselves were not victimized. This reluctance to report occurs mainly because of the frequent interchangeability of offender, victim, and witness roles: the next time they might be the offender and need to count on the discretion of others. Snitching is not likely to result in violent sanctions. Although the Amsterdam criminal milieu does know liquidations: lethal revenge would be considered definitely inappropriate by all parties at this particular level of interaction.
All of these factors make it extraordinarily difficult to catch an offender. Initially, the inner city had its own regulatory system, ensuring that things prohibited by law did not cause any nuisance to the neighborhood. Both the individual and the neighborhood profited from these law violations. When the neighborhood began to resist because of the nuisance mainly caused by drugs, this symbiotic relationship was transformed into parasitism. Nowadays it is still acceptable that a person slips into the role of an illegal or semi-illegal profit seeker every once in a

while, but the interests of the individual and the neighborhood no longer coincide. Among the many cafes in the city center, several are doing very poorly. When a dealer becomes a good customer of a cafe and one then discovers later what the nature of his profession is, it is very hard to get rid of him. Bartenders are "convinced" by a big tip and many employees are bought with a sample of hash or coke. Different from the earlier days, when this kind of thing took place outside the reach of the police and appeared beneficial to the neighborhood, these law violations seem to have mostly negative consequences for this community. Still, most area residents do not want to be a traitor and it remains very difficult for the police to arrest offenders. Moreover, the form in which the current parasitism manifests itself has changed and this suggests that, perhaps, there is an even more subtle and closer interconnection between the legitimate and illegitimate domains than before.

"At the corner of the Lange Niezel it was very dark for years because the building was empty. In front of the door, addicted prostitutes hung around 24 hours a day. Many residents breathed a sigh of relief when they heard that a big snackbar would be established there. From the start, however, it became obvious that this business would be a meeting place for whores and their customers, their addicted boyfriends and numerous users and dealers. It goes without saying that they represented the biggest market for the fast food."

"The stands that were placed on the bridges in the Damstraat found their customers among the very population that was to be removed from this particular area. The fritters and the sweets from the candy stand fit perfectly in the daily menu of the junkies hanging around in this street. A foreign drug expert sincerely inquired whether these stands were put there to accommodate the scene."

"Whenever possible I walk by McDonalds, for their straws are the best to chase the dragon", a Surinamese user stated.

5. Conclusion

For centuries, the Amsterdam inner city has been a tough neighborhood. In addition to the fast food culture, prostitution and gambling, drug dealing also has become firmly entrenched in this area. We have described the development of the drug business in two Amsterdam inner city streets from 1970 to the present.

On the Zeedijk, heroin dealing initially took place in the cafes and continued on the street after the police intervened. The family structure that existed in the cafes was replaced by individual dealers and dealers with assistants. During the second half of the 1980s the police began to act with increasing force against the drug trade and the dealers had to hire a growing number of helpers to practice their profession efficiently.

In the Damstraat, from the early 1970s, hash had been offered to young tourists. When the sale of cannabis was transferred to the coffee shops, the street business took on another character. Hard drugs were now for sale and dealers also began using helpers. In this street, during the second half of the 1980s, a lively pill trade developed involving a large number of users who took turns as buyers or sellers.

Up until the early 1980s, virtually no nuisance was caused by drugs in downtown Amsterdam. This changed, however, when a clearly recognizable group of addicts (a group which incidentally continued to get smaller in size) became increasingly conspicuous outside the Zeedijk. Protests from the neighborhood were initially quite playful and not well organized. Gradually, however, neighborhood actions became better organized, more extensive and harsher. Local authorities responded with extended police powers, more police patrol, and an economic restoration plan for the affected Zeedijk area.

Because of these developments, the inner city of Amsterdam is no longer a dope fiend's paradise for the street scene. Present users increasingly view the normalization policy of Dutch government as a tight strait-jacket; this notwithstanding the easily available needles and methadone. The efforts of city government have caused a number of the dealers and users to continue their daily business somewhere else. Yet, until the present day, there remain many people in downtown Amsterdam who earn their money from drug dealing. They are easily recognizable (also by the non-initiated out-of-towner) and they determine for a significant part the image of the city center.

The persistent nuisance associated with drug use and dealing in illegal drugs is only partly a result of the local, national and international drug conjuncture. The ambiguous attitude among many with regard to petty illegal and semi-illegal advantages were (and continue to be) a fertile ground for illegal behavior. In the past, the excesses of this flexible moral stayed within acceptable boundaries and formed an essential component of the tolerant climate of the inner city. The individual could benefit without being too costly for society; the community profited from the illegal drug trade. Gradually, this symbiosis changed into parasitism because individuals began to pursue personal profit with little or no con-

167

cern for the resulting problems within the neighborhood. Through this process, the benefits of drug-related activities are increasingly overshadowed by the resulting nuisance and disturbance of the local habitat.

References

Cohen, H.: *Drugs, Druggebruikers en Drugs-scene.* Alphen a/d Rijn: Samson, 1975
Fromberg, E., Kalkhoven, S., Haverkamp, G., Steegers, J. and De Jong, T.: *Stichting Kontakt Sentra, Verslag over 1975 en 1976.* Amsterdam, 1976
Koster, L.: *Wandelaars in de Nieuwmarktbuurt; een Onderzoek naar de Invloed van de Harddrugsscene op het Wonen in een Oude Binnenstadsbuurt.* Amsterdam: Instituut voor Sociale Geografie, Universiteit van Amsterdam, 1987
Middelburg, B.: *De Mafia in Amsterdam.* Amsterdam: de Arbeiderspers, 1988
Musto, D.F.: *The American Disease; Origins of Narcotic Control.* New Haven: Yale University Press, 1973
Perry, Ch.: *The Haight Ashbury, a History.* New York: Vintage Books, 1985
Stoute, R.: *Uit het Achterland.* Amsterdam: de Arbeiderspers, 1985
Van Breenen, K., Dijkstra, H., Van Erkel, F., Jeager, E., De Jong, J., Mulder, C., Rekers, A. and Verwaaijen, J.: *De Zeedijk, Nieuw Elan Oude Problemen; Samenwerking tussen Gemeente en Bedrijfsleven als Wondermiddel.* Amsterdam: Studiegroep Stedelijke Revitalisering, Instituut voor Sociale Geografie, Universiteit van Amsterdam, 1987
Van Gemert, F.: *Pushen, Rippen en Versnijden; Dealers in de Amsterdamse Binnenstad.* Doctoraal scriptie. Amsterdam: Antropologisch Sociologisch Centrum, Universiteit van Amsterdam, 1985
Van Gemert, F.: *Pallina, Pallina (Ball, Ball). La Strada* 11(15):4-7, 1987
Van Gemert, F.: *Mazen en Netwerken; de Invloed van Beleid op de Drugshandel in twee Straten in de Amsterdamse Binnenstad.* Amsterdam: Instituut voor Sociale Geografie, Universiteit van Amsterdam, 1988
Verbraeck, H.: *De Staart van de Zeedijk; een Bliksemonderzoek naar enkele Effecten van het Zomerplan 1987 in het Wallengebied.* Amsterdam: Instituut voor Sociale Geografie, Universiteit van Amsterdam, 1988
Verhey, E.: De Binnenbantammerstraat. *Vrij Nederland* 14-11-1985, pp 2-25, 1985

IX. THE DEVELOPMENT OF A "LEGAL" CONSUMERS' MARKET FOR CANNABIS: THE "COFFEE SHOP" PHENOMENON

A.C.M. Jansen

"Coffee shop": place where one may buy small quantities of hashish and marihuana for personal consumption....

1. Introduction

This chapter focuses on the uniquely Dutch institution of the "hash coffee shop". Hash coffee shops represent a commercialization of the cannabis trade – a trade which, although in principle still a penal offense, is in practice tolerated at the retail level. The commercialization of cannabis sales – especially when conducted in establishments comparable to traditional bars or "normal" coffee shops, played an extremely important role in the gradual acceptance by Dutch society of cannabis as "just another stimulant", comparable to alcohol.

As this chapter will show, the commercialization of cannabis took place only gradually and under conditions imposed by the government. Soft drug policy in the Netherlands, as in many other countries, was fairly repressive throughout the 1960s. The 1970s showed the beginning of more tolerance towards the use of soft drugs, culminating in the revised 1976 Opium Act. In Amsterdam, as in other large Dutch cities, there were initially numerous frictions between the operators of the coffee shops and the authorities. Gradually, a policy of "toleration" developed, characterized by fairly strict conditions imposed on the operation of the coffee shops.

This chapter describes how Dutch drug policy has been fairly successful in the integration of soft drugs into Dutch society. The semi-legal entrepreneurs running the coffee shops, without ever losing sight of their economic interests, have been important contributors to the achievement of one of the main aims of Dutch drug policy: a strict separation between the trade in soft and hard drugs.

After a brief discussion of developments in Dutch soft drug policy, the chapter provides a description of Amsterdam hash coffee shops. After that, we attempt to account for the fact that the "hash coffee shop" appears to be a phenomenon which exists only in the Netherlands. Finally, the "success story" of the hash coffee shops should not blind us to the fact that there still exist many cases of misunderstanding, ignorance, and ambiguity concerning cannabis in the Netherlands – the focus of the last section of this chapter.

2. Soft drugs policy and the emergence of coffee shops in the Netherlands

By the 1980s, drug use had become such a pervasive phenomenon in the Netherlands that law enforcement priorities had to be set, resulting in prosecutorial guidelines even more lenient than originally envisioned by the 1976 law. The development of guidelines with regard to the investigation, prosecution and sentencing of drug offenses is based on one of the basic foundations of Dutch criminal procedure: the expediency principle. This principle (Van Vliet 1989:8) empowers the Public Prosecutor's Office to refrain from initiating criminal proceedings "on grounds derived from public interest". In 1980, the Ministry of Justice issued a set of guidelines for the investigation and prosecution of offenses under the Opium Act. These guidelines are interpreted at a local level in the different judiciary districts of the country through a process of "triangular consultation" (*i.e.,* consultation between the Public Prosecutor, the Mayor, and the Chief of Police). This decentralized approach results in a variable prosecution policy, ranging from rather strict to lenient. Typically, the policy is less strict in major cities than in the smaller towns and villages, reflecting differences in community standards, extent of drug problem, and so on. Generally speaking, soft drug policy is most tolerant in the urbanized western part of the Netherlands.

Soon after the "Guidelines for the investigation and prosecution of offenses under the Opium Act" had been issued, the Mayor of Amsterdam announced that "relatively low priority" would be given to the investigation of the commercial retail trade in cannabis products taking place in "certain places", provided that some conditions were met. Two of the more important conditions were a ban on public advertising, and absolutely no sale of hard drugs. Violation of the latter condition would not only result in possible incarceration, but in economic sanctions as well: the establishment would be closed immediately. In this manner, the city of Amsterdam used both a "carrot" and a "stick": the opportunity to make a profit and to conduct business in a relatively undisturbed way represented the carrot; a relatively harsh penalty when violating the ban on the sale of hard drugs represented the stick. This policy which essentially condoned and "normalized" the use and retail sale of soft drugs, was a weighty factor in the rapid proliferation of hash coffee shops in the larger Dutch cities.

The "coffee shop" was not newly invented just for the consumption of cannabis (Korf 1990). To the contrary, the "koffiehuis" is one of the traditional Dutch public places - a place where one goes to have coffee, eat, read a newspaper, and meet friends. It is an alcohol-free cafe. Compared to places with a liquor license, there are virtually no rules or regulations regarding its establishment. In the late 1970s, the owners of some of these coffee shops tolerated the occasional sale of soft drugs by small dealers. The sale of soft drugs gradually became an essential part of the income of coffee shops. Coffee shops that were selling soft drugs in the pre-regulation days soon established "house rules": No hard drugs allowed. No dealing in stolen goods. No violence. In case of violation of any of these rules, the police would be called. Sometimes a square-shouldered person was hired to enforce compliance with the house rules, and these "enforcers" were anything but superfluous: keeping hard drugs out of the soft drug use and trade was not accomplished without, literally, striking a blow.

This means that the local interpretation of the expediency principle in the city of Amsterdam (as well as in other cities) was more or less determined by existing practice: a number of coffee shops, serviced by a

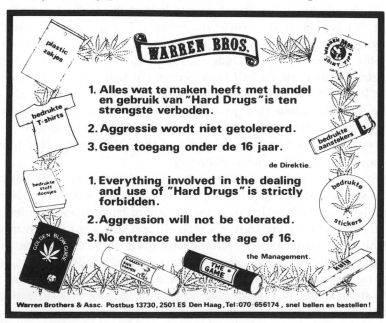

Fig. 1.

(small) number of soft drugs dealers, tradesmen who were soon considered as "personifications of the "separation of markets"-policy" (Van Vliet 1989:9). After the policy shift of 1980, the number of hash coffee shops rapidly increased: "House rules" were mass-produced (Fig. 1). In a fashion, these "house rules" represented a form of "hidden advertising", since they indicated the availability of soft drugs at certain establishments. In the 1980s, the Amsterdam hash coffee shops had found numerous other ways of evading the official ban on advertising (see Jansen 1991).

3. Hash coffee shops in the center of Amsterdam

At the time of this writing, more than 1,000 hash coffee shops exist in the Netherlands. In Amsterdam alone, more than 300 of these coffee shops are currently in business. Not surprisingly these establishments are mainly to be found in the cities. In the smaller towns and villages, hash coffee shops do not exist; these places lack an economic (and possibly a social) basis necessary for their subsistence. Dealing from private houses is still common practice for these areas.

I have studied the gradual emergence of the soft drugs retail business in the inner city of Amsterdam (comprising some 110 coffee shops, see Fig. 2) during the 1980s. In the second half of the 1980s I visited coffee shops on a regular basis. Whenever possible, I would initiate conversations with dealers and customers; on other occasions, I simply observed. My observations always included a registration of the amount of drugs changing hands during a half-hour period. (At that time, all coffee shops in the inner city of Amsterdam carried out their trade quite openly – due to the formally stated "low priority policy". It was typically fairly easy to register the exact amount of drug sales.) A random sample of 887 observations of half-an-hour each during the 1985-1989 period provides the basis for the following conclusions.

First of all, it appears that the policy aimed at the (spatial) separation of the sale of hard drugs and the sale of soft drugs was very successful. In a relatively short period of time, the sale of hashish and marihuana on the streets became comparatively insignificant and was taken over by the "established" trade of the coffee shops. Over 95% of the sale of soft drugs in downtown Amsterdam now takes place in coffee shops, where it is, incidentally, as absurd to ask for hard drugs as it is to ask for a zebra steak at the average butcher's. It is not known to what extent this spatial division of the worlds of soft and hard drugs has also occurred outside the inner city of Amsterdam.

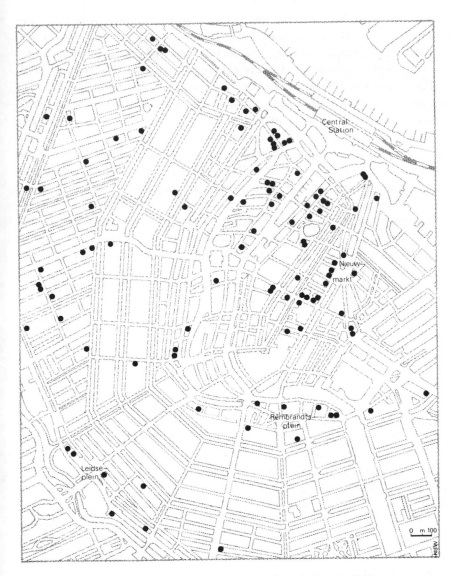

Fig. 2. Hash coffee shops in the inner city of Amsterdam, January 1, 1989.

A second conclusion concerns the importance, both economically and socially, of hash coffee shops. In the inner city of Amsterdam (as in other larger cities), there now exists a large variety of coffee shops. There are coffee shops with a youthful public as their major patronage, and there are coffee shops which are mainly frequented by somewhat older people. There are coffee shops visited mostly by people from Surinam, or from

Turkey, or from the richer neighborhoods of Amsterdam. And there are coffee shops mainly for tourists. There are coffee shops which are viewed as "take-out" places, and there are coffee shops which function as youth centers, where visitors spend hours playing chess, table football, or pool.

The 1980s not only showed a strong growth in the number and types of coffee shops; they also showed an increase in the variety of cannabis products for sale. Within a period of less than ten years, cannabis was imported from virtually all cannabis-producing countries in the world. Most hash coffee shops in the inner city of Amsterdam offer more than five types of marihuana and more than five types of hashish. Neither the variety, nor the price of the goods in coffee shops are influenced by occasional confiscations of shipments of cannabis by the police.

In a social sense, hash coffee shops increasingly resemble those other establishments in Dutch culture which exist mainly because of the profitability of another psychotropic substance: alcohol. From a social scientific perspective the social functions of pubs and bars may easily be viewed in positive terms. A Dutch sociologist concluded his study of the "public house" throughout history with the statement that the quality of life of a society may be inferred from the quality of its pubs (Jansen 1976). As the integration of soft drugs into Dutch culture progresses, G.H. Jansen's criterion of a "liveable" society might include the quality of its hash coffee shops.

The most recent developments in the soft drug sector in Amsterdam show that the original spatial separation between the coffee shops selling hashish and the public establishments with a liquor license, is now fading. At this moment, approximately 25% of the hash coffee shops in the inner city of Amsterdam also offer alcoholic beverages. In addition, we see an increase in the number of pubs where the use of cannabis is tolerated, although the substance is not sold by or in the establishment. In other words, there is some evidence that the soft drugs sector is "dissolving" into the long existing world of liquor establishments. Whereas in the 1980s the profitability of the hash coffee shop was almost entirely based on the sale of cannabis, we now see more establishments where cannabis is but a part of its income.

The "dissolving" of the soft drugs sector has yet another dimension: the "sinsemilla guerilla". From the early 1960s, people in the Netherlands have been experimenting with the growing of cannabis. As a result of these experiments, over the years a home-grown brand of "Netherweed" has entered the market. Most of it is "sinsemilla" (a Spanish expression indicating that the marihuana does not contain seeds). This soft drug can easily win a quality contest with imported marihuana; the price of Netherweed in coffee shops is, therefore, higher than that of imported varieties. According to Dutch law, the growing of cannabis seed is allowed; however, not with the intention to grow a crop of marihuana. It is not forbidden to deal in cannabis seed, nor is it illegal to deal in cannabis plants. This is the basis for what has become known as the "sinsemilla guerilla". The initiators of this "guerilla" promote "home growing" as a means of removing the marihuana trade from the hands of large-scale dealers who, in effect, are violating the Opium Act by importing drugs. High quality seeds or "clones", in combination with an instruction manual for outdoor or indoor growth (Cervantes 1984; Wiet 1983; Wernard 1987), enable a financially attractive small-scale production.

It is impossible to pinpoint exactly where and how the available amounts of Netherweed have been produced. However, since almost every Amsterdam coffee shop is selling Netherweed, it is reasonable to speculate that the commercial production of Netherweed has reached a considerable volume. The same conclusion may be drawn from the lowering of the price of Netherweed: during 1990, the price has been sliced in half. It should be noted, however, that the same holds true for most imported kinds of hashish.

4. An explanation of the "coffee shop culture"

The hash coffee shop is a phenomenon which only exists in the Netherlands. An obvious question remains: Under what conditions did the Dutch "coffee shop culture" develop? Clearly, the legal distinction between soft and hard drugs has been of strategic importance for the development of the phenomenon. However, the Netherlands is not the only country which has introduced a legal distinction between soft drugs and hard drugs (*e.g.*, Spain, Denmark). Is it then perhaps the expediency principle as applied in Dutch criminal law which facilitated the emergence of the Dutch coffee shop culture? The expediency principle made it possible that in the Netherlands, against the stated intentions of the law of 1976, in certain places a cautious beginning could be made with the commercialization of the cannabis trade. However, since the expediency principle is characteristic for criminal law in many European countries (Van Vliet 1989), this could not explain the uniqueness of the Dutch hash coffee shops.

We have to understand how the expediency principle interacted with what was happening in the Netherlands during the 1970s - a period which may be described as "a strange and brief time when middle-class kids had involved themselves in illegal business and felt they were doing the right thing" (Warner 1986:264). The 1970s was the decade of challenging authorities by rebellious (middle-class) youngsters becoming involved with a relatively new phenomenon in their culture: drugs. In cities like Amsterdam (and other university towns in the Netherlands) the protest movements were more powerful than in many other European cities, which may explain why Dutch local authorities were willing to make a rather tolerant use of the expediency principle.

Another factor to consider is that the 1980 prosecutorial guidelines leave considerable leeway for local interpretation. The Dutch have a "built in" aversion against a too strong central power (Schama 1987). The history of policies with regard to hashish and marihuana in Amsterdam confirms this tradition: Differences of opinion between the mayor of Amsterdam and the Minister of Justice in the Hague did not always get resolved in favor of the Minister.

Although the coffee shop culture came into being against the stated intentions of the 1976 revised Opium Act, it should be noted that there was already sound public support for a more tolerant policy with regard to soft drugs. As has been pointed out by Van Vliet (1989) and Engelsman (1989), the changing of the law in 1976 took place in a stable democracy where the changed law was the tail end of a wide public debate.

Our brief discussion of the uniquely Dutch circumstances associated with the emergence of the hash coffee shop culture implies that the Dutch experience cannot easily be generalized to other countries. The primary importance of the hash coffee shop may be the fact that it expresses the possibility of cultural integration of the use of illegal (be it soft) drugs into mainstream society. Over the last few decades, some of the marginality typically associated with drugs has been removed from cannabis in the Netherlands. At this point, cannabis is put in the same category as alcohol: simply another stimulant, rather than an illegal drug. The Dutch government, by (somewhat reluctantly) allowing a legal outlet for the use and purchasing of soft drugs, has taken an active role in the redefinition of cannabis as an ordinary product subject to the demand/supply mechanisms of the legal economic marketplace.

5. Cannabis in the Netherlands in the 1990s: Still some unresolved issues

During the first part of 1990, several interesting events involving cannabis took place in the Netherlands. For example, in early February, the 24-year-old manager of a hash coffee shop in Groningen reported to the police the theft of her entire supply of hashish intended for sale at the coffee shop. The newspaper reporting the event (Haarlems Dagblad, February 5 1990) quotes a spokesman of the Groningen Police Department as saying that such information is rarely received because trafficking in hashish is still officially forbidden. This remark is only partly correct. True, possession of hashish "for retail purposes" is officially prohibited, but it is not true that informing the police of a robbery of hashish or marihuana is such a rare occurrence. It may seldom happen in Groningen, a city in the agricultural northern part of the Netherlands, but in Amsterdam it is not unusual at all for the police to receive a report of a robbery involving hashish or marihuana. As a matter of fact, the Amsterdam police take these (armed) robberies very seriously.

In the same month that the above incident was reported in local newspapers, 45,000 kilos of hashish were confiscated on the premises of an international transportation firm (Volkskrant, February 26 1990). According to the newspaper, it was the largest shipment ever discovered in the Netherlands. The police remarked that the shipment represented a "street trading value" of 450 million guilders (about 230 million dollars). The police comments on this case were rather peculiar. First, they exaggerated the total value of the shipment (which was worth 360 million guilders at the most). However, this form of official exaggeration is the rule rather than the exception and appears to be an almost universal characteristic of law enforcement agencies anywhere in the world. Secondly, the use of the term "street trading value" is odd in the Dutch context where dealing in hashish and marihuana on the streets is virtually a relic of the past. With the establishment of coffee shops, the sale of hashish and marihuana has been taken off the streets and has literally become the domain of "established business".

A few weeks earlier, a remarkable demonstration had taken place in the center of Amsterdam. This demonstration focused on the proposed unification of Europe in 1992 which, in the view of many, forms a direct threat to the liberal Dutch drug policy. Under the proposed plan, European Community member states would no longer be separated by national boundaries, thereby greatly facilitating international trafficking between countries. Concern about the consequences of the Schengen Agreement caused several hundred soft drug users (including coffee shop owners) to demonstrate to express their support of the Dutch drug policy. National television broadcasted the Amsterdam demonstration during the evening news. During the demonstration, a picture was taken of a few police officers accepting marihuana cigarettes from the public. This picture appeared in newspapers and weekly magazines in France, Germany, and Great Britain – doubtlessly reinforcing the popular foreign image of

Amsterdam as the "drug mecca" of the world. During the press conference held in conjunction with the demonstration, the mayor of Amsterdam, in a video-taped interview, emphasized his intentions to do
whatever was necessary to preserve the liberal soft drug policy in his
city. His main argument was that neither hashish nor marihuana are addictive substances.

Another significant event, though much less publicized, was the ruling
by the Dutch High Court that growing hemp plants for their fibers and
their seeds is not in conflict with the Opium Act. A grower of 555 hemp
plants was acquitted by this ruling. Although this ruling was reported in
a very brief notice by a few papers (*e.g.*, NRC-Handelsblad, March 8
1990), this High Court decision will have far-reaching consequences for
the production of cannabis in the Netherlands: the production of seeds
practically coincides with the production of marihuana. For several
years, the Dutch police has routinely confiscated hundreds of kilos of
hemp plants growing in garden plots, hothouses, homes, and on roof gardens. In the Dutch context, however, this 1990 High Court ruling does
not automatically put an end to this practice. To this very day, even very
small "home growers" occasionally see their plants destroyed by the police. Again, the expediency principle can be referred to for explaining this
remarkable practice. It should be noted, though, that currently confiscations of small productions do not normally result in imprisonment; a fine
is more likely.

Another hallmark of the gradual acceptance of soft drugs into mainstream Dutch culture was an extensive report about the phenomenon of
the hash coffee shop published by Elsevier, a middle-of-the-road, if not
somewhat conservative widely read weekly magazine, in March of 1990.
The article speaks of the "success story of a democratized stimulant". In
this article, coffee shop owners are not depicted as criminals, but rather
as worried shop keepers and small business entrepreneurs, afraid of the
consequences of a United Europe. For this article, interviewed coffee
shop owners no longer tried to conceal their identity - openly stating
their names and so on.

The Elsevier article includes some evidence that the Dutch soft drug
policy is still not a perfect success story. For example, the owners of an
Amsterdam coffee shop "The Golden Stamp" were taken to court in the
early months of 1990 because 10.3 grams of hashish and 1.2 grams of
marihuana were confiscated during a police raid. The possession of up
to 30 grams of cannabis is permitted under current prosecutorial guidelines and therefore not ordinarily a valid reason for criminal prosecution.
Rather, the real reason for the prosecution was the fact that the coffee

shop displayed stickers on its windows with a picture of the hemp leaf and with the text "Amsterdam Hash It". In November of 1987, Amsterdam authorities began to place restrictions on advertising by coffee shops. This more restrictive policy was the result of pressure from abroad (particularly Germany) where concerns were expressed that coffee shop fronts decorated with pictures of a hemp leaf were too enticing to young tourists visiting "Europe's Drugs Center Number One".

The Elsevier article quotes a psychotherapist of the Amsterdam Jellinek Center (an alcohol and drug treatment clinic) who notes an increase in the number of people treated for an addiction to cannabis: approximately 200 cannabis users contact the clinic for help each year. Typically, it is the better educated cannabis users who enter therapy: students, doctors, lawyers, journalists. Only seldom do cannabis users from a lower socio-economic background report to the clinic for treatment of their cannabis addiction. Self-reported prevalence statistics on cannabis users (Kersloot and Musterd 1987) suggest that this psychotherapist has touched upon a hidden problem. In the Netherlands - and presumably abroad (Warner 1986) - a relatively greater number of cannabis users are found among the lower socio-economic classes. Although there is no reason to believe that there is cause for alarm, it suggests that the democratization of the "new" stimulant needs to be accompanied by a democratization in the education about the effects and problems of this stimulant. The opinion of one of the psychotherapists of the Jellinek Center is well worth mentioning here:

"As far as I am concerned, hash and weed may be legalized. We should not act as hypocritically as those who feel that a joint is worse than a beer, and hash is as bad as heroin. Parents do not have to worry if their child smokes a joint from time to time; nor if the child drinks a beer once in a while. But with both products they have to fulfill their parental duty and explain the risks. More information is required. If they can talk about being addicted to television, why then can't they talk about hash addiction? Marihuana - it is just too good not to be a problem."

The Dutch press reports on hashish and marihuana in a rather businesslike manner, unlike the very sensational type of reporting on drugs typically found in the American mass media. These Dutch newspaper stories show that the philosophy behind Dutch drug policy, based on "the necessity to integrate the drug phenomenon into Dutch society" (Engelsman and Manschot 1985:61 in the official explanatory note accompanying the new Opium Act) has slowly become a well-accepted reality, particularly with respect to cannabis. On the same token, however, the discussed events also reveal the often chaotic, ambiguous and contradictory nature of Dutch soft drug policy. Indeed, despite a certain degree of cultural acceptance of marihuana and hashish, the behavior of the police and the Department of Justice at times may be characterized as thoughtless, inconsistent, and unfortunate. The lack of clarity with regard to the policy on soft drugs is to a large extent explained by the aforementioned expediency principle. In the view of many, the Dutch soft drug policy is obscure and as tricky to figure out as a cryptogram (Smits 1987:4).

In another context I have called the Dutch soft drug policy an "accidentally intelligent policy" (Van Harten and Meijer 1990:13). This is not meant as a pejorative term, dismissing Dutch drug policy as a failure. On the contrary, in spite of its shortcomings and ambiguities, the soft drug policy in the Netherlands is more reasonable, more humane and more effective than in any other European country. What I do mean is that Dutch drug policy is not solely the result of a preconceived policy goal, rather it reflects the process of "muddling through", a process of trial and error. The particular shape of a drug policy in a democracy is influenced by a number of different "forces", conflicts between authorities at the legislative and executive levels, and conflicts between national and local authorities. In addition, both soft drug dealers and consumers, through their method of "civil disobedience" constitute another important force in the shaping of the Dutch drug policy. As a result of the interplay between these different interest groups, cannabis use has been redefined during the last several years in the Netherlands: it is increasingly considered to be one of the available (legal) stimulants, instead of a (illegal) drug.

A final observation. Although the Dutch soft drugs policy, when compared with virtually all other countries in the Western world, is less repressive, this policy has not resulted in an explosive increase in the use of soft drugs. As a matter of fact, between 1970 and 1979 – a period of growing tolerance of soft drug use (Driessen et al. 1989) – the use of cannabis among youngsters showed a slight decrease. Since 1979, the use of cannabis has shown a minor increase, and if the full period (1970 to 1987) is considered, it appears that the use of cannabis has remained stable. Prevalence figures for Norway and Sweden – countries with a considerably more strict soft drugs policy – are about at the same level as those in the Netherlands. Comparable figures for the United States are significantly higher. In the Netherlands, the use of marihuana among school-age youth (between 10 and 18 years of age) amounted to 6.1% in 1989 (cf. Plomp, Kuipers and Van Oers 1990).

181

References

Cervantes, J.: *Indoor Marihuana Horticulture.* Portland: Interport, 1984

Driessen, F.M.H.M., Van Dam, G. and Olsson, B.: De ontwikkeling van het cannabis gebruik in Nederland, enkele Europese landen en de VS sinds 1969. *Tijdschrift voor Alcohol en Drugs* 15(1):2-13, 1989

Engelsman, E.L.: *Drugs: a Case for Normalization.* Paper presented at the Conference on Drugs Control: Legal Alternatives and Consequences, 10-12 November. Melbourne, Australia, 1989

Engelsman, E.L. and Manschot, R.J.: *Toelichting op de Opiumwet B,* pp 1-61. Lelystad: Vermande, 1985

Jansen, A.C.M.: *Cannabis in Amsterdam. A Geography of Hashish and Marihuana.* Muiderberg: Coutinho, 1991

Jansen, G.H.: *De Eeuwige Kroeg; Hoofdstukken uit de Geschiedenis van het Openbaar Lokaal.* Meppel: Boom, 1976

Kersloot, J.M. and Musterd, S.: *Leefbaarheid en drugs in Amsterdam. De Spreiding van Drugs Scenes over en de Relatie met de Leefbaarheid in de Stad.* Amsterdam: Instituut voor Sociale Geografie, Universiteit van Amsterdam, 1987

Korf, D.J.: Cannabis retail markets in Amsterdam. *International Journal on Drug Policy* 2(1):23-27, 1990

Plomp, H.H., Kuipers H. and Van Oers, M.L.: *Roken, Alcohol- en Drugsgebruik onder Scholieren.* Amsterdam/Utrecht: Vrije Universiteit/Nederlands Instituut voor Alcohol en Drugs, 1990

Schama, S.: *The Embarrassment of Riches. An Interpretation of Dutch Culture in the Golden Age.* New York: Knopf, 1987

Smits, H.: Het beleid ten aanzien van softdrugs is geleidelijk aan verscherpt. *Vrij Nederland, jrg 48* (21 November), 1987

Van Harten, C. and Meijer, R.: Hoe hashiesj en marihuana ingeburgerd raakten. *Elsevier, Jrg 46* (3 March), pp 13-17, 1990

Van Vliet, H.J.: *The Uneasy Decriminalization. A Perspective on Dutch Drug Policy.* Paper presented at the Third International Conference on Drugs Policy Reform, November 2-5, Washington DC, 1989

Warner, R.: *Invisible Hand. The Marihuana Business.* New York: Beech Tree, 1986

Wernard: *Wietologisch Handboek voor de Buitenteelt.* Personal Publication. Amsterdam, 1987

Wiet: *Kweek zelf je Nederwiet.* Amsterdam: Stone-Productions, 1983

X. THE DRUG-RELATED CRIME PROJECT IN THE CITY OF ROTTERDAM[1]

Bert Bieleman and Jolt Bosma

1. Introduction

This chapter describes the Rotterdam Drug-Related Crime (DRC) Project, a program funded by the Dutch government emphasizing cooperation between local city government, the District Attorney's Office, police, and drug assistance agencies. The DRC Project functioned as an umbrella for four smaller programs aimed at the prevention of drug-related criminality. The following four DRC programs were implemented within a three-year time period (1988-1990): a research study describing the extent and nature of the Rotterdam drug-using population; a work project aimed at the re-integration of addicts into society; a "target hardening" project to reduce drug-related property crime in parking garages; and a shelter for addicts near Central Station aiming at the reduction of nuisance associated with the concentration of drug addicts in that area.

2. Development of the Rotterdam drug policy[2]

Rotterdam, the second largest city of the Netherlands (575,000 inhabitants) has been the world's largest harbor for quite some time; for example 20,000 containers pass through this large harbor every day. Rotterdam is situated near the mouth of the Rhine, which is one of Europe's most important waterways. This river divides the city into two very distinct sections. The center of the city is in the northern part. At the start of the Second World War, German bombardments virtually destroyed the center of Rotterdam. After the war the city had to be rebuilt, thereby significantly changing its character. Narrow streets with old fronts were replaced by wide traffic arteries and high rises. Whereas Amsterdam is considered to be the cultural center of the Netherlands, Rotterdam's reputation is more that of a blue-collar city. Rotterdam has fewer foreign European drug users than Amsterdam. Most of the foreign European drug users in Rotterdam come from neighboring Belgium. Additionally there is a notable influx of Moroccan[3] drug users from (through France) Belgium.

Up until the mid-1970s Rotterdam's drug problem was virtually non-existent. However, starting in 1976, the nuisance created by drug users and drug dealers began to increase sharply. To pressure city government into dealing with the problems in the area, downtown citizens started an action group ("the Old West"). By the end of the 1970s, the city of Rotterdam published its first reports on the drug problem.[4] These reports clearly indicated that the city did not view addiction as a disease, rather it was seen primarily as a social problem. The problem exists because the addicts behave themselves in a manner which the community experiences as alarming. This troubling behavior is due, at least in part, to the fact that drugs are illegal and are subject to very high prices on the black market, which in turn leads to the so-called "junkie syndrome": stealing, lying, blackmailing, manipulating, and an inability to take responsibility for one's actions.[5]

Dealing with the problems experienced by the addicts is primarily the task of social service and treatment agencies. On the other hand, dealing with the problems caused by addicts is considered to be the primary responsibility of the police and the criminal justice system. The city has no illusions about solving the drug problem. Consequently, the city should focus its efforts on "containing addicted behavior within the social dimension and, if possible, eliminating it" (Gemeente Rotterdam 1980). The city expressed this premise in the three objectives of its drug policy:
- to prevent the onset of drug use by non-users which may lead to addiction;
- to offer assistance to those who want to overcome their drug habit;
- to offer assistance to those who wish to continue their drug habit by establishing programs which enable addicts to live a socially acceptable life (the so-called low-threshold assistance programs).

In these reports, the city requested more prevention, more low-threshold assistance programs and more after-care and rehabilitation programs. Programs and facilities for assistance and treatment aimed at Surinamese addicts, who are typically in a socially disadvantaged position and who are often beyond the reach of social service agencies, need to be adjusted and expanded. The delivery of services should be based on the so-called "circuit notion". The circuit principle implies that the city must offer a large variety of assistance provisions and programs; every program or agency fulfills one or more partial function in the circuit. The activities of the different agencies should not overlap, but rather complement each other. In addition, there should be a well coordinated referral system of clients throughout the agencies. It is this particular organizational framework which will provide the basis for the Rotterdam (and other Dutch cities') drug assistance services. A drug policy coordinator should be appointed to support local drug policies and to coordinate drug-related services. In addition, an advisory commission should be established to report to the mayor and the city council. Representatives of drug-related assistance programs, criminal justice agencies (police, court, District Attorney's office), and city government should participate in the advisory commission. There should also be routine consultations with the staff of the various methadone programs. These programs get their methadone supply from the city pharmacy, which is part of the Municipal Public Health Service.

In spite of the implementation of the city's drug policy plan, drug-related problems persisted into the early 1980s. Residents of urban renovation projects such as "the Old West" continued to exert pressure on the city to address the problem. In the Old West neighborhood clearly visible street drug dealing continued to flourish. Local residents complained about neighborhood decline and criminality. Previously concealed (*i.e.,* latent) feelings of discrimination became apparent (*i.e.,* manifest) which further complicated and intensified the problem. Street trafficking of heroin was partly in the hands of (often addicted) Surinamese. The many Surinamese residents of the neighborhood were often automatically identified with heroin dealers by the autochthonous residents. This perception threatened to escalate into an open conflict in the Old West. The action group "the Old West" pursued a variety of actions, such as refusing to pay rent and appealing to the (local) mass media to pressure the city.[6] The city's response to this public pressure was two-pronged. On the one hand, police become more active, resulting in dispersing the drug-related problems and making the dealers more cautious. On the other hand, more drug-related assistance programs were established to ensure that the user would not become the victim of the increased law enforcement efforts. These newly created drug-related assistance programs catered to the needs of specific categories of addicts (*i.e.,* Surinamese addicts, chronic psychotic addicts and very young addicts).

In sum, in the early part of the 1980s, the city policy emphasized combatting drug dealing, decreasing drug-related nuisance problems and drug-related crime, as well as establishing comprehensive, easily accessible assistance programs with relatively limited emphasis on programs aimed at breaking the drug habit.[7] The circuit principle remained the organizing framework for delivery of services. Treatment services aimed at abstinence were considered to be very costly in terms of both money and efforts, and were viewed as relatively unsuccessful. Therefore, the emphasis shifted more from a concern with the termination of addiction to an acceptance of addiction. Increased attention was given to the improvement of the social and medical conditions of addiction. Drug-assistance agencies relied heavily on methadone-maintenance programs. The belief was that methadone, in conjunction with social work and rehabilitation programs, would enable drug users to lead more normal lives.

By the late 1980s, city officials agreed that Rotterdam had a sufficient number of drug-related services.[8] There was a consensus that the emphasis should shift in the direction of maximizing the efficiency of the existing circuit of services.

In order to administer and coordinate the methadone programs, the Rotterdam Drug Information System (RODIS) was established in 1988. The city no longer attempted to develop assistance programs specifically designed for minority groups (i.e., Surinamese users). The working assumption was that these groups made sufficient use of existing social service programs and that they were no longer at a disadvantage compared to autochthonous users with regard to access to assistance and treatment. There remained one minority group, however, which still appeared to be virtually beyond the reach of the existing network of services; the users from Morocco.[9] Policy makers decided that the position of the Moroccan addicts would get extra attention within the existing constellation of services, without establishing separate programs for this particular group.

3. Background and origins of the Rotterdam Drug-Related Crime Project

The Rotterdam Drug-Related Crime Project was a local pilot project in the context of the administrative prevention of criminality.[10] In a way the Rotterdam project was an outcome of the social policy plan of the 1983 Government Commission on Petty Criminality (also referred to as the Commission Roethof).[11] The concept of administrative prevention followed from the Commission's conclusion that the sharp increase in criminality was probably related to post World War II developments such as the increased freedom of movement, urbanization, increased anonymity, de-pillarization,[12] decreased importance of traditional authority relationships, and increased prosperity. The Commission listed several additional criminogenic factors: unemployment; alcohol and drug use; decreased personal supervision in many public or semi-public areas, such as department stores, train stations, public transportation, parking garages, apartment buildings. Schools exerted less control over the adolescent population, as demonstrated by an increase in truancy and the increased tendency to cancel classes. The Commission noted that social control had lessened in conjunction with a decrease of functional supervision. To complicate things further, Dutch society witnessed a transition from traditional family life – where parents imposed strict norms on their children – to negotiation-based families – where norms are established in mutual interaction. This shift placed a significant and often unrealistic demand on the ability of youth to exert self-control. All too frequently, educators and parents failed to clearly establish normative boundaries and to provide positive examples.

The 1985 government policy document, "Society and Criminality" referred to the work of the Commission Roethof for the prevention of frequently occurring "petty" crime.[13] The policy plan specified integration and supervision as the core elements of the required prevention strategy for frequently occurring petty crime.

At the same time it stressed the importance of administrative prevention policy instead of police-based preventive measures. Thus Society and Criminality distinguished the following three main components:
- Strengthening the social bonds (family, school, work and leisure) of the young.
- Expanding functional supervision of potential law-breakers by security guards, store personnel, and for instance athletic coaches.
- Designing the material environment in such a manner that supervision is facilitated and criminality is inhibited.

The government document emphasized that alleviating petty criminality required a certain degree of decentralization and local government bodies and social organizations took on tasks which were formerly the domain of the national government. In 1985, administrative prevention was still a fairly novel policy concept and the government felt that a certain amount of experimentation was necessary to establish its utility. Initiatives for such experiments were expected to come primarily from local administrations. For this purpose, the national budget provided 45 million guilders to stimulate local pilot projects. In 1987, the Rotterdam Drug-Related Crime Project was funded as one of the local pilot projects.

The main objective of the project was to deal with the nuisance, public order and crime problems, associated with drug use.[14] The project was also intended to convince local citizens that the city was doing something about the problem of hard drugs. The Rotterdam DRC Project consisted of four smaller projects. First, there was a research component which studied the incidence and seriousness of deviant drug addiction in Rotterdam. This research would provide the necessary baseline for further local drug policy actions. Second, the DRC Work Project attempted to find a way of breaking the vicious circle of social decline connected to deviant drug addiction. For a small experimental group legal procedures were adapted to allow better opportunities for re-employment and further re-socialization. Third, increased supervision and security measures were installed to prevent thefts from cars in parking garages. Finally, a shelter for drug addicts was placed next to the Central Station in order to decrease the visual nuisance associated with the concentration of drug addicts near the train station. The DRC Project was completed within two years (1988 and 1989). The four project components will be discussed further in the next sections.

4. Research component of the Rotterdam Drug-Related Crime Project: The current situation on hard drug use in Rotterdam

The first extensive drug study in Rotterdam was primarily intended to provide information to City Hall, the Police, the Prosecutor's Office and other agencies dealing with drug use and its related problems. The research documents the dispersion of drug use and drug dealing in the city; provides a typology of Rotterdam drug users; and speculates about future developments.[15]

In this study quantitative and qualitative methods of social-scientific research were combined. Several key informants (*i.e.* police officers, drug and youth social workers, street-corner workers) were interviewed about the local hard drug situation. On the basis of this information Rotterdam was divided into several districts, each with their own characteristic features. This provided insight into how to obtain the best possible sample of drug users within each district. Most respondents were identified by using the technique of snowball sampling. Some of the in-depth interviews were conducted by drug aid agencies and drug dealers. Furthermore, participant observation was used: two researchers worked for a period of time in the portable cabin (designed to function as a shelter for drug users) next to the Central Station; several meeting places of drug users were frequently visited (*i.e.,* the St. Paulus Church, the homes of dealers); and some addicts were visited in their own homes. The estimation of the extent of heroin use and the number of heroin users was based on different calculation techniques like the nomination technique. Use has been made, for example, of figures from drug care agencies and police files. Finally, in order to obtain a general notion of the amount of crime committed by drug users, police files were analyzed.

4.1 Dispersion of drug use and drug dealing in Rotterdam

The study (conducted in 1988) suggests that heroin use is dispersed over the entire city of Rotterdam. Of course, there are a few locations in the city where use and dealing in hard drugs is more prevalent than in other areas. For example, in the immediate proximity of the Central Station (CS) is a so-called "street scene", which consists of about 250 hard drug users who hang out or buy drugs. This group is quite diverse with respect to drug use: the majority are opiate-addicted poly-drug users who also use a combination of cannabis, alcohol, cocaine and sleeping pills and/or tranquilizers. An estimated 500 users come to the CS on a regular basis (on average once a week) to sell methadone or to buy drugs. Remarkable is the relatively large proportion of Moroccans and Surinamese hanging out in the Central Station area. There is a rather intensive trade in methadone and in sleeping pills and tranquilizers, particularly Rohypnol and Valium. Heroin and cocaine dealing takes place primarily inside buildings near the CS. The Central Station drug scene is the most visible and disquieting part of the Rotterdam drug problem.

In the lower-class residential district of West Rotterdam, drug dealing and use are concentrated in four neighborhoods. A fairly large number of Surinamese are part of the street scene in this area. These neighborhoods have a significant number of "deal houses". It is estimated that about 700 drug addicts live here. In the district of North Rotterdam, the drug problem is concentrated in four other neighborhoods. This region does not have a real "street scene"; dealing and using mostly occur inside private dwellings. About 600 hard drug users live in this area. Roughly the same situation exists in the South Rotterdam district. However, in this last district drug addiction is more scattered among a fairly large number of small, closely knit groups of individuals. It is estimated that approximately 700 hard drug users live in this part of the city.

4.2 Typology of hard drug users

Using the dimension of drug use/criminality, three categories of opiate users were empirically distinguished in Rotterdam.[16]

4.2.1 Non-criminal users

These users did not commit any crimes before their addiction, nor did they get involved in crime while they were addicted. Less than 10% of drug users belonged to this crime-free group. Interestingly, this category did not include any Dutchmen. The socio-economic position of the users' family was typically good. Few had completed their education. For most of the users in this group, the motives for initiating heroin use were either boyfriend troubles (for the females) or the difficult adjustment to Western society (for the non-Dutch users). About half of this group indicated less heroin use and a more regular and relaxed life during periods of methadone treatment. Nearly all respondents in this group received some form of public assistance sufficient to support their (moderate) heroin use.

4.2.2 Drug delinquents

This category includes users who developed a criminal pattern of illegal and semi-legal activities after they initiated hard drug use. Approximately half of the users fit this category. The socio-economic background of the parents typically varied between unskilled laborer to middle class. It appears that as much as two-thirds of the users in this group had a rather unhappy childhood, for example, because of alcohol problems of one or both parents. Associating with (older) friends who were either already using or experimenting with different drugs was the reason for first involvement with drugs for half of the respondents in this group. Approximately half of these users indicated that their lives were much more relaxed and their involvement in drug-related property crime virtually non-existent during periods of involvement with methadone programs. The frequency of illegal and semi-legal activities depended strongly on the extent of heroin use. All of the respondents in this group had been involved with the police during their addiction. Approximately half of the users in this group were married or lived with a partner, who was usually an addict. Two-fifths of this group had one or more children; however, only the two respondents with a non-using partner raised their child(ren) themselves.

4.2.3 Original criminal drug users

This category includes users who committed crimes both prior to and during their drug use. Their drug use was an extension of an already-developed criminal lifestyle. About one-third belonged to this category, which consisted primarily of autochthonous Dutch people. The socio-economic position of the parents varied from unskilled workers to (lower) middle class. Nearly half of the respondents spent the largest part of their youth in youth homes. More than half were habitual truants and many of them first became involved in criminal behavior while truant. Only very few had no contact with the police prior to heroin use. Over one-third had been detained at least once prior to heroin use. Initiation of involvement in heroin use was consistent with a criminal lifestyle and environment. For over half of this group, the use of methadone produced positive results allowing them to live a more quiet and normal life. The extent of drug use was largely determined by the amount of illegal income; the causal link between drug use and income for this group of offenders is thus exactly the reverse of the drug use/income link for drug offenders. The large majority had received one or more prison sentences. Three-quarters of the users committed violent crimes. Almost one-third of the respondents lived with a partner or was married. One-third had one or more children. Again, only those users who lived with a non-using partner raised their own children.

4.3 Recent increase in hard drug use

The study further suggests that an increase in hard drug use in Rotterdam may be expected to come from the following categories (not included in the previous typology):
- Juvenile delinquents: They become involved with drugs because they associate with (juvenile) delinquent peers. Prior to their opiate use, they have committed all types of crimes. Once they start using, their criminal activity accelerates significantly.
- Moroccans: For most of the group of Moroccans, the marginalization process began in their homeland. For a variety of reasons, they did not complete their education there and they frequently had family problems. After arrival in the Netherlands, their social disadvantage only increased, primarily because they speak very little or no Dutch. In the Netherlands, the Moroccan marginalization process is speeded up because they lack the knowledge and competence to take advantage of the opportunities offered by the different social agencies. Furthermore, as a rule, the re-unification of the family in the Netherlands causes additional problems. Young Moroccans frequently have problems with their father. In a few cases, this results in family conflicts of such magnitude that the youth runs away from home prior to his or her introduction to hard drugs. In short, at the time of their first heroin use most of these respondents already find themselves in a problematic social situation. When their parents find out about the drug use, serious conflicts usually result. The amount of criminality varies considerably. Prior to first heroin use, Moroccan youths are relatively unin-

volved in illegal activities. Following the onset of heroin use, however, about half of this group violates the law on a regular basis.

To conclude this section, a few remarks about cocaine use are necessary. It seems that cocaine use among youths is on the increase. The research suggests that, outside the circles of opiate addicts, there appears to be a category of youths who heavily use soft drugs, drink alcohol, experiment with cocaine or even use cocaine on a regular basis. Cocaine use takes place primarily at discos and youth centers and other places where youths regularly meet.

5. The other three components of the DRC Project

In addition to the provision of information about the nature and extent of hard drug use, the DRC Project developed some experimental measures to remedy drug-related problems. While trying to reduce drug-related problems, the DRC Project also aimed at improving the social position of criminal drug users by employing an alternative criminal justice approach. A program was initiated to introduce incarcerated drug users to a legitimate job. This project was referred to as the DRC Work Project. In order to alleviate drug-related crime and public order problems a project was initiated to improve the security of parking garages, which are very vulnerable to criminality: the Functional Surveillance Parking Garage Project. Also, an already existing drop-in shelter for drug users in and around the Central Station was incorporated as part of the Drug-related Crime Project: the Central Station Project.

In addition to the desire to do something about drug-related crime, the DRC Project had another objective: to encourage the cooperation between the various agencies involved in working with drug use and its problems. Over the last few years, an awareness has developed that the only way to reduce nuisance problems caused by drugs is through joint efforts.

National government is very supportive of this notion of teamwork. It should be noted that while the inter-organizational cooperation was of primary importance in the DRC Project, it was also the source of most of its problems.[17]

5.1 The DRC Work Project

In Rotterdam there was a sense of dissatisfaction with the typical criminal justice approach to drug-related crime. Incarcerated addicts usually do not kick their habit when detained; upon release from custody they often go straight to the dealer and are forced to fund their drug use by criminal means. The DRC Work Project was conceived in an attempt to break this vicious circle. By means of a getting-used-to-work project, an alternative was created for a small number of users. The goal was to motivate the drug users to adopt a socially better integrated lifestyle, without criminality and drug use. The experiment consisted of several stages; participation in the labor market was one of its central objectives. This project was considered the showpiece of the DRC Project, absorbing most of the efforts and finances. It represents a rather unique example of cooperation between law enforcement, city government, rehabilitation, and drug-assistance agencies.

The foundations of the work project were: (1) drug use was not allowed (the exception being a maintenance dose of methadone); (2) in addition to work and restoration of a daily routine, there was room for education and training; (3) if a participant did not follow the rules, he/she would be incarcerated once again. The project was meant for incarcerated drug users in the Rotterdam House of Detention who had been sentenced to an unconditional prison sentence of between five months (minimum) to 12 months (maximum). The DRC Work Project consisted originally of three phases:

1. *A residential stage.* For about six weeks, the clients sailed on an inland vessel. This arrangement was devised as a transition phase between a closed system (House of Detention) and an open system (society).
2. *A training stage.* This stage consisted of a stay of approximately three months in a training center to get used to a normal daily routine.
3. *A work stage.* The clients participated for about 18 months in different work projects, thereby increasing their chances on the labor market.

5.1.1 Selection

Several organizations cooperated in the selection of participants: the Rotterdam House of Detention, the District Attorney and the Courts, the Rehabilitation Division of the Consultation Office for Alcohol and Drugs, and the leaders of the project. In 1988, the Rotterdam jail agreed to participate only with inmates from the drug-free wing (D wing) of the jail[18]. As a result of this restriction, only 22 offenders were recruited for the project, instead of the 40 originally planned for the first year of implementation (1988). Selection was continued in 1989 on a less restrictive basis. Detainees from other than the drug-free wings were included. The new participants in the Work Project had generally been sentenced to a lesser jail sentence of between three and six months, instead of the sentence of between six and 12 months for the old participants. For those participants who started in 1989 the residential and training stage was skipped. They started immediately with the work stage. Forty-three participants were selected in 1989.

5.1.2 Work projects

Finding a location and suitable projects was a very time-consuming enterprise. It was not until May 1988 that an old building belonging to the Holland-America Line was found which could serve as the main location. Attracting appropriate projects took even more time. In the fall of 1988 the first work project was initiated: the assemblage of small "sound houses". These are wooden frameworks containing all kinds of noise-making objects, used for music education in schools and hospitals. During 1989 several outdoor projects were taken on, such as the construction and painting of playgrounds and the reinforcement of the foundation of a small Rotterdam island. Some of the participants fixed up the portable cabin for the drop-in shelter for drug users near the Central Station.

Other re-socializing activities included vocational and educational courses. A course on "bureaucratic competence" (*i.e.,* how to deal with organizations, how to write letters, and so on) was one of the most popular activities of the work project. Organizations such as the Municipal Labor Service and the drug team of the Municipal Social Service were utilized to help participants (re-)enter the regular labor market.

5.1.3 Enforcing the rules

Rule violation, usually illegal hard drug use, was the main reason for termination of the program in the first year (1988). However, during its second year of operation (1989), departure from the program was primarily on the participants' own initiative. The drop-out rate was high especially during the first week of the program. The sudden change from prison conditions to the new work-oriented environment, without much time for adjustment, was probably too much of a problem. In 1989, the program coordinators began to adopt more flexible rules. However, at the insistence of the District Attorney and the court, the more stringent rules with regard to drug use soon were re-introduced.

5.1.4 Results

Six of the 22 participants selected in 1988 completed the program; five of them were able to find a job in the labor market. This means that for 27% of the 1988 participants the project was successful. Incidentally, this percentage is significantly higher than that typically obtained in prisons and therapeutic drug treatment centers (with an average success rate of around 10%). Eighteen of the 43 offenders who started the project in 1989 successfully completed the program by early 1990 (a 42% success rate). Five of these 18 program graduates were able to secure employment on completion of the program. The higher success rate in 1989 can be attributed to the fact that the selection in 1989 was less restrictive, as mentioned before, and to the adoption of more flexible rules during some months of 1989.

5.1.5 Organization and cooperation

The project had an advisory commission consisting of representatives of all participating organizations and the project manager, who was in charge of the daily management of the project. At times, cooperation left something to be desired. This was partly the result of the project's complexity, where the activities of a diversity of agencies had to be coordinated. Sometimes the most unanticipated complications occurred during the selection process of the project participants. Inter-agency problems resulted in the initial selection of a smaller number of participants than was originally intended. To some extent the participating organizations had divergent views on how to deal with drug use and the problems associated with drug use. For example, drug assistance and drug treatment organizations aim at the improvement of the health of the individual (ex-) user, while criminal justice personnel are primarily interested in enforcing the law. It is not surprising that these divergent positions at times result in conflicting assessments of certain situations. This, for instance, led to different ways of compiling information on the participants, disputes over the desirability of supplying methadone, and a late discussion on sanctions on drug-using participants.

5.2 Functional surveillance parking garage

In the two remaining DRC Projects, the notion of "surveillance", a concept re-introduced by the Commission Roethof, plays a crucial role, albeit in two different ways. While the preventive effect of functional surveillance was particularly important in the Functional Surveillance Parking Garage Project, in the Central Station Project informal control was much more important. In the first project the emphasis was on simple technical "target hardening". The latter project, however, dealt with the much more complicated issue of containing the undesirable social behavior of a group of highly problematic street addicts within certain limits.

The municipal parking garage in question, with a capacity of more than 600 cars, is located in the city center (Sint Jacobsplaats). Because of its many entrances and exits, and due to the absence of any form of surveillance, the garage was very vulnerable to crime. According to 1987 data collected by the municipal police, breaking into cars occurred about twice a week. As the garage's lack of security was well known to the public, its level of occupancy was fairly low (64% in 1987). To counter the problems of theft and visual nuisance associated with drug users, several changes were made in the parking garage. Guards were employed during the most vulnerable hours (especially in the evening, at night and during weekends). Only one entrance and one exit were made available. A closed-circuit monitoring system was installed consisting of 12 cameras and monitors. The garage was (partially) repainted and the lighting was improved.

According to police records the results of this project are very encouraging: the 1987 number of 99 thefts from cars decreased between April and December 1988 to 12, and in 1989 only two thefts from cars were reported to the police. In addition, the number of thefts from cars in the six neighboring streets decreased from 286 in 1987 to 99 in 1989. (The total volume of thefts from cars throughout Rotterdam did not decrease during this period.) A 1989 evaluation study indicated that feelings of insecurity were strongly reduced among the users of the garage.[19] The occupancy figures also increased. In 1987 about 50% of the places were reserved for parkers with a long-term permit; in 1988, 80% and in 1989, 90%. The total occupancy rates also increased. The project may be seen as one of the rare and happy occasions where all parties benefit from establishing functional supervision. The garage became a safer and more attractive place for car owners, supervision could largely be financed by higher occupancy rates and, last but not least, job opportunities were created for the unemployed.

5.3 Project Central Station

As in many other cities, Rotterdam's central railway station is a popular hang-out for various kinds of marginal groups in the population. Addicted hard drug users form no exception to this rule. For some years the entrance hall to the railway station, the area just in front of the railway station, and the corridors leading to the metro functioned as one of the most important meeting and copping areas for the Rotterdam drug scene. Due to the rather isolated setting of this public transport complex the drug scene was highly conspicuous. Not unexpectedly, the (growing) presence of this problematic subculture led to more and more complaints from travellers and consequently to growing concern by the city administration regarding the crime and public order situation in this critical city area. That this concern was warranted is borne out by police figures on public order and crime problems in this area. According to the police the criminality has been slightly reduced in and around the Central Station but not, however, the nuisance caused by marginal groups.

As an attempted remedy (but certainly no cure) for this inevitable city problem, a shelter for drug addicts was established at the east side of the Central Station. It consisted of a portable cabin which provided drug addicts (who, at the same time, are often alcoholics, homeless persons or ex-psychiatric patients) with an opportunity to sit down, have coffee or tea and spend some time together. The shelter was opened from two p.m. to eight p.m., from Monday to Saturday. All kinds of games could be played and some activities, such as drawing and painting, were organized. It was also possible to exchange dirty needles for clean ones. From the preventive point of view, this arrangement was meant to supervise and regulate the social behavior of this group. The project used two part-time professionals and about ten volunteers. In the portable cabin, better known as "Perron Nul" ("Platform Zero"), several house rules existed, of which, as the most important rule, the prohibition of the use and dealing in drugs or alcohol and the selling or buying of goods. Furthermore, the police were always allowed to visit the shelter. The establishment of "Platform Zero" was supported by the municipal police and by the St. Paulus Church, one of the main social assistance organizations caring for city drop-outs in Rotterdam. This parish has, under the charismatic leadership of Reverend Visser, acquired a national reputation for opening its doors to illegal immigrants, junkies and other down and out city dwellers. Welfare workers from this church organization participated in the daily management of Platform Zero. Support for this project has not, however, been unequivocal. Many railway travellers, people working in offices in the vicinity of the railway station, and occasionally the local mass media remained critical. The Dutch Railways were rather ambivalent about the shelter project. They expressed concern that Platform Zero would attract more addicts than would normally be present.

In the early stages of the project, the problems which were mainly encountered were with those people who work in the direct proximity of Platform Zero, such as cab drivers and employees of the Station's Currency Exchange Office. Due to the intervention of the municipal police and workers from the St. Paulus Church there were only a few incidents. The visitors consisted mainly of young addicts of ethnic minority groups, Surinamese, Antilleans and Moroccans. In later days people from other problematic marginal groups, such as the homeless and ex-psychiatric patients, began to frequent Platform Zero in increasing numbers. The professional employees were mainly involved with the strenuous task of the daily management of the shelter. Recruiting and coaching volunteers was another important element of their task. In 1989, the portable cabin was remodelled, the rest room was closed and volunteers were no longer recruited from among the visitors. All of these measures contributed to a more favorable atmosphere, less aggression and fewer violations of house rules. A local work group was established which formulated proposals to improve the Central Station and its surroundings. Since 1990, the Central Station Project has been funded in full by local government.

Until this day the shelter is still in existence, despite the occasional but inevitable crises, such as its co-existence with the outside world, the continuous frictions regarding the enforcement of house rules, the heterogeneity of its visitors, the growth in the number of its visitors, and the problems with recruitment of capable volunteers. In 1992, the shelter was made an integral part of a comprehensive plan for the whole area. It was moved to another site in the vicinity of the railway station, next to the police post, which serves as a base for surveillance of the area.

6. Conclusions

The main aim of the DRC Project was the prevention of drug-related crime and public order problems through several smaller projects in which city administration, District Attorney's office, police, and drug-assistance agencies cooperated. Although the project has not accomplished all its objectives, the project has contributed substantially to the reduction of drug-related nuisance. To summarize, the most significant positive effects of the project are the following:

1. Increased insight into opiate use: The research component has provided valuable information regarding the extent and nature of opiate use in Rotterdam. Attention has been focused on the extent of criminality by drug users, drug use amongst Moroccans and the danger of drug use by youths. In addition, the growing use of cocaine in Rotter-

dam has been recognized.

2. Actual reduction of nuisance: Improving the security ("target hardening") of the parking garage Jacobsplaats resulted in the most visible
reduction of nuisance: the number of larcenies from cars was drastically reduced. The occupancy rate of the garage increased and the public appears to feel more relaxed than before the start of the experiment.
Project Central Station has contributed, in all probability, to keeping
the situation around the Central Station manageable. Finally, the DRC
Work Project has provided some ex-addicts with the opportunity to
break out of the vicious circle of drug use, criminality, detention,
using, and so on. This project has acquired a more permanent organizational and financial footing during the most recent years.

3. Symbolic function: In addition to the actual reduction of drug-related
nuisance, the DRC Project also served another function: it showed the
public that policy makers are seriously interested in doing something
about drug-related criminality. Of course, this symbolic function only
keeps its value in the long run if it is accompanied by an actual
decrease in nuisance resulting from drugs: a ritual alone does not work
(anymore).

4. Improved cooperation between agencies: Finally the project has promoted cooperation between several agencies at the level of (drug)
policy. Presently there is, for instance, a more concerted effort to make
the Central Station and its surroundings more livable and several organizations are attempting to improve the situation for the Moroccans.
In its inventory of prevention and intervention channels, the final DRC
Project report argues in favor of increased field work, keeping drug
users out of the criminal justice circuit as long as possible, and increasing inter-agency cooperation. The main contribution of the DRC
Project has possibly been the role it has played as a pioneer in inter-
organizational coordination of drug-related services.

Endnotes

1. The authors thank drs. P.M. Koedijk and G.A.P. Spierings for their comments on an
earlier draft of this chapter.
2. This description draws heavily on Ettema, A.: *Eerst Beheersen dan Beëindigen. Een
Onderzoek naar Doelstellingen en Werkwijzen van de Rotterdamse Drughulpverlening.*
Groningen: Sociologisch Instituut, 1990.
3. Young Moroccan (North-African) males, who either migrated themselves or who are the
children of recently migrated parents, have become a new marginal minority group in
some West European countries.
4. City of Rotterdam: *Verslaving en Hulpverlening. Nota Verslavingsproblematiek.* Rotterdam, 1979; City of Rotterdam: *Notitie Heroïneverslaving.* Rotterdam, 1980.

200

5. Van Epen, J.H.: *Drugsverslaving en Alcoholisme. Diagnostiek en Behandeling.* Amsterdam/Brussel: Elsevier, 1983.
6. De Jong, W. and Van der Valk, P: *De Geschiedenis van de Rotterdamse Drugshulpverlening van 1972 tot en met 1985 vanuit een Machtstheoretisch Perspectief.* Rotterdam: Erasmus Universiteit, 1986.
7. City of Rotterdam: *Vierjarenplan 1983-1987 Drugshulpverlening.* Rotterdam, 1983.
8. City of Rotterdam: *Vierjarenplan Verslaafdenzorg 1987-1991.* Rotterdam, 1987.
9. In the 60s and 70s, in addition to workers from Turkey, large numbers of Moroccans were hired for the Dutch labor market. During that time, there was a shortage of workers for low-paid and manual work. They were primarily people from the mediterranean area who came to the Netherlands for this type of manual labor. It is the children (born in the Netherlands or in their home country) of these workers who sometimes have drug problems.
10. "Administrative" crime prevention refers to control activities not primarily based on law-enforcement activities. For more information, see articles in *Justitiële Verkenningen 13* (August), 1987.
11. Commissie Kleine Criminaliteit: *Interimrapport Commissie Kleine Criminaliteit.* The Hague: Staatsuitgeverij, 1984.
12. Until the Second World War, Dutch society could be described as a "pillarized" society. A pillarized society is comprised of groups (pillars) that (1) each have their own politically relevant philosophy, religion, or ideology; (2) have little mutual contact; (3) are internally tightly organized. This separation was evident in all facets of social life (social, political, religious, educational, media). After World War II, this was radically changed; Dutch society was no longer characterized by these pillars. The process leading up to the abolishment of the pillarized society is called "de-pillarization". De-pillarization implies de-confessionalization (*i.e.,* the weakening of religion as such and as a factor in politics), de-ideologization, increasing social conication and contacts, and the loosening of ties between the different pillar organizations (political parties, interest groups, mass media, and so on). For a more detailed description, see Lijphart, A.: *The Politics of Accommodation; Pluralism and Democracy in the Netherlands.* Berkeley: University of California Press, 1975.
13. Ministry of Justice: *Society and Criminality. A Policy Plan.* Tweede Kamer, Vergaderjaar 1984-1985. The Hague, 1985.
14. We may distinguish three types of nuisance: (a) Criminal nuisance: This is experienced by victims of a crime committed by drug users, for example, theft, pick pocketing, burglary and robbery. (b) Public order nuisance: This refers to the nuisance directly resulting from drug dealing and drug use. It disturbs the physical conditions of every day life. For example, interrupted sleep because of activities in a neighboring house where drug dealing takes place, or used needles on the street. (c) Visual nuisance: This refers to observations of norm-violating behavior which may instill feelings of unsafety.
15. Intraval: *Hard Drugs and Crime in Rotterdam.* Groningen: St. Intraval, 1989.
16. See, for example: Gandossy, R.P. et al: *Drugs and Crime: a Survey and Analysis of the Literature.* National Institute of Justice, Washington DC: US Government Printing Office, 1980; Inciardi, J.: *The Drugs-Crime Connection.* Beverley Hills: Sage, 1981; Johnson, B.D. et al: *Taking Care of Business: the Economics of Crime by Heroin Abusers.* Lexington, Mass/Toronto: Lexington Books, 1985.
17. Intraval: *Minder Hinder. Eindrapport van het Rotterdamse Drug-Related Crime Project.* Groningen-Rotterdam: St. Intraval, 1990.

18. The D wing has about 30 cells for inmates who consciously have chosen to live in a section of the institution where drug use is not present, and where urine tests are used to check for drug use. The inmates of this wing are subdivided into three categories: recent arrivals (group 3); those who want to be involved in therapy (group 4); and those who do not want to be involved in therapy, but who do want to remain drug-free (group 5). The Consultation Bureau for Alcohol and Drugs (CAD) is in charge of the treatment provided in this wing.

19. Intraval: *De Veilige Jacob. Effecten van Preventie in een Rotterdamse Parkeergarage.* Groningen: St. Intraval, 1989.

PART III

INTERNATIONAL AND SUPRANATIONAL DIMENSIONS

XI. DRUG PREVENTION IN THE NETHERLANDS: A LOW-KEY APPROACH

Ineke Haen Marshall and Chris E. Marshall

1. Introduction

This chapter describes Dutch policies aimed at the prevention of substance use and the reduction of harm resulting from use. We examine three components of prevention policy: (1) the philosophy of drug prevention as expressed by Dutch policy makers and drug experts; (2) the major types of drug prevention programs; and (3) the organizational structure of drug prevention. In the last section of the chapter, we briefly contrast the Dutch approach to drug prevention and education to that of the Americans. Since these policies are so sharply different, this contrast serves well to illuminate important aspects of each.

2. Philosophical foundation of Dutch drug prevention

The basic tenets of Dutch drug policy have extensively been discussed in earlier chapters. It is obvious that drug prevention efforts reflect the philosophical assumptions of drug policy in general. A complication arises when examining drug prevention policy: there is not one, single Dutch drug prevention policy carried out everywhere and every time consistently and uniformly (Van Amerongen 1987:91). However, it is possible to identify five key tenets guiding virtually all Dutch drug prevention programs. (The following discussion of the philosophical foundation of Dutch drug policy draws from Marshall, Anjewierden and Van Atteveld 1990.)

2.1 Tenet 1: Drug use is primarily a public health problem

The government commission instrumental in designing the basic outlines of current Dutch drug policy stated in its 1972 report that the goal of the government's drug policy should be "…. to contribute to the prevention of drug use as a component of the general public welfare approach" (Baan 1972:66). This statement continues to portray the basic philosophy of Dutch drug policy and suggests two important things: drug

The authors thank Wim Buisman for his expert review and helpful suggestions.

use is a public health problem and drug use cannot be effectively controlled by criminal justice measures. In a public health model of drug use, prevention is of primary importance and is best served by education and more information. A Dutch drug expert comments, "Learning how to cope with risk-involving behavior (including alcohol and tobacco use) and how to be responsible for one's behavior and choices, is better than simply deterring and warning people" (Engelsman 1988:15).

Since use is viewed as a health problem, the Opium Act assigns the main responsibility for drug policy to the Minister of Welfare, Health, and Cultural Affairs (WHC), and prevention is exclusively the responsibility of the Ministry of Welfare. The Opium Act regards the contribution of the Minister of Justice as complementary and as focused primarily on combatting (international) drug trafficking (Reitsma 1989). Furthermore, a public health approach to drugs implies that education about illegal drug use should be integrated into more general education issues of developing a healthy lifestyle and making healthy choices (Buisman 1988:17; Becherer and Zwinderman 1990:111).

Selective attention to the issue of drugs, particularly in education would result in a credibility gap because youth is very sensitive to the double standard of adults: "your drugs are killers, but ours are pleasures". Therefore, specialized organizations for drug education do not receive government funding. The premise of drug prevention policy is that education about drug use must not be separated from education about other forms of risky behavior (e.g., alcohol and tobacco use and sexual practices) (Engelsman 1992:146).

Dutch drug prevention education does not consider heroin and cocaine as separate, "dangerous" drugs; rather, alcohol and psychopharmaceuticals are also counted as hard drugs along with tobacco in a comprehensive approach to drug prevention (Van Amerongen 1987:91-92; for examples of this approach see pamphlets distributed by Stichting Nederlandse Onderwijs Televisie 1974; Stichting Preventieprojekt Drugs 1986; CAD Haarlem 1984). A typical example of this approach is a comic strip for youth and their parents about "risky behavior and forms of addiction", where in addition to hard drug use also alcohol, tobacco, eating disorders, and addiction to television are discussed (Geene and Zweverink 1987).

2.2 Tenet 2: Drug use should be normalized and demythologized

In 1985, "normalization" became the key concept of governmental drug policy. In that year the Interministerial Steering Group on Alcohol and Drug Policy (ISAD) published a memorandum titled *Drug Policy in Motion: Towards a Normalization of the Drug Problem*. The concept of normalization entails a gradual process of controlled integration of the drug phenomenon into society. The 1985 report makes a set of recommendations for a "heroin policy aimed at socially integrated use" (ISAD 1985:32). While integration does not mean acceptance of drug use, the recommendation that drug use should be "shorn of its sensational and emotional overtones" (Engelsman 1988:15) is emphatic in this report. In order to accomplish this, one of the things needed is the "demythologization of heroin and heroin users through a more carefully balanced transmission of information" (ISAD 1985:32). Thus, ISAD endorsed the importance of a differentiated and rational education of the drug phenomenon.

Normalization requires great public interest in the drug problem: it is only through this interest that the desirable degree of acceptance and normalization can be attained. Paradoxically, a substantial part of the drug problem is the overwhelming public and media attention that is paid to the "drug problem". Public interest should not be roused by *dramatic* campaigns because "dramatization does not draw closer, but results in expulsion [of the drug user]" (Van Amerongen 1987:92). The ISAD report pointed out that, although most Dutch people have not been directly confronted with drug use, they do have an opinion about it – an opinion shaped mostly by the media which tend to focus mainly on "deviant" cases. In this manner, opinions and myths develop about drugs which influence ordinary social institutions and contribute to the processes of social exclusion. An early government report (Commissie Hulsman 1971) already stressed the importance of providing the public with *correct* information and preventing selective attention to the drug phenomenon. This report noted that high-level government officials play an important role as opinion-leaders. It is essential, in the view of this report, that they are continuously supplied with objective and complete information. "It should be possible to clarify misunderstood statements" (Commissie Hulsman 1971:56).

Current drug policy is explicitly aimed towards trying to remove the exciting, the dramatic, and the deviant images of drug use and users; instead, it emphasizes that the drug user is, first and foremost, a normal citizen who has to be responsible for the consequences of his actions. Consequently, drug prevention efforts try to de-emphasize the "differentness" of the drug user; they aim to portray drug use as a not very dramatic, exciting event. The drug phenomenon should remain outside the realm of the emotional, sensational, and negative atmosphere (Engelsman

1992:145). Drug prevention programs are, therefore, characterized by a matter-of-factness about drugs and its effects; they present information in a businesslike, objective fashion. Dutch experts commonly denounce the often emotional language used by the American mass media and stress that Dutch drug prevention does not want to use such language: "In our present-day linguistic usage terms like narcotics brigade, drug team and war on drugs are used much too easily" (Van Amerongen 1987:92). One should avoid these terms because they evoke fear and emphasize the negative aspects of drug use (Van Amerongen 1987:92-93). It is important, therefore, to have "…. no horror stories, no threats, no strong emphasis on dangers of using substances because it is supposed that this will lead to more experiments with drugs" (Buisman 1988:17).

Normalization does not imply condoning drug use; indeed, drug use should be discouraged, but preferably through measures other than the criminalization of the user. Normalization represents some type of compromise between decriminalization and legalization on the one hand, and a repressive "war on drugs" on the other (Engelsman 1992:144). Normalization suggests that drug use, although not viewed as "normal" or acceptable, has become an integral part of society – a "normal" social problem, one among many. Engelsman (1992:144) draws a parallel with alcohol: it continues to exist, but it has been reduced from a collectively experienced, social problem to an individual problem. A similar result may be achieved through the demystification of drug use.

One of the results of the normalization approach and the tolerant approach to drug use and addiction is that people in the Netherlands are quite accustomed to the sight of disheveled looking addicts walking the streets, apparently oblivious of police presence. It may be argued that this highly visible addict population, in some fashion, conveys a message to the public more powerful than any educational program. Exactly what this message is remains an open question: is it that using drugs is not very glamorous, or that drugs, even though illegal, may be used without any fear of formal police intervention?

2.3 Tenet 3: Major goal of drug policy is harm reduction

In its 1985 report, the ISAD stated that there was ambiguity concerning the objective of Dutch prevention policy: should the objective be to prevent the *use* of drugs, or to prevent *problems with use* (p 11)? Consistent with the notion of normalization, it is now generally accepted that the second objective should be the guiding principle:

".... The general aim of drug policy should be the reduction of drug problems. In that context, preventive policy has as its aim to prevent the emergence of drug problems among people *or* to prevent that already existing problems get worse...." (ISAD 1985:38)

It is not expected that it will be possible to stop all people from using or trying illegal drugs; rather, the explicit aim is to minimize the risks associated with drug use including those risks to the user, the environment, and society. (See, for example, Van der Stel 1992:127.) Consequently, the emphasis of prevention programs is on the need to make choices, and to make these choices as a well-informed person. Importantly, it is not implied that the *only* right choice is *never to try any illegal drugs*; education programs allow for the fact that some people will make the choice to use particular drugs. Prevention programs aim to provide the (potential) user with clear and useful information that allows the person to use or experiment (if he/she *chooses* to do so) with drugs in a manner that minimizes the risks to themselves and their environment.

Buisman and Geirnaert (1992:78) represent the prevalent Dutch view that promoting absolute abstinence ignores the reality of the "drug taking society" in which we live; a more realistic policy goal is responsible drug use where an individual makes a personal and socially responsible choice with respect to use, varying from non-use, delay of use, to use under certain conditions. The Dutch have generally accepted this policy goal with regard to soft drugs and XTC.

A good example of the harm reduction emphasis is a recent pamphlet on XTC, published by the Institute for Alcohol and Drug Prevention Amsterdam (IADA 1991). The drug XTC (also known as "Ecstasy"), is since 1988 on the list of illegal drugs. In practice, this means that the production of and trade in this product are illegal. The five-page pamphlet describes the chemical properties of the drugs, the effects (physical, psychological), and the risks. The pamphlet provides tips for safer use: "If you don't want to run any risks, do not use XTC. XTC remains a drug you must be careful with. If you decide you want to use it anyhow, it is good to keep the following in mind...." Then follows a list of recommendations to reduce risks associated with XTC use: ".... XTC is illegal. Therefore, you are never sure what it is you are buying. If you buy XTC you may prevent unwelcome surprises by not buying it on the streets or in a disco, ask other users for "good" pills and a reliable dealer, try the pill you bought by first taking only one-quarter or half a pill.... Like any other drug, the effect of XTC is partly determined by the conditions and mood of the user and the setting in which you use it. Make sure that you feel well physically and mentally and that you are around the right people in a comfortable atmosphere.... Use selectively (not more than one monthly).... Don't combine it with alcohol, medicine, or other drugs.... Carry condoms with you...." (IADA 1991).

One implication of the harm reduction emphasis for prevention programs is that they tend to shy away from the absolutely-never-under-any-condition approach. In a recent publication intended for users who experience problems with drug use, it is made clear that, for some users, complete abstinence is an unrealistic or undesirable choice; instead, the pamphlet stresses the need to realistically and rationally compare the costs and benefits of complete abstinence. It suggests that for some users "controlled use" may be the preferred approach: "If you can reduce your dependency to such a degree that you can live with it reasonably, that is also progress" (Posma 1991:19). This particular pamphlet is a good example of the practical implementation of the normalization approach; it attempts to show how to integrate drug use in a normal life pattern in such a way as to minimize any harmful effect.

2.4 Tenet 4: Soft drugs and hard drugs are two different things

Dutch drug policy aims to keep users of soft drugs (*i.e.*, drugs with "acceptable risks" such as hashish and marihuana) separate from users of hard drugs (*i.e.*, drugs with "unacceptable risks" such as heroin, cocaine, LSD, amphetamines). This policy is reflected in the *de facto* decriminalization of trading and possessing small quantities of marihuana and tolerating the sale of soft drugs in "coffee shops". The policy with regard to the pseudo-legal retail trade aims to prevent the blending of hard and soft drug markets.

Consistent with this policy, drug prevention efforts stress that the risks of using soft drugs are lower and more acceptable than the risks of using hard drugs. Rather than arguing that not taking any drugs is the only acceptable alternative, Dutch drug prevention efforts tend to stress the difference between soft drugs and hard drugs, thereby implicitly rejecting the "stepping stone theory" of drug use. Actually, most Dutch experts do not view the occasional use of soft drugs as any kind of problem; consequently, prevention efforts do not place much emphasis on marihuana and hashish. The differentiation between soft and hard drugs appears to have had great preventive utility: today, for most Dutch people there is a qualitative difference between soft and hard drugs – that is a line not to be crossed lightly (*cf.* Van der Stel 1992:15). This conscious differentiation between soft drugs and hard drugs is reflected in the government's "message" on heroin and cannabis:

"Heroin – a quickly and intensively addicting substance. Any experimenting must be dissuaded.... Cannabis – a psychotropic substance, and consequently not without risks.... No panic about experimental and functional-recreational usage. Encouragement to cannabis usage is ill-advised" (Van Amerongen 1987:94).

2.5 Tenet 5: Dutch drug policy is pragmatic, not moralizing

Current Dutch drug policy is pragmatic and mainly guided by cost-benefit principles (see Marshall *et al.* 1990:393). This is not to say that moral considerations have never played an important role in Dutch public policy with regard to mind-altering substances. To the contrary, drug prevention efforts had to break away from strongly moralistic concepts, in which moral theology played a predominant role (Van Amerongen 1987:93). In its early years, drug education was an extension of rather old-fashioned information about alcohol. For a long time, Dutch alcohol information showed a very rigid and threatening character, in which the main lines were drawn by total abstinence (Van Amerongen 1987:93). Paralleling information about alcohol, drug education initially focused on information in combination with warnings and moral remarks. But presently there is support for the notion that young people, *knowledgeable* young people, who want to experiment should get the latitude to do so and not be thought immoral having made that choice.

Today's drug prevention programs aim to steer away from moralizing practices. For example, Buisman (1988:16) states that there is a consensus among prevention officials that there should be ".... less emphasis on moral aspects, more on individually accountable choice of risky substance and risky habits". Consistent with the pragmatic philosophy, most drug education efforts are devoid of moralizing messages and value judgements; rather, they stress the need to be able to rationally calculate the "costs" versus the "benefits" of using drugs. In a recent discussion of an American education program ("Skills for Adolescence"), Akveld and Buisman (1992:160) conclude that, although generally speaking this appears to be a solid program, the part concerning drugs reflects the very moralizing American background: "This segment definitely needs further adjustment for the Dutch situation." (Akveld and Buisman 1992:160)

This non-moralizing stance is a cornerstone of government policy. However, whether this formal policy is always reflected in actual practices, is, of course, another matter. In this context, it is useful to distinguish between official government policy (pragmatic, non-moralizing) and the beliefs of "John Q. Public". The Dutch public is not necessarily as tolerant, understanding, and open-minded as formal policy would suggest. The public is tolerant with regard to cannabis; however, there is a fairly widespread disapproval of hard drugs, particularly in the big cities. Thus, as the ideas and values of prevention efforts "trickle down" from government policy makers, scholars, and legislators to individual police officers, school teachers, and health education staff, a substantial part of their non-moralizing character is often lost. It seems only reasonable to expect, then, that value judgements of individual health workers, counselors, teachers, and police officers *are* inevitably incorporated in the final "messages" transmitted to the audience (see, for example, Van Amerongen 1987:93 for a discussion of moralizing by the police); these value judgements may be closer to the American "drugs are evil" ideology than the Dutch may like to think.

3. Types of prevention programs in the Netherlands

Policies aimed at the demand side of drug use draw heavily from medical (public health) literature, which makes a distinction between primary prevention efforts and secondary prevention efforts (*cf.* Mulder 1978:98). Primary prevention interventions are those designed to reach individuals before they have developed a specific disorder or disease. Dutch drug policy's primary objective is minimalization of risk and harm associated with drug use, rather than to prevent *any* use or experimentation. Therefore, translated into Dutch drug policy terms, primary prevention programs are those designed to reach individuals before they have developed *problems* with drug use. We may further distinguish between (1) primary prevention efforts aimed at the total population (particularly the young), and (2) primary prevention efforts aimed at high-risk groups.

Secondary prevention interventions are those designed to decrease the number of existing cases with the "disease" in a particular population (Botvin 1990:465). Applied to the Dutch situation, secondary prevention programs are designed to prevent drug abuse problems among (high) risk groups who are not current users, but who are likely to start using or abusing drugs (*e.g.*, immigrants, school dropouts, children of addicted parents, youngsters in residential youth care facilities, unemployed youth), or groups that (already) have adopted a rather high and risky pattern of drug consumption, which could lead to severe drug abuse in the near future (Buisman 1992). The general aim is to decrease the number of users who experience *harmful* consequences of their use.

3.1 Prevention efforts aimed at total population (mostly youths)

Primary prevention efforts targeted at the total population by means of mass media campaigns are not common in the Netherlands. It is commonly believed that programs aimed at a general audience are unnecessary and not justified in cost-benefit terms. It is also thought that these kinds of programs may cause several unintended negative side effects. Because the main target group of young people at risk is probably no greater than 10% of the total population, experts believe that there are more appropriate prevention methods available to risk groups than the execution of big mass media campaigns (Buisman 1988:22). Although, unlike the English and American situations, there is not much support for high profile mass media campaigns in the Netherlands (Buisman 1988:22), a large mass media drug information campaign was initiated in 1980 by a non-profit group (SIRE) which lasted for more than five years. Akveld and Buisman characterize this campaign as a "low profile" campaign (1992:166). The campaign consisted of advertisements in newspapers and magazines urging frank, open discussion about drugs and to become as well informed as possible. Headlines in the ads included: "Fear is a bad advisor" and "Ignorance does not help". The readers were invited to cut out a coupon entitling them to a free booklet "What everybody should know about drugs" (Buisman 1988:21-22; also Buisman 1990). A total of more than 500,000 booklets were distributed in this manner. The main targets for this media information campaign were parents, teachers, youth workers, and health professionals. The effect of this campaign was evaluated in 1985, and it was found that mostly well-educated people and people who already were involved in the topic asked for the pamphlet. Mostly the campaign was effective in increasing knowledge and interest in drugs (Van Berkum *et al.* 1986) (For more information on this campaign, see Buisman and Kok 1983.)

There have been some other small-scale, fairly simple campaigns with as a common denominator that they are informative, slightly cautionary, but not threatening or judgmental (Akveld and Buisman 1992:167). However, after the SIRE campaign, there have only been two other broad-based mass media drug-related education programs. First, in 1986, the Ministry of Welfare, Health and Cultural Affairs initiated a national anti-alcohol campaign with as slogan, "Be honest.... how much do YOU drink....?" (see: Van de Vrie 1988; Zandbergen 1987 for more details). More recently, a comprehensive media campaign was initiated on the HIV virus and AIDS.

The recent media campaigns on AIDS clearly illustrate how the Dutch attempt to avoid negative approaches, included those intended to have emotionally charged shock effects. As compared to American and British campaigns, the Dutch are more explicit in their campaigns and humor is often used to get people's attention (Cohen 1989:15). For example, "I do it with...." posters (showing prominent Dutch public figures) convey the double meaning of having sex using condoms as well as the suggestion that one is about to reveal the identity of one's sex partner. The focus of Dutch media campaigns is "less on what not to do and more on what you can be doing" (Cohen 1989:15).

Perhaps the Dutch approach to drug prevention is best characterized as "low-key". This low-key approach is not only reflected in the relative unimportance of general mass-media anti-drug campaigns, but also in the low priority given to drug education to school-age youth. Buisman, a leading Dutch expert on drug prevention, argues that alcohol and tobacco education should be started in primary schools, at the age of ten (1988:17). These educational efforts should be repeated in the first year of junior high, and at this time cannabis education should be included in the curriculum. In the higher classes of secondary schools, tobacco and cannabis education should be repeated, possibly including other drugs at this time; however, alcohol education at all times should continue to be an integral aspect of the education plan (Buisman 1988:17). Consistent with this advice, there *are* some examples of broad-based programs integrated in general health education programs, but drug education ".... is far from completely integrated into the regular school curriculum" (Cohen 1989:11). A WHO (World Health Organization) survey of 29 countries with regard to prevention programs for drugs, indicates that school drug education in the Netherlands was merely "incidental" (Smart *et al.* 1988: Table 2). (It should be noted that this survey was conducted in the early eighties and employed very global and rough measures.) Curriculum education, teacher training, and teacher counseling training for primary and secondary school children are not uniformly incorporated in schools throughout the Netherlands, although more than 60% of the high schools pay attention to drug education during 2 hours a year on the average (Mesters and Buisman 1987).

The National Institute of Alcohol and Drugs (NIAD) has developed the main primary school program at a national level, targeting 11- and 12-year olds. Some of the school-based programs have been evaluated. Included among these is the evaluation of the effect of drug and alcohol education on fifth and sixth graders which shows an increase of knowledge, but no change in attitude (Jessen and Winkel 1989). Also, Becherer and Zwinderman (1990) found that a drug prevention project in high-school affected knowledge, but not attitudes about drugs.

A number of Dutch cities run their own local programs, sometimes adapting the NIAD materials and involving police and addicts (Cohen 1989). Involvement of police in school drug education remains controversial in the Netherlands. Beginning in the 1970s, numerous police officers started to provide drug education to schools. Typically, education by the police tended to emphasize the sensational tale and the horror-stories of drug use (Van Harten 1988). Concerned with the possible negative effect of police involvement in drug education, the Education and Prevention branch of the former FZA (Federation of Institutions for Alcohol and Drugs, the former government-funded umbrella organization for drug programs) formally protested against police involvement in drug education. Consequently, an agreement was reached in 1984 between the Ministry of Justice, the Ministry of the Interior (in charge of local police), and the Ministry of Welfare, Health and Cultural Affairs to distribute an order designed to end police involvement in education. For reasons not entirely clear, this order was never executed and Dutch police continue to actively participate in drug education. For example, in 1986 the Amsterdam police initiated a prevention project for 12-year-olds (6th graders) which involves a confrontation with a drug addict in jail (De Keijser 1989). In 1988/1989 about 75% of all Amsterdam schools participated in this program. In Rotterdam a policeman organizes programs with primary schools in his area. It includes talks by the police and addicts. It should be noted that Dutch experts continue to strongly reject police education as being "counterproductive" (see also Buisman 1988:16).

3.2 Prevention programs targeted at high-risk groups

Most Dutch experts agree that drug prevention efforts are most efficient if focused on specific high-risk target groups, rather than aiming at a broad-based audience (e.g., media and school programs). Indeed, in the Netherlands today, the main focus has shifted from primary prevention to specific (secondary) drug abuse prevention (Buisman 1992:6). From a cost-benefit analysis, general primary prevention (expensive, with limited success) is not as useful as a more focused prevention targeted at high-risk groups where more intense intervention may be planned with a greater chance of a positive result (Buisman and Geirnaert 1992:79). Some Dutch prevention programs are aimed at such high-risk target groups as those already experimenting, which makes it hard to make a clear distinction between primary prevention programs aimed at high-risk youth and secondary prevention programs. Other high-risk groups are those in youth homes, or those already involved with social service agencies. Buisman (1988, 1992) and Buisman and Van der Stel (1992) list prevention programs aimed at adolescents who have left school, youngsters who go out a lot at night, migrant children, cannabis users, children of addicted parents, as well as hard drug users. In this context, the term "marginalized youth" (randgroepjongeren) is used to refer to youths (16-25 years) who are socially disadvantaged in several ways. It is this category of youths who are at high risk for problematic drug use (Akveld and Buisman 1992:162). The policy objective for these high-risk groups is to prevent premature exclusion from assistance programs, school, community centers, and other significant reference groups and, relatedly, to prevent marginalization and stigmatization (Borghuis 1990:21). Furthermore, the primary goal of these programs is to prevent *problematic* use or to promote the sensible use of alcohol and drugs (*ibid.* p 21).

One of the first programs of this kind was the Amsterdam Stichting Preventieproject Drugs which targets high-risk youths between the ages of 12 and 20. Another example of recent preventive work with high-risk youths is the Prevention Alcohol and Drugs (PAD) team in The Hague where youth centers now have permanent prevention workers. This worker makes weekly visits to the center and develops specially adjusted programs for these centers. Program methods vary from distribution of pamphlets and posters, and unstructured conversations about the topic, to showing videos, organizing information evenings, a competition in fixing alcohol-free drinks, and beer tasting contests (including, of course, alcohol-free beer)(De Ruijter 1989:10-11).

In his recent overview of Dutch (secondary) prevention programs, Buisman (1992) describes a program aimed at cocaine use among high-risk youths (Amsterdam youngsters between 14 and 21 years, low-income, poorly educated, frequent disco and coffee shop visitors): the Amsterdam Cocaine Prevention Campaign conducted by the Jellinek Institute for Alcohol and Drug Prevention Amsterdam in 1986-1988. Activities in the first stage of the campaign were aimed to change the general belief among the target group that cocaine is a safe drug when used carefully. The slogan of "Coke, the white hammer" was displayed on eye-catching posters, and information booklets (in both Dutch and English) were distributed to disco's, coffee shops, and youth centers. In the second stage of the campaign the notion was challenged that use of cocaine increases your status among your peers. Other posters and booklets were distributed with the slogan: "Cocaine, the illusion of being strong". The last stage of the program involved three videos specially designed for the target youths. Although no formal evaluation study has been conducted, there are reasons to believe that the campaign had some positive effects. Different groups requested campaign materials (including bar-owners who like to hang the posters on the doors of the toilets). People are no longer openly using cocaine in disco toilets. The campaign slogans are still favorite and frequently used. The prevalence of cocaine use in Amsterdam was reduced from 1.6 in 1987 to 1.3 in 1990. (For more details on this program, see Jamin 1991.)

Special efforts are made to communicate with young foreign tourists visiting Amsterdam, a notoriously high-risk group because of the international reputation of this city as the low-threshold access drug capital of the world. A special pamphlet is available in places where these young visitors tend to congregate, providing information and caution on drug use in this city. [Amsterdam Institute for Alcohol and Drug Prevention, IADA] Because it is well known that young migrants (*i.e.,* Surinamese, Antillians, Moroccans, and Moluccans) have an increased risk of problematic drug use, a small number of prevention programs targeting these groups have been developed (Akveld and Buisman 1992:164).

Of course, AIDS has added a special urgency to programs aimed at the reduction of the harmful consequences of drug use. Since the mid-eighties, the Dutch have developed a very pro-active AIDS prevention policy – a policy explicitly trying to effect realistic changes in the lifestyle (*i.e.,* safer drug use and safer sex) of as many drug users as possible, as quickly as possible (Kerssemakers and Kramer 1992:195). Needle exchange has been a mainstay of AIDS prevention. The Dutch have been pioneers of street/outreach work around drugs issues. One advantage is that drug use in the Netherlands, with more facilities where drug-using people may openly congregate, is much less underground than in either the US or UK (Cohen 1989:17). An example of an innovative outreach program is project "NO Risk" where drug users are used as "paraprofessionals" who, for pay, do outreach work focused on drug using prostitutes and other users (Kerssemakers and Kramer 1992).

In addition, training programs have been developed for police officers, community workers and volunteers. In collaboration with the Foundation of Parents of Drug Addicts, special training programs are carried out for counseling and guiding of self-help groups of parents of drug addicts. These programs are supported with educational and audio-visual materials, developed and distributed by national organizations (Buisman 1988:23).

4. Organizational structure of drug prevention programs

The Netherlands is an economically rather healthy and prosperous country with one of the world's best developed systems of social welfare and health services. It is thus not surprising to find that a large variety of organizations and individuals are involved in "doing something about drugs". It is estimated that there are about 100 full-time prevention officials, engaged in preparation, development and management of educational and preventive programs (Buisman 1988:18). Often, prevention and treatment services are integrated in that the same organization employs specialists in both fields (Cohen 1989:8). Several hundreds of health education officials attend to drug education as part of a more comprehensive general health education program. Additionally, an unknown number of other professionals like doctors, community workers, youth club workers and volunteers are conducting education programs having strong components of drug prevention (Buisman 1988:18).

It is not simple to provide a comprehensive overview of all organizations involved in drug prevention in the Netherlands since both governmental organizations and non-governmental organizations (usually subsidized by the government) consider prevention of drug-related problems one of their responsibilities. In the following, we will limit our discussion to only the most important national and regional organizations. Part of alcohol and drug information is given by organizations with ideological principles, namely, the National Committee against Alcoholism, originally a total abstinence organization, and the People's League against Excessive Drinking, a temperance organization (Van Amerongen 1987:95). Prior to 1940, a great part of the assistance and treatment of alcoholics was in the hands of volunteers and these volunteers were mostly strong opponents of alcohol use (Otto 1984:120). After World War II, volunteers almost completely disappeared, and alcoholism came to be viewed as a disease – a disease best attended to by "experts". Presently, by far the greatest part of alcohol and drug instruction is planned and carried out by the CADs (Consultation Bureaus Alcohol and Drugs). These CADs utilize virtually no volunteers. They are non-governmental organizations, but fully subsidized by the Ministry of Welfare, Health and Culture. There is a network of CADs in the Netherlands; nearly all large and medium-sized towns have a CAD. The initial CAD activity was assistance to people with alcohol problems. Since 1970, these CADs also have taken responsibility for assistance to drug addicts. Today, the main tasks are: ambulant care and treatment for people with alcohol and drug problems, probation supervision for those convicted of drunken driving or drug offenses; and, since 1979, prevention (Van Amerongen 1987:95).

While prior to 1979, CADs did some prevention work, it was not done systematically. Pioneering work in prevention was done by the FZA (Federation of Institutions for Alcohol and Drugs, the government-funded umbrella organization to which all CADs and alcohol and drug clinics belonged). In 1973, the FZA appointed three people to travel through the country and educate agencies about prevention (Van Dalen 1987:55). It was not until 1975 that the CADs started to pay attention to systematically organized prevention activities. In 1979, funding was provided for CDAs to appoint their own prevention staff (Van Dalen 1987:55). At that time, the job of prevention workers was not fully described; the role had developed by way of trial and error. In 1981, there were five professional prevention staff at the FZA, and 36 at the CADs; in addition, general CAD staff was expected to spend 10 percent of their time on prevention activities (Otto 1984:122).

Since 1979, the FZA has assigned primary responsibility for local and regional prevention projects to the CADs. In the early 1980s, emphasis was placed on secondary prevention (*i.e.*, the promotion of early recognition of addiction *problems*). In 1987, the FZA ceased to exist as an independent organization. Together with two other institutions it merged into the NIAD (National Institute for Alcohol and Drugs). Its activities, in the field of promoting, developing and evaluating alcohol and drug prevention programs were continued within this new organizational context.

In addition to CADs, the GGDs (Municipal Health Departments) play an important role in drug prevention. Operating within these GGDs are departments of Health Education (Gezondheidsvoorlichting en Opvoeding - GVOs) that focus on drug education and prevention. The exact role of CADs and GGDs varies from area to area and is further complicated by recent re-organization and the involvement of a number of voluntary organizations in the field. Ideally, the preventive activities of the CADs and GGDs complement each other.

5. American drug prevention

As described earlier, the Dutch view drug use or abuse as a public health issue. With this view, the Dutch expect that most policy emphasis be placed upon the following: (1) recognition of the need to normalize and demythologize drug use; (2) harm reduction; (3) a sharp distinction between soft drugs and hard drugs; and (4) maintenance of a pragmatic, not moralizing drug policy. As we have seen, the Dutch have, by and large, attempted to seriously incorporate these basic elements in their prevention programs.

Present drug policy in the United States reflects sharply different goals and premises than those of Holland. The difference between these countries lies in large part with the apparatus which each country sets loose on the "problem": in Holland, the choice is social workers, psychologists, physicians, prevention professionals, and community workers; in the United States the choice is police, judges, and lawyers. Rather than viewing drug use as a public health matter, Americans tend to see these activities as a moral/legal issue. Based upon this moral/legal perspective, American drug policy emphasizes: (1) repression of all drug use even to the point of "zero tolerance"; (2) moral stigmatization of all involved with drugs from suppliers to users; (3) dramatization of the negatives of the lives of those involved with drugs by means of media, government propaganda, or any other vehicles available; (4) blurring the distinction between soft and hard drugs so as to simplify the moral message to "hate all drugs"; and, finally (5) use of the criminal justice apparatus rather than public welfare and medicine to deal with the problem of drug use.

5.1 The "war on drugs"

Both Musto (1987) and Conrad and Schneider (1980) have provided detailed and interesting histories of narcotic control in the United States. The pre-1914 attitude of most Americans was one in which no stigma was attached to opiate use or addiction (Conrad and Schneider 1980:116). The Harrison Act of 1914 was the first major effort to place narcotics use under federal control. It was a tax act and not a direct prohibition of narcotics. The intent of the bill was to place opiates and addicts completely in the hands of physicians. However, in placing the enforcement of the act in hands of the Treasury Department, the implementation of the Act quickly took on the character of a moral crusade and resulted in harassment of physicians and druggists (Conrad and Schneider 1980:124). Moreover, two Supreme Court decisions, *Jin Fuey Moy vs United States* (1920) and *United States vs Behrman* (1922), continued to take away the control of the medical profession over opium use and distribution.

Another significant event in the history of narcotic control in the United States is the creation of the Federal Bureau of Narcotics (FBN) in 1930 within the Justice Department. Henry J. Anslinger, a former Prohibition official, became the head of the FBN and an archetypical "moral entrepreneur". His efforts to cause the public through major propaganda efforts to view narcotic addiction as clearly a criminal problem and the addict as a moral degenerate are legendary. Anslinger and his agency had an enormous effect upon national drug policy for 30 years; he finally resigned in the early 1960s and national drug policy began to shift away from the law enforcement model toward the treatment model (Abadinsky 1989:66-67). In the late 1960s and early 1970s, there was greatly expanded funding of drug rehabilitation programs and also a growing popularity of the "therapeutic community" approach – for example, Synanon in California and Daytop Village, Phoenix House, Odysey House, and others in New York – to addiction (Rouse 1991).

Thus, the law enforcement approach to drug control has not always dominated American drug policy. For example, President Carter, in an address to Congress in 1979, expressed his support for lessening the law enforcement approach to drug policy:

"Penalties against possession of a drug should not be more damaging to an individual than the use of the drug itself; and where they are, they should be changed. Nowhere is this more clear than in the laws against possession of marihuana in private for personal use" (Carter 1979:66-67).

President Carter's narrow electoral victory in 1976 was a premonition of the increasing general conservativism in the country, including its views of drug use. Ronald Reagan's landslide presidential victory in 1980 completed the cycle. President Reagan and his administration aimed at the supply of drugs in the United States with increased appropriations for law enforcement. Moreover, Nancy Reagan represented the "zero tolerance" attitude by directing disdain at the demander/user of drugs. She states: "Each of us has a responsibility to be intolerant of drug use anywhere, any time, by anybody.... We must create an atmosphere of intolerance for drug use in this country".

In the view of some, the drug war attempted to create a new morality, one with a clear "right" and "wrong". It is arguable that the American loss of the Vietnam War and the frequent questions of moral impropriety regarding the actions taken during its conduct left a country in need of moral guidelines upon which to rely. The drug war, then, was an attempt, through federal, state, and local policy to "create" a morality in what was perceived to be a moral void. The perceived crisis of drugs provided the perfect vehicle for the badly needed moral crusade. Other important factors arose in the decade of the 1980s. First, in 1981, the acquired immune deficiency syndrome (AIDS) was discovered. This fatal disease could be transmitted by contaminated needles which were used to inject drugs. Secondly, in 1985, "crack", a smokeable and relatively cheap form of cocaine, appeared in several areas of the US (Musto 1987:274). These two developments were used as political justifications for the Anti-Drug Abuse Act of 1986. As Musto describes the political aspects of this act: "..Congress and the President vied with one another to show their hatred of drugs and to state how much money they were willing to pit against the drug issue" (*ibid.* 1987:274). The first debate regarding the Act occurred in August 1986 at which time a public furor over cocaine had peaked; the Act was signed into law by Reagan shortly before the November elections. This Act authorized $4 billion for the battle against drugs and most of this was directed at law enforcement. (It should be noted that the AIDS argument was used similarly – as a political justification – but with the opposite effect in the Netherlands: not to increase law enforcement efforts, but as a legitimation of *pragmatic* drug policy.)

A few years ago, the White House issued the report: *National Drug Control Strategy* (1989) which sets forth the Bush Administration's policy regarding illegal drugs: "The main thrust and heart of the report, measured by proposed expenditures and emphasis, centers largely upon law enforcement, interdiction efforts, and increased and heavier penalties for convicted offenders" (Kittel 1992:107). This report recommends a vast expansion of the criminal justice system at both the state and federal levels. Specific recommendations include more street-level drug law enforcement; expanded efforts to eradicate the domestic marihuana crop; drug testing of arrestees, prisoners, and individuals under court supervision; more judges, prosecutors, and police; more vigorous prosecution of misdemeanor drug offenders by the states; greater coordination of federal, state and local efforts; and massive increase in prison space (Kittel 1992:113).

Drugs are viewed as one of the primary causes of street crime in the United States, where fear of crime is at an all-time high. In American society, people's fear of crime, now more so than ever before, appears to focus on racial minorities, African-Americans in particular. Many people associate gangs, drugs, assault and public disorder with black inner city violence. The "war on drug" pictures the drug user/addict as a violent person, to be feared:

"Reflecting on the earlier wave of drug intolerance, one cannot help but be concerned that the fear of drugs will again translate into a simple fear of the drug user and will be accompanied by draconian sentences and specious links between certain drugs and distrusted groups within society, as was the case with cocaine and Southern blacks in the first decade of this century" (Musto 1987:277).

In the US drugs have become a highly politicized issue, a central focus of the mass media and a main concern of the public. Because of its perceived links with violence, crime, and deteriorating race relations, the war on drugs was one of the main campaign issues in the 1992 presidential platforms. In the US, drug abuse is a very salient, high profile issue – much more so than in the Netherlands; this is reflected in the much more intense efforts to prevent and combat drug use. In 1992, the American federal budget for drug control was 12 billion dollars; approximately 70% of the drug control budget was allocated to law enforcement and other supply-reduction strategies. It should be noted, however, that President Clinton, the Democratic successor of George Bush, has called for a re-evaluation of the current drug war, with increased emphasis on treatment alternatives.

5.2 American drug use prevention programs

Although the American national preoccupation with drugs is of a more recent origin, the US has been experimenting with substance abuse prevention programs for more than two decades. (The following description draws from Botvin 1990.) A large variety of programs exist. Many of these prevention programs focus on school populations. As in the Netherlands, in the US, information dissemination is the most widely used approach. These approaches generally focus on the provision of factual information concerning the nature and pharmacology of specific substances, the ways in which these substances are used, and the adverse consequences of use (Botvin 1990:474). School programs involve the teaching of factual information in drug education classes, school-wide assembly programs featuring guest speakers (frequently police officers or health professionals), and films. In some programs, student involvement has taken the form of organizing a showing of film strips, conducting poster contests, developing anti-drugs public service announcements, or producing anti-drug plays and skits (Botvin 1990:475).

As Botvin points out (1990:475), in contrast to approaches designed to merely disseminate factual information, some have attempted to emphasize and even dramatize the risks associated with tobacco, alcohol and drug use. The underlying assumption is that evoking a simple, visceral fear would be more effective in repressing use than would volumes of "facts" and information about drugs. There is a clear and unambiguous message that drug use is dangerous, and those individuals foolish enough to disregard warnings by parents, teachers and health professionals will be left to suffer the consequences (Botvin 1990:475).

There is no doubt that the fear arousal approach is a mainstay of American drug prevention policy and has become more prominent over the last few years.

Another approach, frequently combined with information dissemination, involves attacking the problem of drug use from a moral perspective (Botvin 1990). This prevention strategy involves "preaching" to students about the evils of smoking, drinking, or using drugs and exhorting them not to engage in those behaviors (Botvin 1990:475-476). Often in conjunction with the above-mentioned fear arousal emphasis, the moral component has recently become increasingly important in drug prevention programs.

American programs have also approached drug education as a process designed to increase affective skills. The focus of affective education programs is on values clarification, teaching responsible decision-making, increasing self-esteem, and promoting participation in alternatives (Botvin 1990:477). (See also Tobler 1986.)

Many current educational programs incorporate a number of the above-discussed approaches (i.e., information dissemination, fear arousal, moral appeal, and affective education.) Two programs which have received considerable attention are SPECDA (School Program to Educate and Control Drug Abuse) in New York City and DARE (Drug Abuse Resistance Education) in Los Angeles. These programs are remarkably similar in objective and assumptions about the precursors of adolescent drug (ab)use (De Jong 1987:21). Both of these involve the close partnership of the schools and the police as a vehicle to intervene and mediate peer, relative, and sibling pressure – these thought to be the key to drug and alcohol use among adolescents. Both SPECDA and DARE are aimed at fifth and sixth graders. The curricula of the programs include such units as: (1) factual information on alcohol, tobacco, and drugs and the consequences of use; (2) promoting self-awareness and self-esteem; (3) assessment of risks and decision-making skills; (4) media and peer influence that encourage substance use; (5) techniques for resisting peer pressure; and (6) positive alternatives to substance use (De Jong 1987:17).

A recent DARE "graduation ceremony" of fifth graders in a public school in a midwestern city provides a good illustration of the importance and nature of drug education in American public schools. Students, dressed up in their best clothes, were called by name, one by one, to come to the front of the auditorium to receive their "diploma". Emphasizing the importance of this event was the presence of several uniformed police officers, a high-level representative of the school administration, the school principal, parents, and other friends and relatives. The fifth graders signed a certificate, promising never to use drugs. Several children had written brief skits for this special occasion. These skits were perhaps the most convincing evidence of the "success" of the DARE program: one took place in a cemetery (drugs kill!!), and several others made it clear that any experimenting with any type of drug (including alcohol) was bound to result in disaster.

While these programs have received much attention and many schools across the country continue to emulate the original ones, systematic evaluation of their success is limited (Moore and Kleiman 1989:11). Botvin (1990:478) notes that, overall, these approaches have not been shown to be effective.

With regard to the role of the mass media, most of these have relied on information-dissemination and/or fear-arousal strategies (Botvin 1990:503; Buisman 1990). Many opinion leaders in the United States including politicians, sports, media and music stars have begun to repeatedly convey the message of the new drug morality: "Just Say No!". The mass media also frequently emphasize the fear arousal aspect. A good example is a television add showing a fried egg: "This is your brain on crack!"

Another important aspect which distinguishes the US from the Netherlands is its grass-roots support of drug prevention programs. As Botvin points out, a growing force in substance-abuse prevention in recent years is the Parents' Movement. This is essentially a grass-roots movement involving concerned parents from communities throughout the country who have organized themselves into local parents groups. The main function of these groups is to provide support for concerned parents, to provide a mechanism for becoming educated about drugs, to increase the awareness of the parents throughout the community, and to serve as a catalyst for change in their communities (Botvin 1990:504). More recently, many of these local parent groups have been drawn under the umbrella of the National Federation of Parents for Drug-Free Youth (NFP), formed in 1980. Another example are Mad Dads, a self-help community group consisting of African-American males whose main purpose is to rid their neighborhood of drug use and violence; an important aspect of their work consists of talking to schools and community organizations about the evils of drugs. In addition to community volunteers, professional associations such as the American Bar Association, the American Medical Association, the American Public Health Association, and the American Psychological Association have all begun taking a greater leadership role in the area of substance-abuse prevention (Botvin 1990:504).

Burden (1990) identifies six major youth groups which, in different ways, are trying to do something about problematic drug use. The Boy Scouts of America, for example, has since 1987 distributed more than 13 million copies of an 18-page brochure, "Drugs: A Deadly Game"; also available from the BSA is a video and a wall-size chart showing the effect of drugs, alcohol, and smoking on the human body, and a discussion guide for parents and teachers. The New York City Police Department's drug awareness efforts have utilized the BSA materials (Burden 1990:9). Other youth organizations which have initiated similar programs include the Boys Clubs of America; the Girl Scouts of the USA ("Take the Lead: Fight Drugs"); Girls, Inc. ("Friendly Peer-suasion"); Camp Fire for Boys and Girls ("I'm Peer-Proof"); Key Clubs, the youth arm of Kiwanis International (Burden 1990).

Finally, the US has several comprehensive community-based prevention projects. Botvin (1990:507-510) describes project STAR (Student Taught Awareness and Resistance) as an exemplary program of comprehensive community-based prevention. The most recent comprehensive community-based drug prevention program is the federally funded "Seed and Weed" program, a program designed to "weed" out drugs and crime in high-crime areas and "seed" these neighborhoods with positive alternatives (*i.e.,* employment, decent housing, and so on).

6. Conclusion

Although there are undeniably parallels between prevention strategies in Holland and the US, they differ in several important ways. First, the national pre-occupation with drugs in the US makes substance use control and prevention a higher priority item. The American mass media, public, politicians, and educators appear to devote considerably more resources and energy to issues related to drugs prevention than is the case in Holland. Differences in intensity of prevention efforts reflect fundamental differences in the definition of drugs as a social problem in the US and the Netherlands: In the US, drugs are viewed as a terrible evil to be fought with heavy arms (both in terms of prevention and repression); in the Netherlands, from a policy maker's viewpoint, drugs are viewed as a "normal" social and health risk controlled by minimal measures or even ignored (*e.g.,* cannabis, XTC). In the Netherlands, both law enforcement and prevention are kept low-key and minimal; in the US, both law enforcement and prevention are more intense. Relatedly, American prevention programs employ fear arousal and moral appeals in a higher degree than in Holland. And finally, there is much more reliance on volunteers, self-help and grass-roots involvement in the US than in Holland.

Our overview of Dutch and American drug prevention programs further suggests the need for a careful evaluation of the role of media and media campaigns: "..the net effect of public service announcements designed to prevent substance abuse.... can only be characterized as infinitessimal compared with advertisements promoting tobacco, alcohol, and drug products" (Botvin 1990:502-503). Indeed, "an overwhelming majority of mass media drug abuse prevention programs have failed to change behavior" (Flay and Sobel 1983, cited by Botvin 1990:503). Moreover, media campaigns can do damage: emotional anti-drug campaigns "inevitably increase the ostracism of drug users, further alienating them from society" (Rhodes 1990:16). As pointed out by Buisman (1988:20), although mass media campaigns have been shown to be non-effective, mass media definitively can have a function in the process of drug communication, because through them it is possible to direct the topics about which people think and talk. This so-called "agenda setting" function is extremely important in raising the proper public concern for the problem (Buisman 1988:21). Importantly, one should not forget that the media play a significant role in the constant glamorizing of drugs.

Further, in view of the fact that drug use is primarily viewed as a lower-class, minority phenomenon, particularly in the US, it is ironical that there seems to be a lack of appropriate preventive means to communicate with these risk groups. The most common preventive means such as booklets, audio-visual materials, and so on are very middle-class oriented and often are of limited utility for members of ethnic minority groups (Buisman 1988:28-29). This problem is also noted to be true for the American situation (Botvin 1990). Interventions are focused primarily on white, middle-class populations. A key question remaining unanswered concerns the efficacy of these programs with high-risk groups (Botvin 1990:510).

The relative success of the Dutch *vis-à-vis* the American approach to prevention may be judged in at least two different manners. The first is through evaluation studies which have been conducted in both countries. (See Botvin 1990, for a listing of American studies.) Interestingly, both Dutch and American studies seem to consistently indicate the relative inefficacy of traditional school-based prevention programs in changing attitudes and behavior. We have to be realistic in our expectations concerning the positive preventive effects of drug education programs, particularly in schools: "If our educational system, that is for almost 100% cognitively oriented, would pretend to be able to prevent a behavioral problem with relatively few cognitive aspects such as drug abuse, through education (*i.e.*, teaching), it would show very little sense of reality" (Van Amerongen 1982:143; see also Buisman and Geirnaert 1992:83). Unfortunately, evaluation studies in both countries suffer from methodological shortcomings and few prevention programs have a built-in evaluation component. At this point, therefore, evaluation studies cannot be used as the basis for our assessment.

A second way of assessing the relative merits of different approaches to substance use prevention is by comparing facts on drug use in the population. In Holland, drug use among young people is lower than in the US. Alcohol use among young Dutch people has increased over the last decade (Reijneveld 1990) while drug use has remained constant or even leveled off. However, cocaine use in the Netherlands is viewed as a growing problem among young people and adults. In the US, according to recent reports, drug use in general has been declining; experimental and casual use have been declining sharply (Kittel 1992:108). However, it is notable that frequent drug use by the poor in inner-city areas is either remaining constant or increasing (Kittel 1992:108). Although one might quibble about the exact figures and statistics, most experts would agree that drug abuse is currently a more pressing social problem in the US than in Holland.

We agree with Engelsman (1992:138) that a pragmatic and problem-oriented policy works better than an emotional, dogmatic approach. The Dutch pragmatic approach has prevented the use of radical measures such as forced treatment, drug testing at the work place, and fear-inducing information campaigns – "solutions" which may give the appearance of a tough approach, but which frequently cause more problems than they solve. Engelsman (1992:149-150) lists several additional accomplishments of Dutch drug policy: addicts are not forced to live an isolated life of social exclusion; the drugs phenomenon is more public and visible and thus controllable; social service agencies are able to reach the majority of users; the social and physical functioning of users is reasonably good; only a relatively small proportion is actively involved in crime; and users have become more cautious in their drug-taking and sexual practices.

It is, however, naive to conclude that this suggests that Dutch prevention programs should be adopted by the United States. Both the nature and extent of the drug problem *and* society's response to it reflect the larger structural and cultural conditions of society. Structural factors conducive to problematic drug use – especially poverty and racism – exist to a greater degree in the US than in Holland. Compared with the US, people in the Netherlands suffer fewer economic hardships, there is less systematic exclusion based on race or ethnicity, there is less polarization of the population into the "haves" and the "have-nots" – all of which are structural causes of persistent hard drug use. The low-key Dutch prevention programs reflect the lower urgency of drug problems, the higher level of social security, the lower incidence of drug-related crime, the lower level of violence, and the more tolerant attitude to drug use.

It does seem that Holland has accomplished a much closer approximation of former President George Bush's "kinder and gentler society" in the area of drug policy than has the United States. However, we should note in concluding that one issue which has remained outside the focus of our analysis in this chapter is the differential roles of Holland and the United States in the world-wide political and economical community and the potential impact of these different roles upon the domestic drug policies and practices of the two countries.

References

Abadinsky, H.: *Drug Abuse: An Introduction.* Chicago: Nelson Hall, 1989

Akveld, F.W.: *Effectiviteit van Drugvoorlichting.* Afdelingsrapport nr. 89. GGD-Rotterdam, afd. GVO, 1988

Akveld, G. and Buisman, W.R.: Drugsvoorlichting in de praktijk: een overzicht. In: Buisman, W.R., Van der Stel, J.C. (Eds.), *Drugspreventie. Achtergronden, praktijk en toekomst.* Houten, the Netherlans / Zaventem, Belgium: Bohn, Stafleu, Van Loghum, 1992

Baan, P.A.H.: *Achtergronden en Risico's van het Druggebruik.* The Hague: Staatsuitgeverij, 1972

Becherer, L.H.J. and Zwinderman, A.H.: Onderzoek naar effecten van drugsvoorlichting. *Tijdschrift voor Alcohol, Drugs en Andere Psychotrope Stoffen* 16:110-116, 1990

Borghuis, M.: Alcohol en drugs: Preventie in de jeugdhulpverlening. *Jellinek Journal* 4(4):20-23, 1990

Botvin, G.J.: Substance abuse prevention: theory, practice, and effectiveness. In: Tonry, M., Wilson, J.Q. (Eds.), *Drugs and Crime.* Chicago and London: The University of Chicago Press, 1990

Buisman, W.R.: *Drug Prevention in the Netherlands. Review and Perspective.* Paper presented at the Anglo-Dutch Debate: Responding to Drug Problems (Royal Society of Medicine, London, United Kingdom, September 15 and 16.) Department of Education and Prevention, Netherlands Institute for Alcohol and Drugs, 1988

Buisman, W.R.: Drugsvoorlichting en massacommunicatie. *Tijdschrift Gezondheidsbevordering* 11:25-32, 1990

Buisman, W.R.: *Drug Abuse Prevention in the Netherlands. An Overview of (Secondary) Prevention Programmes.* Unpublished paper, 1992

Buisman, W.R. and Geirneart, M.: Theorieen en modellen voor drugspreventie. In: Buisman, W.R., Van der Stel, J.C. (Eds.), *Drugspreventie. Achtergronden, Praktijk en Toekomst.* Houten, the Netherlands / Zaventem, Belgium: Bohn, Stafleu, Van Loghum, 1992

Buisman, W.R. and Kok G.J.: Alcohol- en drugsvoorlichting: Een zwak middel? *Tijdschrift voor Alcohol, Drugs en Andere Psychotrope Stoffen* 9:137-145, 1983

Buisman, W.R. and Van der Stel, J.C. (Eds.): *Drugspreventie. Achtergronden, Praktijk en Toekomst.* Houten, the Netherlands / Zaventem, Belgium: Bohn, Stafleu, Van Loghum, 1992

Burden, O.P.: Youth groups join the War on Drugs. *CJ the Americas* 3:9-10,32, 1990

CAD Haarlem: *Drugs.* Haarlem, the Netherlands: CAD Haarlem, 1984

Carter, J.: President's message to the Congress on drug abuse. In: *Strategic Council on Drug Abuse's Federal Strategy for Drug Abuse and Drug Traffic Prevention,* pp 66-67. Washington, DC: General Printing Office, 1979

Cohen, J.: Drugs & AIDS prevention and education. Work with young people in the Netherlands. *The International Journal on Drug Policy* 1(3):19-23, 1989

Commissie Hulsman: *Ruimte in het Drugbeleid.* Rapport van een werkgroep van de Stichting Algemeen Centraal Bureau voor de Geestelijke Volksgezondheid. Meppel, the Netherlands: Boom, 1971

Conrad, P. and Schneider, J.W.: *Deviance and Medicalization. From Badness to Sickness.* St. Louis: the C.V. Mosby Company, 1980

De Jong, W.: *Arresting the Demand for Drugs:* Police and School Partnerships to Prevent Drug Abuse (National Institute of Justice: Issues and Practices). Washington, DC: US Department of Justice, 1987

De Keijser, R.P.: Drugsvoorlichting op een andere wijze. *Algemeen Politieblad* 21:75-77, 1989

De Ruijter, J.: Drugpreventie in het jongerenwerk. *Jongeren & Conditie* 10:10-11, 1989

Engelsman, E.: *Responding to Drug Problems: Dutch Policy and Practice.* Paper presented at the International Conference on Drug Policy Reform. Washington, DC: Drug Policy Foundation, 1988

Engelsman, E.: Overheid en preventie. In: Buisman, W.R., Van der Stel, J.C. (Eds.) *Drugspreventie. Achtergronden, Praktijk en Toekomst.* Houten, the Netherlands / Zaventem, Belgium: Bohn, Stafleu, Van Loghum, 1992

Geene, P. and Zweverink, H.: *Alex in Wonderland. Een Werkstrip voor Jongeren en hun Ouders rondom Riskant Gedrag en Vormen van Verslaving.* Zutphen, the Netherlands: Project Preventie en Hulpverlening, 1987

IADA (Instituut voor Alcohol en Drugpreventie Amsterdam): XTC. *IADA Bulletin* 4(3), 1991

ISAD (Interdepartementale Stuurgroep Alcohol en Drugbeleid): *Drugbeleid in Beweging – naar een Normalisering van de Drugsproblematiek.* The Hague: Staatsuitgeverij, 1985

Jamin, J.: *Verboden Vruchten, Drugspreventie op Maat.* Amsterdam/Utrecht, 1991

Jessen, E.H.C. and Winkel, N.J.: Drugs.... Weet je er genoeg van? *GGD Nieuws* 4:99-101, 1989

Kates, N.D.: *REACH: Fighting Crack and Crime in Pilgrim Village, Detroit* (Kennedy School of Government, Case Program). Cambridge, MA: President and Fellows of Harvard College, 1990

Kerssemakers, R. and Kramer, A.: Aids en drugspreventie. In: Buisman, W.R., Van der Stel, J.C. (Eds), *Drugspreventie. Achtergronden, Praktijk en Toekomst.* Houten, the Netherlands / Zaventem, Belgium: Bohn, Stafleu, Van Loghum, 1992

Kim, S., McLeod, J.H. and Shantzis, D.: An outcome evaluation of refusal skills program as a drug abuse prevention strategy. *Journal of Drug Education* 19(4): 363-371, 1989

Kittel, N.G.: Public policy toward illegal drugs. *Criminal Justice Review* 17:107-117, 1992

Kundberg, K.: *The Philadelphia Anti-Drug Coalition* (Kennedy School of Government, Case Program). Cambridge, MA: President and Fellows of Harvard College, 1990

Marshall, I., Anjewierden, O. and Van Atteveld H.: Toward an "Americanization" of Dutch drug policy? *Justice Quarterly* 7(2):391-420, 1990

231

Mesters, F. and Buisman, W.R.: Alcohol and drugsvoorlichting in het voortgezet onderwijs. *Tijdschrift voor Alcohol and Drugs* (13)4:122-128, 1987

Moore, M.H. and Kleiman, M.A.R.: *The Police and Drugs* (National Institute of Justice: Perspectives on Policing). Washington, DC: US Department of Justice, 1989

Mulder, W.G.: Voorlichting en preventie. *Tijdschrift voor Alcohol, Drugs en Andere Psychotrope Stoffen* 4(3):97-99, 1978

Musto, D.F.: *The American Disease: Origins of Narcotics Control* (Expanded Edn). New York: Oxford University Press, 1987

Otto, M.F.: De preventie-activiteiten van de Consultatiebureau's voor Alcohol en Drugs. *Feiten over het Alcohol- en Drugsprobleem* 20(4):120-134, 1984

Posma, R.: *Het Afkickproces. Een Spiraal naar Boven*. Nijmegen, the Netherlands: Vakgroep Klinische Psychologie en Persoonlijkheidsleer, Katholieke Universiteit Nijmegen (Experimentele versie), 1991

Reijneveld, M.: Rock & roll high school. *Amsterdams Drug Tijdschrift*: 5-6, 1990

Reitsma, T.: De rol van de politie inzake de drugsproblematiek. In: Groenhuijsen, M.S., Van Kalmthout, A.M. (Eds), *Nederlands Drugsbeleid in Westeuropees Perspectief*. Arnhem, the Netherlands: Gouda Quint, 1989

Rhodes, T.: The politics of anti-drugs campaigns. *Druglink* 5 (3):16-18, 1990

Rouse, J.J.: Evaluation research on prison-based drug treatment programs and some policy implications. *The International Journal of the Addictions* 26(1):29-44, 1991

Smart, R.G., Murray, G.F. and Arif, A.: Drug abuse and prevention programs in 29 countries. *The International Journal of the Addictions* 23(1):1-8, 1988

Stichting Nederlandse Onderwijs Televisie: Leerlingenkrant bij de schooltelevisie-serie Drug-knopen. The Hague: Stichting Nederlandse Onderwijs Televisie, 1974

Stichting Preventieprojekt Drugs: *Aan Jou de Keus*. Informatie over alcohol en drugs. Amsterdam, the Netherlands: Stichting Preventieprojekt Drugs, 1986

Tobler, N.: Meta-analysis of 143 adolescent drug prevention programs: quantitative outcome results of program participants compared to a control or a comparison group. *Journal of Drug Issues* 16:537-567, 1986

Van Amerongen, B.: Cinderella's portrait: Some observations on Dutch drug prevention policy. In: Kaplan, C.D., Kooyman, M. (Eds.), *Proceedings of the 15th International Institute on the Prevention and Treatment of Drug Dependence*. Rotterdam, the Netherlands: Institute for Preventive and Social Psychiatry, Erasmus University, 1987

Van Berkum, G., Buisman, W.R., Kok, G.J. and Siero, F.: Massacommunicatie en drugsvoorlichting. *Tijdschrift voor Alcohol, Drugs en Andere Psychotrope Stoffen* 12:223-231, 1986

Van Dalen, W.E.: Alcohol- en drugspreventie op de CADs. *Dienblad* 4(3):55-56, 1987 and *Tijdschrift Alcohol en Drugs* 3:121-128, 1987

Van de Vrie, R.: Nieuwe alcoholmatigingscampagnes. *Tijdschrift Gezondheidsvoorlichting* 5(9):12-13, 1988

Van der Stel, J.C.: Druggebruik en preventiebeleid: een caleidoscopisch overzicht. In: Buisman, W.R., Van der Stel, J.C. (Eds), *Drugspreventie. Achtergronden, Praktijk en Toekomst*. Houten, the Netherlands / Zaventem, Belgium: Bohn, Stafleu, Van Loghum, 1992

Van Harten, C.: Averechts. *Elsevier* 122:30-32 (January 16, 1988)

Zandbergen, G.: Alcohol is te gewoon geworden. *Trefpunt* 6/7:27-29, 1987

XII. LEGALIZATION, DECRIMINALIZATION AND THE REDUCTION OF CRIME

M. Grapendaal, Ed. Leuw and H. Nelen

1. Introduction

Although the debate on the possible effects of legalization of illicit drugs can be characterized as somewhat murky at times and definitely polemic, both sides agree on one thing: the expected decrease of drug-related crime after legalization. In this chapter we will have a closer look at this assumption. We will do so on the basis of an empirical study conducted among Amsterdam opiate addicts. Because this study was done in the relatively *decriminalized* context of illegal drug use in the Netherlands, its conclusions cannot be generalized to other countries.

The chapter starts with an outline of the general pros and cons of legalization. The next section contains a review of theoretical assumptions about the different hypothetical links between drug use and predatory crime. These theoretical models allow for different predictions about the influence of legalization on the level of criminality among drug users. We will present results of the Amsterdam study that are relevant to both the theory of drug-related crime and the possible effects of legalization.

2. Pros and cons of legalization

After decades of a vigorous but futile fight against the use and trafficking of illegal drugs, a discussion has developed about the advantages and disadvantages of legalizing or decriminalizing illicit drugs (Nadelmann 1991; Inciardi and McBride 1989; Karel 1991; Trebach 1982, 1987, 1989; Szasz 1991; Schmidt-Semisch 1990; Miller 1991; MacCoun 1991; Michaels 1991 and many others). In this discussion a limited number of topics invariably surface.

When making the case for legalization people argue that *crime* will decrease substantially; both crime related to trafficking and dealing, and criminality by users who commit crimes to maintain their addiction. The price of drugs would fall significantly (Nadelmann 1991) and so would the profits from the illegal trade. This would make trafficking in drugs less and less attractive. Users would be able to buy their desired drug at reasonable prices and would no longer be forced to commit crimes.

The focus of the pro-legalization argument is not only on crime, however; the *health* consequences of legalization are also addressed. Typically, advocates of legalization foresee a significant improvement of the physical condition of drug users. Because sterile needles and syringes would become readily available for IV users, the spread of contagious diseases like AIDS and hepatitis would slow down. The quality of the drugs would improve and the danger of adulterants would diminish.

There is also a *philosophical* side to the debate. Referring to John Stuart Mill's essay "On Liberty", those in favor of legalization argue that the state may not interfere with individual behavior that does not harm other individuals or, for that matter, is not detrimental to society at large.

Apart from the primary pharmacological risks in terms of addiction and toxicity, all secondary negative effects of drugs (crime, marginality of users, insecurity produced by violent drug markets, drug-related infections, and so on) are linked to the illegal status of the drugs. There is no inherent property to illegal substances themselves that causes these negative outcomes of drug use. According to the legalization argument, abolishing the illegal status of drugs would reduce the harmful effects to a level comparable to legally available stimulants such as alcohol and tobacco. Contrary to popular belief, it may be very hard to decide whether these legal drugs are potentially less harmful to health and society than the illegal drugs (Byck 1987). The pro-legalization side argues that the supposedly exceptional danger of illegal drugs is a culturally determined, social construction for which there are no good, valid or objective arguments.

Alternatively, proponents of legalization may point to social-scientific and historical analyses, which demonstrate that prohibition of drugs primarily serves moral value and political power interests (Gusfield 1966; Musto 1987; Scheerer 1992; Williams 1991). The historical prohibition of alcohol in the United States serves as a case in point.

More pragmatically, legalization is favored because of the *costs* of prohibition. The government spends huge amounts of money to fight the war on drugs with no apparent success. While the "war on drugs" may have had some constraining effects on recreational drug use by the conventional middle class (youth), there is no indication that decennia of fierce law enforcement has had any effect on the spreading of deviant, addictive and problematic drug use in marginal segments of society (Reuter 1992). After legalization resources could be re-allocated to more sensible targets: treatment, education, prevention.

And last but not least, because the powers of law enforcement authorities and other government officials have been substantially extended in order to better "fight" the war on drugs, citizens' *civil liberties* are in danger. The very nature of the drug problem causes law enforcement agencies to apply an aggressive and pro-active approach. This problem of increasing violation of civil liberties is debated most in the United States, where the war on drugs undoubtedly is fought with the most perseverance.

In the case against legalization, authors primarily warn against the possibility that the *number of users* would increase markedly. The higher the availability of a commodity, the more it will be used, they argue. In a free market, manufacturers and sales companies would launch advertisement campaigns to attract potential users. Because drugs are *dangerous* this is an undesirable situation. Not only do drugs inflict physical harm – one can die from an overdose of heroin for example – they also impair the social, productive and responsible behavior of users. In this respect drug use itself, but also the policy option of legalization is deemed to be inherently *immoral*.

A more practical consideration concerns the argument that proponents of legalization fail to recognize the complexities of the matter at hand. A concrete and specific proposal on how to legalize and under which conditions drugs may be produced, sold, and used has yet to be formulated. According to a common objection, legalizers *oversimplify* the subject in presenting legalization as a panacea for all problems revolving around drug use, drug violence and drug trafficking.

A few words on the relation between legalization and decriminalization are in order. Regardless of additional restrictions and other practical considerations (licensing, minimum consumption age, level of government control, quality demands *etc.*), legalization would imply that formerly illegal drugs would get the same legal status as alcohol and tobacco. Decriminalization means that drugs remain illegal, but that the *use* of drugs, and to a certain degree possession of drugs are not prosecuted as a criminal offense. Both concepts indicate the degree to which penal law control is removed. More importantly, in both concepts societal normalization is the central issue. Normalization may be understood as a social process in which informal social control by moral rejection, stigmatization and exclusion is diminished. Because the relaxation of penal law control is only one element of normalization, legalization does not necessarily indicate a higher level of social "acceptance" than decriminalization.

On the Dutch demand side of the drugs problem there is a substantial degree of decriminalization. Using hard drugs is not prohibited by law. The police and the Public Prosecutor's Office are explicitly instructed not to act against possession of hard drugs for personal use. This means that only those Dutch drug addicts who are involved with dealing and/or trafficking are caught up in the criminal justice system (not counting drug-related property crimes, of course). In a broader sense, decriminalization of drug addiction and drug use in the Netherlands may be understood as a manifestation of increased integration and acceptance of illegal drug use and addiction as a "normal" social adversity (Leuw 1991; Van den Wijngaart 1991).

The more tolerant social conditions of illegal drug use and addiction in the Netherlands are relevant for the issue of legalization and its possible effects on drug-related crime. As will be discussed later in this chapter, to some extent the results of our study concerning the issue of drug-related crime might be a function of ongoing social processes in the Netherlands – social processes of which legalization is the final stage.

3. Theoretical perspectives on the drug-crime nexus

The possible benefits of legalization with regard to the predicted reduction in drug-related criminality can only be addressed sensibly in the context of theoretical models for explaining the relation between illegal drug use and criminal behavior.

The existence of a close relationship between illegal drug use and criminality has been proven time and again (Parker 1989; Dobinson and Ward 1985, 1987; Dobinson 1989; Korf 1990; Ball 1982; Hammersley and Morrison 1987; Hammersley *et al.* 1989). At the same time it has widely been recognized that criminality is no more than a *secondary* characteristic of illegal drug consumption. Perhaps apart from some very specific instances, there are no inherent effects of illegal drugs which force its users into delinquency. This implies that criminality, along with most other social and health consequences connected to illegal drug addiction, is essentially *not* related to the pharmacological properties of the substances, but to the social conditions surrounding this kind of drug taking. Acknowledging the secondary character of drug-related criminality has not solved basic interpretational issues of the empirical evidence of its existence.

There are three major theoretical positions. According to the first model, drug addicts are driven to criminal behavior because they have to pay large sums of money for their drugs. This model assumes that addicts are physically dependent on their drugs and if they do not receive the required amount every day they will become sick. This position is widely known as the "inevitability hypothesis" (Goldman 1981) or enslavement theory (Inciardi 1991).

In contrast, the second model holds that drug use is caused by crime. According to this perspective, involvement in delinquency provides the context, the reference group and definitions of the situation that are conducive for subsequent involvement with drugs (Clayton and Tuchfield 1982).

The third model maintains that drug use and criminality are mutually reinforcing expressions of deviance. Deviance is viewed as the result of individual and collective reactions to the fundamental social-economic and cultural conditions of society. In this theoretical context, drug-related crime is partly explained in terms of the moral status of drug use and the social conditions under which illegal drug use has materialized. The perceived roots of evil are shifted from alien substances to the fabric of culture and social-economic structure (Inciardi 1974; Leuw 1986; Parker 1989).

Each of these theoretical models probably will prove to have some validity for some types of users and for certain circumstances and conditions. Important though, is that each model predicts a different effect of legalization on the level of crime among addicts.

Assuming that the crimes committed by drug addicts are purely instrumental and serve no other purpose than to provide money to buy drugs, the "inevitability hypothesis" predicts that legalization would have a major impact on the level of crime as the price of drugs would fall substantially. This is exactly the same result that was expected from large scale methadone supply to addicts. If addicts are able to substitute an expensive drug (heroin) for a free or cheap one (methadone), there would no longer be any necessity to steal and rob.

According to the second and third models, the effect of legalization on the level of crime would be more ambiguous. If crime does cause drug use, it can not be expected that drug users will immediately cease to commit crimes when their preferred drugs are legally available. Similarly, the impact of legalization on the level of crime is questionable when, according to the third model, both the use of drugs and criminal behavior are integral components of a deviant lifestyle.

To establish an empirical basis to evaluate these theoretical viewpoints, we need answers to specific questions: At which point in time did drug addicts start their criminal career, was it before or after their first drug use? Does methadone supply reduce criminal activity? How (in)elastic is the demand for drugs? In other words, do drug addicts need a fixed amount of drugs at fixed time intervals? Do drug addicts cease to commit crimes in periods of abstinence? Do all drug addicts engage in serious criminal activity?

The study we conducted in Amsterdam was not in the first place intended to solve basic theoretical issues, but rather to gain insight in the economic behavior of heroin addicts. Nevertheless, the study provides enough information to answer the questions mentioned above.[1] Consequently, we are able to provide the empirical basis to address the issues raised in this chapter.

4. Design of the study

The fieldwork of the study started mid 1987 and ended two years later. The sample consisted of 150 hard drug users. Respondents were recruited from the hard core of the Amsterdam (street) junkie scene. In line with population estimates, the sample was divided so that two-thirds of the subjects were ambulant methadone maintenance clients. The remainder were not involved in methadone prescription. The first subsample was randomly approached on the premises of the methadone maintenance agencies, while the second subsample was recruited by snowballing techniques, mostly starting in the drugs area of Amsterdam: central Amsterdam which also includes the red light district. This is a relatively small and well-defined area where drug use and the retail trade in drugs are clearly visible.

The design allowed for a maximum of seven interviews of each respondent, over a period of about 13 months, about drug taking and economic behavior (*i.e.*, how they obtained and spent money). All standard interviews referred retrospectively to the preceding seven days. The first three interviews took place in the first three weeks after initial contact, the next four quarterly. Respondents were interviewed in a field station, a bar or - depending on the weather - on a bench in the street. In addition to collecting quantitative information, a life history interview was conducted. Respondents were asked about their family backgrounds, peer group, criminal and drug careers and their motivation to maintain their deviant lifestyles. The field workers and researchers also spent considerable time observing the daily activities on the streets of central Amsterdam. The experiences and observations were recorded in a personal diary.

The design of the study is much like the Johnson *et al.* study, conducted in New York (Johnson *et al.* 1985). The major differences are the number of - and time intervals between - the interviews and the emphasis on qualitative data. In the Amsterdam study we paid more attention to the life history interviews and participant observation.

5. Empirical evidence

5.1 The start of a criminal career

One of the major questions to be answered concerns the point in time at which the criminal career starts, relative to the onset of drug use. Many researchers addressed this question (Korf 1990; Swierstra 1990; Erkelens *et al.* 1979; Intraval 1989; Johnson *et al.* 1985; Stephens and McBride 1976; Nurco *et al.* 1985; Inciardi 1986). Especially in the Dutch literature there seems to be strong consensus about the percentage of drug addicts who committed crime before they started using drugs: All (Dutch) studies report a figure of about 50%. This is not different in our study: 51% of our respondents engaged in crime before they started using drugs. For 8% drug use and crime occurred simultaneously, 20% eventually started committing crimes after they first used drugs and 21% says that they never engaged in criminal activity despite their obvious addiction. Moreover, when we take a closer look at the recent criminal behavior of our subjects, we find that the respondents who display pre-drug criminality belong to the most criminal group in our sample. This suggests that there exists a certain continuity in the lifestyle and crime patterns people develop before they start using drugs.

Logically, the paradigm that criminal behavior is caused by drug use (the first model), can only be true for the relatively small proportion in our sample that began committing crime after they started using drugs. A remarkable finding is that 21% never engaged in (property) crime either before or after initiation into drug use. This finding is not uncommon in Dutch literature (see for an overview: Korf 1990) and perhaps typical for the Dutch situation. Because popular belief tends to be that every drug addict at some stage in his career commits at least some crime, this finding needs some explanation. The Netherlands have a rather elaborated system of social welfare. Everyone who is not able to work is, under certain conditions, entitled to a monthly governmental support that amounts to the Dutch equivalent of approximately $600.[2] A large proportion of our sample receives a monthly welfare check.[3] In addition they often do odd jobs. Given the fact that many addicts save money on the more conventional expenses, such as housing, heating, meals, clothes and so on, they can spend almost their complete monthly income on drugs. Considering the price of one bag of heroin or cocaine (about $15 for one-tenth of a gram, enough to make it through the day at a moderate level of use combined with methadone supply) some addicts can maintain their habit with a relatively low budget and without crime.

5.2 Methadone maintenance and the reduction of crime

The next important question is whether or not methadone maintenance results in a reduction of property crime committed by drug addicts. In fact, methadone is a legal opiate. According to the classical psycho-physiological theory of methadone maintenance this "treatment" should remove the major drive for criminal behavior of heroin addicts. The Amsterdam case, where about two-thirds of the addict population is estimated to be registered with methadone programs, may be especially suitable to test the impact of this mode of "legalization".

During the first years of methadone maintenance programs in the United States, spectacular successes were claimed. Clients were said to improve dramatically. Not only did abstinence or a serious reduction of illegal drug intake occur in most clients of methadone maintenance programs, it was also estimated that between 50% and 85% showed marked progress in social functioning (Senay 1985).

In later years, news from America on methadone maintenance became more moderate in tone, but there remained a relatively strong consensus that methadone maintenance programs lead to a reduction in the use of illegal drugs and to a (connected) reduction in illegal income acquisition (Edwards 1979; Sechrest 1979; Anglin et al. 1981).

The predominantly positive results of evaluations of methadone programs on drug-related crime in the US should be approached with caution. Two points should be considered: (1) reliability of reported illegal drug use and delinquency and (2) selectivity of participants in methadone maintenance programs in the US. There is an extensive literature on the reliability and validity issue, but here we will limit ourselves to questioning the reliability of (self-report) data on illegal drug use and crime, obtained within the context of (criminal justice) maintenance programs that attach severe penalties to illegal drug use and undesirable social behavior (Ausubel 1983).

The reported success of methadone maintenance in the United States would certainly fade considerably once the question of double selectivity is taken into account. The "double selectivity" refers to both the criteria to be admitted into the methadone maintenance program, as well as the requirements addicts must meet to stay in the methadone maintenance programs. Certainly in comparison to the situation in the Netherlands (Amsterdam), methadone maintenance programs in the United States have a high threshold and impose a large number of conditions. For example, one of the most important programs in Baltimore only takes clients who have been employed for at least two years.[4] Using illegal drugs (besides methadone) or committing criminal offenses usually are grounds for refusing admittance to the program or removal from the program. To a certain extent, therefore, a decrease in crime rates should be regarded as an artefact of the strict criminal justice context of many methadone (maintenance) programs in the US. In this context, they could be compared to the successes often claimed by drug-free therapeutic communities. Addicts who are able to remain in such programs for any length of time indeed do have a good chance to improve. But then we are talking about an extremely small selection from the population of drug addicts.

To conclude simply that the reduction in crime reported for the American clients of methadone programs has no meaning at all would be unwarranted. However, the results do imply that the relationship between methadone and crime needs more careful consideration. Before we may conclude that there is a biological-causal link between methadone maintenance and reduced criminality, more careful research in other social settings needs to be conducted.

What about the Amsterdam situation of methadone prescription? Perhaps most importantly, the threshold to participate in a methadone maintenance program in Amsterdam is much lower than in the US. The distribution of methadone in Amsterdam is mainly in the hands of the drug department of the local health authorities (GG&GD). There are several different modalities of distribution, each with its own character. First, there are the methadone buses. Initially, old public transportation buses adapted for use as methadone maintenance centers were used, but in the spring of 1989, new specially designed buses were put into service. Seven days a week, two of these buses follow two separate routes through the city, making stopovers at special bus stops at set times for set periods.

These buses provide the lowest threshold service available in Amsterdam. There are barely any requirements that a client has to meet to be able to register with a methadone bus program: there are no urine tests for illegal drugs, addicts are not required to show up every day and they are not expected to change their lifestyle. If a client at one of the buses is "functioning well", he may be promoted to a community station. The three community stations are situated at the edge of the old city center. They are open on working days; clients are given pills for the week-end. The community stations differ substantially from the buses. Their explicit aim is abstinence from illegal drugs. To that end, urine tests are conducted twice a week, contact with doctors and social workers is mandatory and active support is available wherever possible and necessary.

Apart from the Municipal Health Service, some general practitioners in Amsterdam also provide methadone. The family doctor occupies the highest rank on the promotion ladder of methadone maintenance: addicts may be promoted from bus to community station, and from community station to GP.[5] Doctors give prescriptions that addicts can take to the pharmacy in order to obtain methadone pills. In general, a client may pick up a prescription every two weeks. This places a heavy demand on the patient's own responsibility, for on the street two weeks' worth of methadone fetches between $115 and $170.

The different forms of methadone distribution in Amsterdam may be differentiated according to the requirements that clients have to meet: these may vary from almost none to obligatory abstinence from illegal drugs; from very low threshold to high(er) threshold modalities.

First we shall examine the relationship between property crime and methadone maintenance in a more general way. In order to examine the relative importance of methadone maintenance as a determinant of criminality, a multiple regression analysis was performed, using amount of crime-generated income as the dependent variable. The total number of independent variables used in the analysis was seven (cocaine consumption, heroin consumption, gender, age, duration of opiate use, receipt of social benefits, and registration with a methadone maintenance program). The percentage of explained variance is small (20%) but statistically significant ($p=<0.001$). Four variables explain 20% of the variance in individual gain from income-generating crime. These variables are, in order of importance: cocaine consumption (the more cocaine one uses, the higher the income from crime), gender (men earn more money through crime than women), age (the younger one is, the more income from crime one has) and heroin consumption (the higher the consumption, the more crime-related income). More important, though, the results show that the influence of methadone programs relative to other variables is virtually negligible. This result is not surprising in view of the fact that the bivariate correlation between criminal gain and methadone distribution is very weak (-.08). Registration with a methadone program nor duration of opiate use, nor the receipt of social benefit make any difference in the amount of gain from income-generating crime.

In general then, participation in a methadone program does not seem to influence the level of criminality. These results may be interpreted as a rejection of the reduction-in-crime hypothesis based on the orthodox, metabolic theory of methadone maintenance. However, as we have seen above, there are important differences between methadone maintenance programs (both in terms of admission and retention criteria). Further analysis is needed to examine whether participation in a methadone program *under certain circumstances* may be related to a decreased level of criminality.

We distinguish between three conditions: (1) high threshold programs (*i.e.*, community stations), (2) low threshold programs (*i.e.*, buses), and (3) no registration with a methadone program. Table 1 shows how clients from the three groups differ from each other in terms of profits from crime: there is a clear relationship between the type of methadone program and income-generating crime.

Table 1. Methadone programs and monthly profits from acquisitive crime

Programs	High threshold	Low threshold	No program	N
Profits				
No crime	60%	33%	41%	69
$1 - $285	24%	31%	34%	43
$ >285	16%	36%	25%	36
N	62	42	44	148

$\chi^2 = 9$; df = 4; $p < 0.05$

Especially noteworthy is that more clients from the low threshold programs (the buses) commit criminal offenses than the other two groups. Two-thirds (67%) of the users involved in a low-threshold program are involved in income-generating criminality, as compared to 59% of those not involved in a program and 40% of those registered with a high-threshold program. Table 1 also suggests that the low-threshold category is more likely to be involved in more lucrative crimes (over $285.00) than the other two groups. In other words, not only has the hypothesis that methadone maintenance always leads to a reduction in crime been falsified, more of those who obtain methadone from the buses commit crime (67%) than those not on methadone maintenance (59%), and clients of low-threshold programs are also more likely to be involved in the more lucrative crimes. We may view this phenomenon as an important indication that *the most relevant factor is not the methadone, but the addict's lifestyle.* A brief description of the three different groups may illustrate this conclusion.

Most clients of the high-threshold community stations are at the end of the line of their drug career and want to moderate their deviant lifestyle. They are drug addicts whose ferocity and socially destructive energy has tapered off. They may be typed as retired or pacified junkies. They cut down on the use of expensive illegal drugs and especially keep away from cocaine. They do commit some crime, but generally at a low frequency and with little financial gain. The pacified junkies succeed in taking illegal drugs within a non-criminal lifestyle by cutting their expenses for "normal" daily subsistence to an extremely low level. They do not spend much money on food or clothing, nor do they pay for public transportation. Their friends and family do not expect the money borrowed to be returned. Some of these drug users make extra money by doing odd jobs for shop keepers: they sweep the pavement, help to unload vehicles, clean windows. Others collect used syringes and needles, exchange these paraphernalia at one of the drug agencies and sell new "shooting equipment" on the street.

Prescription methadone fulfills an important role within the lifestyle of the pacified junkie. The daily use of this synthetic opiate not only prevents the well-known withdrawal symptoms but has social-psychological functions as well: the fact that a client has to show up every day structures his life. He has a reason to get out of his bed, he meets friends at the community station and regularly stays for a chat. If he has problems, he can contact the professionals - both doctors and social workers - who are present at the station.

Turning to the low threshold programs (*i.e.,* the methadone by bus project), we observe a totally different kind of client. These drug users are often hyperactive addicts, who are still fascinated by the deviant lifestyle. They are poly-drug users with a predilection for cocaine. Their visits to the methadone bus are characterized by irregularity and speed. Methadone serves as an insurance against the feared withdrawal symptoms when they have difficulty in obtaining other drugs. At these "bad" moments they will rush to the bus, drink their methadone and leave at once. They do not have time to hang around; they have to go to "work". In the vocabulary of hyperactive addicts, "work" is synonymous to "committing crimes". A large proportion of their income is generated from property crime.

Most of the drug users who do not subscribe to any methadone program are active on the drugs market, either as a small-time dealer, a lookout or a middleman. These drug users are commonly being paid in drugs, thus they require less (cash) money than other drug users.

5.3 Inelasticity of demand

The third question pertaining to the legal availability of opiates and criminal behavior concerns the widespread belief that drug addicts need a physiologically and pharmacologically fixed amount of heroin each day. In other words, the demand for opiates is said to be invariable and inelastic. The idea is that the use of (in this case) heroin over a long period of time causes physical tolerance of the drug to increase until an individually determined optimum has been reached. This level is thought to determine the daily amount of opiates necessary to prevent withdrawal symptoms and to function normally. Legalization may be expected to have more impact on drug-related crime if the demand for heroin is indeed as inelastic as the psycho-physiological theory of heroin addiction implies.

Data from our study reveal that the level of consumption of drugs varies widely. We developed a method of measuring the extent to which drug use varies. A calculation was made for each respondent of the average drug use for all of the days in the first interview cycle (*e.g.,* the first three weeks). Subsequently, variability in consumption – expressed as the standard deviation from the daily average – was calculated. As the standard deviation increases, so does variability in consumption. To allow for large variations in absolute size of daily amounts, the standard deviation was expressed as a percentage of the daily average (variability=s/m*100; in which "s"=standard deviation and "m"=daily average).

Table 2 shows the frequency of deviation percentages of heroin use.

Table 2. Deviations in heroin use as a percentage of average use

Deviations		N	%
Constant*		23	16
Deviation	1- 25%	25	17
	26- 50%	18	12
	51- 75%	19	13
	76-265%	63	43
Total		148	100

*: no heroin use (*n*=13) or constant use (*n*=10)

The apparent large variability in consumption of the illegal drug heroin is partly explained by a strong relation with participation in a methadone program. A relatively easily accessible distribution network for methadone in Amsterdam offers drug users a way of replenishing opiate deficiencies on "bad days" with this synthetic opiate. Due to the availability of free methadone as an insurance against sickness, addicts obviously have much latitude to obtain or not to obtain heroin.

Addicts do indeed cut their coats according to their cloth (Grapendaal 1992). They will obtain the amount of illegal drugs depending on their daily fortunes. This is likely to be the result of the limits they set on activities they are prepared to undertake in order to obtain heroin and/or money. In this sense, a beneficial effect of methadone prescription on crime may not necessarily be a lower individual level, but a reinforcement of individual limits to criminal behavior. "Everybody" including the drug addict, has his (moral) restrictions with regard to his (criminal) behavior. Availability of free methadone helps addicts to respect these personal normative limits. In similar vein, we may hypothesize that legalization of heroin will put some limits to "excessive" criminality.

5.4 Reduction of crime in periods of abstinence

Criminalization of using and selling drugs inevitably implies that drug users must cross the normative borders of legality. In many respects they must also cross the social borders of deviance. It is quite inconceivable that persons who are "forced" to enter an illegal subculture will *not* lose constraints against criminal behavior. Therefore, in this broad societal sense, legalization may be expected to decrease criminal behavior. On the other hand, the present study (as well as other ethnographic studies of deviant drug users) suggests that criminal behavior offers its own attractions to drug addicts. To a large extent this attraction depends on the lifestyle of the addict, and the particular stage he is at in his career of deviance. If a drug addict is heavily involved in a deviant lifestyle, abstinence will be less conducive to a decrease of criminal behavior. In this case, drug use or addiction is no longer an incentive or catalyst for criminal behavior, but criminal behavior remains motivated by other deviant interests. In other words, a devoted junkie, deeply involved in an absorbing and rewarding deviant lifestyle, cannot be expected to be transformed into a conventional law-abiding citizen, once his drug taking has stopped.

We will now turn to the relevant empirical results of our study. Periods of abstinence or seriously reduced use were calculated for those respondents with complete information for an entire year (*n*=85). The level of crime during these periods was compared with the level of crime during periods in which a high level of drug use was reported (of more than two grams a week).

We were able to identify 51 respondents (*i.e.* 60%) with at least one such period of abstinence in the course of the research project. For our analysis, we compared income from crime by means of a *t* test for paired samples.[6] In a week during which they used a lot of heroin, these 51 respondents generated four times as much income from crime as they did in a week during which they used little or no heroin. When using a lot of heroin, the average income from crime was $95.00; in the low-use week, the average income was reduced to $22.00 ($t=2.30$; $p=0.03$). This difference is statistically and substantially significant.

For cocaine, the picture is more or less identical. There were 59 respondents with periods of abstinence or greatly reduced cocaine use. During such periods, income from crime for this group averaged $30.00. During the period of heavy cocaine use, the average climbed to $85.00. The corresponding t value (2.29) has a level of significance of 0.03.

The conclusion will be obvious: during periods of abstinence, considerably less income is generated from acquisitive crime than during periods of drug use. This finding is consistent with the results of Anglo-Saxon research (Nurco *et al.* 1985, 1988; Dobinson 1989). However, finding a clear link between the use of hard drugs and the level of crime does not necessarily imply that more drug use leads to more crime, or conversely, that less drug use results in less crime. It might well be that the mechanism described in the previous section is also operative here: the abstinent addicts are generating less money – for whatever reason – and are therefore using less or no drugs.

The big difference between our study and other (foreign) research is that drug users in other countries show a proportionately much larger decrease in criminal activities during periods of abstinence. This may be partly explained by the different operationalizations of the concepts of crime and abstinence. In the present study, crime was defined in the narrow sense of acquisitive crime (excluding drug dealing), while our "abstinence" category also includes some periods of a very limited and strongly decreased drug use.

A more theoretically relevant explanation for the difference in results may be found in the social circumstances of Dutch society. Because of the relatively generous social welfare system, Dutch addicts are less dependent on crime as a source of income anyway; this is suggested not only by the (lower) percentage of crime-generated income, but also by the (smaller) number of addicts who commit criminal offenses (Grapendaal *et al.* 1991). It is likely that this is partly (or even mainly) due to the system of social security. As dependence on crime as a source of income decreases, there will, by definition, be smaller fluctuations in criminal activity.

In Table 3 a comparison of three studies (Johnson *et al.* 1985; Parker *et al.* 1988) with regard to the level of crime among drug users is offered. This table shows that Dutch addicts commit less crime than their foreign counterparts. It is plausible that in case of legalization the reduction of crime would be less in countries where addicts are less dependent on crime as a source of income.

Table 3. An international comparison

Source of income	Percentages of total income		
	This study	Johnson et al. 1985	Parker et al. 1988
Welfare check	29%	11%	11%
Salary	4%	9%	7%
Drugs market	20%	17%	11%
Prostitution	15%	7%	4%
Property crime	24%	43%	65%
Others	8%	12%	2%

Apparently, committing crimes is less typical of drug addicts in the Netherlands than in some other countries. In a deeper sociological sense this may not only be contingent on available sources of income. A weakened link between drug use and crime may also be explained by the relatively more decriminalized and (therefore) less deviant circumstances of hard drug use in the Netherlands. As has been suggested above, the effect of drug use on criminal behavior may depend on the extent that more general deviant interests are served by this illegal drug use. This would imply that legalization may only result in a strong reduction of criminal behavior when this occurs under the conditions of severe repression and stigmatization of illegal drug use. It is reasonable to speculate, therefore, that legalization might thus result in a considerable decrease of criminal behavior in the USA, while it would have less impact on criminality in the Netherlands.

6. Discussion

The results presented above cannot be fully explained by one of the causal theoretical models. It is not tenable that drug use does cause crime (or *vice versa*), it is more likely that drug use intensifies and perpetuates criminality. We find the strongest support in the observation that drug addicts do commit less crime in periods of abstinence, but that an important proportion continues to commit crime at a lower level. The results do confirm, however, the notion that there is a strong relationship between drug use and crime. This relationship can best be explained by applying the theoretical approach that both drug use and crime are expressions of an underlying dimension, related to both crime *and* drug use.

We will consider the possible effects of legalization on crime committed by addicts in the light of the deviant career perspective that we found to be the most plausible explanation for the results of this study.

The perspective implies that hard drug users play an active role in beginning and continuing a life with drugs, that they make choices and that they are usually well aware of the (direct) consequences of such choices. There are both theoretical and empirical reasons for maintaining that, in a sense, they aspire to a deviant existence, because it provides a solution to individual problems that concern both social position and personal development. The illegality of the drugs used, and the illegality that therefore surrounds a life with drugs, is not a coincidental property of a drug that is sought after solely for its pharmacological effects. In other words, people who are attracted to illegal drugs are looking not only for dope, but also for illegality.

Logically, of course, this is a strong argument in favor of minimizing penal repression. However, for precisely the same reason, it is not a compelling argument for totally doing away with penal repression. Legalization may remove one of the elements of a deviant lifestyle, but it will not influence the "search", the motivation, and the (social) conditions that underlie that lifestyle. Nowadays, an interest in deviance may be satisfied by taking drugs, thanks to legislation, moral codes and fashion. In this sense, being an addict is no more, nor less, than an historical form of deviance; a bed along which a river of criminal behavior flows. A different fashion or change in legislation may divert the course of the stream, but this does not necessarily imply that it will run dry.

The results of this study show that addicts, at a certain stage in their development, are able to live "quiet" lives (having periods of abstinence, participating in high threshold methadone programs, not committing crime at all) despite the current illegal status of hard drugs. It seems that an optimal reduction of drug-related crime can be achieved if the criminalization of drug addicts is as moderate as possible. From the point of view of crime prevention, legalization is not necessary for those who have had enough of an illegal existence, and not enough for those for whom that existence still fulfills many functions. The assumption that legalization would immediately reduce drug-related crime derives from the same causal assumption underlying the (rejected) hypothesis that methadone maintenance in and of itself will lead to a reduction in crime rates.

The most relevant arguments for and against legalization concern the tension between primary and secondary prevention of drug addiction. This theme is especially relevant to *social* drug policy and only partially affects *penal* policy. For that reason we shall deal with it very briefly. In the Netherlands, social drug policy has two aims: (1) restricting the spread of drug-taking, and (2) limiting the adverse effects of drug-taking that is already established. It is highly likely that legalization would have contradictory effects on these important policy goals. Lifting the prohibition on drugs will reduce the taboo on drug-taking and increase the availability of drugs through different channels. One needs only look at the (pseudo) legalization of pornography and cannabis in the Netherlands. They are offered for consumption very much more frequently than they were in the days when they were still banned, and the ban was enforced. There is no reason at all to suppose that things would be different for heroin and cocaine.

Legalization would not only increase the availability of drugs, it would also lead to changes in the attraction and significance of hard drugs. It is difficult to estimate what changes in the functions of hard drug use would take place and to what extent these would result in changes and increases in the consumer population. At least two important factors are at work here. On the one hand, drugs would be less attractive as an expression of a deviant style of life, and this could mean that the number of users would decrease. Or, as Nadelmann (1991) puts it with regard to Dutch cannabis policy: "The policy has succeeded (...) in making drug use boring". On the other hand, greater accessibility could lead to more experimental users. However, experimental use needs not to become problematic use (Zinberg 1984; Cohen 1990). The greatest social (public health) risk attached to legalization may well be the greatly lowered threshold (both practical and psychological) for "normal" populations. We do not really want adolescents, at odds with school, their parents and themselves, to be able to escape too easily to a pharmacologically created other world. The "coffee shops" are already a place of asylum for some of these kids. The question of whether horse and coke would appear there on the menu after legalization is not just a figment of the imagination.

By the same token, it is indisputable that the problems faced by hard drug users would be greatly diminished after legalization. The illegality and marginality of being an addict would largely disappear. The significance of drug scenes would be greatly diminished. The quality of drugs would be controllable, the conditions under which they are taken more hygienic and developments around infectious "drug diseases" such as hepatitis B and AIDS more easily monitored.

On the demand side, the social problem of drugs can be defined as the product of two variables, the number of drug users and the extent of the problems per user. The question then arises as to the necessity of making concessions to the primary prevention of hard drug use for the sake of the secondary prevention of risk. There are many reasons for assuming that there is no great need to legalize drugs in the Netherlands. From an epidemiological point of view, problematic drug use is a reasonably restricted and stable phenomenon. Pragmatic Dutch drug policy allows a variety of control strategies. Legalization is the obvious option if the "war on drugs" is lost. Contrary to the United States, there is, fortunately, no such war in the Netherlands.

References

Anglin, M.D., McGlothlin, W.H. and Speckart, G: The effect of parole on methadone patient behavior. *American Journal of Drug and Alcohol Abuse* 8(2), 1981

Ausubel, D.P.: Methadone maintenance treatment; the other side of the coin. *The International Journal of the Addictions* 18(6), 1983

Ball, J.C.: Lifetime criminality of heroin addicts in the United States. *Journal of Drug Issues* 3, 1982

Byck, R.: Cocaine, Marihuana and the meanings of addiction. In: Freedman, A.F. and Hamowy, R. (Eds), *Dealing with Drugs*. San Francisco: Pacific Research Institute for Public Policy, 1987

Clayton, R.R. and Tuchfield, B.S.: The drug-crime debate: obstacles to understanding the relationship. *Journal of Drug Issues* 2, 1982

Cohen, D.A.P.: *Drugs as a Social Construct*. Utrecht: Elinkwijk, 1990

Dobinson, I.: Making sense of the drug and crime link. *Australian and New Zealand Journal of Criminology* 4, 1989

Dobinson, I. and Ward, P.: *Drugs and Crime*. Sydney: NSW Bureau of Crime Statistics and Research, 1985

Dobinson, I., and Ward, P.: *Drugs and Crime: Phase 2*. Sydney: NSW Bureau of Crime Statistics and Research, 1987

Edwards, E.D.: Arrest and conviction histories before, during and after participation in a substance abuses treatment program. *Drug Forum* 7:3/4, 1979

Erkelens, L.H., Haas, P.D.J. and Janssen, O.J.A.: *Drugs en Detentie; een Beschrijvend Onderzoek naar Harddrug Gebruikers in een Zestal Huizen van Bewaring*. Groningen: Rijksuniversiteit, Kriminologisch Instituut, 1979

Goldman, F.: Drug abuse, crime and economy; the dismal limits of social choice. In: Inciardi, J.A. (Ed.), *The Drugs-Crime Connection*. Beverly Hills: Sage Publ, 1981

Grapendaal, M.: Cutting their coat according to their cloth: economic behavior of Amsterdam opiate addicts. *The International Journal of the Addictions* 27/4, 1992

Grapendaal, M., Leuw, E. and Nelen, J.M.: *De Economie van het Drugsbestaan; Criminaliteit als Expressie van Levensstijl en Loopbaan*. WODC-reeks, 115. Gouda: Quint bv, 1991

Gusfield, J.R.: *The Symbolic Crusade, Statuspolitics and the American Temperance Movement*. Urbana/London: University of Illinois Press, 1966

Hammersley, R., Forsyth, A., Morrison, V. and Davies, J.R.: The relationship between crime and opioid use. *British Journal of Addictions* 84, 1989

Hammersley, R. and Morrison, V.: Effects of polydrug use on the criminal activities of heroin-users. *British Journal of Addiction* 82, 1987

Inciardi, J.A.: The vilification of euphoria; some perspectives on an elusive issue. *Addictive Diseases* 1, 1974

Inciardi, J.A.: *The War on Drugs: Heroin, Cocaine, Crime and Public Policy*. Palo Alto: Mayfield, 1986

Inciardi, J.A.: *The Drug Legalization Debate. Studies in Crime, Law and Justice*, 7. Newbury Park: Sage Publ, 1991

Inciardi, J.A. and McBride, D.C.: Legalization: a high risk alternative in the war on drugs. *American Behavioral Scientist* 32(3), 1989

Intraval: *Harddrugs en Criminaliteit in Rotterdam*. Groningen: Drukkerij Gerlach, 1989

Johnson, B.D., Goldstein, P.J., Preble, E., Schmeidler, J., Lipton, D.S., Spunt, B. and Miller, T.: *Taking Care of Business; the Economics of Crime by Heroin Abusers*. Lexington: Lexington Books, 1985

Karel, R.B.: A model legalization proposal. In: Inciardi, J.A. (Ed.), *The Drug Legalization Debate. Studies in Crime, Law and Justice*, 7. Newbury Park: Sage Publ, 1991

Korf, D.J.: Jatten alle junkies? *Tijdschrift voor Criminologie* 32(2), 1990

Leuw, E.: Heroïnegebruik, criminaliteit en de mogelijke effecten van methadonverstrekking. *Tijdschrift voor Criminologie* 28(3), 1986

Leuw, E.: Drugs and drug policy in The Netherlands. In: Tonry, M. (Ed.), *Crime and Justice: A review of Research*, Vol. 14. Chicago: The University of Chicago Press, 1991

Musto, D.F.: *The American Disease, Origins of Narcotic Control*. Oxford/New York: Oxford University Press, 1987

MacCoun, R.J.: *Would Drug Legalization open the Floodgates? Understanding the Effects of Legal Sanctions on Psychoactive Drug Consumption*. Santa Monica: Rand-Corporation, 1991

Michaels, R.J.: The market for heroin before and after legalization. In: Hamowy, R. (Ed.). *Dealing with Drugs*. San Francisco: Pacific Research Institute for Public Policy, 1991

Miller, R.L.: *The Case for Legalization*. Westport: Praeger Publ, 1991

Nadelmann, E.A.: The case for legalization. In: Inciardi, J.A. (Ed.), *The Drug Legalization Debate. Studies in Crime, Law and Justice*, 7. Newbury Park: Sage Publ, 1991

Nurco, D.N., Cisin, I.H. and Ball, J.C.: Crime as source of income for narcotic addicts. *Journal of Substance Abuse Treatment*, 1985

Nurco, D.N., Rosen, L., Flueck, J.A., Hanlon, T.E. and Kinlock, T.W.: Differential criminal patterns of narcotic addicts over an addiction career. *Criminology*, 3, 1988

Parker, H.: Young heroin users and crime: how do the "new users" finance their habits? *British Journal of Criminology* 29(2), 1989

Parker, H., Bakx, K. and Newcombe, R.: *Living with Heroin; the Impact of a Drugs "Epidemic" on an English Community*. Milton Keynes/Philadelphia: Open University Press, 1988

Reuter, P.: *Hawks Ascendant*. Santa Monica: Rand-Corporation, 1992

Schmidt-Semisch, H.: Ueberlegungen zu einem legalen Zugang zu Heroin fuer alle. *Kriminologisches Journal* Heft 2, 1990

Sechrest, D.K.: Methadone programs and crime reduction: a comparison of New York and California addicts. *The International Journal of the Addictions* 14(3), 1979

Senay, E.C.: Methadone maintenance treatment. *The International Journal of the Addictions* 20(6/7), 1985

Scheerer, S.: Political ideologies and drug policy. *European Journal on Criminal Policy and Research* 1(1), 1992

Stephens, R.C. and McBride, D.C.: Becoming a street addict. *Human Organization* 35, 1976

Swierstra, K.E.: *Drugscarrières; van Crimineel tot Conventioneel*. Groningen: Stichting Drukkerij C. Regenboog, 1990

Szasz, T.: The morality of drug controls. In: Hamowy, R. (Ed.), *Dealing with Drugs*. San Francisco: Pacific Research Institute for Public Policy, 1991

Trebach, A.S.: *The Heroin Solution*. New Haven: Yale University Press, 1982

Trebach, A.S.: *The Great Drug War*. New York: MacMillan, 1987

Trebach, A.S.: Tough choices: the practical politics of drug policy reform. *American Behavioral Scientist* 32(3), 1989

Van de Wijngaart, G.F.: *Competing Perspectives on Drug Use, the Dutch Experience.* Amsterdam: Swets & Zeitlinger, 1991

Williams, J.C.: *Drug Control: a History of Good Intentions.* Paper presented at the Law and Society Congress: Law in the Global Village. Amsterdam, June 1991

Zinberg, N.E.: *Drug, Set, and Setting; the Basis for Controlled Intoxicant Use.* New Haven/London: Yale University Press, 1984

Endnotes

1. In the study we made a conceptional distinction between property crime, drug offenses and prostitution. In the Netherlands, prostitution is neither a criminal offense, nor a misdemeanor; therefore, this activity is not included in the crime figures. Since dealing in drugs is a crime without victims, drug-dealing offenses are also excluded from the figures we are about to present.

2. The used conversion rate for Dutch Guilders to US Dollars is 1.75.

3. Eighty-seven percent of the sample received at least part of their income from the social security system.

4. Information obtained from Richard Lane, executive director of this program.

5. Recently, the system of distribution has been changed drastically. Urine tests at the community stations have been stopped. This means that the health authorities have moved away almost entirely from the graduated model. Community stations are now meant to cater to addicts who need extra attention, the extremely problematic cases. The special station which previously existed to deal with these highly problematic cases has been abolished. In principle, clients of both buses and community stations must submit to a (social) medical examination once every three months. Because the data for this study were collected at a time when the health authorities still adhered to the promotion system, the results should be viewed in that context.

6. "Paired samples" means that we are not dealing with independent samples, but with a comparison of two values for the same respondent, namely income from crime during two different weeks. The differences between these values provide the so-called t value.

XIII. THE FUTURE OF THE DUTCH MODEL IN THE CONTEXT OF THE WAR ON DRUGS

Tom Blom and Hans van Mastrigt

1. Introduction

From the beginning of this century, various international treaties have been closed aimed at a uniform drug policy in all countries of the world. The most important recent agreement in this respect is the Single Convention of New York. Virtually every country in the world (including the Netherlands) is now a party to this treaty. Beginning in the mid-seventies, the Netherlands started to deal with drug problems in a manner quite different from elsewhere in the world. Because of its unique drug policy, the "Dutch model" has attracted international attention. Often, the international opinion was negative, and the Dutch tolerance was met with an apparent lack of understanding. Over the last few years, however, more positive assessments of Dutch drug policy are heard more frequently.

Although respect for the Dutch model is certainly growing, there are several developments - particularly internationally - which possibly may threaten its continued survival. In this chapter, we describe a number of these developments. First, we place Dutch policy as it has developed since the mid-seventies in the context of the Single Convention. Then we describe a number of recent international developments in the United Nations and Europe. Finally, we summarize our discussion and speculate about the likelihood that the Dutch Model will survive in the international War on Drugs. In our discussion, we also include relevant domestic developments in the Netherlands.

2. The Dutch model and the Single Convention

Recent Dutch drug policy has been developed within the context of the Single Convention of 1961. This United Nations convention replaced the nine international drug-related treaties which existed prior to 1961 and is generally considered to be the foundation of both national and international developments in this area.

2.1 The Single Convention of New York[1]

As is clearly stated in the preamble, the main goal of this convention was to protect humanity from the evil of drugs:

"The Parties, Concerned with the health and welfare of mankind, (...). Recognizing that addiction to narcotic drugs constitutes a serious evil for the individual and is fraught with social and economic danger to mankind, (and) Conscious of the duty to prevent and combat this evil, (and) Considering that effective measures against abuse of narcotic drugs require coordinated and universal action, (and ...) calls for international co-operation."

Article 4 of the convention lists several general obligations of the parties to the treaty. The parties must take the legislative and administrative measures needed to put into operation and implement the stipulations of this convention, and must, consistent with the clauses of this treaty, limit "...the production, manufacture, export, import, distribution of, trade in, use and possession of drugs..." to medicinal and scientific purposes only. Parties to this convention are not only required to take legislative action but also to take an active role in its implementation. Supervision over the execution of the obligations of the convention is in the hands of the International Narcotic Control Board (INCB) - which has the right to conduct local inspections (Article 14, 1c) - and the Commission on Narcotic Drugs (CND). By its very nature, the Single Convention primarily targets the supply side of the drugs problem. Through administrative controls and criminal sanctions it aims to combat production and distribution of illegal drugs, thereby preventing people to get involved with illegal drugs. In addition, the Convention allows countries to "...take all practicable measures for the prevention of abuse of drugs and for the early identification, treatment, education, after-care, rehabilitation and social reintegration of the persons involved and shall co-ordinate their efforts to these ends...".[2]

2.2 The Dutch latitude to maneuver

A direct consequence of the convention is that it restricts the latitude of the parties to the treaty to develop their own policies. However, Article 36, paragraph 4 of the Convention provides some room to develop unique, national emphases in prosecution and penalization policy:

"Nothing contained in this article shall affect the principle that the offenses to which it refers shall be defined, prosecuted and punished *in conformity with the domestic law of a Party.*" (Emphasis added)

It is this provision the Netherlands used in its 1976 Revised Opium Act with regard to the de facto decriminalization of the possession of cannabis and a limited amount of other illegal drugs for personal use. Prior to the 1976 revision, the Netherlands had always acted in complete conformity with the manner in which other countries had implemented the Single Convention.

The drafters of the Revised Opium Act of 1976 did realize that the Netherlands should not expect much international understanding for the liberalization of its drug policy, which represented a more lenient approach to drug users in particular. The legislature feared negative international economic consequences, especially from its neighbor Germany, a country of extreme economic importance to the Netherlands. It was partly because of this reason that the revised legislation introduced a substantial increase of the maximum sentences for (inter)national trafficking in hard drugs; there should be absolutely no question that the Netherlands would be backing out of its international obligations. Consequently, the guidelines with regard to the investigation of drug offenses assigned the highest priority to the trafficking in hard drugs (and the large scale trafficking in hemp products). In this manner, the Netherlands met its obligations of the Single Convention, while at the same time creating some latitude to develop its own policy. The (partial) departure from the dominant international repressive ideology with regard to cannabis and the use of illegal drugs in general was thus compensated by the absolute conformity to the letter and the spirit of the international drugs legislation with respect to illegal drug trafficking.

These legislative adjustments did not insulate the Netherlands from foreign pressure and threats to give up its "tolerant" policy. For example, a rapidly escalating conflict developed when the Dutch town of Enschede decided to tolerate a small dealer in hemp products on the premises of the youth center "de Kokerjuffer". Germany, in particular, objected to the presence of a pseudo-legal dealer close to its border with the Netherlands. In response to this conflict, the International Narcotic Control Board visited the Netherlands to determine if the provisions of the Single Convention had been violated. They took no action, however; they accepted the argument that this component of Dutch policy was trying to prevent that youth would get involved in more dangerous and harmful drug use.

Germany was also twice involved in a conflict about the prosecution and punishment of Harm Dost, a Dutch small-scale dealer in soft drugs operating in Arnhem (a city close to the German border) who sold hashish to youth from Germany. On the insistence of German authorities Harm Dost was prosecuted and convicted for these facts in the Netherlands. However, when Harm Dost was on a vacation in Spain, West Germany requested and obtained his extradition from Spain because of his dealing in illegal drugs in Arnhem. In Germany he was tried and convicted to 10 years incarceration for the very same offenses for which he already had been tried and convicted in Holland. High-level diplomatic protests against the kidnapping and unlawful conviction of a Dutch citizen were of no avail. Dost had to serve many years of his prison sentence. Not only was he incarcerated in Germany for offenses that were exclusively committed in the Netherlands, but for actions which were typically not prosecuted under Dutch legal practice.

In spite of conflicts with its neighbors, the Netherlands managed to continue its unique drugs policy and thus built its unique reputation abroad. In 1985 the notion of "normalization" was introduced to provide a philosophical foundation for the policy; at the same time, a high priority was assigned to convincing other countries of the effectiveness and legitimacy of the Dutch model.[3]

3. Recent international developments

Policy developments at the international level have not remained at a standstill since the Single Convention in 1961. Within the same United Nations context new treaties important for national drug policy – and thus also for the Dutch model – have been developed.[4] In addition to these developments at the global level, several things have happened in Europe.

The obvious starting point for our discussion of European developments is the European Community (EC). Within the European Community framework, drug policies are developed and implemented. The EC has a parliament which has the authority to make decisions concerning the European approach to drug problems. Furthermore, within the EC context treaties are developed which may have a direct impact on the legislation and practices of the member states. Finally, a substantial number of groups concerned with policy making, coordination, information exchange, and so on, in the field of drug problems have emerged in Europe. To an important degree, these forums have been developed within the framework of the EC; some function within other international contexts, such as the Council of Europe.[5]

3.1 International drugs legislation within United Nations context

Since 1961 two important treaties have been developed within the context of the United Nations: The Convention on Psychotropic Substances of 1971[6] and the Convention against the Illicit Trafficking of Narcotic Drugs and Psychotropic Substances of 1988.[7] The Convention on Psychotropic Substances of 1971 may be viewed as a further expansion of the criminalization of substances not included in the Single Convention. The Convention against Illegal Trafficking focuses specifically on the legal means to combat the illegal drugs economy and may be viewed as the formal legal codification of the current War on Drugs.

The Netherlands had always taken the position that it was not necessary to enter into the Convention on Psychotropic Substances because the most important non-medical products (hallucinogens and amphetamines) of this agreement were already included in Schedule 1 of the Dutch Opium Act. With regard to the remaining drugs included in the 1971 Convention (barbiturates and tranquilizers), the Dutch did not see a need to participate in this particular international treaty; they considered the existing non-penal regulation of these drugs through the Medicine Act sufficient. However, pressured from several sides (the Schengen Agreement discussed later in this chapter, European Parliament, and the Convention against the Illicit Trafficking), the Netherlands has revised its earlier position on this matter and has entered the Convention on Psychotropic Substances. The legislative proposal to revise the Opium Act to make it consistent with this development is currently discussed in the Dutch parliament. A peculiar development is that, because the Netherlands has to abide by the conditions of the 1971 Convention, barbiturates and tranquilizers will be included in Schedule 2 of the Opium Act, while formerly, schedule 2 exclusively included solid blends of the cannabis plant.[8]

The Convention against the Illicit Trafficking of Narcotic Drugs and Psychotropic Substances is an instrument aimed against the illegal drugs economy. This agreement focuses on the law enforcement attack of trafficking in illicit drugs, in particular international cooperation with regard to international trafficking. The core of the Convention is Article 5. This article obliges all parties to the treaty to take the necessary measures to allow forfeiture of all profits from actions deemed illegal by this Convention.

To a large degree, the Convention against the Illicit Trafficking definitions are consistent with the current Dutch Opium Act. However, a new element is the obligation to criminalize the so-called laundering of profits from drug trafficking. Although the Convention still has to be ratified, the Minister already has proceeded to implement it in a number of new legislative measures.[9] These new legislative provisions include: the creation of a criminal financial investigation to determine the amount of the illegally obtained profits; the introduction of the seizure of the suspect's property as security, to ensure that upon conviction the high monetary fine or required amount to compensate for illegally obtained profits is paid; a sentence of maximally six years of incarceration may be imposed in those cases where there is no possibility of redress on property; the separation of the procedure to determine guilt or innocence from the procedure to determine the amount of profits (in the latter procedure the burden of proof is based on a "balance of probabilities"[10]); the possibility to seize anything that somehow was obtained illegally, independent of the charges and convictions.[11]

The Dutch minister has been severely castigated for the manner in which he wants to implement this convention.[12] Critics focus on the proposed violation of the legal principle that only one judicial body deals with the entire legal case; the violation of the *praesumptio innocentiae*[13] in the procedure to determine the amount of illegal profits; and the reduction of the role of the Public Prosecutor to only represent the government's interests in this procedure.[14] Many fear that a substantial portion of Dutch criminal procedural law will be turned upside down because of the War on Drugs. Yet, it appears likely that the Netherlands will ratify the Convention, and that parliament will accept without much resistance the legislative proposals associated with this treaty.

3.2 Developments in Europe

At the European level, the European Community (EC) is of course of special importance. In order to secure the envisioned future economic, monetary, and (partly) political unification in the year 2000, EC countries desire extensive mutual cooperation in a multitude of areas. The desire for unification is formalized in the Treaty on European Union (February 7, 1992), also referred to as the Maastricht Treaty.[15] This Treaty contains several interesting statements concerning the organization of future European drug policy[16]; however, it appears at present that the chance that this Treaty will survive is highly uncertain. Therefore, for the present situation in Europe, other developments are currently of more importance.

In the section which follows, we discuss two European Parliament reports completed in the last several years. Although formally its powers are limited, the discussion in the European Parliament is important because it serves as a good indicator of how, at the level of (party-)politics, the individual member states think about drug policy. Next, we discuss the Schengen Agreement and how it deals with drugs problems. At the conclusion of this section we focus on a number of groups within the EC and the Council of Europe, and their concern with drugs.

3.2.1 The European Parliament (EP)

The European Parliament has twice occupied itself with drug problems, resulting in two reports: the Stewart-Clark Report (1986) and the Cooney Report (1991). First, in October 1986 the British conservative Sir Stewart-Clark presented the report of the investigative commission on the drug problems in the EC.[17] Then, in early 1991 the EP established another investigative commission to study the increase of organized crime in the member states of the EC associated with illegal drug trafficking. At the end of the same year, rapporteur Cooney presented a report of its findings.[18] Because the Parliament in plenary session has taken positions different from those discussed in the report, the Presidium of the EP no longer allows distribution of the report. In this chapter, we use the Dutch version of the report. Neither commission has succeeded in presenting to parliament a unanimous final report; both have final reports with a majority and a minority opinion.[19]

The Stewart-Clark Report: The Stewart-Clark Commission started its work on drug problems in Europe in October 1985; exactly one year later Parliament was able to evaluate its final report. The report consists of a majority position (with as its central focus the repressive approach to drugs), and a minority position (linking the emergence of organized illegal drug trafficking primarily to existing repressive policies). Although both parties agreed on a strict enforcement policy with regard to illegal large-scale dealing, the minority allowed for the possibility that legalization could be an effective tool to control this problem.

The Dutch policy was discussed in the debate concerning the desirability of legalization of heroin and cocaine. The majority referred to the Netherlands - together with Spain and Sweden - as an example of the failure of a "brief period of greater liberalization (with an) attendant high increase in the number of addicts".[20]

The majority position referred also explicitly to the Netherlands in its discussion of the possibility of legalization of cannabis: As one of the arguments against legalization is mentioned that it is illogical to keep dealing in cannabis illegal while decriminalizing its consumption.[21] Yet, the report admits that the Dutch approach has not resulted in an increase in the number of users, and that "psychological problems connected with those illegally consuming the drugs have disappeared" (p 48).

For the minority in the Stewart-Clark Commission, the Dutch model shows that it makes sense to consider the legalization of certain drugs. The minority favors decriminalization of use, possession, and small-scale dealing. They argue: "It is incomprehensible that possession, use, manufacture, cultivation and marketing should be criminal offenses in the case of one drug and not in the case of another, when (illegal drugs and alcohol, nicotine, and mind-altering pharmaceutical drugs) are equally damaging to health..." (p 93).

After a lengthy debate, the European Parliament agreed to organize a European conference on drugs policy; at this conference the effects of the existent approach would be discussed. In addition, it was decided to recommend educational programs and the establishment of research centers. Finally, the report recommended the improvement of the coordination of police activities of the member states, and the establishment of a European Narcotics Brigade. Now, six years later, the proposed Narcotics Brigade is about to become reality.

The Cooney Report: On January 24, 1991 the European Parliament decided to establish an investigative commission specifically focusing on illegal drug trafficking. The commission started its work in February and finished its report on December 2, 1991. Again, the commission was divided, with a minority report signed by six members (among others, Stewart-Clark and rapporteur Cooney) and a majority position (nine members). Chair was the British Bowe.

Consistent with its specific assignment, the commission focused on how to approach organized illegal drug trafficking; in doing this, it beats it usual repressive drum. Police and customs must increase their cooperation; they argue in favor of the establishment of the European Drug Intelligence Unit (EDIU), and the establishment in each individual member state of a national Office of Narcotics, including a special department for financial crimes to investigate money laundering. They further favor mandatory registration for project development companies, the tourist industry, construction, and the arts because it is assumed that considerable money laundering takes place in these areas.

However, in several of its sections, "Dutch" ideas surface. For example, the report discusses a distinction between categories of drugs, varying from "ultra-hard" to "ultra-soft".[22] Drug addiction is viewed primarily as a public health problem, and next to cracking down on dealers, the report gives the highest priority to prevention, and assistance of addicts: "...The key to a definitive victory in the battle against drugs is at the level of demand..." (p 50). In the opinion of the majority there would need to be a more even balance between the expenditures for demand reduction and supply reduction. More facts would need to be collected about AIDS, social and medical problems and how to lower demand for drugs. Free treatment, needles and sometimes substitute drugs should be available. The recommendations even noted that, in view of harm reduction, a pragmatic approach needs to be followed where drugs in pure form are available in the right doses.[23] However, the report rejects legalization of presently illegal drugs, partly because the United Nations (*i.e.,* "the world") has declared drug use and drug trade illegal because these substances are harmful to body and mind, and disrupt family and society. The EC – itself a constitutional union – must accept and appreciate this (p 51).[24] Nevertheless, in its recommendations an important breakthrough surfaces: Possession for personal use should no longer be viewed as an offense.[25]

Again, a European conference is proposed in order to examine, not only the phenomenon of drug trafficking, but also the consequences (for democracy, and the safety and freedom of the citizens) of drug enforcement itself, including the harmonization of legislation resulting from the far-reaching economic unification as originally anticipated by the end of 1992 (but now postponed to the end of this decade). Finally, the CELAD (discussed later in this chapter) has to develop an integrated program of education of the population of all EC countries. At the same time, initiatives must be taken to provide drug information through the radio, television, and press.

Actually, the minority position deviates from the majority position in only one aspect, namely with regard to the decriminalization of possession for (own) use. The minority considers a certain degree of repression of users appropriate and feels that possession for private use should remain illegal. Furthermore, the minority believes that "...against the backdrop of a common EC policy (...), we must put a halt to the illogical policy that currently exist in a number of countries where trade in and supply of cannabis are illegal, but where the sale and possession of small amounts of cannabis are legally permitted..." (p 70).

At the parliamentary discussion of the resolutions on May 11, 1992, the majority opinion was rejected. The resolution that is finally accepted states that one does not believe "...that any form of legalization offers a practical solution for the drugs problem..." and one "...reaffirms support for the legal order as expressed in the UNO treaties and the legislations of the member states..." Incidentally, the Dutch model is also used as a (usually terrifying) example during the plenary session. A French delegate (Lehideux) referred to the Cooney report as "scandalous": "Through the lax measures it advocates in the direction of the Dutch model, it has sadly proven itself. It trivializes drug use and it facilitates drug trafficking..." (preliminary verbatim report of proceedings, Strasbourg, May 11, 1992, p 36). Another delegate believed that the Dutch (and the Spanish) government should realize that the lenient approach has devastated the lives of many young people and their families, among others because one believed that soft drugs were harmless. In the opinion of this delegate, there was now conclusive evidence that the use of soft drugs will lead to experimentation with hard, addictive drugs (*ibid.* p 33).

As the preceding discussion shows, opinions within the European Parliament with regard to drug policy remain greatly divided. However, it appears that the general tendency within this supranational organ is predominantly prohibitionist, and support for the preservation of the Dutch model or its spreading to other European countries is not to be expected from this side, at least not in the near future.

3.2.2 The Schengen Treaty[26]

It goes without saying that the European Parliament is an important organ within the EC. However, it is definitely not very powerful, it is often internally divided, and it is probably mostly of symbolic significance. This is different for the treaties that have been made (and are still being made) in the context of European unification. We already referred briefly to the Maastricht Treaty, but the importance of this agreement for practical Dutch drug policy remains, for the time being, purely theoretical. This is definitely not the case for the more regionally oriented cooperation between several EC countries with regard to border traffic. In an agreement between Belgium, the Netherlands, Luxembourg, Germany and France entered into on June 14, 1985 (the so-called Schengen Treaty), the gradual abolition of checkpoints at the common border crossings was advocated. The treaty was meant to be a precursor of European unification in 1992.[27]

The 1985 treaty devotes much attention to the potential negative consequences of the abolition of customs inspection at the borders. It proposes measures to prevent illegal drug trafficking across national borders. In 1985, the parties to the treaty had committed themselves to a more efficient coordination of drug enforcement (Article 8), including the exchange of information about capital movement (Article 9). At the same time, it was agreed that, eventually, the participating countries would strive towards harmonization of legislation, specifically in the area of drugs (Article 19). Finally, the parties committed themselves to an exchange of all information useful "...to the coordination of their actions to combat the trade in narcotic drugs..."[28]

In the view of Dutch government officials, the treaty posed no special threat to the continuation of a specific "Dutch" drug policy. They were of the opinion that the Opium Act revised in that same year (Revised Opium Act of 1985) had satisfied Article 8, through the criminalization of illegal preparatory acts (Article 10a) and expanded judicial powers with regard to the prosecution of preparatory acts committed by foreigners abroad (Article 13). In their interpretation, Article 9 merely encouraged exploration of intensification of existing forms of cooperation. Finally, the explanation accompanying Article 19 noted that the Single Convention already provides the necessary foundation. Since all Schengen parties have entered into the Single Convention, the legislation is already harmonized, or so the Minister seemed to think.[29]

Since 1985 the countries involved have been in continued deliberation to work out the Schengen Agreement. The semi-annual reports indicate that the other Schengen partners view the Dutch cannabis prosecution policy as problematic. Germany, in particular, takes exception to the coffee shops, particularly in the border regions. Meanwhile, in order to escape this foreign pressure, the Netherlands has proposed a variety of measures to prevent foreigners from taking advantage of its relatively mild legal and penal climate. An example is the proposal to bar foreigners from Dutch drug assistance agencies. Incidentally, in some cities this policy has already been implemented: in Amsterdam, for instance, only in acute emergencies is methadone provided to foreigners who are not Amsterdam residents. Another Dutch concession is that coffee shops would no longer be allowed to sell soft drugs to "...subjects from other Schengen countries as well as foreigners in general..."[30] This condition would be added to the already existing requirements for coffee shops: no dealing in hard drugs, no sales to minors, no advertising, no significant nuisance problems for the neighborhood.

After five years of talks, in 1990 the Schengen Implementation Agreement[31] came about. On June 25, 1992, the Dutch parliament concurred. The Agreement rests on two pillars. The parties to the agreement are responsible for their own national policy, but they share responsibility for the consequences of this policy for the other Schengen countries. With respect to drug policy, this notion is reflected as follows: "...In as far as one of the Parties in the context of its national policy regarding the prevention and treatment of addiction to narcotic drugs deviates from the principle established in Article 71, paragraph 2 (*i.e.* the administrative and legal prevention of illegal export, sale, provision and delivery of those substances – added by authors), all parties will take the necessary legal and administrative measures in order to prevent the illegal import and export of these substances (...)."

The Dutch minister has interpreted this clause to mean a need for increased domestic control of drugs in order to compensate for the elimination of the border controls. Consistent with this view, he has already announced that the policy with regard to coffee shops will be strictly enforced.

The most important provisions in the area of drug policy are Articles 70-76 (narcotic drugs) and 39-47 (law enforcement cooperation). In these stipulations, the Agreement creates several obligations, such as the intensification of the scrutiny of border-crossing persons, goods and means of transportation to prevent the illegal import of narcotic drugs (Article 71, paragraph 3); provisions to confiscate the monetary gains from illegal drug trafficking (Article 72), and finally, provisions allowing the use of undercover drug agents and "controlled delivery" (provided that these tactics do not violate the national constitution and legal order).[32]

Of importance for the investigation of violations of the Opium Act are also Articles 40-43 of the Agreement regulating the conditions under which observation and pursuit of suspects may cross national borders. The authority to follow suspects is restricted to a list of serious offenses, including the illegal trafficking in narcotic and psychotropic drugs. Except in emergencies, drug enforcement agents are required to obtain prior permission of the national authorities of the country where the pursuit takes place. Under certain conditions are drug enforcement authorities allowed to continue the pursuit on foreign territory of drug dealers caught red-handed in their jurisdiction. Clearly, these provisions expand to a considerable degree the freedom of foreign law enforcement agents to work on Dutch territory.

In addition to increasing repressive measures, the Agreement also pays some attention to the treatment aspect of drug problems. In Article 71 (paragraph 5), the Parties commit themselves to do whatever is in their power to prevent and counteract the negative effects of the illegal demand for drugs. However, it remains a matter of individual responsibility of the parties to determine exactly how that obligation is to be realized.

The joint statement accompanying Article 71, paragraph 2 obligates the Netherlands to make sure that the Schengen partners are not inconvenienced by Dutch drug policy. According to the Dutch ministers, this means a thorough surveillance of the sales points of drugs, in particular in the border regions where many foreign addicts come to buy their drugs.[33] The already mentioned stricter guidelines with regard to sale of cannabis to foreigners in coffeeshops reflects this effort. On the other hand, it remains Dutch prosecutorial policy not to turn over to foreign authorities criminal cases which would not be prosecuted in the Netherlands, for example for possession of user amounts of illegal drugs. In spite of this principled decision of the top officials of the Office of Public Prosecution, the Minister of Justice did establish a working group to develop guidelines on this matter.[34]

Apart from the just discussed changes, the harmonization of drugs legislation and policy anticipated with so much fear by the Dutch, has not (yet) become reality. Harmonization has definitely taken place with regard to illegal trade in and possession of weapons; however, with regard to drugs, the emphasis has primarily been on improving cooperation. The question remains, however, whether the threat to the continued survival of the Dutch model indeed has past. Only experience will be able to tell the true extent of mutual tolerance between the parties.

3.2.3 European advisory groups

Finally, it is important to discuss the variety of groups (both inside the EC as well as those independent of the EC) where drug problems are under discussion. After all, decisions formally taken at the European level, for example by the Council of Ministers, often may be the result of discussions held in these forums in an earlier phase.

Figure 1 provides a schematic overview of the different organizations involved directly or indirectly in the debate concerning the drug policy in Europe.

Historically, the Council of Europe has been the most important forum for the shaping of European criminal justice cooperation, exchange of information and harmonization of regulation. It was within this structure that in 1971 the first European-level advisory group was established by George Pompidou (commonly referred to as the Pompidou Group). Presently, this advisory body has grown to include ministers of public health and justice from over 25 countries.

This body devotes attention to all aspects of the drugs problem, such as prevention, epidemiology, repression, law enforcement and juridical cooperation. As part of the Pompidou Group's activities, there is an an-

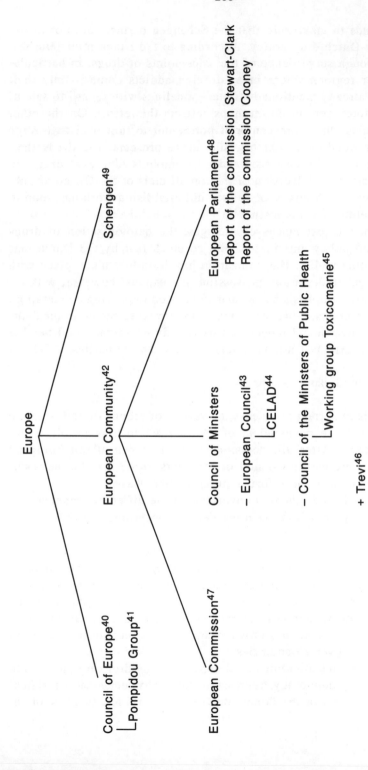

Fig. 1. Schematic overview of drug advisory bodies in Europe.

nual conference of chiefs of police in charge of international airports, where the participants keep each other informed of recent developments in the area of smuggling methods and routes, as well as efficient investigation techniques and equipment.

There exist additional advisory bodies and ad hoc working groups in the field of drug problems within the European Community context. Unfortunately, these groups present a rather muddled picture. Since 1976, there is the Trevi Group whose goal it is to combat international terrorism (resolution of the EC ministers of June 29, 1976).[35] In 1985 her task was expanded to include the exchange of information about law enforcement techniques and tactics for the combatting of other serious forms of (organized) criminality with international aspects. The purpose here was not only to improve the infrastructure of the investigation through exchange of information and expertise but also the development of repressive and preventive strategies.[36] At the suggestion of the Trevi ministers, the European Summit of Maastricht decided in 1991 to establish Europol. For the time being, Europol consists only of a European Drugs Unit (formerly referred to as the European Drugs Intelligence Unit (EDIU)), which is currently without any executive tasks. Using information provided by the member states, this agency would analyze information about internationally organized, serious drug criminality, to improve and coordinate the joint investigation.[37]

Apart from the Trevi Group, drug problems are also discussed in other groups. For instance, there is the group Toxicomanie, associated with the Council of Ministers of Public Health. Over the past years, this group has been involved in activities related to the ethical and technical aspects of urine testing, drug use prevention, establishment of a European data network, development of alternatives for incarcerated addicts, and so on.

In addition, there is a group named Juridical Cooperation, another one by the name of Mutual Cooperation, and a group named RELEX, which involves itself with drug-related "relations extérieures".

In order to impose some semblance of order in this gamut of advisory bodies, the Comité Européen pour la Lutte Anti-Drogue (CELAD) (the European Committee for the War Against Drugs (proposed by French President Mitterand), was established in 1989. This intergovernmental coordinating group is directly accountable to the European Council (consisting of government leaders and heads of state).[38] However, more and more the CELAD is operating as yet another new club developing its own activities. In 1990, CELAD drafted a European plan against drug addiction accepted by the European Council (in Rome).[39] Although this plan is primarily targeting the supply side of the drugs problem, it does raise the issue of the desirability of providing a more central place to harm reduction in view of the AIDS epidemic. In addition, CELAD has worked to establish a European Drugs Monitoring Centre; in its Guidelines for a European Plan to Combat Drugs (May 1990), CELAD clearly indicated that it did not want to limit itself to "social and health aspects, but also other drug-related aspects, including trafficking and repression". The criminal justice component, in particular, encountered considerable resistance, among others in the Netherlands. As a compromise, agreement was reached that in the first years the data network will primarily include data concerning use, prevention, and assistance. It concerns scientific data on epidemiology, assistance (number of clients, types of assistance and organization) and data on (national) policy. The Center will obtain these data by means of an infrastructure of one or more national centers (so-called Focal Points), named REITOX (European Information Network on Drugs and Drug Addiction). The intention is that every EC country participates, under the jurisdiction of the Council of Ministers.

Trying to characterize the activities and focus of these advisory groups, it becomes very clear that they are mostly oriented towards aspects related to the coordination, cooperation, and organization of the combatting of illegal drugs trafficking. Of much less concern are prevention and assistance or treatment – the public health aspects which are of primary importance in the Dutch model. Furthermore, there is no question that the great diversity of groups and the unclear authorities and procedures are definitely unconducive to the effectiveness of the whole.

4. The chances of survival of the Dutch model

So far, we have described several international developments which may have an effect on the chance of survival of the Dutch Model in the international War on Drugs. In order to speculate about the preservation of the Dutch drug policy within an increasingly uniform international political system based on prohibitionism, we have to consider two issues. On the one hand, we have to estimate the power of international forces in shaping Dutch policy; on the other hand, we have to assess the degree to which the Netherlands can muster the internal power and force to resist these international pressures.

4.1 International pressures

The effects of the previously described supra-national developments are hard to estimate. For instance, it is hard to predict the consequences of the Maastricht Treaty for European drug policy. The role of the European Parliament is also hard to place in this respect. Its two commissions (Stewart-Clark and Cooney) and the two plenary sessions devoted to their reports stood out through their contradictions, with alternating positive and negative opinions about elements of the Dutch model. And although the majority opinion in the recent Cooney report appears to take a step forward (particularly in comparison to the majority opinion of the Stewart-Clark report), the European Parliament in its plenary meeting was not able to arrive at a majority position.

Other developments, however, leave no doubt that the Dutch model has come under severe international pressure. Many countries have joined the American War on Drugs. The War on Drugs has been transformed from an American war into a world war, increasing international pressure on the Netherlands to adjust its drug policies. Dutch participation in the international fight against drugs trafficking, started in 1976, has continued even stronger in the early 1990s. The Convention Against Illicit Trafficking has been completely endorsed by the Netherlands, and has already resulted in severely criticized legislative proposals. And, although the original reasons for non-ratification have not changed, the Convention on Psychotropic Substances has also been signed by Holland.

Two spearheads of Dutch drug policy, the allowance of possession of small amounts of cannabis for own use, and coffee shops, appear most vulnerable to international pressures. For example, the problems surrounding coffee shops and drug-related public order problems in the Dutch-German border region seriously impaired negotiations related to the Schengen Agreement. In order to arrive at uniform policies several cities in the Dutch-German border area have recently started deliberations about the best approach to drug addiction.

Although the impact of the Schengen Agreement does not necessarily have to be detrimental to present Dutch drug policy, it is an undeniable political fact that the Netherlands is dependent on the tolerance of its neighbors, Germany in particular. The Kokerjuffer and Harm Dost incidents discussed earlier are not encouraging in this respect. Also, the entering into the Convention on Psychotropic Substances further complicates matters: while previously (from 1976) the drugs in the Opium Act were listed on two separate lists allowing separate policies for hemp products and other illegal drugs, now the list for hemp products (Schedule II) has been "polluted" by all kinds of barbiturates which in practice will fall under another policy. This muddling of the waters makes the legitimation of the policy - both nationally and abroad - more problematic.

Finally, danger also lurks from the institutional context of the Single

Convention. In 1992, the INCB – the investigative organ of the Convention – paid another visit to the Netherlands aimed primarily at Dutch cannabis policy. This was triggered by the frequent stories in the international press concerning the greenhouse cultivation of high quality Dutch varieties of the hemp plant. In its annual report, the INCB concludes that the Dutch policy is not "in conformity" with United Nations conventions, in particular with respect to possession of cannabis for personal use.[50] The Commission also questioned whether the Dutch policy indeed has resulted in the intended separation of the illegal markets in cannabis and other illegal drugs (*e.g.*, heroin). The Commission did ask the Netherlands to reconsider its policy in view of the feared negative repercussions for the international community. In response, the Netherlands referred to the positive effects (*i.e.*, low rate of fatalities, relative decline in number of minors addicted to drugs). The Dutch did consent to sharpen the control of coffee shops.

4.2 Dutch domestic developments

Whether the Netherlands ultimately will be able to resist international pressures generated by the War on Drugs depends also on developments on the home front, in particular the extent to which the Dutch model is able to preserve its national support. We are somewhat disheartened by recent developments. The primacy of public health aspects in the Dutch model implies that the Ministry of Public Health functions as coordinator of Dutch drugs policy; theoretically at least, an integrated policy is guaranteed through the Interdepartmental Steering Group Alcohol and Drugs Policy (ISAD), with representatives of the Departments of Justice, Public Health, and Foreign Affairs. It characterizes current developments in the Netherlands that this coordinating commission has not met for years; recently it was even discovered that this commission has ceased to exist altogether.[51] This is consistent with the observation that in national debates on drugs the law enforcement approach is becoming more important, at the expense of the public health approach.

Several factors are involved in this shift in policy debate, but there is no question that the international developments described in this chapter play a substantial role. After all, the War on Drugs is primarily prepared and executed by the justice departments of the different countries. Although occasionally, the Ministry of Public Health has participated in international discussions, primarily the officials and political leaders of the justice department are the persons who have been instrumental in shaping the role of the Netherlands in international developments. There is an increasing quest for more intensive international cooperation, particularly in the field of trafficking in illegal drugs. This is quite different in the area of public health, where international coordination is limited and there is much less striving towards a uniform policy.[52] That is why internationally the public health approach has been more and more pushed to the background, and the initiative is primarily in the hands of the departments of justice. Not surprisingly, the international leadership position of the justice departments has ramifications for the position of the Ministry of Public Health in the Dutch government bureaucracy.

The position of the Ministry of Public Health is further undermined by other developments in general government policies. For example, recent budget cuts spared judicial agencies and law enforcement, unlike the "soft" areas of public health and welfare. Indeed, several budget cuts have affected the Public Health Department responsible for drug problems over the last several years. Furthermore, the central government now assigns high priority to decentralization of authority (including budgets) to the local level. Consistent with this policy, substantial amounts of money - occasionally earmarked for particular purposes - have been deposited in general funds from which individual municipalities receive their budgetary allotments. It is quite likely that future funds for assistance and treatment of drug addicts will be distributed in this manner. This means that the budget - and thus an important administrative tool in the setting of policy - of the Ministry of Public Health will be strongly reduced.[53] Within certain boundaries, municipalities will be able to determine their own policy with regard to the public health aspects of the drug problems. In some cases this may provide an impetus for daring experiments consistent with the Dutch model. However, without central government intervention through budget restrictions, other local governments may start implementing policies much less concerned with harm reduction. In view of this, it is not unlikely that Dutch drug policy may begin to develop in a very fragmented and locally differentiated manner.[54]

A recent change of personnel in key positions of the Ministry of Public Health may also affect the current shift in emphasis: two of the architects of the Dutch policy of normalization have left for other public health fields.[55] In one fell swoop, a wealth of experience has disappeared, including expertise related to drug-related negotiations with the Ministry of Justice.

In sum, it seems that the Ministry of Public Health is losing its grip on developments in drug policy to the Ministry of Justice. It appears likely that its future role will be restricted primarily to funding of national experiments, research, training and provision of information.[56]

If we are correct, and the formulation of drug policies becomes primarily the domain of the Department of Justice, then it becomes of vital importance for the survival of the Dutch model that the political and official leaders of this ministry genuinely support this policy model. However, recent international and national reports, policy plans, and memos reflect a different spirit among Ministry of Justice officials: a more forceful attack of illegal trafficking, no matter what the costs.

Next to the priority assigned to drug trafficking (and organized crime in general), increasing importance in the Dutch national debate is given to the fighting of public order problems – primarily a local responsibility – resulting from drug dealing and use. Amsterdam has played a leading role in this area, which is not surprising in view of the relatively large number of users (also from abroad) residing in this city.[57] An additional powerful impetus to the national debate were the disturbances (in 1989) in the neighborhood of Klarendal in Arnhem (a town close to the German border) where most of the drug-related nuisance was blamed on (German) drug tourists. In part as a response to the problems in Arnhem, in 1990 a national working group was established to take inventory of available administrative and legal means to deal with drug-related nuisance and public order problems. In January 1991 this group presented a report including both an inventory and a set of recommendations. Central to this report (titled "Drugs and Nuisance") is an "integrated approach", favoring a policy which employs a combination of criminal law, civil law, alien law, and administrative law.[58] This report is significant because of its proposal to make use of criminal justice measures in order to control drug-related public order problems – including when it involves people who only possess small amounts of illegal drugs. Significantly, the Working Group thinks no distinction should be made between soft drugs and hard drugs; they argue that for the citizens who experience nuisance problems it is irrelevant whether the problems are caused by the use of hard drugs or soft drugs.[59] This report recommends almost exclusively repressive measures as solutions for public order problems, with particular emphasis on a harsh approach to foreigners.

Although the recommendations of the Working Group have not yet been translated into actual policy, the final report is a good illustration of the present philosophy of the Ministry of Justice – a philosophy which takes more and more distance from the policy foundations aimed at normalization expressed in the 1985 document "Drug Policy in Motion". The Department of Justice now questions important assumptions of the Dutch model (*e.g.,* protection of users by allowing possession of small amounts for personal use). There is, incidentally, yet another reason why this particular Working Group exemplifies our pessimistic expectations with regard to the future of the Dutch model: the group spent a whole year studying public order problems and drug use, while the Ministry of Public Health (still the formal coordinator of Dutch drug policy) was never even informed of the existence of this commission.

As a final indication of the trend in Dutch drug policy, we mention the statements repeatedly made by the political leadership of the Ministry of Justice. In statements to the press, making reference to the need to develop policies consistent with neighboring countries, the Minister of Justice has expressed the desire to "sharpen" Dutch policy. Although these statements have rarely been translated in actual policy, they create a climate more and more receptive to changes in current policy. A recent example is a speech by the Minister in December 1992, arguing in favor of the introduction of mandatory "afkick programs" as well as a harder approach to the growing and trading of "nederwiet" and other hemp products. He stated: "The Netherlands cannot afford to become the laughing-stock of Europe in this already very delicate area of policy."[60]

5. Concluding comments

It should be obvious by now that our general expectations concerning the future of the Dutch model are bleak. Dutch drug policy is in real danger of changing into a war on drugs (aimed primarily at drug dealing and public order problems). The likely negative impact of this repressive policy on users of illegal drugs (as explained in the 1985 policy document favoring normalization) appears to play a slowly diminishing role in the decision-making process. Indeed, it seems that the containment of public health problems associated with drug use is no longer the center piece of Dutch drug policy; instead, drug trafficking and public order problems are gradually becoming the focal concerns of Dutch policy.

Yet, we want to conclude this essay with a few more hopeful signs, for not all international developments need to be interpreted as a threat to the Dutch model. A recent interesting development is taking place at the level of European cities. In order to develop a channel to influence (international) drug policy, a policy advisory consortium for cities was established in 1990. The thought behind this development is that drug policy is developed internationally and nationally, while drug problems mostly are concentrated in big cities - cities that typically are not able to exert a real influence on policy. Meanwhile, this consortium has drafted a proposal to decriminalize the purchase, possession and use of hemp products and the non-prosecution of use, purchase, possession and consumption of small amounts of other illegal drugs. Together with Frankfurt (Germany), Hamburg (Germany) and Zurich (Switzerland), Amsterdam was among the first to endorse this proposal; recently the Dutch cities of Rotterdam and Arnhem also signed the resolution. Perhaps this initiative provides a new impetus to preserve or further expand the Dutch model at the local level. To compensate for the declining influence on local policy of the Ministry of Public Health, this organization of municipalities may stimulate Dutch cities to more innovative experiments. Rotterdam, for instance, for some time now has had "user rooms", and there has been talk about initiating experiments with the supply of heroin.[61]

Internationally, there are also signs indicating a growing support for the Dutch model. In the past, the international opinion of Dutch policy was mostly negative, and "the Dutch tolerance" was met with incomprehension. However, lately more positive accounts of Dutch drug policy are voiced in the international arena. An important example of this growing understanding is Germany, formerly one of the staunchest adversaries of Dutch policy. There are a number of developments in Germany which reflect a partial adoption of the Dutch way of thinking. In particular after the AIDS epidemic, a number of the German federal states have started experimenting – albeit on a small scale – with methadone. In several German states, needle exchange or needle supply programs have been established, including needle machines, and German officials have expressed a desire to integrate elements of Dutch drug policy into the German approach to drugs. Illustrative of the recent change in climate was the admission of a government delegation of Bundesland Reinland-Westfalen that in the past Germany often had unjustly criticized Dutch drugs policy. This comment was made at a press conference during a visit to the Netherlands. Primarily because of the efforts of the SPD (German Socialist Party) which favors a more liberal policy, politicians have begun to question German drug policy. Furthermore, in 1992 an important development has taken place in German jurisprudence: the Lubeck court challenged the constitutionality of the punishability of cannabis relative to the absence of legal penalties for more dangerous substances such as alcohol and nicotine.

Finally, even within the United Nations some encouraging signs may be noted. For example, in the final statement of the 1990 World Ministerial Summit to Reduce Demand for Drugs and to Combat the Cocaine Threat held in London under the auspices of the United Nations, the participating ministers stated that demand reduction (prevention, treatment and assistance, re-socialization) must have the same priority as supply reduction, and that, therefore, more funds should be allocated to the former. Also, in 1991 the Commission on Narcotics Drugs formally assigned a high priority to demand reduction (possibly reflecting the fact that the Commission was under Dutch chairmanship).

It is even possible to detect encouraging signs in the official United Nations Documents, which are not able to ignore some of the positive aspects of the Dutch model. For example, the 1991 Annual Report of the INCB mentions the Netherlands in one of its few positive references when describing the world drug problem: "The Netherlands is one of the few countries in Europe where the number of drug-related deaths continues to decline."[62]

In conclusion, internationally the Dutch model is under pressure, particularly because of developments in the field of law enforcement with regard to drugs trafficking. It appears that in this respect, the Dutch want to follow the repressive UN model, with all its negative consequences, including those for the position of users. As a countervailing trend, however, we see developments suggesting that more and more people outside the Netherlands are convinced that the War on Drugs does not provide a realistic solution to the drug problem; other countries have proposed (and sometimes even actually implemented) components of the Dutch model as realistic alternatives. The ultimate fate of the Dutch model will depend on the interplay between these two opposing developments.

Endnotes

1. Single Convention on Narcotic Drugs, New York, March 30 1961; and Protocol to Modification of the Single Convention on Narcotic Drugs, Geneva, March 25, 1972.
2. Article 38 of the Convention as Modified in the Protocol to Modification of the Single Convention; Geneva, March 25, 1972.
3. *Drug Policy in Motion, Toward a Normalization of Drug Problems*, p 42. Interdepartementale Stuurgroup Alcohol en Drugs (ISAD). The Hague: Government Printing Office, 1985.
4. At the global level, in addition to the United Nations, other organizations concerned with drug use exist; for instance, within the context of the so-called G-7 Conference. The G-7 Conference consists of six important industrialized countries from the West, (US, Canada, UK, France, Germany and Italy) and Japan. The G-7 Conference has two Task Forces dealing with drug-related issues: the Financial Action Task Force and the Chemical Action Task Force both of which deal with the trade in chemicals necessary for the production of particular drugs. The present paper excludes these groups from further discussion.

5. The Council of Europe consists of approximately 25 countries that cooperate in the areas of culture, public health, criminal justice and social welfare. The European Community, on the other hand, consists of three coalitions historically united by predominantly economical interests: the European Community for Coal and Steel, European Economic Community, and European Community for Atom Energy. Presently, the European Community has 12 member states (France, Germany, Great Britain, the Netherlands, Belgium, Luxembourg, Italy, Spain, Denmark, Ireland, Portugal, and Greece).
6. The Convention on Psychotropic Substances, Vienna, February 21, 1971.
7. Convention against the Illicit Trafficking of Narcotic Drugs and Psychotropic Substances, Vienna, December 20, 1988.
8. Minutes of the Dutch Parliament, 1990-1991, 22090, nos. 1-3. It should be noted that the guidelines will not tolerate the sale of barbiturates in the coffee shops.
9. It concerns the new legislation to supplement the Criminal Code and Criminal Procedure with provisions to fight fencing, and the expansion of the conditions under which illegally obtained profits may be seized.
10. The judge may base the probability that illegal profits are involved on the prosecution's (proven) argument that the convicted person has considerable material goods which reasonably cannot be assumed to result from his legal income, *and* the convicted person cannot present a plausible claim that his profits were obtained in a legitimate manner.
11. This is possible if a special criminal-financial investigation shows that it is reasonable to assume (*i.e.,* it is not necessary to prove it) that additional illegal acts somehow resulted in illegal profits for the convicted person.
12. We provided an overview of this in another publication: Blom, T. and Van Mastrigt, H: Kroniek rechten en criminologie: het verdrag tegen de sluikhandel. *Tijdschrift voor Alcohol, Drugs en andere Psychotrope Stoffen*, 17(3):110-113, 1991.
13. This principle implies that every person, prosecuted for a criminal offense, is presumed to be innocent until proven guilty by law.
14. In the inquisitorial system of the Netherlands, the role of the Public Prosecutor is broader than in the adversarial American legal system. First, the Dutch Public Prosecutor functions as an administrator whose central concern must be to protect the government's interests. An example of this prosecutorial task is found in the prioritizing of prosecution of violations of the Opium Act (possession for personal use versus large scale dealing). Second, the Public Prosecutor functions as a magistrate, whose obligation it is to represent the interests of all parties involved in a case - including those of the accused. This two-fold responsibility even allows for the possibility that a Public Prosecutor requests acquittal. The proposal under discussion will minimalize the importance of the magistrate role of the Public Prosecutor.
15. *Treaty on European Union.* Europe Documents, nos 1759/60, February 1, 1992.
16. The Maastricht Treaty includes, in addition to the establishment of the Council of Ministers of Home Affairs and Justice (K3) and the Coordinating Group (K4), the creation of the European Police Office (Europol) (Art. K.1 paragraph 9) and the European Drugs Intelligence Unit (EDIU). The Council of the Ministers of Justice and Home Affairs has been assigned an important role in the fight against drug addiction and unlawful drug trafficking. However, this topic is also discussed in the section on Public Health (title X, Article 129), where drug dependence is the only "major health scourge" explicitly referred to. (This may be related to the fact that the final text was formulated under Dutch chairmanship.)
17. "Report drawn up on behalf of the committee of enquiry into the drug problem in the member states of the community on the results of the Enquiry". Reporter: Sir Jack Stewart-Clark, European Parliament, Working Documents, 1986-87, Document A 2-114/PE 106.715/B/fin./corr.

18. "Report drawn up by the commission of enquiry into the spread of organized crime linked to drug trafficking in the member-states of the European Community". Reporter: P. Cooney, European Parliament, meeting documents A3-0358/91.
19. To illustrate our point: during the last meeting of the Stewart-Clark Commission (September 1986), the recommendations were finally passed with 300 amendments.
20. We have absolutely no idea to which "brief period" the Commission refers.
21. The other two arguments concerned the fact that the cannabis trade still remains in the hands of criminal organizations, and the danger that more potent varieties will be cultivated, or that chemical substances (*e.g.,* PCP) will be added.
22. They somewhat over-differentiate between ultra-hard (heroin, crack), hard (morphine, cocaine, methadone), medium-hard (amphetamines, LSD, barbiturates), medium-soft (opium, hashish, tobacco, distilled alcohol), soft (cannabis, fermented alcohol, mushrooms, tranquilizers) and ultra-soft drugs (tea, coffee, chocolate) (p 9).
23. Unfortunately, it remains unclear exactly what the commission has in mind with this.
24. Apparently the members of the commission believe it is no longer possible to be critical or to conduct a rational analysis simply because the United Nations has taken particular decisions in the past.
25. The minority position opposes this majority viewpoint based on the argument that in most of the rest of the world possession for personal use is illegal.
26. Agreement between the Netherlands, Belgium, Federal Republic of Germany, France and Luxembourg with regard to the gradual abolition of check points on common border-crossings, June 14, 1985.
27. Meanwhile, the following countries have joined the Schengen agreement: Italy, Spain, Portugal and Greece. Only the EC member states of Denmark, UK and Ireland have not (yet) joined the Schengen Agreement.
28. Appendix 3 of the treaty: "Measures concerning the fight against drugs trafficking."
29. Minutes of the Dutch Parliament 1985-1986, 19326, no 1, p 8.
30. These proposals may be found in the Annual Report of the Office of Public Prosecutions: "*Law Enforcement and Open Borders*". The Hague: Government Printing Office, 1987.
31. Treaty to implement the agreement between the Netherlands, Belgium, Germany, France and Luxembourg of June 14, 1985. Schengen Agreement with regard to the gradual abolition of the check points on common border crossings; June 19, 1990.
32. In view of the jurisprudence on the agent-provocateur and the secret pursuit of people, the Dutch judge is unlikely to object to this method.
33. Minutes of the Dutch Parliament 1991-1992, 22140, no 12, p 28. Although it concerns users of cannabis, the minister talks about "addicts" - a label considered inappropriate by most Dutch policy makers since the 1970s.
34. Minutes of the Dutch Parliament 1991-1992, 22140, no 12.
35. The intergovernmental consultation of the EC ministers who are responsible for domestic security and combatting of crime.
36. Minutes of the Dutch Parliament II 1986-1987, 20031, nos 1 and 2, p 31 *f.f.*
37. An important point of debate is where this agency will be located. The Netherlands would like to house this prestigious agency. Of course, the image of Dutch policy abroad is an influential consideration. France - not entirely coincidentally also interested in housing this agency - complained [through the Minister of the Interior (Quiles)] that the Netherlands has a lax drug policy and therefore would not be suitable to provide the seat for this agency. This comment resulted in a diplomatic scuffle between the two countries.
38. The group is strongly law-enforcement oriented. An official of the Ministry of Justice represents the Netherlands, the Ministry of Welfare, Public Health and Culture provides the substitute.

39. European plan to combat drugs. DOC CELAD 126, November 22, 1990. In June 1992 the European Council instructed the CELAD to present a report about the implementation of the program before the end of that year.
40. Consists presently out of more than 25 countries which cooperate in the areas of culture, public health, criminal justice and social welfare.
41. This is the consulting body of the ministers of Public Health and Justice within the Council of Europe. This body devotes attention to all aspects of the drugs problem, such as prevention, epidemiology, repression, law enforcement and juridical cooperation.
42. Consists of three unions: The European Community for Coal and Steel, The European Economic Community, and the European Community for Atom Energy.
43. Consulting body between government leaders and ministers of Foreign Affairs.
44. Comité Européen pour la Lutte Anti-Drogue, established by the European Council in 1989 in order to coordinate the activities of the EC member states in the area of prevention, health, social policy with regard to addicts, and the combatting of (international) drugs trafficking. In 1990 they drafted the European Plan to Combat Drugs. It is this committee that originated the plan to establish a European Drug Observation Post and a European network for information about drugs and drug addiction (REITOX).
45. Working group of the Council of Ministers of Public Health. This group has been involved in activities related to the ethical and technical aspects of urine testing, drug use prevention, establishment of a European data network, development of alternatives for incarcerated addicts, and so on.
46. Existing since 1976, this advisory body of the ministers in charge of police and security, has been organized outside the EC organs. Initially it was established to fight international terrorism; however, since 1985 its task was expanded to include the exchange of information about law enforcement techniques and tactics for the combatting of other serious forms of (organized) criminality with international aspects, such as drugs trafficking. In June 1990 in Dublin, Trevi initiated the proposal for "national drug units", which resulted in the establishment of the EDIU (European Drug Intelligence Unit), later renamed to Europol Drugs Unit.
47. The Commission presents her plans to the Council of Ministers and ensures that the decisions of the Council are implemented. In addition, the Commission may propose directives and regulations. A directive obligates the member states to adjust their national legislation according to that particular directive (for example, the Directive of October 6, 1991, on the prevention of the use of the financial system for the purpose of money laundering - 91/308/EEC). An ordinance is even more far-reaching. It replaces national legislation (for example, Regulation (EEC) No 3677/90 of December 13, 1990 mandating measures to be taken to discourage the diversion of certain substances to the illicit manufacture of narcotic drugs and psychotropic substances).
48. The institution which involves the citizens of the member states in the activities of the community. It plays only a modest role. It can give non-binding advice to the Council of Ministers and the European Commission (*e.g.*, the reports of the commissions Stewart-Clark and Cooney).
49. Agreement signed by almost all EC members (except Denmark, Great Britain and Ireland) states to abolish the internal borders between the participating countries.
50. *Report of the International Narcotics Control Boards for 1992.* United Nations, 1992.
51. Minutes of the Dutch Parliament, *Nota Verslavingsproblematiek*, 1991-1992, 22684, no 2, p 40.
52. See, for instance, the relevant articles in the Schengen Agreement (Article 71, paragraph 5) and the Single Convention (Article 38), and the statements in the commission reports of the European Parliament.

53. At present, a (temporary) transitional provision (the so-called TFV – Temporary Financial Regulation Addiction Care) is in effect which still offers the Ministry (some) power to direct local or regional policy.

54. This opinion was also expressed in a recent interview of Eddie Engelsman, the former head of the division of the Public Health Ministry responsible for drug policy (NRC, July 2, 1992).

55. We refer here to Eddie Engelsman, (former) director of the Division of Alcohol, Drugs and Tobacco, and Léon Wever, (former) head of the section policy development (both in the Ministry of Public Health).

56. Minutes of the Dutch Parliament, *Nota Verslavingsproblematiek*, 1991-1992, 22684, no 2, p 40.

57. For several years now, a few areas in the center of Amsterdam have been declared emergency zones, which authorizes the police to prohibit people to be in these areas during a certain period (from 8 hours to 14 days). In addition, the police can take action against the possession of users' amounts of drugs and all paraphernalia related to drug use, such as lighters, spoons, and so on. Because of AIDS prevention, an exception is made for clean needles.

58. *Drugs en overlast; een inventarisatie van de mogelijkheden om op te treden tegen overlast als gevolg van drugshandel en -gebruik, die geboden worden door het strafrecht, de vreemdelingenwetgeving, het bestuurlijk instrumentarium en door het civiele recht.* Presented by the Work Group "Drugs Tourism" to the Commission of Attorney-Generals, The Hague, January 1991.

59. "Drugs and Nuisance", p 6. In our view this undermines the rationale for drug-specific regulations in the realm of public order; it would be sufficient to employ general public order (local) ordinances. However, the Working Group does not follow this reasoning. See for a more extensive discussion of this report: "Kroniek rechten en criminologie: Drugs en overlast". Blom, T. and Van Mastrigt, H, *Tijdschrift voor Alcohol, Drugs en andere Psychotrope Stoffen* 1991 17(5):183-188.

60. As cited in Trouw, December 4, 1992.

61. In September 1992, the annual report of the Rotterdam municipal police argued in favor of experiments with heroin distribution in the context of public order and criminality prevention.

62. Report of the International Narcotics Control Board for 1991, United Nations, 1991, p 33.

XIV. AN ECONOMIC VIEW ON DUTCH DRUGS POLICY

D.J. Kraan

1. Introduction

In this Chapter, a description and analysis is given of Dutch policy with respect to illegal drugs from an economic perspective. However, in contrast to previous explorations in this direction (Stigler and Becker 1977, Pommerehne and Hartmann 1980, Becker and Murphy 1988, Pommerehne and Hart 1991), the focus will not exclusively be on drug consumers or drug producers and dealers, but also on the politicians and agencies who are responsible for the shaping and execution of drugs policy. In this approach these officials will not be treated as benevolent outsiders who seek to improve the outcomes of market behavior in accordance with some conception of the common good, but rather as participants in a system of politico-economic interaction on their own behalf. This can be characterized as a "public choice" approach to public policy, as opposed to a welfare-theoretical approach.

The analysis focuses on three different illegal drugs: cannabis, cocaine and heroin. Although there are many other illegal drugs, these three are the most important in terms of both market turnover and costs of government involvement. The analysis is based on already existing information. Availability of quality data is usually a problem in research on illegal drugs. Fortunately, in the Netherlands there is a relative wealth of data compared to other countries. On the one hand, data are collected by the care-providing institutions as part of their regular tasks; on the other hand, a small but very valuable empirical research tradition has developed in universities and specialized institutes, which aims at data collection among the drug users themselves. However, the relative abundance of data does not apply to all relevant behavior. As far as the drugs markets are concerned, much more is known about the demand side than about the supply side. Obviously, this reflects the higher degree of repression at the supply side.

The Chapter is organized as follows. First, I provide an economic characterization of the instruments of Dutch drugs policy. The next section describes the markets for cannabis, cocaine and heroin, first for the city of Amsterdam (where most data are being collected), and subsequently for the Netherlands as a whole. The descriptions include the regulatory regime which the government has put in place for each market. Thereafter, a description follows of the services which the government supplies in the areas of law enforcement and health care, as well as a cost estimate of these services. The next section describes the net benefits of the regulation of the drugs markets and the provision of law enforcement and health care services to politicians and the public. Subsequently, I discuss the ways in which the improvement of information about costs and benefits may alter the nature of public policies, given the objectives of decision makers and given the prevailing decision rules. In order to provide an international perspective, the next section compares some important economic characteristics of Dutch drugs policy with those of the radically different drugs policy of the USA. The final section presents some conclusions.

2. An economic characterization of the instruments of drugs policy

From an economic point of view, the instruments of Dutch drugs policy may be distinguished into (1) the regulation of markets and (2) the provision of services.

In a formal sense, in the Netherlands "regulation of markets" implies, for each of the three drugs, the extreme case of complete prohibition in all markets (import, export, distributive and retail markets). However, according to Dutch criminal law (*i.e.*, through the so-called "expediency principle"), there is a certain latitude for discretion in the sphere of law enforcement. Since this latitude is frequently used, for all practical purposes the nature of regulation must be identified on the basis of the factual prosecution policy. This policy is partially determined by the prosecution guidelines for which the Minister of Justice is politically responsible. The guidelines have the status of recommendations to the prosecutors associated with the district courts. These prosecutors consult with the local mayors and the chiefs of police about the application of the guidelines. As will be explained below, as a consequence of this arrangement the nature of regulation is strongly dependent on local circumstances. Furthermore, it differs for each of the three drugs, with a particularly marked difference between "soft" drugs (cannabis) and "hard" drugs (heroin, cocaine).

Publicly provided services in the area of drugs policy can be distinguished into (1) enforcement of the regulation of drugs markets (*i.e.*, law enforcement), and (2) health care services for drugs consumers. Law enforcement services can be characterized as public goods. Furthermore, these services are produced by public agencies and funded by public means. They should be distinguished from the enforcement of common criminal law and the repression of public nuisance among the consumers of drugs. It will appear below that, from an analytical point of view, this distinction is rather important because of a strong interdependency of the benefits of both kinds of law enforcement services.

Health care services can be characterized as private goods with strong "external effects" (effects on the welfare of people other than the primary beneficiaries of the services). The drug consumers are the primary beneficiaries. Health care services are funded entirely by politicians from public means. Furthermore, in the Netherlands they are produced by health care institutions outside the government.

3. The drugs markets

3.1 Cannabis

3.1.1 Prevalence in Amsterdam

Table 1 presents prevalence data for cannabis consumption in Amsterdam, as estimated in a recent survey.

Table 1. Prevalence of cannabis use in Amsterdam in 1990

	Percentage of population of 12 years and over	Number of consumers
Last month prevalence	6	35,500
Last year prevalence	9.9	58,500

(From: Sandwijk et al. 1991; last column computed by the author.)

In the present Chapter, "current consumption" is interpreted as "last month" prevalence. According to this survey, in 1990 the estimated number of current consumers of cannabis in Amsterdam was 35,500.

3.1.2 Turnover and prices

It is estimated that the largest part of the total turnover at the retail stage can be attributed to the so-called (hashish selling) "coffee shops" (Jansen 1991:60). The remainder is sold by "house dealers". Street dealing has virtually disappeared. In 1990 there were 110 coffee shops in the city center and about 300 in Amsterdam as a whole (Jansen 1991:60). On the basis of systematic observation, total sales in the city center were estimated at approximately 42 million guilders in 1990 (Jansen 1991:56). Assuming that the average turnover in coffee shops outside the center is comparable to that of shops in the city center, total sales in Amsterdam in 1990 may be estimated to have been about 115 million guilders.

Coffee shops typically sell hashish and marihuana from various countries and of different qualities (Moroccan, Columbian, Dutch sinsemilla, and so on). Prices vary accordingly. Most brands sell for between four and 15 guilders per gram. The average price is eight guilders per gram (Jansen 1991:61,67). Given the estimated turnover of about 115 million guilders, the total physical turnover of the coffee shops in Amsterdam can be estimated at 14,000 kilograms per year. Since buying from coffee shops rather than from house dealers has clear advantages from the point of view of quality reliability and price information, it is generally assumed that in recent years the turnover of the coffee shops has surpassed the retail turnover by house dealers by far. If the house dealers would still sell half as much as the coffee shops – which in view of the mentioned development is probably an inflated estimate – the total physical turnover in the retail market of Amsterdam would amount to 21,000 kilograms of cannabis, and a total monetary turnover of 170 million guilders per year.

On the basis of prevalence studies, it is estimated that the total number of current consumers of cannabis in the Netherlands is presently about 400,000 (Stichting Informatievoorziening Verslavingszorg 1993). Assuming that the average use per consumer outside Amsterdam is equal to that of the average consumer in Amsterdam, the turnover of drugs in the Netherlands as a whole would be 11 times the turnover in Amsterdam. This would amount to a national estimate of about 230,000 kilograms and about 1900 million guilders per year.

3.1.3 Structure of the retail branch

The retail sector for cannabis in the center of Amsterdam consists of large, intermediate and small enterprises. The four largest enterprises exploit ten coffee shops with a total market share of about 30%. The 12 intermediate enterprises manage 18 coffee shops with a total market share of about 25%. The 71 small enterprises exploit 82 coffee shops with a total market share of approximately 45% (Jansen 1991:78).

Typically, coffee shops are set up by former street dealers who have become "sedentary" (Jansen 1991:64). In 1980, the number of coffee shops was still less than 20 (Cohen 1981). At the present time, a stage of complete commercialization has been attained. Competition is strong but focuses on quality assortment, mode of delivery (weight variety of prepacked portions, possibility of weighing out on the spot), location and atmosphere, rather than on price. This type of competition is comparable to that of the sector of bars and pubs.

The profit margin of successful coffee shops is probably comparable to that of bars and pubs: about 50% (Jansen 1991:62). This would amount to total gross profits of the coffee shop sector in the Netherlands of about 950 million guilders. While cannabis, in itself, being an illegal substance, cannot be taxed, the profits of the coffee shops are subject to income tax.

3.1.4 Regulation of the retail market

Formally, the possession of small quantities of cannabis is a misdemeanor; possession of larger quantities is a felony. Materially, because of the expediency principle discussed earlier, there are considerable differences depending on local circumstances. Important factors determining the local law enforcement response are the tolerance of the population (which tends to be greater in big cities than in smaller towns and villages), and the presence of a hard drug problem (which draws attention away from cannabis). Furthermore, the personal preferences of district court prosecutors or judges (*i.e.*, lenient or strict), represent an important factor.

In the big cities, the possession or sale of less than 30 grams of cannabis is materially "legalized". In 1987, Amsterdam tightened its policy. Now the limit of 30 grams is taken more seriously than before. The Amsterdam police has occasionally raided coffee shops in order to check their inventory. However, it cannot be said that, at the present time, the limit of 30 grams is strictly enforced in Amsterdam or elsewhere. Much depends on the good relations of coffee shop owners with the neighborhood and the responsible police officers.

3.1.5 Structure and regulation of markets for import, export and distributive trade

Much less is known about the import, export and distribution of cannabis than about its retail trade. It is assumed that 10 to 20% of the turnover in the retail market is produced domestically ("nederwiet"; Jansen 1991:145).[1]. This would amount to 18,000 to 36,000 kilograms per year. Production takes place in greenhouses in the country and, more and more, indoors using artificial light. The quality of the domestic product has improved markedly in recent years. Accordingly, its retail price has risen to as much as 25 guilders per gram (for the top quality of Dutch sinsemilla), which is considerably higher than the normal prices of the imported variety.

Next to nothing is known about import, export and transit of cannabis. In some publications, estimates are based on quantities seized by the police and customs office (84,292 kilograms in 1991). This quantity is then multiplied by a factor of ten in order to obtain an estimate of total sales (export, transit and retail) in the Netherlands. This estimation method must be considered entirely arbitrary and unreliable. It is likely that quantities seized are strongly dependent upon the priority given to police investigation in this area and that strong random factors are involved.

Most imported cannabis enters the country by ship. The import trade is thought to be interwoven with the international trade in legal products, such as oranges and furniture. The Netherlands is an important transit country for cannabis from Morocco destined for Germany, Denmark and England (Driessen and Jansen 1991:31).

In view of the severe risks involved, activities in the higher levels of the trade column will be more profitable than the exploitation of coffee shops or dealing at the retail level. Possibly, profit margins are comparable to those of large-scale trade in cocaine and heroin, which in some studies have been estimated at 200 to 300% per independent trader (Cachet 1990).

3.2 Cocaine

3.2.1 Prevalence in Amsterdam

Table 2 presents prevalence data for cocaine use in Amsterdam, as estimated in a recent survey.

Table 2. Prevalence of cocaine use in Amsterdam in 1990

	Percentage of population of 12 years and over	Number of consumers
Last month prevalence	0.4	2500
Last year prevalence	1.3	7500

(From: Sandwijk *et al.* 1991; last column computed by the author.)

The survey from which these data were taken was not directed at the group of "problematic consumers"; that is, consumers with a problematic pattern of drug consumption indicated by involvement in health care services or conviction of a drug-related felony.[2] The number of problematic drug consumers in Amsterdam is estimated at 7000 (De Zwart 1992). A substantial part of this group consists of so-called poly-drug users (users of more than one drug). Seventy-five percent of this group uses cocaine in combination with heroin. This adds approximately 5000 consumers of cocaine to the 2500 non-deviant current users that can be extrapolated from the Sandwijk et al. (1991:54) survey, bringing the total of current consumers of cocaine in Amsterdam to about 7500.

3.2.2 Turnover and prices

The most reliable method of estimating the turnover of cocaine for domestic consumption is probably to deduce it from the level of use per consumer. On the basis of a recent study, it may be estimated that the average use of a non-problematic current consumer of cocaine in Amsterdam amounts to 2.4 grams per month (Cohen 1989). The average level of use of the problematic consumer has been estimated at 14.6 grams per month (Grapendaal et al. 1991:128). Given the estimated numbers of consumers (2500 non-problematic; 5000 problematic), this amounts to a total physical turnover of approximately 950 kilograms per year for consumption in Amsterdam (70 kilograms (7%) by non-problematic consumers and 880 kilograms (93%) by problematic consumers).

There is a considerable variation in price. This is typical of a market of a strongly repressed consumption good, where supply is irregular and strongly dependent on the random factor of seizures in all chains of the trade column. A 1987 study suggests that prices may vary between 120 and 220 guilders per gram, with an average of 180 guilders per gram (Cohen 1989). Given this average price and the already mentioned estimated physical turnover, total monetary turnover for cocaine consumption in Amsterdam amounts to 170 million guilders per year.

On the basis of prevalence studies, it is estimated that the number of consumers of "hard drugs" (cocaine, heroin) in the Netherlands as a whole is three times that of Amsterdam (De Zwart 1992). Assuming an equal average use per consumer, this amounts to an estimated physical turnover of 2850 kilograms and a monetary turnover of 510 million guilders per year for domestic consumption.

3.2.3 Structure of the retail market

A recent study shows that 21% of non-problematic consumers buy cocaine from dealers in bars and discos (who make a profit), 34% from other dealers (who also make a profit) and 45% from "friends" (who do not make a profit) (Cohen 1989). Assuming that the "friends" buy it from dealers in bars and discos and from other dealers in the same proportion as the consumers not buying it from friends, this would amount to a market share of 38% for dealers in bars and discos and of 62% for other dealers. As far as the group of problematic consumers is concerned, it seems plausible to assume that the role of bars and discos in the retail market is smaller, and that most of these consumers buy it either from other dealers or from friends.

In view of the comparable risks, the profitability of retail dealing in cocaine may be similar to that of dealing in heroin, which in some studies has been estimated at about 20 to 30% (Cachet 1990); this would amount to 100 to 150 million guilders in the Netherlands as a whole.

Due to the relatively lenient judicial policy towards the possession of small quantities of cocaine, the retail trade is quite dispersed. There is a relatively large group of consumers who can make a living out of street dealing and related mediation services concerning cocaine and heroin. The later discussion on heroin will expand on this.

3.2.4 Regulation of the retail market

Regulation of the retail market is strongly dependent on local circumstances. Formally, the possession or sale of any amount of cocaine is a felony. Practically, repression by law enforcement is focused on large-scale trade and on consumers who are causing a nuisance (usually problematic consumers). However, when cocaine or heroin consumers are arrested in possession of small quantities, apparently for own consumption or small-scale street dealing, no further steps are taken and often the cocaine or heroin is not even seized.

3.2.5 Structure and regulation of markets for import, export and distributive trade

Very little is known about import, export, production and distributive trade in cocaine. Since rumors about coca cultivation in glass-houses are probably untrue, it may be assumed that the entire domestic turnover is imported, almost exclusively from South America. Again, the estimates of transit based upon quantities seized by the police and customs service (4288 kilograms in 1990) must be considered entirely unreliable. The Netherlands is thought to be an important transit country but, according to a recent study, its transit share is diminishing as a consequence of increasing repression (Driessen and Jansen 1991). At the present time, Dutch judicial policy with respect to large-scale trade is comparable to that of other West European countries and in some respects even more repressive.[3] Obviously, the presence of a large harbor in Rotterdam remains an important determinant of transit trade, but other European countries also have large harbors (Hamburg, Bremen, Antwerp, Marseille, Le Havre, Bilbao, Lisbon). To the extent that the consumption of cocaine in the hinterland of those harbors will increase, the relative importance of Rotterdam will diminish. Another important factor consists of the traditional ties that the Netherlands has with the Latin American country of Surinam. A substantial proportion of the Surinam population has relations with the Surinam community in the Netherlands. The significance of Surinam for the Dutch cocaine trade depends partially on the regulatory policy and the effectiveness of law enforcement in that country. At the present time, new forms of cooperation in the area of law enforcement are being developed between the Netherlands and Surinam.

It is characteristic of the lack of knowledge about large-scale trade in cocaine that key experts hold widely divergent views about the relative importance of large criminal syndicates (Driessen and Jansen 1991; Korf and De Kort 1990). According to one view, large-scale trade in cocaine and heroin is predominantly in the hands of permanent, large or medium-sized organizations consisting of one or two leaders, a group of five to ten insiders and a larger group of associates available for temporary jobs. In this view, some of these organizations may be connected to the large Columbian drug cartels such as "Medellin" and "Cali". According to an opposing view, the trade of cocaine and heroin is largely in the hands of transient small groups and family enterprises. According to this view, there is a minimum of organization and the recruitment of assistants is often arranged around the preparation and execution of a particular deal.

According to an internal memorandum from the Dutch Criminal Investigation Information Service, 130 drug trading groups are known to the police (Driessen and Jansen 1991). At most, 25 of these groups are believed to include from 20 to 30 people and no more than 20 include more than 30 people. These numbers do not provide a conclusive answer to the opposing views about the market structure of the large-scale trade. It seems undeniable, however, that at the level of import and export trade a large number of small, poorly organized and primitively operating groups are in business alongside a number of more sophisticated organizations. This is obvious from the large numbers of poorly dressed, foreign traffickers, often women, who are picked up from international flights and arrested with relatively small quantities of packaged cocaine and heroin in their luggage, clothing or stomachs.

There is more agreement among experts that the large-scale trade in drugs is horizontally diversified: trading groups specialize in drugs, and often deal only in one single type of drug (Driessen and Jansen 1991:16). The cocaine trade is mainly in the hands of Dutch groups (although recently some small-scale networks of South American traders have been observed). However, in order to spread risk and to protect the import and export networks, the trade column serving the domestic retail market is vertically rather diversified. There will often be two or more distributive traders between the importer and the retail trader. Each trader will only know his immediate supplier but is kept ignorant of the higher chains in the trade column.

In view of the comparable risks, the profit margins in the large-scale trade of cocaine are probably similar to those of heroin, which in some studies have been estimated at 200 to 300% per independent trader (Cachet 1990).

3.3 Heroin

3.3.1 Prevalence in Amsterdam

Little is known about heroin consumption outside the group of "problematic consumers". Furthermore, in typical survey studies, the consumption of heroin appears to be virtually non-existent, in contrast to cocaine. It may be the case that heroin consumption outside the problematic group is relatively insignificant. Whatever the case may be, for the purpose of estimating prevalence and market turnover, it is appropriate to work with data about the relatively well-researched heroin consumption patterns in the problematic group. The number of current problematic consumers of heroin in Amsterdam is estimated at about 7000 (De Zwart 1992), which amounts to 1.2% of the population of Amsterdam of 12 years and over.

3.3.2 Turnover and prices

As was true for cocaine, the most reliable method for the estimation of the total turnover for domestic heroin consumption is probably to deduce it from the level of use per consumer. In a recent study, the average use per consumer was estimated at 7.7 grams per month (Grapendaal *et al.* 1991:128). Given the estimated 7000 consumers of heroin, this would amount to a total physical turnover of about 650 kilograms per year in Amsterdam.

Retail prices of heroin, like those of cocaine, are rather volatile, due to the strong repression of the entire heroin trade sector. The Criminal Investigation Information Service reported an average retail price ("street value") of 92.50 Dutch guilders per gram in 1987 (Driessen and Jansen 1991). Given this price and the estimated physical turnover of 650 kilograms per year, the total monetary turnover for heroin consumption in Amsterdam would amount to 60 million guilders.

Given an estimated number of consumers of "hard drugs" in the Netherlands as a whole of approximately three times that in Amsterdam (De Zwart 1992), and assuming an equal average use per consumer, the physical turnover for heroin consumption in the Netherlands would amount to approximately 2000 kilograms per year, and the monetary turnover for heroin would be about 180 million guilders.[4]

3.3.3 Structure of the retail market

In the seventies and early eighties, a large part of the heroin retail trade in Amsterdam took place in the so-called heroin cafés on the Zeedijk and their immediate environment (the "drug scene"). Because of the increasing nuisance these establishments were creating in the neighborhood, concerted action was taken by the police and the municipal authorities in the mid-eighties to improve the situation. The heroin cafés were shut down and the police intensified its surveillance of the neighborhood. As a consequence, the heroin retail trade moved to the streets. Since street dealing in a closely patrolled area requires quick and simple transactions with a minimum of risk per transaction, this policy definitely enhanced the dispersion of the heroin retail trade.

A recent study provides a sketch of the typical trading practices in the drug scene of Amsterdam (Grapendaal et al. 1991). Two or three times a day the principal dealer appears on the market. In a safe place, he divides his stock among a small number of trusted street dealers, who usually obtain the merchandise on consignment. Each street dealer receives between ten and 20 rolls of "brown" (heroin) or "white" (cocaine). A roll consists of either a tenth or a quarter of a gram. The street dealer usually earns one roll for himself for every five rolls he sells. He can use his earnings either for his own consumption or sell it on his own account. The next time the principal dealer appears, the street dealer hands over the money and receives the new merchandise. The street dealers often work for more than one principal dealer at the same time. In general, they have a busy life (one of the attractions of the drug scene for otherwise unemployed adolescents). In order to spread the risk further, the street dealers often make use of assistants as package carriers and lookouts. Package carriers carry the rolls of white and brown for the street dealers (and thus run the risk of arrest), but are not allowed to handle money. Lookouts are stationed in the vicinity of where deals are taking place and warn the street dealers when the police is approaching. Package carriers and lookouts are paid in kind by the street dealer, just as he himself is paid in kind by the principal dealer.

The drugs market provides an income not only to street dealers, package carriers and lookouts, but also to service branches such as "garbage men" and lessees of "shooting galleries". Garbage men collect used needles and exchange them for new ones at health care posts. Shooting galleries are safe places for using drugs. In all, around 15% of the problematic consumers of heroin earn a living from street dealing and mediation services in the drugs market.

Principal dealers typically do not consume heroin themselves. In contrast to coffee shop owners, they have low costs, but the risks of arrest and imprisonment are much higher. In some studies, profit margins at the heroin retail level have been estimated at 20 to 30% (Cachet 1990), amounting to 40 to 60 million guilders in the nation as a whole.

3.3.4 Regulation of the retail market

Just as for cannabis and cocaine, heroin regulation is strongly dependent on local circumstances. Although formally the possession of any quantity of heroin is a felony, materially repression is targeted on large-scale trade and on those consumers who cause a nuisance. The possession of small quantities heroin for personal consumption or small-scale street dealing is not prosecuted. Criminality to property by heroin consumers is prosecuted, but only a minority of the problematic consumers engages in such behavior (Grapendaal et al. 1991: Ch. 6). In general, no judicial action is taken against the majority of problematic consumers who do not harm other people. Nevertheless, there is a grey area in the sphere of repeated and extensive petty drug peddling, in combination with creating a public nuisance; local circumstances determine the kind of response these drug consumers face.

3.3.5 Structure and regulation of markets for import, export and distributive trade

Generally speaking, what has already been said about the structure and regulation of the large-scale trade markets for cocaine applies to heroin as well. Here too, there is a strongly diversified trade column serving the domestic heroin market and a mixture of more or less sophisticated trading groups for distribution, as well as for import and export. The quantity of heroin seized by the police in 1990 was 532 kilograms. A major difference is that, while the large-scale trade in cocaine is mainly a Dutch business, the large-scale trade in heroin has traditionally been in the hands of Chinese, Turkish and Pakistani nationals. At lower levels in the heroin trade column, many people of Surinam descent are also active (Driessen and Jansen 1991:20).

4. The costs of regulation and collective services

4.1 Real and apparent costs

One of the basic premises of the economic theory of bureaucracy is that in public agencies the incentives to improve the efficiency of production are much smaller than in private enterprises. In particular, it is very likely that in public agencies there will be a discrepancy between the real costs of services ("opportunity costs") and the financial means which are actually spent to produce the services. The latter may be termed "apparent costs". The difference between apparent and real costs is known as "managerial discretionary profit". From a normative point of view, this margin can be considered pure waste. If the margin is zero, production is technically efficient, otherwise the technical efficiency of production can be improved. In general, administrators of public agencies will seek to enlarge managerial discretionary profit because this can be used for discretionary purposes, for instance, a larger work force than necessary to produce the services or luxurious office equipment (Migué and Bélanger 1974).

Not all collective services are supplied by public agencies. In the area of drugs policy, law enforcement services are mostly provided by public agencies, but in the Netherlands publicly funded legal assistance and the entire cluster of drug-related health care services are provided by private agencies. From an economic point of view, supply by private agencies has two advantages. Firstly, a private agency has a better incentive to produce efficiently, because it is allowed to keep its exploitation surplus even when this cannot be transferred in the form of "profit" to private "residual claimants" (shareholders or owners); take, for instance, private foundations in the sphere of ambulant health care which can keep and re-invest their exploitation surplus. Secondly, it is much easier to open up the market for competition. Often, there are various agencies in the same area which can supply the same services. In that case the government can grant the contract to the agencies which offer the services at the lowest costs. Furthermore, even when agencies hold a regional monopoly, it is possible for government to compare performances and to equalize public financial contributions at the lowest level. This implies that profits in private agencies tend to be eliminated either by competition or by governmental action and that the apparent costs of these agencies can be used as a reasonable approximation of real costs.

4.2 The costs of regulation and law enforcement services

The following approximation is based on the assumption that there are no other costs of regulation than enforcement costs; in other words, it is assumed that the costs of decision making about regulation are negligible. The enforcement of regulation involves: (1) police services; (2) judicial services (prosecution, adjudication and legal assistance); and (3) penitentiary (i.e., correctional) services.

With the exception of legal assistance, all these services are provided by public agencies in the Netherlands. The discussion in the previous section suggests that apparent costs, as reported in governmental budgetary documents, may substantially exceed real costs (i.e., contain waste). In view of the fact that the political demand for enforcement services in the area of drugs is probably inelastic, it is likely that the agencies supplying these services are able to extract a margin of managerial discretionary profit that is even higher than average among public agencies.

No information is available about the real costs of law enforcement services (with the exception of a few specific studies about particular agencies). Therefore, apparent costs will be estimated in order to obtain an idea of the financial burden related to drugs policy. The estimates in Table 3 are based upon the following assumptions:

a. The apparent costs of the police for the enforcement of drugs laws amount to 7% of the total apparent costs of the police; this percentage is based on the estimate that drug felonies account for 28% of the time that the police devotes to the investigation of felonies; in turn the investigation of felonies accounts for 26% of the total time of the police.[5]

b. The following divisions of the police are seen as being involved in the enforcement of criminal law: the Criminal Investigation Information Service, the Corps National Police, the Advisory Center for the Administration of Police Vehicles, the Police Communication Service, the Police Logistic Service and the municipal police; 7% of the special national budget for criminal prevention projects by the police is taken to be the apparent costs of these branches.

c. The apparent costs of the offices of the public prosecutors, judiciary and bar for the enforcement of drugs laws account for 3.6% of the total apparent costs of these agencies, relating to the enforcement of criminal law; this percentage is the proportion of the total number of final dispositions regarding violation of sections 10 and 11 of the Opium Law.[6]

d. It is assumed that 44% of the salary costs of judges, 32% of the salary costs of supporting court personnel, and 40% of the material costs of the courts are apparent costs of the judiciary, relating to the enforcement of criminal law; the cost of criminal procedures (*i.e.*, costs of bailiffs, witness examinations, and so on) are also taken into account. These figures are estimates of the proportion of the total apparent costs of the judiciary, relating to the adjudication phase of criminal procedures.[7]

e. The apparent costs of the penitentiary services relating to the enforcement of drugs laws represent 18% of the total costs of common public correctional institutions (not including institutions for pathological delinquents), public institutions for juvenile delinquents, and private institutions for juvenile delinquents; this percentage represents the proportion of the institutionalized population convicted for violation of sections 10 and 11 of the Opium Law on 30 September 1990.

Table 3. Costs of the enforcement of drugs laws

Police	266 million
Judicial services	
- offices of public prosecutors	7 million
- judiciary	9 million
- legal assistance	3 million
Penitentiary services	125 million
Total	410 million

(Computed by the author on the basis of the state budget for 1992 and the assumptions mentioned above.)

4.3 The costs of health care services

In the Netherlands, the following drug-related health care services are available:

1. Twenty clinics and departments of general psychiatric hospitals for addiction treatment with 1060 beds.
2. Sixteen Consultation Bureaus for Alcohol and Drugs with 105 offices.

3. Thirty-six regional agencies for social and medical care to drug users with offices in 45 municipalities.
4. Methadon programs at seven municipal health care services.
5. Three clinics for addiction treatment of special groups.
6. Three institutes for research, information and development of expertise.
7. An action program for projects and experiments in the sphere of prevention (including prevention of AIDS), addiction among ethnic minorities, associations of users, research and international cooperation.

All these services are provided by private agencies and fully funded by the central government. The clinics and hospital departments mentioned under subsection 1 are paid for by income-dependent premiums on the basis of a social insurance law which covers special medical services. The social and medical services mentioned under subsections 2, 3 and 4 are provided by private agencies and municipalities and are funded by grants-in-aid to the municipalities. The clinics and institutes mentioned under subsections 5 and 6, and the action program mentioned under subsection 7, are funded directly by the central government.

The cost estimates in Table 4 for the services of clinics and departments of general hospitals for addiction treatment, the Consultation Bureaus for Alcohol and Drugs and the national institutes for research, information and development of expertise, are based on the assumption that 48% of the total costs of these agencies can be attributed to drug-related services (the remainder is for alcohol-related services).

Table 4. The costs of health care services for drug users

Clinics and departments of psychiatric hospitals	36 million
Consultation Bureaus for Alcohol and Drugs	36 million
Regional agencies for social and medical care	56 million
Municipal methadone programs	7 million
Clinics for addiction treatment of special groups	3 million
Institutes for research, information and development of expertise	5 million
Action program	4 million
Total	157 million

(Computed by the author on the basis of the cost data provided by the Minister of Welfare, Public Health and Culture and the Minister of Justice in the "Memorandum Problems of Addiction" ("Nota Verslavingsproblematiek" 1992) and the above-mentioned assumption about the percentage of drug-related services of the Consultation Bureaus for Alcohol and Drugs.)

5. The net benefits of regulation and collective services

5.1 The net benefits for politicians

The standard methodology of cost-benefit analysis exclusively takes into account the costs and benefits of public policy to the population at large. However, the population does not decide on public policy. Politicians do. A positive analysis must, therefore, focus on the preferences of politicians rather than on those of the population.

Public choice theory distinguishes two main kinds of political motivation: "followers" attempt to maximize votes and "leaders" attempt to maximize their own gain from public policy. Accordingly, followers will consider primarily the net benefits for the electorate; leaders will look primarily at their own net benefits. However, leaders cannot entirely neglect the benefits for the electorate because they, too, have to win elections in order to get their favorite policies implemented. The main difference between followers and leaders is that leaders will spend more time on policy advocacy in order to influence the preferences of the electorate, and will have less interest in a larger than necessary majority for re-election.

The prevailing political views on the net benefits of drugs policy are partially reflected in official statements which appear in electoral programs and governmental policy documents. As far as the government is concerned, the official objectives of drugs policy are stated as the advancement of public health and the prevention of common criminality. In the Netherlands, reduction of drug consumption is not a policy objective *per se*. Consequently, there is no official policy with respect to non-problematic drug consumption. This is typical of Dutch political culture, which is consensus-seeking and averse to conflict. Also, it is possible that socially conservative politicians, who in principle would favor such a policy, refrain from advocating it because they have been convinced of either its non-feasibility or its huge costs.

Obviously, the prevailing agreement about the officially stated objectives of drug policy does not imply that all politicians (or even the politicians in the cabinet coalition) hold identical views about the desirable nature and extent of governmental activities. There are continuous discussions about such things as coercing criminal drug users to accept treatment, imposing more conditions on participation in methadone programs, the controlled supply of heroin, and legalization of production and domestic trade of cannabis. These discussions show that, below the surface of general agreement on the stated general objectives, there are considerable differences of opinion on objectives at a more specific level of policy development. These differences are due to two factors. Firstly, there is a lack of knowledge about the relation between repression and the policy objectives of public health and prevention of criminality. Secondly, a political motive exists which is not reflected in the official policy objectives, namely the motive to attain electoral gains from a "tough stand" on drugs.

As far as the knowledge of politicians is concerned, the most common prejudices overstate the effectiveness of repression in relation to the policy objectives. Therefore, well-informed politicians tend to hold more tolerant attitudes than their less-informed colleagues. In the next section, the most harmful prejudices and the role of information in this respect will be dealt with further.

As far as the electoral gains from a "tough stand" on drugs are concerned, much depends on the intensity of external effects (other than on health and crime), such as public nuisance and the visible presence of a "drugs scene". In general, the benefits for the public from drug policy will parallel those for politicians. They, too, will be interested in public health and prevention of criminality. A conservative group may also consider drug consumption as an evil in itself which ought to be suppressed by government, regardless of its effects on health and crime. However, apart from these preferences and convictions, many inhabitants are annoyed by the nuisance caused by some forms of drug consumption and by confrontation with the non-conformist lifestyles of drug consumers. Furthermore, because of the greater lack of knowledge among the general public, support for the repression of supply is greater among the population at large than in the political community. These circumstances cause permanent tension between politicians and the public. Often, politicians are exposed to the temptation of submitting to public sentiment. In the Netherlands, politicians usually do not give in to this temptation. Informal understandings between politicians preclude electoral polarization in this area. On the other hand, the very existence of a discrepancy between the prevailing views of politicians and the public exerts an immobilizing effect on policy in which politicians cannot afford to deviate from existing policy in the direction of less or more repression. Deviation in the direction of less repression is punished on election day and deviation in the direction of more repression is excluded by informal agreements that decent and responsible politicians are expected to honor. It is the paradox of drug policy that while the best way to reduce the social isolation of drug consumers and to eliminate the lack of knowledge in the population would consist of full legalization for supply, the very existence of this isolation and ignorance impedes such a step from being taken.

6. The role of information in political decision making

Information can have an impact on public policy when it enables politicians and the public to gain better insight into the costs and benefits of the choice alternatives. It is the responsibility of the research community to provide such information. The impact of information will be greater to the extent that it reaches lesser informed people, and to the extent that it focuses on themes where the prevailing misunderstandings are more serious.

Two of the most serious and harmful misunderstandings are: (a) that consumers of "hard drugs" are generally "addicted" and that they will therefore engage in criminality to property when they lack the necessary means to pay for their drugs; and (b) that additional investment in the repression of supply contributes to public health and the prevention of criminality to property through its effect on the number of drug consumers.

The idea that consumers of cocaine or heroin will engage in criminality to property when they lack the necessary means to pay for their needs is based upon an oversimplified causal model of drug-related criminality. Firstly, there is growing evidence that the demand elasticity of cocaine and heroin is much higher than the very concept of "addiction" suggests. Most cocaine and heroin consumers are able and willing to adjust their average consumption to their current income. In general, average individual consumption is subject to large fluctuations due to changes in external circumstances (Hoekstra 1984; Cohen 1989; Grapendaal et al. 1991). This does not only apply to income changes but also to other occurrences, such as changes in the pattern of personal relationships or in living conditions. Methadone programs are helpful because they can provide for partial compensation of fluctuations in consumption of heroin. The "grey" (illegal) methadone market fulfills a similar function. As far as criminal consumers are concerned, the connection between drug consumption and criminality to property is more complicated than one way causality. Although it is true that drug consumption may contribute to the degree of criminality of a certain group, most criminal consumers have been in contact with the police or the judiciary before they started consuming drugs. Models in which participation in a criminal subculture is conceived as a possible cause of drugs consumption, or in which factors of social and psychological deprivation (chronic unemployment, bad housing, alcoholic parents, violence in the family, and so on) are proposed as the common causes of both participation in a criminal subculture and drugs consumption, are more realistic than models that hypothesize on an exclusive one-way link between drugs consumption and criminality to property.[8]

The idea that additional investment in the repression of the supply of drugs will contribute to the policy objectives of crime reduction and health improvement through its effect on the number of consumers, is inconsistent with available evidence. We now know that the problems of health and criminality stemming from drug consumption are concentrated in a subgroup of problematic drug consumers who are not affected by repression of supply. Furthermore, studies suggest that the relation between the repression of supply and the number of consumers is not linear. Only when repression becomes so severe that any possession of an illegal drug involves a sizable risk of arrest and imprisonment will the number of non-problematic consumers decline. In particular, recent experience in the USA indicates that consumption among school-age youth is probably affected in this way.[9]

On the other hand, repression has a large effect on price. Therefore, it tends to increase rather than decrease the extent to which those drug consumers who are not deterred by the risk of arrest commit crimes against property. Not only must criminal drug consumers obtain more money to pay for their needs, but also the repression of supply criminalizes everybody who possesses drugs, thereby diminishing the threshold between common criminality and mere possession.[10] The additional common criminality caused by an increase in repression of supply involves huge social costs to society. Furthermore, an increase in repression tends to reduce the number of cocaine and heroin consumers who can pay for their needs out of revenues from street dealing and mediation services (see above). When criminality to property becomes a safer way to collect income than drug-related mediating services, a number of suppliers will probably opt for criminality to property. Finally, the retail market will become more concentrated and will be taken over by individuals and organizations which are willing to take the higher risks involved. This will not only contribute further to property crime but also encourage the more serious forms of violent criminality related to the very risky large-scale trade.

Once a process of normalization has set in, the chances are high that it will be self-reinforcing. On the one hand, normalization changes the characteristics and environment of drug consumption. On the other hand, normalization will improve available information about the costs and benefits of repression. When this information is provided to growing numbers of politicians and inhabitants, the panic will tend to subside; existing forms of regulation will be eyed with increasing skepticism until they are finally restricted or abolished. In the Dutch case, the history of cannabis is exemplary in this respect.

7. An international comparison

Reuter has made a useful distinction between three kinds of political attitudes towards the drug problem: those of hawks, doves and owls (Reuter 1992). "Hawks" consider the nature of the drug problem as one of amorality of consumers and sellers and they seek the solution in the repression of supply. "Doves" see the nature of the drug problem in the bad effects of prohibition and they seek the solution in legalization and information. "Owls" see the nature of the drug problem in addiction and disease and they seek the solution in prevention and treatment while maintaining prohibition. Heroin and cocaine drug policy in the Netherlands appears to fit in the "owl" category, whereas it wavers between that of owls and doves with regard to cannabis. The clearest example of a country where drug policy is in the hands of hawks is the USA. From a comparative point of view, it is illuminating to look at some conspicuous differences between policies in these two countries, as well as at the consequences of these differences for costs and net benefits.

As far as regulatory policies are concerned, the differences between the USA and the Netherlands are moderate.[11] Owls and hawks both support prohibition. Only the dove-like quasi-legalization of cannabis in the Netherlands contrasts with the federal regulatory regime in the USA, which does not discriminate between "hard" and "soft" drugs. The major contrasts are regarding law enforcement and health care services. The intensity of law enforcement has increased enormously in the USA during the last decade. Table 5 presents some data on convictions and imprisonments for both countries.

It should be noted that the data are presented per 1000 inhabitants (per capita *1000); presentation per consumer c.q. seller would be more appropriate. In view of the non-reliability of drug use prevalence data, however, the current presentation is preferable.

Table 5 shows that the number of convictions and prison sentences per 1000 persons is more than five times higher in the USA than in the Netherlands; the USA per capita prison population (incarcerated for drug felonies) is even sixteen times higher than the proportion of Dutch persons incarcerated for drug felonies. It should be noted that the latter ratio partially reflects longer terms of imprisonment.[12]

Table 5. Convictions and imprisonment sentences on account of drug felonies[11] in the USA and the Netherlands

	USA (1988 c.q. 1990)		The Netherlands (1989)	
	total	per capita *1000	total	per capita *1000
Convictions	225,000	0.90	2550	0.16
Prison sentences	155,000	0.62	1758	0.12
Prison population	400,000	1.60	1518	0.10

(Computed by the author on the basis of estimates by Reuter (1992) for the USA and on the basis of data from CBS (1991) for the Netherlands. The data for the USA concern convictions and imprisonment sentences by state courts (1988) and the prison population in federal, state and local prisons (1990). The share of federal courts in convictions and imprisonment sentences is relatively small. However, in view of the severity of federal offenses, the share of total expected prison time generated by the federal courts is not small: 50,000 years compared to 150,000 years generated by the state courts (33%) in 1988.)

As far as health care services are concerned, in the USA there is less emphasis on the prevention of AIDS among drug consumers and on methadone and needle-exchange programs. The scale of health care activities can best be judged from cost data. Table 6 presents some data about apparent costs of both health care programs and law enforcement

Table 6. Some data on apparent costs of publicly funded health care and law enforcement services per inhabitant in the USA and the Netherlands

	USA		The Netherlands	
	$ millions	$ per capita	$ (Dfl.) millions	$ (Dfl.) per capita
Law enforcement				
federal/central	7157	29	230 (410)	15 (27)
(USA 1991, Netherlands 1992)				
state and local/local	5240	21	0 (0)	0 (0)
(USA 1988)				
Health care	898	4	90 (157)	6 (10)
federal, state and local/				
central and local				
(USA 1989, Netherlands 1992)				

(Sources: USA: Bureau of Justice Statistics 1992; the Netherlands: see source description Table 3. For the health care services in the USA, only the publicly funded part (52%) of the total reported treatment costs is presented. The figures for these services are underestimates, mainly due to a lack of response from 22% of known drug and alcohol treatment and prevention units in the annual survey from which the data are taken. The cost data for the Netherlands are presented in dollars on the basis of the average dollar exchange rate in 1992, which was Dfl. 1.75. Costs cannot be totalled because the methodologies and years differ.)

programs in the USA and the Netherlands, taken over all levels of government.

These data indicate that the absolute amount of dollars spent per person for law enforcement is much higher in the USA than in the Netherlands. Even if the volatility of the dollar exchange rate is taken into account, it can safely be concluded that per capita costs for law enforcement are more than four times as high in the USA as in the Netherlands. On the other hand, the costs of publicly funded health care services are of the same order of magnitude (note that the health care figures for the USA are underestimates because of the lack of response mentioned in the source description).

It also appears from Table 6 that the ratio of law enforcement to health care costs is very different in both countries. Even if the fact that health care costs for the USA are underestimates and that they refer to a different year than the law enforcement costs, is taken into account, it seems plausible that they make up less than 15% of the total public budget in the area of drug control. In the Netherlands, health care services made up circa 30% of the total public budget for 1992 in this area. This difference is remarkable, the more so if the fact that, due to relatively favorable living conditions in Dutch prisons, the costs of imprisonment per inmate in the Netherlands are about twice as high as in the USA, is taken into account.[13] If Dutch imprisonment costs were equal to those in the USA, the ratio of health care to law enforcement costs would still increase by about 3%.

The prevailing political views on the net benefits of drug policy in the USA are very different from those in the Netherlands. The USA has a long tradition of political activism against drug consumption. This tradition has its roots in puritan religious beliefs of a socially conservative nature, and in the ideas of progressive emancipation movements among working class people and women at the beginning of the century. The essence of these beliefs is that the consumption of drugs is, in principle, a morally degrading and evil activity; it is not only the right but also the obligation of the government to repress such an activity, regardless of the effects that this repression exerts on other persons. There is a straightforward and well-documented connection between the political movements which were responsible for the alcohol prohibition of 1919, and the narcotics and marihuana prohibitions of 1914 and 1937.[14]

Moreover, the political culture in the United States is in general less averse to conflict and less consensus-seeking than in the Netherlands. As a consequence, there has always been an open political debate between prohibitionists and libertarians about the means and objectives of public drug policy. Another explanatory factor may be that, compared to their Dutch colleagues, American politicians are typically less afraid of the large costs involved in public endeavors deemed morally worthy. Thus, the restraint of political polarization that is characteristic of Dutch drug policy does not exist in the USA. Moreover, the American two-party system and the pressure on Republicans with libertarian views to hold the ranks closed, has contributed to the enormous escalation of repression which occurred in the Reagan and Bush eras and which resulted in the bizarre situation that in 1990 400,000 American men and women (40% African-Americans) were incarcerated under extremely problematic penitentiary conditions for drug-related felonies (see Table 6).

Although the Democratic camp in the presidential election of 1992 has not openly distanced itself from the raging "war on drugs", the Clinton administration is clearly willing to take a fresh look at prevailing policies. There are indications that there now is a certain retreat from the hawkish approach in a more moderate direction. Although anti-drug activism is deeply rooted in American political culture, the history of alcohol prohibition (and its subsequent defeat) shows that American policy makers are able and willing to bring about a fundamental policy change as soon as they become convinced of its advantages and moral acceptability. It is hard to predict whether such a fundamental policy change will occur with respect to drug policy in the near future. However, it does seem clear that the huge costs of the hawkish approach, in combination with its apparent lack of success, will keep the debate alive in the years to come.

8. Conclusions

This Chapter was written from a "public choice" perspective, which focuses attention on the motivation and behavior of public officials, especially of politicians. Decisive for the development of drug policy are the costs and benefits of regulation and collective services as they are perceived by politicians and the public. Costs have to be paid for out of taxes and social security premiums. Benefits lie in the sphere of prevention of criminality, public health, and low visibility of a small and unpopular subculture.

Information can have an important impact upon policy. To that purpose, information should particularly be directed at existing prejudices and misunderstandings. The single most important theme in this respect relates to erroneous beliefs about the effect of the repression of supply on property crime and on forms of professional criminality. Step-by-step reduction of suppression is a learning process that tends to be self-reinforcing because it enhances the dissemination of information about the reality of drug use. It is important that the trend towards normalization predominant in Dutch drugs policy for some decades should be extended to the areas of cocaine and heroin. One may only hope that new forms of international cooperation do not pose unwanted barriers in this respect.

References

Becker, G.S., Murphy, K.M.: A theory of rational addiction. *Journal of Political Economy* 9:675-700, 1988

Bureau of Justice Statistics, US Department of Justice: *Drugs, Crime and the Justice System.* Washington: US Government Printing Office, 1992

Cachet, A.: *Politie en Sociale Controle: over het Effect van Politie-Optreden: een Vergelijkend Onderzoek naar Verkeersdelicten, Gezinsgeweld en Drugsgebruik.* Arnhem/Gouda: Quint, 1990

Cohen, H.: De hashisch cultuur anno 1980: een overlijdensbericht. *Tijdschrift Alcohol Drugs* 7:3-8, 1981

Cohen, P.: *Cocaine Use in Amsterdam in Non-Deviant Subcultures.* Amsterdam: Instituut voor Sociale Geografie, University of Amsterdam, 1989

De Zwart, W.M.: *Alcohol, Tabak en Drugs in Cijfers.* Utrecht: Nederlands Instituut voor Alcohol en Drugs, 1992

Driessen, F.M.H.M., Jansen, H.F.A.: *Drugshandel na 1992.* Utrecht: Bureau Driessen Sociaal Wetenschappelijk Onderzoek en Advies, 1991

Grapendaal, M., Leuw, E., Nelen, J.M.: *De Economie van het Drugbestaan.* Arnhem/Gouda: Quint, 1991

Centraal Bureau voor de Statistiek (Central Bureau of Statistics): *Criminaliteit en Strafrechtspleging 1989.* The Hague: SDU Uitgeverij, 1991

Hoekstra, J.C.: De illegale heroinemarkt. *Economisch Statistische Berichten* 68:1188-1192, 1984

Hulsman, L.H.C.: Het Nederlandse heroïnebeleid in internationaal perspectief. *Tijdschrift Criminologie* 26:76-97, 1984

Jansen, A.C.M.: *Cannabis in Amsterdam: A Geography of Hashish and Marihuana.* Muiderberg: Dick Coutinho, 1991

Korf, D.J.: Jatten alle junkies. *Tijdschrift Criminologie* 32:105-123, 1990

Korf, D.J., De Kort, M.: *Drugshandel en Drugsbestrijding.* Amsterdam: University of Amsterdam, Criminologisch Instituut Bonger, 1990

Migué, J.L., Bélanger, G.: Toward a general theory of managerial discretion. *Public Choice* 27:37-54, 1974

National Drug Control Strategy. Budget Summary. January 1992, The White House, Washington, Executive Office of the President

Nota Verslavingsproblematiek. Kamerstuk 1991-1992 22684 No. 1. The Hague: SDU-Uitgeverij

NRC Handelsblad: Strakkere regels voor hennepteelt. *NRC Handelsblad* 19 August, 1992

Pommerehne, W.W., Hart, A.: Drogenpolitik(en) aus ökonomischer Sicht. In: Grötzinger, G. (Ed.) *Recht auf Sucht? Drogen, Markt, Gesetze.* Berlin: Rotbuch, 1991

Pommerehne, W.W., Hartmann, H.C.: Ein ökonomischer Ansatz zur Rauschgiftkontrolle. *Jahrbuch Sozialwissenschaft* 31:102-143, 1980

308

Reuter, P.: Hawks ascendent: the punitive trend of American drug policy. *Daedalus*
121/3:15-22, 1992
Sandwijk, J.P., Cohen, P.D.A., Musterd, S.: *Licit and Illicit Drug Use in Amsterdam*. Amsterdam: Instituut voor Sociale Geografie, University of Amsterdam, 1991
Sociaal en Cultureel Planbureau (Social and Cultural Planning Bureau): *Doelmatig Dienstverlenen*. Rijswijk: Sociaal en Cultureel Planbureau, 1989
Stichting Informatievoorziening Verslavingszorg: *Some Information and Statistical Data about the Addiction Treatment Services in the Netherlands, based on the National Information System "Ladis"*. Utrecht: Stichting Informatievoorziening Verslavingszorg, 1993
Stigler, G.J., Becker, G.S.: De gustibus non est disputandum. *American Economic Review*
67:76-90
Thornton, M.: *The Economics of Prohibition*. Salt Lake City: University of Utah Press, 1991

Endnotes

1. A report from the Criminal Investigation Information Service of August 1992 reports that in 1991 the police identified 37 rural cannabis farms with a total annual production capacity of 8160 kilograms of hashish and marihuana (*NRC Handelsblad* 19 August, 1992).
2. A drug-related felony is a felony against a drug law or other felony in which the consumption, production or trade of drugs is presumed to contribute to the offence (*e.g.*: theft in order to acquire money to be spent on drugs, or violence among drugs traders).
3. For an international comparison, see Hulsman 1984.
4. Estimates for earlier periods were much higher. For example, Hoekstra estimates a monetary turnover of 650 million in the Netherlands in 1982 (Hoekstra 1984; see also, Cachet 1990). The differences are mainly due to the higher prices of heroin prevailing at the beginning of the eighties (Hoekstra assumes 300 guilders per gram in 1982).
5. These percentages were computed by the Social and Cultural Planning Bureau on the basis of the report by the Project Quantification Police Work (Social and Cultural Planning Bureau 1989).
6. These percentages were computed by the author on the basis of data collected by the Central Bureau of Statistics (Central Bureau of Statistics 1989).
7. These percentages were computed by the author on the basis of data provided by the Ministry of Justice.
8. For discussions on the validity of the models discussed, see Grapendaal *et al.* 1991 and Korf 1990.
9. According to general population surveys, 11% of high school seniors reported using marihuana on a daily basis in the previous month in 1978; less than 2% of seniors reported such use in 1991 (Reuter 1992). The decline has been spread evenly between age, sex and race groups.
10. The connection between drug prices and damage by criminality to property is well established in empirical studies. Some of these are cited in Cachet 1990 and in Pommerehne and Hart 1991. See also Hoekstra 1984.
11. In both countries, distribution offenses are always felonies, possession offenses can be either felonies or misdemeanors.
12. In view of the discrepancy in the data base mentioned in the source description in Table 6, the difference between the ratios for imprisonment sentences and prison populations cannot exclusively be attributed to longer terms of imprisonment.

13. The costs per inmate in federal prisons and correctional institutions contracted by the Federal Bureau of Prisons were $23,000 in 1991 (National Drug Control Strategy 1992). The costs per inmate in Dutch penitentiary institutions (including institutions for juvenile delinquents) were Dfl. 82,000 (circa $47,000) in 1992.

14. A very interesting survey of the history of the prohibitions and their mutual connections is provided by Thornton (1991).

XV. IS DUTCH DRUG POLICY AN EXAMPLE TO THE WORLD?

C.D. Kaplan, D.J. Haanraadts, H.J. Van Vliet and J.P. Grund

1. Introduction

The papers in this Volume have provided an understanding of the socio-historical factors which have led to the construction of the Dutch definition of drug problems. This final Chapter moves from inspection and introspection to the more risky work of projection. The first sections of this Chapter set the stage for a flight into the future of international drug policy development. This flight is directed towards a deceptively simple question: Is Dutch drug policy an example for the world? As a point of departure, this question could be answered by specifying and evaluating what can be drawn from the Dutch experience that is relevant in the new era of international drug policy development. This era has been signalled by the pronouncements for demand reduction at the Vienna convention of 1988.[1]

In our view, the Dutch experience (with some local adaptations of course) is indeed a markedly relevant example to the world. Support for our view stems from a number of local, national and international movements which are rallying under the banner of *public mental health/crime prevention* reforms to respond to a perceived failure of the international control system. This movement involves a compromise position between what Peter Reuter (1992) has recently termed the replay of the post-Vietnam war international relations scenario of the "hawks" versus the "doves". The war on drugs movement represents the hawks while the movement for legalization plays the role of the doves. In this deadlock nothing really pragmatic for the resolution of the drug problem can be suggested and a policy collapse not unlike the debacle of the Vietnam war is a real possibility. What Reuter proposes is a new kind of bird on the horizon. Drawing from the book on the prevention of nuclear war edited by Nye, Allison and Cornesale, he sees the ascendant bird as an owl. The owl offers a public mental health/prevention intervention alternative.[2] Reuter views the European drug policy development as the prototype of the owl alternative. Within this international "owl" movement, the official drug policy of the Netherlands has played a definitive role simply because it was the first clear and consistent commitment of a government to a change in the direction of international drug policy development. The recent appointment of Professor Hamid Ghodse,[3] Chairman of the Addiction Research Department of St. George's Medical School in London, a psychiatrist and scientist, as Chairman of the International Narcotics Control Board is a significant sign of the emergence of an alternative way of controlling the international situation; formerly, this position was routinely given to a professional international diplomat.

The importance of a single nation's experience in turning the tide of international drug policy cannot be underestimated. For example, in the inaugural Thomas Okey Memorial Lecture, Jerome H. Jaffe, first architect of America's national strategy on drugs, provides a personal perspective of the American experience which indicates how a single national experience can provide the pivot on which to move world drug policy in a different direction (Jaffe 1987). Situating his analysis of the American strategy in terms of its "British origins", he shows how British drug policy was able to influence the American national response through the forum of the World Health Organization. The prestigious World Health Organization Expert Committee on Drug Dependence provided a mechanism whereby leading British ideas could obtain an international legitimacy and influence. This process – the use of official international bodies for legitimating and extending national interests – has been characteristic of international drug policy development from its beginning (see Stein 1985; Escochado 1989; Musto 1973). Therefore, it is not surprising that Jaffe (1987:598) bases his lecture on the seminal idea of the WHO working paper that "all the elements making up a national response ... are always in a state of dynamic equilibrium" and that this equilibrium involves a process of subtle international relations. Thus, the international character of drug policy makes a national response an action that usually has consequences far beyond its legal borders.

The formation of drug policy at the international level always involves an uneasy consensus of competing interests (see Kaplan 1984). Nevertheless, as Jaffe (1987:598) recommends, the best approach for achieving consensus is based upon an open-minded, "learning" attitude to drug problems.

"It would be presumptuous to assume that those in other countries can learn important lessons from a so brief and personal perspective on the American national response. Yet nations do not usually have the capacity to conduct controlled experiments with alternative national responses to drug problems. If they are to reduce the costs of drug use and misuse, they must learn either from their own history or from the experiences of other nations."

A rigid and dogmatic state of mind will normally lead to the isolation of a national approach and, eventually, as a result of international pressure, readaptation to the fragile, albeit legitimate international standards. In contrast, and significant for the arguments put forward in this Chapter, in order for a nation to start the essential development of opening another nation's mind, research that takes a self critical look at the origins and consequences of the historical experience of that nation's drug use must be set in motion. Along with this fundamental critical attitude, scientific curiosity must be stimulated as to how the experiences of other nations may function as comparison and control conditions.

In an earlier paper Jaffe (1983) presented a fundamental conceptual framework in which he scientifically situated the assessment and international comparison of drug problems and policy responses. The first step was the stimulation of multidimensional information systems about drug users, the drugs they use and the real effects these drugs have on the user and society. The next step was to situate this information in a qualitative context of the history of the social response to drug use and the functions drug use has in society and culture. Once this work has been done, finer distinctions such as that between drug use and drug abuse can be made.

Conceptually, the physician Jaffe argues in his paper for "the limited relevance of the pharmacological dimension". In an age where biological psychiatry is making major pharmacological breakthroughs, this limitation may be forgotten. Thus, the important pharmacological scientific results have their practical relevance mainly as adjuncts to the evolving social systems of drug use and control. In Jaffe's own research of a wide variety of national experiences documented in the case studies of a major WHO collaborative study, the only common factors to be identified were "deviance" and "impairment". Thus, in Jaffe's conception, the dimension of the social definition of drug use is at least as important as the pharmacological dimension in formulating an appropriate "international response" to the wide variety of national experiences. Jaffe (1983:110) clarifies his position:

"Firstly, a pattern of drug use is seen as a problem when it deviates from a traditionally accepted or an emerging cultural norm. And, secondly, it is seen as a problem when it impairs health or social functioning ... Developing appropriate responses requires an understanding of the specific society, its history, its dynamics and its aspirations: factors that must be understood at least as thoroughly as we understand pharmacology and specific drug-induced pathologies."

2. The Dutch definition

The statements of Jerome Jaffe, urging a multiple and multidimensional approach for responding to international drug problems, is familiar to Dutch scientists as well as to cabinet members. For example, the former Minister of Justice of the Netherlands, Frits Korthals Altes, addressing the United Nations International Conference on Drug Abuse and Trafficking in Vienna urged that "international cooperation is indispensable. However, an attempt to reach an internationalization of drug policies in the sense of a single, non-differentiated approach is bound to be counterproductive for many countries..." (cited in Van Vliet 1990:463). This commitment to finding a "cooperation in diversity" has been a cornerstone in the development of the national drug strategy in the Netherlands. This policy approach has also been a significant contributor to the dynamic equilibrium of the international drug control system. Much like the earlier influence of the British through international organizations, the Dutch have maintained an influential role despite the widespread opinion that the Netherlands is somehow in violation of the existing international order. Going beyond this popular and at times official misconception, the Netherlands was one of the signatories of the 1988 Vienna agreement and contributes significantly to its mandate (Article 14) for the adoption of appropriate measures for eliminating and reducing demand. The newly defined international emphasis on demand reduction is not at all strange or even innovative with reference to Dutch national policy. Demand reduction has been the self-conscious aim of Dutch drug policy for the last two decades. This definition provides the basis for the controversial Dutch drug policy innovations of the separation of drug markets and the normalization of drug problems (Van Vliet 1990).

The current Dutch definition did not develop in a social vacuum. On the contrary, the Dutch experience in drug use control can be found in the context of broad civilization and collectivization processes which have a global scope, but have always been openly and clearly expressed in Dutch society. Dutch drug policy can be seen as part of a broad sociohistorical movement which the Dutch sociologist Abram de Swaan (1988:244) termed "the collectivization of arrangements for coping with adversity and deficiency" which has characterized all modern industrialized societies. the Netherlands has always had an historical role as a fore-runner of Western social development. It was the Netherlands which pioneered the great social transformation of civilization from the Middle Age feudal structure to the modern capitalist structure, the so-called "civilization offensive". Politically, the United Provinces of Holland became an example for a variety of modern state organizations, such as the United Kingdom, the United States of America and the French Union. In the contemporary world, the Netherlands can be seen to be pioneering the social development of the immense and gradual shift from modern to post-modern society – a phenomenon that only very recently has been measured and evaluated by social scientists.

Despite this unique historical role, it would be mistaken to conclude that, as a society, the Netherlands is an exception to "the rule". Rather, Dutch society represents a particular national adaptation to broad sociocultural processes that are omnipresent in the world. The tendency of the Dutch to define drug problems as they do is not a unique idiosyncrasy, but rather a re-organization, selection and retention of social potentials that exist in different degrees and combinations in contemporary societies. Despite obvious national differences, De Swaan (1988:244) can conclude that these processes have even become quite irreversible:

"The underlying consensus about the basis of the welfare state is still so encompassing that it remains largely unnoticed ... Even determined conservative regimes, such as Thatcher's or Reagan's, have not undone the basic tenets of collectivization and transfer capital accumulation. The "welfare backlash" has been more of an ideological exercise in verbiage, than an effective or consistent policy."

Of course, there is a great amount of diversity in these irreversible processes. The "welfare backlash", for instance, in the United States, became a dominant ideological pillar for the former Republican administration, with the result that real changes in society were made. But these changes were perceived to increase the social misery of the American people. This may have contributed to the defeat of the Republicans in 1992 and the election of a Democratic administration which was more likely to get America back on a progressive ideological track. Under the Republican administration, substantial social investment was made in drug control. In the Republican decade of 1981 to 1991 federal government spending on drug control increased almost seven-fold, growing from $28 million to $1.016 billion (Bureau of Justice Statistics 1992:130).

Funds for drug enforcement increased 14-fold while funding for drug treatment only increased four-fold. Spending on drug prevention, however, had the greatest relative growth over the decade, increasing 17 times. However, despite this relatively high increase in the funding of law enforcement, its share of the entire drug budget had leveled off after the early 1980s to a modest increase of from around 60% of the budget to around 70%. This supports the "irreversibility" hypothesis of De Swaan: lots of ideological noise, very modest real reversals. The real loser in the decade was drug treatment which fell from just under 40% of the budget in 1981 to just over 20% in 1991, but this decline was compensated by a relatively high increase in drug prevention to almost 20% of the budget.

The American "war on drugs" rhetoric did have a modest material base in that drug problems were being used to channel the accumulation of transfer capital away from classical welfare state institutions to new "warfare" state experiments. Thus, drug problems were used to stimulate the growth of the federal prison program and the military. Federal prisons were budgeted in 1988 for $445.9 million, raised to $630.7 million in 1989 and $1 billion and $476.5 million in 1990. The Department of Defense, which had always been very ambivalent about the drug problem,[4] were given the incentive to become involved in the drug war with their budgetary allowance growing in the interdiction category from $94.7 million in 1988, to $308.3 million in 1989 and $313.2 million in 1990, and in the international category from zero funding in 1988 to $117.5 million in 1990. To European thinking, the use of military and prison institutions to provide "warfare" alternatives to welfare state functions is almost unthinkable, but this has been a persistent mechanism both in North and South America for maintaining social control. For example, in traditional American society, delinquent youths were frequently given the choice after apprehension by the police of either going to jail or joining the army. A more modern form of this American practice is illustrated by the emergence of "boot camps" for first-time violators of drug laws. These camps, largely organized by the prison system, have been termed "shock incarceration" and involve the combination of "personally challenging" military-like basic training with some sort of drug treatment (Center for Substance Abuse Research 1993; Mackenzie 1990). By March 1992 there were 41 correctional boot camps in 25 states, including one run by the Federal Bureau of Prisons. These programs have the wide support of the American people (49% in a recent Associated Press survey) and can be said to represent the legacy of the war on drugs in the decade of the 1990s (Bureau of Justice Statistics 1992:96). In short, in the Netherlands, problematic drug users tend to be provided with social and medical services while, in the United States, they are more likely to be dealt with through the criminal justice system.

The Dutch definition can also be seen as an expression of certain global historical cultural changes which have been characterized as the shift from "materialist" to "post-materialist" value orientations (Inglehart 1977, 1990; see also Van Deth 1983a, 1983b for critical remarks pertaining to the Netherlands). These value orientations involve a continuum of basic commitment to the maintenance of national order ("materialism") to setting the priority on freedom of expression ("post-materialism"). The Netherlands has perhaps the strongest intact tradition of relative tolerance, pragmatic compromise and social welfare and can be seen as the earliest national forerunner of the post-materialist value orientation. The living Dutch tradition springs from the ethical norms of gentleness, temperance, kindness and the pursuit of knowledge and spiritual development expressed by the early 16th Century Rotterdam scholar and humanist Erasmus. During the Dutch "Golden Age" these norms were upheld by the ruling orders of the urban patriarchate against the rigidness of the Calvinistic clergy and the so-called uneducated masses. They provided the means for the crystallization of a distinct Dutch value system built upon orientations beyond the materialist transformations which were changing the global social structure.

This humanitarian value system was not, however, simply idealistic. It was tied to a commitment to utilitarianism and value pluralism that was the basis of Dutch mercantilism. This attitude allowed for experimentalism in both social ends and means. For example, unlike many other prosperous nations, riches was not seen as an end in itself to be displayed in ostentatious status symbols, but rather as an "embarrassment" to be subsumed under other ends such as sobriety and modesty (see Schama 1988). With this value system in operation, the immense prosperity during the 17th Century of the Republic of the United Netherlands enabled the absorption of different ethnic cultures, religions and traditions. For example, persecuted Jews from Spain and Puritans from England were offered refuge in the Dutch Republic in the interests both of utilitarianism and humanitarianism. They were permitted and encouraged to maintain their original backgrounds and cultures. It was expected that these tolerated groups would provide Dutch culture with the most beneficial intellectual and material parts of their own without fundamentally changing the Dutch status quo. In exchange, their traditions and cultural practices were tolerated. Dutch tolerance then as today means not only freedom of religion but also the allowance of different

expressions of lifestyle, attitudes and behavior in accordance with one's
ethical beliefs. To use a metaphor, in order for Dutch society to expand
its prosperity, the mainstream needed fresh input from new springs which
reinforced the strength of the current.[5]

Roughly summarizing the last century of societal development in the
Netherlands, four groups based either on religion (mainly protestantism
and catholicism) or ideology (socialism and liberalism) created their own
so-called "pillars" of institutions of education, religion, leisure activities
and media. These pillars gave a distinctive identity to their members
while, through a democratic process of persistent compromise, created a
modern welfare state. This system of institutional "living-apart-together-
ness" imploded after the Second World War under the influence of
secularization, the "cultural revolution" of the 1960s and the process of
"global villagization". Traditional community life and social control
gave way to new waves of urbanization and immigration and the development of individualized lifestyles. During the "cultural revolution" of the
1960s, patronizing control over people's personal lives by religious,
political and community leaders was rapidly replaced by self-determination at the family and individual levels. This shake-up in individual and
social values impacted on all Western countries in one way or another.
Yet this effected the Netherlands some years earlier (in 1965) and in a
more playful way than most of its neighbors. Moreover, the social shake-
up contributed to new forms of national consciousness and social
responsibility, rather than dividing society along the simple lines of
young/old, left/right and pro/contra. When the violent protest movements
of the late 1960s shook the world, the Dutch had the advantage of having
already renovated their social and cultural infrastructure. Filling the gap
left by the implosion of the pillar system, a strong national welfare state
in cooperation with many professional and interest groups emerged as the
end result of what Abram de Swaan (1988:210) has called "a long sizzle
and a late bang". This "caring state" left intact the strongly knitted fabric
of social, economical and mental interactions between citizens and
institutions, preventing major tensions and disruptions. On the foundations of prosperity and enlightenment laid down in the 1960s, the Dutch
government and society further developed the welfare state towards what
the Dutch called the "well-being state" (*welzijn*) in the 1970s. By adding
a general "quality of life" criterion to a renovated welfare state apparatus, the new Dutch well-being state provided a critical departure from
the rigid and ineffective welfare state bureaucracies which were already
rotting in many Western societies. This renovation prevented the growth
of anti-welfare state ideologies such as Thatcherism and Reaganomics.

The well-being state, while providing basic material prosperity and security for all through an extensive system of social security, medical care and educational programs, was still not considered sophisticated enough for the management of the growing complexity of Dutch society. Citizens should be embedded in an encompassing structure in which intra-personal, interindividual, group and class conflicts are preferably solved by the "soft policing" of social, youth, cultural and community workers and neighborhood policemen, instead of by harder legal, administrative or even military interventions. Although this type of social management was increasingly criticized and was partly dismantled in the 1980s on financial and ideological grounds, the well-being state continued in its function as a social manager appointed by its citizens.

Although Dutch drug policy is not currently dominated by moral overtones, it does not necessarily mean that morality has not played a part in response to certain substances. Similarly to many other countries which were adapting themselves to the new demands of industrialization of the mid-19th century, the Netherlands' "fight" against the "evils" of alcohol paralleled other European countries which moved in the direction of temperance in contrast to the prohibition of alcohol. In southern Europe, alcohol became completely normalized and integrated in the fabric of society. This broad European response became the analogue for policies towards other drugs.

Comparing the success of American and European temperance movements, the major difference was that in Europe the anti-alcohol reform movement did not lead to national legal prohibition like the 18th Amendment to the American constitution. Thus, although local Dutch regulations restricting opening times and locations of bars were issued, legislation was not used as the major tool to fight alcohol. Instead, the emphasis was put on improving the living and working conditions of the people who were most likely to be unable to control their drinking habits. The analogy between alcohol and drug policies is that regulation of the problem was preferred to aggressively fighting it. Policies based on creating fear for the dangers of drugs, on forcing drug users into illegality or incarcerating them are considered in the Netherlands to be counter-productive and costly – to be bad policies and therefore immoral in their consequences.

The rising global concern for drug abuse and trafficking should be viewed embedded in this particular sociopolitical context. Compared with most other countries, room was created for experimentation with different policies including those aimed at incorporation and control rather than aggressive attack and elimination. Dutch social life and legal regulations are strongly oriented towards normalcy. Dutch tolerance and permissiveness are based on a strong desire by state and citizens alike to be able to see what your fellow citizen is doing, where he is doing it and why. This highly sophisticated form of social control grew out of the desire for social equality. Groups or individuals who act deviantly are under constant pressure to become part of the normal mainstream. The much vaunted "typical" Dutch tolerance and permissiveness are, in reality, a generally accepted public policy strategy of holding a juicy carrot in front of groups, promising them the tolerance of their existence, providing them an identity and even financial support, if (and only if) they are willing to subscribe to some basic unwritten rules: as far as possible to act openly and, in public, not to force differing beliefs and lifestyles on anybody else – implying the acceptance of the moral and legal dominance of the mainstream. Consistent with this, current Dutch "drug problems" are not centered so much around the pharmacological negative effects of drug use, but rather around the reluctant attitude of "extremely problematic" drug users to become controllable by the social and healthcare systems. Much of drug problem solving, therefore, is referred to in a pragmatic and tolerant model of society which manages social experiments in realizing its collectivization and civilizing goals. This response is consistent with an experimental attitude that has been applied to the management of virtually all types of social problems including drugs as well as other tricky, moral issues, such as homosexuality, abortion, euthanasia and age of sexual consent.

3. The shift to different goals strategy: the grand experiment of the Netherlands

As the American political scientist Ronald Inglehart (1990) maintains, in times characterized by an increasing gap between aspiration levels and the perceived situation, two kinds of adaptations are possible – a "more of the same" adaptation strategy or a "shift to different goals" strategy. The pronouncements at the conference in Vienna 1988 have opened a new era in the international drug field in which this credibility gap becomes the pivotal point of future proceedings. The conference simultaneously adopted a "more of the same" strategy in focusing upon narcotrafficking; that is, supply reduction which had become the calling card of the American approach. At the same time, the conference adopted a "shift to different goals" by recognizing the fundamental importance of demand reduction; that is, prevention and treatment services, interventions and experiments. The convention has provided the frame of reference for a new socio-historical era where multiple and different goals for international drug policy can be defined. The uneasiness in the new period is precipitated by the inherent tensions between the two strategies. The old era's aspiration of achieving consensus on drug control through supply elimination and containment strategies does not fit well in a situation of a continuous and steady growth in the world market of psychoactive drugs. The emergence of the new strategy of demand reduction becomes intelligible as a necessary adaptation to the world market situation.

The Netherlands was an early representative in the international community of nations of this "shift in different goals" strategy. The Dutch strategy, built on a post-material value orientation, involves a process of incorporation rather than alienation of the social groups linked to drug-related problems. As a recent Dutch ministerial white paper contends, the national strategy should seek to depoliticize the drug problem by reconceptualizing the problem as one of individual responsibility instead of mass public concern (Engelsman 1989, 1990). The Netherlands exemplifies a concrete case of a government interpreting its international obligations in the framework of a public mental health and prevention perspective fundamentally grounded on a shift to the new and different goal of demand reduction. Underlying this commitment is the wish to maintain a stable and controllable society through the provision of services friendly to drug users and minimizing the potential harm of drug abuse.

The concern for unintended effects of overly repressive national drug policies that would alienate illegal drug users into uncontrollable, enclosed subcultures was one of the main reasons for reforming the Opium Act in 1976. These reforms provided for the strategic principle of the separation of markets for drugs with an acceptable risk (*e.g.,* cannabis) from other drug markets (*e.g.,* heroin, cocaine, amphetamine). This reform allowed public exposure of soft-drug use in the "normal" environment of the coffee shops. These coffee shops functioned as public places where cannabis users could meet, buy and smoke without being threatened by police (Jansen 1989). This principle is founded upon the view that certain "new" (and illegal) drugs such as cannabis had gained a firm footing in everyday life in post-modern society comparable to alcohol, tobacco and coffee in earlier times. In such a situation, legally to "favor" alcohol and tobacco while prohibiting cannabis is akin to an act of civil rights discrimination (see Ehrenberg 1991). The consistent conclusion from this analysis is that to build a policy on the prohibition of illegal drugs is neither realistic nor conducive to a modern democratic society. Rather, a strategy of "normalization" is a more adequate legal fundament; a shift (consistent with provisions regulating legal drugs) attempting to find formulas for the conditional integration of drug users in society in order to minimize the harm caused by their drug use.

In contrast, these Dutch strategic goals can be compared to an opposing strategy which has also been highly visible within the community of Western industrialized nations. The United States *National Drug Control Strategy* drafted under the Bush Administration (The White House 1989) represents, in a most sophisticated form, the "prohibitionist expectancy" underlying the international drug control order (see Kaplan 1984; Van Wijngaart 1991). The current American "war on drugs" response is a concrete example of a countervailing strategy in which the situation is "hyperpoliticized" and the government attempts to mass mobilize its population towards supporting a "more of the same" adaptation to the increasing credibility gap. In direct contrast to the Dutch strategic principles, the American strategy tends towards "unifying" drug markets by arguing for uniform criminal and social sanctions across *all* drugs. Within this strategy, the prohibitionist expectancy logically is extended to the socially acceptable drugs of alcohol and tobacco. The current American anti-smoking and drunken driving campaigns can be seen as preliminary attempts to *criminalize* tobacco and alcohol use. And the American policy of "user accountability" and "zero tolerance" can be seen as being diametrically opposed to the normalization of the drug problem principle. Here the drug user is singled out by the government for segregation from society despite the rhetoric of treatment. Drug users' civil and social rights are made contingent upon their willingness to alter their drug preferences. In this way, the power of public definition is being mobilized to raise the thresholds of social tolerance to the point where the very act of using a drug is tantamount to *immoral* behavior – what might be called the "*ab*normalization of drug problems".

In choosing an adaptive strategy of "shift to different goals", the drug policy in the Netherlands is demonstrating itself to be in accord with the "experimentalist expectancy", the countervailing pillar of the prohibitionist expectancy, beneath the international drug control order. The American social psychologist Donald T. Campbell (1988) has coined the phrase "the experimenting society" to describe a society founded on the principles of "applied social science, on treating the ameliorative efforts of government as field experiments" (Campbell 1988:291). The image of such a society is "...one that would vigorously try out possible solutions to recurrent problems and would make hard headed, multidimensional evaluations of outcomes, and when the evaluation of one reform showed it to have been ineffective or harmful, would move on to other alternatives."

In the experimenting society, there must be a spirit of social learning with the goal of knowing more about innovations decided upon by political decisions. Thus, Campbell (1988:301) can conclude: "To learn about the manipulation of relationships one must try out manipulation. The scientific, problem-solving, self-healing society must be an experimenting society." The apparent uniqueness of the Dutch drug policy is largely the outcome of applying the principles of the experimenting society to drug problems. This can be contrasted with many other countries which may provide lip service to experimentation and policy evaluation, but which still decide their policies towards drug problems primarily on "ends idealism"; *i.e.,* morality. The experimenting society, in contrast, places the premium on "means idealism". Thus, to cite one cogent example, in the early 1970s, the Netherlands' and the United States' governments independently established expert commissions to provide recommendations on drug policy issues. The Baan Commission in the Netherlands developed the risk criterion which was the basis for the 1976 policy reforms. In the United States, the Shaffer Commission came to many similar conclusions and recommendations. In the American case, these scientifically grounded recommendations were tabled and "ends idealism" prevailed. The new Republican American government under the leadership of Richard Nixon instead declared a war on crime and drugs, an expedient alternative to the collapse of the former Democratic administration's "war on poverty" in the wake of Vietnam.

An experimental laboratory is in most cases rather small and simple compared to overall reality and the Netherlands is a small country compared to most others. This compactness coupled with a thorough registration system needed for the management of the Dutch well-being state has provided the Netherlands with optimal conditions to experiment in the drug policy field. These optimal conditions have been recognized in all sectors of Dutch society; from the business community to the social services.[6]

The design of the Dutch drug policy experiments has largely been in the form of field trials and program evaluations rather than clinical trials and laboratory experiments. Following Campbell's (1988:308) principle of "means idealism", these social policy experiments have focused on policies and programs which can be applied in more than one setting (*e.g.,* in different cities) and *not* on the evaluation of persons and clients. Social experiments are not real social experiments unless the people effected *comply.* In laboratory animal experiments, the animals have no choice in the matter. In contrast, true social experiments are based on volunteerism and informed consent which function, in turn, as basic design conditions. Thus, with regard to drug policy, social experimentation requires an acceptable level of compliance of drug users themselves – the program must be user friendly. The real challenge is to design experiments that are sensitive to drug users; that involve, in operation, a real research alliance between the subjects and the researchers (see Kaplan *et al.* 1990). This "volunteerism" principle in social experimentation requires specific and special methodologies. Campbell (1988:307-308) has described these methodologies as evaluations legitimated and facilitated by non-professional participants and professional observers.

4. An evaluation of the Dutch approach

Recently, the application of evaluation methodologies to national drug policy has become a top level scientific priority further emphasizing the critical importance the issue has gained in the contemporary world. For instance, the prestigious American journal *Science* has published an article by two highly regarded emeritus professors of pharmacology with long experience in the field of drug abuse (Goldstein and Kalant 1990). In this article an evaluation of American drug policy is presented with a cost-benefit analysis based on pharmacological, toxicological, sociological and historical facts. This article represents an important milestone in the development of a rational valuative approach to assessing a national drug strategy. The choice of a cost-benefit analysis, however, is only one of a variety of options available for conducting evaluation research (see Rossi and Freeman 1985). Cost-benefit methods of evaluation have the limitation of relying upon accepted "net benefit" formulas combining sufficiently reliable quantitative indicators. Furthermore, in terms of Campbell's criteria for social experimentation, the cost-benefit analysis may be sufficient in terms of scientific independence, but insufficient from the viewpoint and interests of the drug users themselves. Without this additional methodological constraint, the evaluation may lose in concreteness and sensitivity what it gains in abstractness and objectivity.

To calculate their net benefit function, Goldstein and Kalant rely upon the indicators of the availability of alcohol in the general population and of opiates to the medical professions. Using these indicators, they are able to demonstrate that alcohol prohibition in the United States did indeed result in a decrease in the use of alcohol and, on the other hand, the ease of availability of opiates by the privileged medical profession can account for their higher use of these prohibited drugs. On the basis of this cost-benefit analysis, they then conclude that "the practical aim of drug policy should be to minimize the extent of use, and thus to minimize the harm" and "that radical steps to repeal the prohibitions on presently illicit drugs would be likely, on balance, to make matters worse rather than better" (1990:1513).

However, drug policy need not necessarily adopt the means of minimizing the extent of use in reaching the goal of minimizing the harm of drugs. An alternative (and not necessarily contradictory) means of reaching the same goal of demand reduction is changing the *nature* of drug use itself. For example, changing the nature of drug use from injection and "basing" to more slowly working forms of self-administration of cocaine, can also minimize the harm and reduce demand (see Bieleman *et al.* 1993). In this case, the extent of use may remain the same, but an unsatisfactory situation would be improved and the dimensions of the problems relating to cocaine would be reduced.

Evaluation of the ideal means for changing the nature of drug use requires a different sort of evaluation methodology. Thus, Goldstein and Kalant's quantitative indicators as suitable measures relevant for an analysis of demand reduction need to be cross-validated with complementary global *qualitative* standards which relate to the nature of drug use in society. This turn in evaluation methodology leads to a critical question. How much of the decrease in alcohol use during the American Prohibition indicates a real reduction in demand and a real improvement in an unsatisfactory condition? Could not the overall demand of drugs have even increased during Prohibition as new substitutes, such as coffee and cigarettes, were found (*i.e.,* the extent of alcohol was reduced without the underlying nature of drug *using* behavior being effected)?

An alternative methodology to cost-benefit analysis for drug policy evaluation is the cost-effectiveness method. With cost-effectiveness analysis, the output is primarily qualitative. With this method, the criterion is not net benefit, but the effectiveness of a policy in improving the quality of life. In this regard, the evaluation of Dutch drug policy has been more concerned with cost-effectiveness; the outcome criteria are not so much reducing demand by decreasing the extent of use, but rather by *improving* the quality of life of *both* drug users and their communities in such a way that the nature of use changes in the direction of reducing harm. To cite one concrete example, the low threshold methadone programs do not aim at blocking all heroin use, but at substituting acceptable drugs (*e.g.,* methadone) and activities (contact with a social medical professional) for unacceptable drugs (*e.g.,* heroin) and unacceptable activities (contact with criminal dealers). These objectives are not realized abstractly, but at certain strategic moments in the daily lives of drug users (see Kaplan *et al.* 1990; Grapendaal *et al.* 1992). Thus, the end of demand reduction is reached not by directly lowering the prevalence of heroin use, but, rather by improving the nature of drug use through a re-organization of the daily and weekly routines of heroin addicts in such a way that the time devoted to the acquisition and self-control of illegal drugs is reduced. Furthermore, with regard to Campbell's recommendation that programs rather than clients should be evaluated, a number of Dutch studies do not look myopically at only the drug user, but also at the relational context created by the impact effect of specific policy innovations (Verbraeck 1988). In summary, the reduction of demand can be globally assessed as the reduction of the negative quality of life conditions that stimulate demand and produce harmful drug use behavior. In this regard, the Dutch use of methadone can be evaluated as a social management innovation aimed at improving the general quality of life in neighborhoods where drug users reside.

Karl Popper's advice, essential for a proper climate for evaluation of "letting our ideas die instead of ourselves", has characterized the pragmatic approach of Dutch policy-oriented research (quoted in Campbell 1988:292). Overall and in terms of its own ends, the drug policy in the Netherlands is seen as functioning positively. The goal of relatively reducing the secondary effects of drug abuse (for example, AIDS, violence) is being reached. For instance, Peter Cohen's (1989) study of cocaine use in non-deviant social groups in Amsterdam, and Intraval's (1992) study of the nature and extent of cocaine in Rotterdam,[7] both provide hard and sound evidence that patterns of use need not necessarily lead to negative secondary or, for that matter, primary effects. These studies provide support for a cocaine policy that is more differentiated than that of other hard drugs. The longitudinal study of Swierstra (1990) of 91 heroin addicts demonstrates that the normalization policy has been effective for diverting the career of heroin addicts from criminal to conventional, but has been less effective in getting heroin users clean. Recent survey data from Amsterdam have shown that the current separation of markets strategy has not led to an increase in cannabis use despite the expansion of the coffee house circuit (Sandwijk *et al.* 1992). However, the preliminary findings of the Netherlands Institute on Alcohol and Drugs from a national survey of 11,000 high school students where alarming increases in cannabis use have occurred over the last eight years are counter-indicative. These results document the limits of tolerance and, therefore, current attention is being placed on the abuse of the coffee house system, and on new programs which focus on the potentially harmful effects of excessive cannabis use in the young. Thus, the coffee house system itself is in need of a comprehensive re-evaluation. On-going evaluations of clinical programs for addicts concentrating on outcomes, retention and the place of psychopathology in the provision of a wide array of treatment services are yielding results which help to improve the care system (Kooyman 1992; Van Limbeek *et al.* 1992; Hendriks 1990). The efficacy of needle exchange as it relates to AIDS' prevention, migrant drug policies and drug prostitution policies has been evaluated with generally positive results (Van Gelder and Sijtsma 1988; Van der Hoek *et al.* 1989; Grund *et al.* 1992).

Finally, all Dutch programs have a built-in mechanism to assess the efficiency of their functioning – the so-called advisory commission, made up of independent experts who monitor most research and intervention programs. The standard procedure for establishing such a commission for every evaluation research project is a unique mechanism which bridges the gap between independent researchers and program managers. These commissions are chaired by a respected expert and are appointed to reflect divergent and often conflicting interests. They meet periodically and issue written minutes of their deliberations. Thus, these commissions function, to use the terminology of evaluation research, as "shadow controls" (Rossi and Freemann 1985:266).

5. The manageable bits of Dutch drug policy

To begin the final approach to answer the question posed by this paper, Dutch drug policy needs to be reformulated in terms of technology transfer. The global themes of Dutch drug policy already outlined in this Chapter would be merely an interesting oddity, if they could not be transformed into a relatively context-free set of tools which could be used elsewhere. In order to do this, the policy must be de-constructed into its "manageable bits" which are transferable singularly or in sets to other social situations. Thus, a corollary to this Chapter's general question is: what specific bits of Dutch drug policy would be transferable to other countries? The transferability of the drug policy of the Netherlands is consistent with its experimental nature. Again, as Campbell emphasizes, the evaluation of programs rather than persons requires a methodology that searches out multiple sites in varying contexts in order fully to assess the program of interest. An answer to this question of transferability starts with the realization that complex and seemingly inextricable social problems (including drugs) must be broken down into discrete areas. By so doing, we do not solve all the problems at once, but we do create situations that can be analyzed separately or in their contexts, that can be managed in a number of cases, and that can be solved sometimes and to a certain extent. Thus, it also becomes possible to break down the so-called "drug problem" into a matrix of microproblems concerning a variety of very different substances, with very different risks involved, to which different sets of rules, measures, instruments can be applied to achieve certain distinct aims. The solutions to these microproblems once packaged and operational become the manageable "bits" of the drug policy. Managers can learn the "bits" of Dutch problem-solving and use them in their own situations.

Table 1. The manageable bits of Dutch drug policy

Problem-solving responses	Problematic factors	
	impairment	deviance
Pharmacology	low threshold methadone	separation of markets
Social definition	normalization	differential criminal law

The manageable bits of Dutch drug policy are schematically represented in Table 1. The common problematic factors defined by Jaffe (impairment and deviance) have been cross-classified by the dimension of problem-solving responses (pharmacology and social definition) also posited by Jaffe. The manageable "bits" of Dutch drug policy can, in turn, be assigned to the cells of the cross-classification, representing four distinct problems faced by policy-makers and four distinct responses made by them to solve these problems. From a dynamic point of view, they also depict four distinct stages of policy development in the Netherlands.

The earliest "bits" appear in the cell pharmacology/impairment. In the 1970s, the pharmacology of drugs was assessed by a government-appointed work group chaired by Dr. Baan, the Head of the Mental Health Inspectorate. The Baan Commission proposed the criterion of socially acceptable risks. By the application of this criterion cannabis was found to be properly classified as pharmacologically acceptable while heroin was not. In order to deal with the impairments associated with heroin use, low threshold methadone programs were established based on community psychiatric models set up in Chicago and London (Trimbos 1973). Thus, at first Dutch drug policy focused on the classical terrain of medicine defined by the impairment/pharmacology cell and designed a novel response through the use of easily accessible methadone.

In the later 1970s, Dutch drug policy developed the "bit" represented in the cell of pharmacology/deviance. In accordance with the differential pharmacology of different drugs, separate markets needed to be created.

The "soft" drug (cannabis) market had to be separated from the "hard" drug (heroin, unacceptable risk) market in order to minimize the social deviance caused by illegal drug use. The Ministry of Justice guidelines created a situation where the deviance associated with cannabis use was officially seen as different from that of heroin use deviance; separation of the markets was devised.

The third cell (impairment/social definition) was filled in by the development in the early 1980s of the normalization of drug problems. Normalization recognized that much of the impairment in social functioning of heroin users was the result of the social definitions they had of themselves and which society supported. Junkie unions and other forms of drug user self-help organization were created in order to provide drug users with the resources to take more responsibility for their own impairments and to define the kind of help they needed. In this way, drug users were coaxed into a process of normalizing their problems and seeking solutions in the sphere of the conventional rather than the criminal world.

The late 1980s saw the developments in the fourth cell (social definition/deviance). In line with the pronouncements of Vienna 1988, the section of differentiated criminal law policy was created in order to provide the means for lowering the intensity of law enforcement on the hard drug user while, at the same time, increasing the intensity of action against international drug trafficking. The result of this can be seen in actions as diverse as the creation of "tolerance zones" by the police, where open small scale drug dealing is allowed, and the cooperation between the Dutch navy and the American armed forces in patrolling the Caribbean to intercept international drug traffic.

6. Conclusions

The two macrosocial science theories of De Swaan and Inglehart have been consulted in order to provide support for the proposition that Dutch society presents a compact adaptation of broad socio-historical processes which *all* modern societies are now undergoing. Given the above discussion on the socio-historical background of Dutch drug policy, it makes no sense to argue, as has been done on numerous occasions, that Dutch policy works for the Dutch, but is so culturally specific that it could not work in other more "representative" places. This would provide the answer to our question "is Dutch policy an example to the world?" with simply a clear "No". However, if the preceding arguments can be accepted and Dutch drug policy is indeed the rational outcome of conscious political decision-making and problem-solving, then Dutch drug policy could be an example to the world. Dutch drug policy is an example to the world insofar as Dutch society is a forerunner in the "shift to different goals" strategy for solving social problems. Dutch society, therefore, functions as the example of a new and innovative well-being state which, in the words of De Swaan (1988), collectivizes treatment, education and caring, extending civilization to the lower social strata while changing the ways emotions are managed and controlled. For the purposes of our analysis, De Swaan provides a view of the basic condition for the transfer of the technology of the manageable bits of Dutch drug policy – the existence and recognition of a well-being state as *both* a collectivizing and civilizing conglomerate. The emotional component of the well-being state as expressed in its post-material value orientation as well as a set of institutions collectivizing the helping services are integral conditions necessary for the effective transfer of the technology of the manageable bits. In Inglehart's analysis of the results over the last two decades of the Euro-Barometer surveys and other national political value surveys, a clear albeit gradual shift in world culture, from materialist to post-materialist values can be measured. Thus, the emotional and cultural conditions for the technology transfer of Dutch drug policy are indeed becoming widespread. Furthermore, these value orientations have been found in a German national survey to have an "extremely orderly relationship" with drug-related attitudes (Kaplan 1987). The measures used in this survey were adopted from Ingelhart's theory using a slightly different terminology. In the study of a national sample of Germans, those holding the equivalent of materialist values (and to a lesser degree a mixed value orientation) had significantly different views on drugs from those who held on to post-materialism.[8]

Focusing on the emotional component, the analysis of the German national sample showed that "fear of the future" was an important variable. The post-materialists were more likely to articulate the emotion of fear of the future in society. This recognition of fear provides a reasonable functional explanation for the widespread use of drugs and makes this use understandable and somewhat acceptable. Thus, at a deep political psychological level, drug policy can be seen to be related to the recognition of fear of the future in society. When fear becomes tied to massive declines in political and interpersonal trust, basic orientations can radically shift (Abramson 1983). The instinct of American politicians to capitalize on this new emotional complex allowed substitution of the war on drugs for a more gentler variety of response. American policy can be seen as a novel attempt to exploit the post-material fear of the future sentiment and separate its association with casual contacts with drug users.

It has become a worn-out truism to argue that drugs play the role of a scapegoat in society (Szasz 1974; Alexander 1990; Reinarman and Levine 1989). Drugs, as Goldstein and Kalant convincingly argue, are indeed potentially dangerous. But fear of the dangerous is no basis for the formulation of a rational and effective policy. There are sufficient international initiatives to draw on for inspiration that are both more optimistic and consistent with Dutch drug policy. One such example is the WHO/EURO program "Health for All in the Year 2000". This document emphasizes positive action and provides a way beyond fear-based thinking. The document notes that "the WHO concept of health as a state of physical, mental and social well-being and not only the absence of disease and disability, views health as a positive condition involving the whole person in the context of his/her situation". The target of reducing health-damaging behavior including illicit drugs by 25% (*i.e.*, demand reduction) is tied to a social context whereby "health-damaging practices should not be thought of as discrete forms of behavior, but rather as aspects of a cultural life, often one of several interacting problems. Risk behaviors can be a way in which people try to resolve conflicts within themselves and between themselves and society".

In the drug area there is a general call "to develop innovative approaches to prevention, taking into consideration a broad range of possible resources in different sectors". In line with the WHO targets, Dutch drug policy includes the mobilization of resources from the broadest possible range of society including active drug users themselves. A primary care orientation with greater degrees of general practitioner and community involvement, more responsibility to the drug user and sensitivity to the conflict resolution function of drugs in a fearful world, has also brought Dutch drug policy in line with other international initiatives such as UNESCO's "preventive education" approach to drug abuse.

In conclusion, broad socio-historical processes can be seen to determine the national response to the drug problem. While every society is unique, the transferability of Dutch drug policy "bits" will be feasible in a country where the value orientation of post-materialism is ascendant; *i.e,* a priority is placed on social and self-actualization needs of esthetics, intellect, belonging and esteem. In any case, since these cultural orientations are now broadly distributed over the globe and are gradually expanding, Dutch drug policy, as an outcome of this value orientation cannot be considered a deviant case with no real transfer potential. Thus, while it is indeed true, as Jaffe (1983:111) maintains "...that the characteristics of society itself are essential elements in developing a useful classification of drug problems ... drug problems need to be defined in the context of the society in which they occur", it is equally true that an international definition of the drug problem must reflect the emergent general characteristics of society. There is still much creative work to do in the future. The limitations of the Dutch and, for that matter, of the American examples of drug policy "for the world" are that neither has struck the right balance between prohibition and legalization, between a "drug free" and a "free drug" society. It will surely take a new bird (call it an owl) to make the flight into the wild blue yonder of future drug policy beyond those now tiring hawks and doves.

References

Abramson, P.R.: *Political Attitudes in America: Formation and Change*. San Francisco: Freeman, 1983

Alexander, B.: *Peaceful Measures: Canada's Way Out of the "War on Drugs"*. Toronto: University of Toronto Press, 1990

Bieleman, B., Diaz, A., Merlot, G., Kaplan, C.D. (Eds.): *Lines Across Europe: Nature and Extent of Cocaine use in Barcelona, Rotterdam and Turin*. Amsterdam/Lisse: Swets & Zeitlinger, 1993

Bureau of Justice Statistics: *Drugs, Crime and the Justice System: A National Report*. Washington, DC: USGPO, 1992

Campbell, D.T.: The experimenting society. In: Overman, E.S. (Ed.) *Methodology and Epistemology for Social Science*. Selected Papers, pp 190-314. Chicago: University of Chicago Press, 1988

Center for Substance Abuse Research: The Maryland boot camp experiment. *CESAR Reports* 3:1,6, 1993

Cohen, P.: *Cocaine Use in Amsterdam in Non-Deviant Subcultures*. Amsterdam: University of Amsterdam, 1989

Coppes, M.: *NRC Handelsblad*, 20 July 1988

De Swaan, A.: *In Care of the State: Health Care, Education and Welfare in Europe and the USA in the Modern Era*. Cambridge: Polity Press, 1988

Ehrenberg, A.: *Individus sous Influence: Drogues, Alcool et Médicaments Psychotropes*. Paris: Ed Espirit, 1991

Engelsman, E.L.: *Individual Responsibility and the Role of Criminal Law*. Presented at the World Ministerial Drugs Summit. London, April 9-11, 1990

Engelsman, E.L.: Dutch policy on the management of drug-related problems. *Br J Addiction* 84:211-218, 1989

Erickson, K.: *Wayward Puritans*. New York: John Wiley & Sons, 1966

Escochado, A.: *Historia de las Drogas 1/2/3*. Madrid: Alianza Ed, 1989

Ghodse, H.A., Kaplan, C.D., Mann, R.D. (Eds.): *Drug Misuse and Dependence*. Camforth, UK: The Parthenon Publishing Group, 1990

Goldstein, A., Kalant, H.: Drug policy: striking the right balance. *Science* 249:1513-21, 1990

Grapendaal, M., Leuw, E., Nelen, H.: Drugs and crime in an accommodating social context: the situation in Amsterdam. *Contemporary Drug Problems* 303-326, Summer 1992

Grund, J.P.C., Blanken, P., Adriaans, N.F.P., Kaplan, C.D., Barendregt, C., Meeuwsen, M.: Reaching the unreached: targeting hidden idu populations with clean needles via known user groups. *J Psychoactive Drugs* 24:41-47, 1992

Hendriks, V.M.: *Addiction and Psychopathology: a Multidimensional Approach to Clinical Practice.* Rotterdam: Erasmus University, 1990

Inglehart, R.: *The Silent Revolution: Changing Values and Political Styles among Western Publics.* Princeton, NJ: Princeton University Press, 1977

Inglehart, R.: Post-materialism in an environment of insecurity. *Am Political Sci Rev* 75:880-900, 1981

Inglehart, R.: *Cultural Shift in Advanced Industrial Society.* Princeton, NJ: Princeton University Press, 1990

Intraval: *Between the Lines: A Study of the Nature and Extent of Cocaine Use in Rotterdam.* Groningen/Rotterdam: Intraval, 1992

Jaffe, J.: What counts as a "drug problem"? In: Edwards, G., Arief, A., Jaffe. J. (Eds.) *Drugs Use and Misuse: Cultural Perspectives,* pp 101-111. London: Croom Helm, 1983

Jaffe, J.: Footnotes in the evolution of the American national response: some little known aspects of the first American strategy for drug abuse and drug traffic prevention. The inaugural Thomas Okey Memorial Lecture. *Br J Addiction* 82:587-599, 1987

Jansen, A.C.M.: *Cannabis in Amsterdam: A Geography of Hashish and Marijuana.* Muiderberg: Dick Coutinho, 1989

Kaplan, C.: The uneasy consensus: prohibitionist and experimentalist expectancies behind the international narcotics control system. *Tijdschrift voor Criminologie* 26:98-109, 1984

Kaplan, C.: Droge und Militär. In: Korczak, D. (Ed.) *Die betäubte Gesellschaft: Suchte: Ursache, Formen, Therapien,* pp 155-165. Frankfurt: Fisher Verlag, 1986

Kaplan, C.D.: The social functions of drugs in the coming decades. In: Kaplan, C.D., Kooyman, M. (Eds.) *Responding to a World of Drugs: Intentional and Unintentional Effects of Control, Treatment and Prevention.* Proceedings 15th International Institute on the Prevention and Treatment of Drug Dependence, pp 15-19. Rotterdam: Institute for Preventive and Social Psychiatry, 1987

Kaplan, C., De Vries, M.W., Grund, J.P., Adriaans, N.F.P.: Protective factors: Dutch interventions, health determinants and the reorganization of addict life. In: Ghodse, H.A., Kaplan, C.D., Mann, R.D. (Eds.) *Drug Misuse and Dependence,* pp 165-176. Park Ridge, NJ: The Parthenon Publishing Group, 1990

Kooyman, M.: *The Therapeutic Community for Addicts: Intimacy, Parent Involvement and Treatment Outcome.* Rotterdam: Erasmus University Press, 1992

Mackenzie, D.L.: Boot camp prisons: Components, evaluations and empirical issues. *Federal Probation* 44-52, September 1990

Musto, D.: *The American Disease: The Origins of Narcotic Control.* New Haven: Yale University Press, 1973

Reinarman, C., Levine, H.G.: The crack attack: politics and media in America's latest drug scare. In: Best, J. (Ed.) *Images of Issues,* pp 115-137. Hawthorne, NY: Aldine de Gruyter, 1989

Reuter, P.: Hawks ascendent: the punitive trend of American drug policy. *Daedalus* 121:15-52, 1992

Rossi, P.H., Freeman, H.: *Evaluation: A Systematic Approach, 3rd edn.* London: Sage, 1985

Sandwijk, J.P., Cohen, P.D.A., Musterd, S.: *Licit and Illicit Drug Use in Amsterdam.* Amsterdam: University of Amsterdam Press, 1992

Schmoke, K.L.: Back to the future: the public health system's lead role in fighting drugs. *Am Oxonian* 77:1-9, 1990

Stein, S.D.: *International Diplomacy, State Administrators and Narcotics Control.* Aldershot, UK: Gower, 1985

Swierstra, K.: *Drugscarriers: Van Crimineel tot Conventioneel.* Groningen: RUG, 1990

Schama, S.: *The Embarrassment of Riches: An Interpretation of Dutch Culture in the Golden Age.* Berkeley: University of California Press, 1988

Szasz, T.: *Ceremonial Chemistry. The Ritual Persecution of Drugs, Addicts and Pushers.* Garden City, NY: Doubleday, 1974

Trimbos, C.J.B.J.: De methadon-onderhoudsbehandeling van heroin verslaving. *Ned Tijdschrift Geneeskunde* 115:262-266, 1973

Van der Hoek, J.A.R., Van Haastrecht, H.J.A., Coutinho, R.A.: Risk reduction among intravenous drug users in Amsterdam under the influence of AIDS. *Am J Publ Hlth* 79:1355-1357, 1989

Van Deth, J.W.: The persistence of materialist and post-materialist value orientations. *Eur J Political Res* 11:63-79, 1983a

Van Deth, J.W.: Ranking the ratings: the case of materialist and postmaterialist value orientations. *Political Methodol* 9:407-432, 1983b

Van Gelder, P., Sijtsma, J.: *Horse, Coke en Kansen. I: Sociale Riscio's en Kansen onder Surinaamse en Marokkaanse Harddruggebruikers in Amsterdam.* Amsterdam: University of Amsterdam, 1988

Van Limbeek, J., Wouters, L., Kaplan, C.D., Geerlings, P.J., Van Alem, V.: Psychopathology in drug-addicted Dutch. *J Substance Abuse Treat* 9:43-52, 1992

Van Vliet, H.J.: Separation of drug markets and the normalization of drug problems in the Netherlands: An example for other nations? *Journal of Drug Issues* 20(3):463-471, 1990

Van Wijngaart, G.F.: *Competing Perspectives on Drug Use (The Dutch Experience).* Lisse/Amsterdam: Swets & Zeitlinger, 1991

Verbraeck, H.: *De Staart van de Zeedijk; een Bliksemonderzoek naar enkele Effecten van het Zomerplan 1987 in het Wallengebied.* Amsterdam: Instituut voor Sociale Geografie, Universiteit van Amsterdam, 1988

The White House: *National Drug Control Strategy.* Washington, DC: USGPO, 1989

Endnotes

1. The Vienna United Nations International Conference on Drug Abuse and Trafficking in 1987 elaborated on a new Convention on Drugs in November/December, 1988 to be ratified by member states. This global effort stands in the tradition of international cooperation begun in 1912 with the signing of the The Hague Convention. Since the founding of the United Nations after the Second World War several protocols and conventions have been adopted to respond to the drug problem. The 1961 Single Convention on Narcotic Drugs amended by a 1972 Protocol moved to modernize the earlier international accords. In 1971 the Convention on Psychotropic Substances attempted to broaden and move forward the international drug control system. By 1981 the UN had accepted the International Drug Abuse Control Strategy which authorized international cooperation in fighting drug abuse and drug trafficking. In the UN Assembly's 1984 Declaration on the Control of Drug Trafficking and Drug Abuse, the drug problem became a maximum international priority. That same year a new convention was proposed that would treat those aspects of the problem not sufficiently covered by the existing instruments. The Vienna Convention is especially significant in that it marks the beginning of the "post-modern" period that goes beyond the terms of the "modernizing" process since the Second World War. This is signalled by its articles on demand reduction which turn the momentum of the instruments away from production and distribution and towards consumption. This is especially important because it promises to unravel an essential paradox noted by Stein (1985:5) that "much of the history of national and international narcotics control can be written without addicts or addiction". The Vienna Convention also signals a new style of work that fits into the post-modern mode: consensus is to be sought through the stimulation of increasing numbers of conferences, meetings, seminars and workshops at all levels and in all regions attended by representatives

from multidisciplinary and multisectorial backgrounds.

2. For another recent and politically informed statement by the Mayor of Baltimore, see Schmoke 1990.

3. See Ghodse *et al.* (1990) for a Volume debating drug policy options in the UK and the Netherlands.

4. Perhaps because their enlisted corps consists of predominantly young males who are traditionally the highest users of illicit drugs (see Kaplan 1986).

5. This kind of gentleman's agreement of mutual respect did not work for all groups. For instance, the prosperity and tolerance of the Republic became an affront to the group of Puritans who had fled from England. As a result, in 1620 they set sail for the New World to establish a new, isolated society based on "pure" Protestantism, protecting themselves and their children from the corrupting influence of worldly temptations. After several years in the "new Providence" frightened by their own insignificance, these "wayward Puritans" resurrected the witch hunt in Salem that had died away in Europe with the civilization offensive (Erickson 1966).

6. Coppes (1988), a business consultant, puts it this way in a newspaper story: "Because no other society has reached the compactness and the complexity of the Netherlands' society, there are no well tried recipes yet for accommodation of various new kinds of business activity and society. They will have to be invented in the Netherlands itself."

7. This has become the model for a later European Community study (Bieleman *et al.* 1993).

8. Materialists were highly unlikely to know a drug user, while half the post-materialists did. The generally more permissive attitudes of the post-materialists to drug users is associated with their greater familiarity with them. This finding was independent of the drug use of the post-materialists which was not much higher than the materialist Germans. However, the post-materialists were nine times more likely to experiment in their lifetime with drugs than the materialists. The post-materialists found drugs more easily available, but, at the same time, found them to be more harmless. Post-materialists also displayed a more differentiated view of drugs having different attitudes than materialists for both cannabis and heroin. Post-materialist Germans seem quite receptive to the "separation of markets" bit while not going so far as the endorsing of the legalization of cannabis.

ABOUT THE AUTHORS

Chapter I   *Marcel de Kort, PhD*

Marcel de Kort is a historian and sociologist. He published a dissertation on the history of Dutch drug policy. As a researcher at the Universities of Amsterdam and Rotterdam, Marcel de Kort was involved in the study of the history of drug use, drug trade and drug policy, and wrote several publications on these subjects.

Chapter II   *Ed Leuw*

Criminologist and former lecturer at the University of Amsterdam, Ed Leuw is currently with the Research and Documentation Center at the Ministry of Justice. Member of the Scientific Board of the European Monitoring Center for Drugs and Drug Addiction. Author of numerous publications on deviant addiction and drug policy.

Chapter III   *Jos Silvis*

Jos Silvis is currently a judge at the court of Rotterdam. Formerly a lecturer at the University of Utrecht. Author of numerous publications on the legal aspects of (Dutch) drug policy.

Chapter IV   *Léon Wever*

Until June 1992, Léon Wever was the Deputy Head of the Alcohol, Drugs and Tobacco Policy Division of the Dutch Ministry of Welfare, Health and Cultural Affairs. Since then, he has held several positions at this ministry, such as Director of Information Policy, coordinator for Health Care Reform and leader of special projects. He is a member of the Board of the largest city-sponsored drug treatment center in Rotterdam.

Chapter V   *Leendert H. Erkelens*

Leendert H. Erkelens studied sociology at the State University of Groningen, where he worked as a reseacher at the Criminological Institute. Since then, he has worked in various fields at the Ministry of Justice involved with (penal) policy administration and research. Currently he is employed in various management tasks, especially in the field of forensic psychiatry.

Vincent C.M. van Alem

Vincent C.M. van Alem studied politicology and worked at the School of Psychology of the University of Nijmegen, where he participated in an evaluation project on penitentiary drug policy. He is the author of several publications on this and related subjects. Currently he is employed as an information specialist at a clinic for drug addiction and as an information advisor for several drug-assistance agencies.

Chapter VI   *Koert Swierstra, PhD*

Koert Swierstra worked as a criminologist in the field of drug studies at the State University of Groningen until 1990. His research focused on the life styles of hard-drug addicts, criminal behavior and drug dealing. He wrote a dissertation based on a longitudinal hard-drug study. He has been working at the Ministry of Justice since 1991 on, amongst other things, probation policy, safe cities projects and drug problems.

Chapter VII   *Dirk J. Korf, PhD*

Dirk J. Korf was an outreaching field worker, working predominantly among foreign (German) drug tourists in Amsterdam. Currently, he is a lecturer at the Bonger Institute of Criminology at the University of Amsterdam, and a Senior Researcher at the Amsterdam Bureau of Social Research and Statistics (O+S). He has carried out extensive research on deviance, drug use and the drug trade. His dissertation entitled "Dutch Treat" traces the development of the formal control and illicit drug use in The Netherlands, and deals with the consequences of the Dutch drug policy.

Chapter VIII   *Frank van Gemert*

Frank van Gemert is a researcher at the University of Rotterdam in the field of urban minority studies. He studied cultural anthropology and worked as a bartender in an inner-city cafe in the Amsterdam drug area. He has produced several publications on the culture of street-level drug dealing.

Hans Verbraeck

Hans Verbraeck is a cultural anthropologist. As a free-lance drugs researcher, he carried out several field studies on the hard-drug scenes of

Utrecht, Amsterdam and New York. More recently, he has published work on the culture of illegal drugs supply.

Chapter IX *Adriaan C.M. Jansen, PhD*

Adriaan C.M. Jansen is an Associate Professor at the Institute of Economic Geography of the University of Amsterdam. His research topics mainly concern the economy of cities and of economic sectors. He has published a book and a number of articles on the Dutch cannabis sector. He is Chairman of a foundation for drug consultancy and advisor to the Dutch federation of cannabis retailers.

Chapter X *Bert Bieleman*

Bert Bieleman studied sociology and is the Director of Intraval, a socio-scientific research and advice bureau with offices in Groningen and Rotterdam. He has been involved in several (evaluation) studies on drug use and crime prevention.

Jolt J. Bosma

Jolt J. Bosma is a sociologist, working at the Criminological Institute of the University of Groningen and with the research and advice bureau Intraval. He has been involved in research on drug use and crime prevention.

Chapter XI *Ineke Haen Marshall, PhD*

Ineke Haen Marshall is Professor of Criminal Justice at the University of Nebraska at Omaha. She is studying sociology at the Catholic University of Brabant (The Netherlands) and obtained her PhD at the Bowling Green State University. She is currently collaborating in an international study of self-reported juvenile delinquency. Her current research interests include criminal careers, ethnicity and crime, the validity of self-report methodology and comparative criminological theory.

Chris E. Marshall, PhD

Chris E. Marshall is a sociologist, working as Associate Professor of Criminal Justice at the University of Nebraska at Omaha. He has published in the areas of victimization, juvenile justice and comparative criminology. His current interests include social control and theory construction.

Chapter XII   *Martin Grapendaal*

Martin Grapendaal is a social and organizational psychologist. Since 1984 he has been employed by the Research and Documentation Center of the Justice Department as a drug and prison researcher.

Hans Nelen

Hans Nelen is a criminologist with a law degree. Since 1986 he has been a researcher at the Research and Documentation Centre of the Ministry of Justice in The Netherlands, mainly involved in drug and fraud research. Recently he has been active in the field of organized crime.

Chapter XIII   *Tom Blom*

Tom Blom is a lecturer on Criminal Law Science at the Erasmus University, Rotterdam. He lectures in the fields of International Drug Law and Dutch Drug Policy.

Hans van Mastrigt

Hans van Mastrigt studied the Sociology of Law and worked as a Lecturer at the Law School of the Erasmus University in the fields of police violence and drug policy. He has been a staff member for drug policy in several municipal health services. Currently, he is working for the City of Rotterdam in the field of drugs and public order, and for the WHO Multi City Action Plan on Drugs.

Chapter XIV   *Dirk-Jan Kraan, PhD*

Dirk-Jan Kraan studied Public Law and Economics. He was a Lecturer on Public Law and Public Administration at the University of Rotterdam. Since 1982 he has worked in several departments of the Ministry of Finance. He is the author of numerous publications on public economics and public choice theory. His most recent book is entitled "Budgetary Decisions: A Public Choice Approach" (Cambridge University Press, 1996).

Chapter XV   *Charles D. Kaplan, PhD*

Charles D. Kaplan is an American sociologist and political scientist. After working in the field of drugs research at Rutgers University in New Jersey, he was invited to be a visiting Professor at the Goethe University in Frankfurt (Germany). In 1984 he moved to the Erasmus University in Rotterdam (The Netherlands) and took up the post of Professor at the Medical Faculty. He founded and directed the European Addiction Research Institute (IVO) at the Erasmus University. Currently, he is working as the Director of the Drug Use and Abuse Division of the International Institute for Psychosocial and Socioecological Research (IPSER) at the University of Limburg (The Netherlands). He is also a part-time Adjunct Professor at the University of Texas at San Antonio.

Dirk-Jan Haanraadts

Dirk-Jan Haanraadts is a historian from Rotterdam. He has been involved in research on alcohol control policy in The Netherlands. He now lives and works in the U.S.A.

Henk-Jan van Vliet

Henk-Jan van Vliet is a lawyer from Amsterdam, who has been working in the fields of drug treatment and drug policy since 1977. Since 1988 he has been an international consultant on drugs and AIDS.

Jean-Paul C. Grund, Phd

Jean-Paul C. Grund is Deputy Director of The Lindesmith Center, a New York-based drug policy research institute, and also Assistant Professor at the Department of Sociology of the University of Connecticut. He is the author of numerous articles and two books on drug use culture, HIV, and their socio-political determinants. In the early 1980s he worked with the Dutch "Junkiebond", the first drug-user self-organization, and he founded and directed Rotterdam's first outreach program for drug users.